Florian Stallmann

**Spicing up Software-Intensive Systems with CurCuMA**

AF092622

Florian Stallmann

# Spicing up Software-Intensive Systems with CurCuMA

A Model-Driven Approach to Multi-Agent System Design

Südwestdeutscher Verlag für Hochschulschriften

**Impressum/Imprint (nur für Deutschland/ only for Germany)**
Bibliografische Information der Deutschen Nationalbibliothek: Die Deutsche Nationalbibliothek verzeichnet diese Publikation in der Deutschen Nationalbibliografie; detaillierte bibliografische Daten sind im Internet über http://dnb.d-nb.de abrufbar.
Alle in diesem Buch genannten Marken und Produktnamen unterliegen warenzeichen-, marken- oder patentrechtlichem Schutz bzw. sind Warenzeichen oder eingetragene Warenzeichen der jeweiligen Inhaber. Die Wiedergabe von Marken, Produktnamen, Gebrauchsnamen, Handelsnamen, Warenbezeichnungen u.s.w. in diesem Werk berechtigt auch ohne besondere Kennzeichnung nicht zu der Annahme, dass solche Namen im Sinne der Warenzeichen- und Markenschutzgesetzgebung als frei zu betrachten wären und daher von jedermann benutzt werden dürften.

Verlag: Südwestdeutscher Verlag für Hochschulschriften Aktiengesellschaft & Co. KG
Dudweiler Landstr. 99, 66123 Saarbrücken, Deutschland
Telefon +49 681 37 20 271-1, Telefax +49 681 37 20 271-0, Email: info@svh-verlag.de
Zugl.: Paderborn, Universität Paderborn, Dissertation, 2009

Herstellung in Deutschland:
Schaltungsdienst Lange o.H.G., Zehrensdorfer Str. 11, D-12277 Berlin
Books on Demand GmbH, Gutenbergring 53, D-22848 Norderstedt
Reha GmbH, Dudweiler Landstr. 99, D- 66123 Saarbrücken
**ISBN: 978-3-8381-0907-7**


**Imprint (only for USA, GB)**
Bibliographic information published by the Deutsche Nationalbibliothek: The Deutsche Nationalbibliothek lists this publication in the Deutsche Nationalbibliografie; detailed bibliographic data are available in the Internet at http://dnb.d-nb.de.
Any brand names and product names mentioned in this book are subject to trademark, brand or patent protection and are trademarks or registered trademarks of their respective holders. The use of brand names, product names, common names, trade names, product descriptions etc. even without
a particular marking in this works is in no way to be construed to mean that such names may be regarded as unrestricted in respect of trademark and brand protection legislation and could thus be used by anyone.

Publisher:
Südwestdeutscher Verlag für Hochschulschriften Aktiengesellschaft & Co. KG
Dudweiler Landstr. 99, 66123 Saarbrücken, Germany
Phone +49 681 37 20 271-1, Fax +49 681 37 20 271-0, Email: info@svh-verlag.de

Copyright © 2008 Südwestdeutscher Verlag für Hochschulschriften Aktiengesellschaft & Co. KG and licensors
All rights reserved. Saarbrücken 2008

Produced in USA and UK by:
Lightning Source Inc., 1246 Heil Quaker Blvd., La Vergne, TN 37086, USA
Lightning Source UK Ltd., Chapter House, Pitfield, Kiln Farm, Milton Keynes, MK11 3LW, GB
BookSurge, 7290 B. Investment Drive, North Charleston, SC 29418, USA
**ISBN: 978-3-8381-0907-7**

# Acknowledgments

I would like to express my thanks to Professor Dr. Wilhelm Schäfer, my supervisor, for supporting me in my work and giving me the opportunity to work in a dynamic and challenging environment. I would also like to thank Professor Dr.-Ing. habil. Wilhelm Dangelmaier and Professor Dr. Hans Kleine Büning for acting as my co-supervisors, and Professor Dr. Mauro Pezzè and Prof. Dr. Gregor Engels for reviewing my thesis. I am truly grateful to Professor Dr. Holger Giese for his guidance and our invaluable discussions – this thesis would not be the same without him.

Thanks go out to my colleagues in the Software Engineering Group and the Special Research Initiative 614 for making my time in Paderborn a positive and pleasant experience: To the B1 team, Dr. Matthias Tichy, Stefan Henkler, Dr. Martin Hirsch, Dr. Sven Burmester, Dr. Daniela Schilling, to the Fujaba team, Matthias Meyer, Dietrich Travkin, and Dr. Lothar Wendehals, to our workgroup, Professor Dr. Ekkart Kindler, Dr. Vladimir Rubin, Björn Axenath, Dr. Robert Wagner, Dr. Matthias Gehrke, Ahmet Mehic, Jutta Haupt, Sabrina Clemens, and Jürgen Maniera, and to my colleagues from the SRI, Benjamin Klöpper, Henner Vöcking, Bernd Schulz, Kathrin Witting, and Christoph Romaus.

For their efforts and enthusiasm, I am indebted to the students who have worked with me: Michael Spijkerman, Andreas Seibel, Holger Mense, Carsten Kröger, Basil Becker, Thomas Janson, Michael Schwier, Stefan Neumann, Eike Rethemeier, Frank Nillies, Andrea Zschirnt, Maik Anderka, Nedim Lipka, Jens Wenner, Timo Wiesemann, Tao Xie, and Sergej Tissen; Dietmar Bielemeyer, Hendrik Renken, and Sven Luzar.

I should not like to forget Eckhard Steffen and his team, who have been working hard to establish the Graduate School of Dynamic Intelligent Systems and the ideas it represents.

I am grateful for Thomas Hädrich and all the friends who have faithfully accompanied me through the years.

Finally, I could not have succeeded without the love, encouragement, and support of my family.

Without my brother Bertram, always ready to lend an ear.

Without Freia sharing my life, her love and faith in me.

Without my loving parents, to whom I am indebted in so many ways.

**II**

# Table of Contents

**Acknowledgments**    I

**Table of Contents**    V

**1 Introduction**    1
    1.1 Motivation . . . . . . . . . . . . . . . . . . . . . . . . . . . . . . . . 1
    1.2 Objectives . . . . . . . . . . . . . . . . . . . . . . . . . . . . . . . . 3
    1.3 Approach . . . . . . . . . . . . . . . . . . . . . . . . . . . . . . . . 6
    1.4 Contribution . . . . . . . . . . . . . . . . . . . . . . . . . . . . . . . 12
    1.5 Structure . . . . . . . . . . . . . . . . . . . . . . . . . . . . . . . . . 14

**2 Foundations**    17
    2.1 Introduction . . . . . . . . . . . . . . . . . . . . . . . . . . . . . . . 17
       2.1.1 Related Work . . . . . . . . . . . . . . . . . . . . . . . . . . 17
       2.1.2 Application Example . . . . . . . . . . . . . . . . . . . . . . 19
    2.2 Story-Driven Modeling . . . . . . . . . . . . . . . . . . . . . . . . . 21
       2.2.1 Notations . . . . . . . . . . . . . . . . . . . . . . . . . . . . 21
       2.2.2 Formalization . . . . . . . . . . . . . . . . . . . . . . . . . . 25
    2.3 Coordination Patterns . . . . . . . . . . . . . . . . . . . . . . . . . . 37
       2.3.1 Notations . . . . . . . . . . . . . . . . . . . . . . . . . . . . 37
       2.3.2 Formalization . . . . . . . . . . . . . . . . . . . . . . . . . . 41
       2.3.3 Integration . . . . . . . . . . . . . . . . . . . . . . . . . . . 44
    2.4 Conclusion . . . . . . . . . . . . . . . . . . . . . . . . . . . . . . . 49

**3 Constraints**    51
    3.1 Introduction . . . . . . . . . . . . . . . . . . . . . . . . . . . . . . . 51
       3.1.1 Related Work . . . . . . . . . . . . . . . . . . . . . . . . . . 54

|  |  | 3.1.2 | Application Example . . . . . . . . . . . . . . . . . . . . . | 56 |
|---|---|---|---|---|
|  | 3.2 | Structural Properties . . . . . . . . . . . . . . . . . . . . . . . . . . | 58 |
|  |  | 3.2.1 | Enhanced Story Patterns . . . . . . . . . . . . . . . . . . . | 58 |
|  |  | 3.2.2 | Story Decision Diagrams . . . . . . . . . . . . . . . . . . . | 62 |
|  |  | 3.2.3 | Formal Semantics . . . . . . . . . . . . . . . . . . . . . . . | 74 |
|  |  | 3.2.4 | Discussion . . . . . . . . . . . . . . . . . . . . . . . . . . | 91 |
|  | 3.3 | Temporal Properties . . . . . . . . . . . . . . . . . . . . . . . . . . | 92 |
|  |  | 3.3.1 | Timed Story Scenario Diagrams . . . . . . . . . . . . . . . | 92 |
|  |  | 3.3.2 | Formal Semantics . . . . . . . . . . . . . . . . . . . . . . . | 110 |
|  |  | 3.3.3 | Discussion . . . . . . . . . . . . . . . . . . . . . . . . . . | 128 |
|  | 3.4 | Conclusion . . . . . . . . . . . . . . . . . . . . . . . . . . . . . . . | 130 |

# 4 System Design 131

|  | 4.1 | Introduction . . . . . . . . . . . . . . . . . . . . . . . . . . . . . . | 131 |
|---|---|---|---|
|  |  | 4.1.1 Application Example . . . . . . . . . . . . . . . . . . . . . | 134 |
|  | 4.2 | Conceptual Framework . . . . . . . . . . . . . . . . . . . . . . . . | 138 |
|  |  | 4.2.1 Approach . . . . . . . . . . . . . . . . . . . . . . . . . . . | 138 |
|  |  | 4.2.2 Environment Specification . . . . . . . . . . . . . . . . . . | 140 |
|  |  | 4.2.3 Social Specification . . . . . . . . . . . . . . . . . . . . . . | 143 |
|  | 4.3 | Formal model . . . . . . . . . . . . . . . . . . . . . . . . . . . . . | 146 |
|  |  | 4.3.1 Environment Specification . . . . . . . . . . . . . . . . . . | 146 |
|  |  | 4.3.2 Culture Specification . . . . . . . . . . . . . . . . . . . . . | 153 |
|  |  | 4.3.3 Community Specification . . . . . . . . . . . . . . . . . . . | 164 |
|  |  | 4.3.4 Agent Specification . . . . . . . . . . . . . . . . . . . . . . | 166 |
|  |  | 4.3.5 System Specification . . . . . . . . . . . . . . . . . . . . . | 170 |
|  | 4.4 | Conclusion . . . . . . . . . . . . . . . . . . . . . . . . . . . . . . . | 171 |
|  |  | 4.4.1 Related Work . . . . . . . . . . . . . . . . . . . . . . . . . | 171 |
|  |  | 4.4.2 Discussion . . . . . . . . . . . . . . . . . . . . . . . . . . | 174 |

# 5 Verification and Validation 175

|  | 5.1 | Introduction . . . . . . . . . . . . . . . . . . . . . . . . . . . . . . | 175 |
|---|---|---|---|
|  | 5.2 | Verification . . . . . . . . . . . . . . . . . . . . . . . . . . . . . . | 178 |
|  |  | 5.2.1 Model Checking . . . . . . . . . . . . . . . . . . . . . . . | 183 |
|  |  | 5.2.2 Invariant Checking . . . . . . . . . . . . . . . . . . . . . . | 191 |
|  |  | 5.2.3 Behavior Verification . . . . . . . . . . . . . . . . . . . . . | 195 |

|  |  | 5.2.4 | Scenario-based Verification . . . . . . . . . . . . . . . . . . . . . . . 199 |
|  | 5.3 | Validation . . . . . . . . . . . . . . . . . . . . . . . . . . . . . . . . . . . . . . 209 |
|  |  | 5.3.1 | Automation . . . . . . . . . . . . . . . . . . . . . . . . . . . . . . . . . . 210 |
|  |  | 5.3.2 | Simulation . . . . . . . . . . . . . . . . . . . . . . . . . . . . . . . . . . 214 |
|  |  | 5.3.3 | Analysis . . . . . . . . . . . . . . . . . . . . . . . . . . . . . . . . . . . 221 |
|  | 5.4 | Conclusion . . . . . . . . . . . . . . . . . . . . . . . . . . . . . . . . . . . . . 225 |
|  |  | 5.4.1 | Related Work . . . . . . . . . . . . . . . . . . . . . . . . . . . . . . . . 226 |
|  |  | 5.4.2 | Discussion . . . . . . . . . . . . . . . . . . . . . . . . . . . . . . . . . . 227 |

## 6 Application     229

- 6.1 Introduction . . . . . . . . . . . . . . . . . . . . . . . . . . . . . . . . . . . . . 229
- 6.2 Tool support . . . . . . . . . . . . . . . . . . . . . . . . . . . . . . . . . . . . . 230
  - 6.2.1 Tool Landscape . . . . . . . . . . . . . . . . . . . . . . . . . . . . . . . 230
  - 6.2.2 Modeling . . . . . . . . . . . . . . . . . . . . . . . . . . . . . . . . . . . 232
  - 6.2.3 Prototyping . . . . . . . . . . . . . . . . . . . . . . . . . . . . . . . . . 236
- 6.3 Deriving Constraint Specifications . . . . . . . . . . . . . . . . . . . . . . . . 239
  - 6.3.1 Specification Pattern System . . . . . . . . . . . . . . . . . . . . . . . 239
  - 6.3.2 Deriving Properties from Textual Requirements . . . . . . . . . . . . . 243
- 6.4 Application in Practice . . . . . . . . . . . . . . . . . . . . . . . . . . . . . . . 252
- 6.5 Conclusion . . . . . . . . . . . . . . . . . . . . . . . . . . . . . . . . . . . . . 259

## 7 Conclusion and Future Work     261

- 7.1 Conclusion . . . . . . . . . . . . . . . . . . . . . . . . . . . . . . . . . . . . . 261
- 7.2 Future Work . . . . . . . . . . . . . . . . . . . . . . . . . . . . . . . . . . . . . 262

## Bibliography     288

# Chapter 1

# Introduction

## 1.1 Motivation

**Software-intensive systems.** Software is increasingly permeating our everyday lives. In little over two decades, it has found its way into our telephones, appliances, and hi-fi racks. It is keeping planes in the air, cars on the road, and trains on schedule. It is powering the Internet, providing an unprecedented degree of world-wide networking. Behind the scenes, it is quietly coordinating the supply chains of a global economy.

These developments have been enabled by advances in electronics and computer science. The available processing power and bandwidth have multiplied, while the cost, energy consumption, weight and size of components have all decreased. This has not only allowed the construction of more powerful and compact electronic devices, but has also led to the integration of significant computing power into systems that had previously been purely mechanical. As a consequence, systems as diverse as cars and washing machines have become safer, more efficient, and easier to use. In order to reflect the increased importance of electronics and software, the label *mechatronic system* [BSDB00] has been proposed for such systems. As wireless technology promises to provide ubiquitous connectivity, ad-hoc networks of such systems are expected to exhibit even more intelligent cooperative behavior in the future. The ultimate vision is to build *self-optimizing* systems [FGK$^+$04] that can reflect on their objectives and adapt their structure and behavior in response to changes in the environment.

Meanwhile, improved software engineering techniques have been developed to address the additional complexity that is introduced by distribution, concurrency, heterogeneity, and requirements concerning real-time behavior, safety, and reliability. These advances have benefited embedded and large scale systems alike: In the enterprise application sector, they have allowed the construction of complex networked information systems dealing with enterprise resource planning, management information, or production planning and control.

The term *software-intensive system* [Sta00] has been introduced to characterize this wide range of applications. Their common trait is that while they are situated in or interacting with the real world, software plays an essential part in the design, operation and evolution of the system.

While software has become a main driver of innovation in this sector, it still is, at the same time, a critical bottleneck, as present design methodologies struggle with handling the ever increasing complexity. The three main challenges in this context are coping with dynamic environments, providing structural and behavioral adaptation, and managing the integration of heterogeneous infrastructures. A fundamental problem in designing the large scale coordination of the system is reconciling predictability and emergent behavior resulting from the distributed nature of control.

**Model-Driven Engineering** [Ken02] promises to boost both productivity and quality by facilitating communication between domain experts and software engineers, allowing the early validation of requirements, providing a foundation for formal verification, and enabling automatic code generation. Models reduce the complexity of a design by abstracting from details of the implementation or the target platform, placing the focus on the domain-specific aspects of the design instead. The more abstract representation facilitates the analysis of the design and reuse in different contexts. However, the model needs to be sufficiently formal, detailed and free from ambiguity in order to support verification activities and an automated operationalization.

Software-intensive systems typically need to meet strict requirements with respect to correctness and reliability. Where software interfaces with mechanical systems, the potential for harm to human beings or physical damage needs to be taken into consideration, subjecting the software to the standards for *safety-critical systems* [Sto96, Lev95]. Even where safety is not an issue, software that is controlling business processes is often mission-critical and therefore held to the more general quality standards for high-integrity systems [BH99].

The *verification* of the system design is therefore indispensable. Due to the complexity of the systems, simulating and testing alone are insufficient as a means of quality assurance, as the achievable coverage is too low. Distribution, reconfiguration and time constraints lead to huge state spaces that cannot be dealt with using brute force. They require formal methods that reduce the complexity of the problem by intelligently decomposing it into units that are tractable using automated verification techniques.

However, as for all model-based approaches, simulating and testing are nonetheless required to ensure that the verified model actually represents a valid abstraction of reality. Moreover, formal verification can usually only establish the safe bounds of complex emergent behavior, especially where the specification allows non-deterministic choice to reflect a component's autonomy. With respect to efficiency, it is generally at best possible to make probabilistic guarantees so that optimized performance has to be achieved through iterative refinements.

The *Unified Modeling Language* (*UML*) [Obj07] is the de-facto standard in software engineering, not least because its visual notations and flexibility make it accessible and useful for the communication with stakeholders. While a certain laxness with respect to semantics is part of its appeal in this context, this becomes a liability when the UML is used as a formal specification language. In response to this problem, the expressiveness of many notations has been increased in the UML 2.0 – however, a comprehensive formal semantics is still missing. In order to enable code generation, the *Model-Driven Architecture* (MDA) [Obj03], the standard for model-driven engineering proposed by the Object Management Group (OMG), uses the concept of an abstract *platform-independent model* (PIM), which is transformed into a concrete *platform-specific model* (PSM) based on a *platform model* (PM) describing the characteristics of the target platform, combined with unambiguous standards for the operationalization of modeling concepts. Code for a target platform can then be generated from the platform-specific model.

*Component-oriented software engineering* [Szy98, Gri98, BRS$^+$00] is a paradigm that is highly relevant for the design of large and complex distributed systems. By strictly enforcing the principle of encapsulation and making all external dependencies explicit, components provide a more adequate unit of reuse and deployment than traditionally offered by designs based on more fine-grained object-oriented techniques. Using components promotes modular designs that make systems more flexible and allow them to adapt to changing requirements, possibly even by performing the necessary reconfiguration at runtime.

While components provide a clear separation between the different parts of a system, the individual interactions between them are fundamentally deterministic and cooperative. For modeling the behavior of independent actors whose reactions are not entirely predictable because they are following their own agenda, *agent-oriented software engineering* [WJ95b] therefore introduces the idea of autonomous agents as a better abstraction. The agent concept has a long tradition in artificial intelligence and, somewhat more recently, distributed intelligence, but has only lately garnered increased attention in the software engineering field. As a consequence, the predominant approaches are still rooted in modal logic, intentional models, and ontology and speech act theory, which makes them difficult to reconcile with established software-engineering practices. Their semantics are often based on a rather limited and idiosyncratic view on the world, which is beneficial when modeling and reasoning about the agents in isolation, but becomes a liability when integrating the agents into traditional software systems or designing a situated intelligence that is capable of complex, unstructured interactions with its environment. Even though the employed models are quite formal, it is therefore rarely possible to formally verify non-trivial properties of the agents' behavior, let alone prove that these results apply in practice.

A competing school of thought sees agent-orientation as an evolutionary extension of object-orientation and takes a more pragmatic approach, primarily focusing on the required infrastructure for agent execution, communication, and mobility. In this context, attempts to establish visual modeling languages that extend the UML with agent-specific concepts abound. However, these approaches are often quite technical and get mired in low-level message passing between agent objects, losing sight of the helpful abstractions that agent-orientation actually set out to provide.

## 1.2 Objectives

The challenge in designing the coordination behavior of adaptive software-intensive systems is therefore to find an approach that reconciles the perspectives of model-driven engineering and agent-oriented software engineering. Together, they could enable an efficient model-driven design process that provides specific support for dealing with the characteristic complexities of these systems.

The Special Research Initiative *Self-optimizing Concepts and Structures in Mechanical Engineering*[1] is developing novel concepts for adaptive mechatronic systems. One of its key innovations is the *Operator-Controller-Module* (*OCM*) [HOG04, OHG04], a layered architecture that decomposes each component into the *Controller* level, which is exclusively responsible for interacting with the hardware, the *Reflective Operator*, which is handling real-time communication and reconfiguration, and the *Cognitive Operator*, which encapsulates high-level functions such as advanced coordination and optimization strategies.

In [FGK+04, p.20f], we differentiate between two types of *structural adaptation*: *reconfiguration*, which modifies the relationships of a fixed set of components, and the more complex *compositional adaptation*, which additionally allows the introduction and removal of components. While a solution that enables safe reconfiguration at the Controller level has been proposed (cf. [Bur06]), there is no approach that supports compositional adaptation. In particular, there is a need for a systematic treatment of the dynamic instantiation of coordination behaviors.

While previous work has focused on the two lower levels of the OCM, a scalable concept for dynamic coordination behaviors is even more important at the level of the Cognitive Operator. It is a precondition for the coordination of large, open systems, which inherently involves compositional adaptation.

Designs that are based on flexible ad-hoc interactions between loosely coupled components are furthermore only feasible if there are binding contracts that constrain the expected behavior, which is evocative of the current trend towards service-based architectures. Contracts depend on the ability to specify behavioral constraints in a form that is viable in practice, amenable to formal analysis, and verifiable at run-time, which is an open issue shared by both domains.

The general objective of this thesis is therefore to provide a model-driven design approach that systematically supports adaptive coordination behaviors in dynamic environments and is capable of capturing precise behavioral constraints for interacting components. We mean to achieve this by integrating agent-oriented concepts into a sound model-driven development process. For this purpose, we take a pragmatic view on *agents*, which are seen as active components with a dedicated thread of control that are striving to achieve certain objectives. This perspective makes existing component-oriented modeling, formal analysis and code generation techniques available. At the same time, it provides a way to introduce the desired abstractions, based on the intuition of describing multi-agent system behavior as social interactions driven by the agents' intentions, as extensions to established software-engineering modeling techniques, thus combining the best of both worlds.

The principle of grounding all aspects of the system in the environment allows us to describe the concrete aspects of a multi-agent system, i.e. agents sensing and acting in physical and virtual environments, and its conceptual aspects, i.e. communication, coordination, relationships, and dependencies, within a single coherent object-oriented framework. The framework is organized in layers, from the concrete to the conceptual, and defines a set of architectural views which provide the context for applying specific *design patterns* that facilitate reuse or encode best practices

---

[1] DFG Special Research Initiative 614, *Self-optimizing Concepts and Structures in Mechanical Engineering*, University of Paderborn. Website: http://www.sfb614.de

## 1.2 Objectives

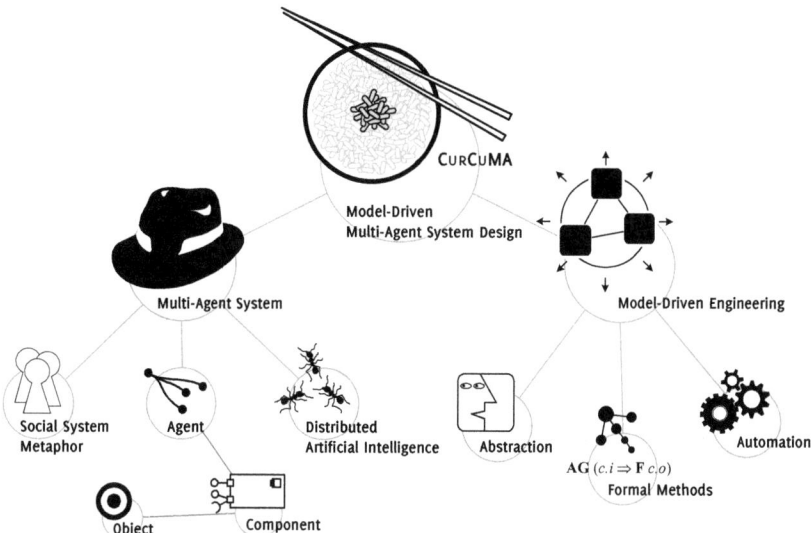

Figure 1.2.1: Reconciling the multi-agent paradigm with model-driven engineering

in software engineering. For capturing advanced coordination behaviors, we extend the concept of *Coordination Patterns* [GTB+03] with a set of well-defined social metaphors which add the ability to discuss system structure and the agents' intentions, resulting in *cultures*, a generic coordination mechanism for governing agent *communities*.

Our focus is on the architectural modeling of complex adaptive systems comprising multiple agents, capturing requirements, and the design of coordination mechanisms. The behavioral contracts that are specified by *cultures* are meant to ensure safe and reliable interaction, not to unduly constrain the implementation of the Cognitive Operator. They only define boundaries for the observable coordination behavior, not the artificial intelligence itself, which is out of the scope of this thesis. We only capture those internal aspects that directly affect coordination behavior such as objectives, which may e.g. determine the choice of basic design pattern (cf. [FGK+04, p.37ff]).

Modeling the system, especially during the early phases when requirements are elicited, should be intuitive enough to allow application domain experts to participate in the effort and fully comprehend the resulting specification. Nonetheless, all employed notations need to be formal in order to enable formal verification and code generation. In order to meet both requirements, we need to improve on existing constraint languages.

Finally, we have to ensure that our designs are correct and robust. Although the verification of the design is of central importance, the complexity of software-intensive systems poses an obstacle to their thorough verification for many practical applications. While an agent-oriented approach is well-suited to the problem domain's actual characteristics, the verification of multi-agent systems is notoriously difficult due to the agents' autonomy. We make this problem tractable by requiring agent behavior to be a valid *refinement* of the applicable *culture* specifications, which can then in turn be verified. By applying compositional techniques (cf. [GTB+03]), results that hold for the overall system can furthermore be obtained from the analysis of partial specifications.

This leads to two different verification problems: Is the specification internally consistent and does it guarantee certain invariants? And is the implementation a valid refinement of the specification?

In order to assert the internal consistency of the specification and prove safety properties, we can build on results for the verification of *Coordination Patterns* [GTB+03, Bur06] and existing techniques for invariant checking [Sch06, BBG+06] and graph-based model checking [RSV04]. If we want to support the capabilities of the employed constraint languages in full, however, we need to adapt and extend them. In particular, the available approaches do not cover liveness properties such as progress or fairness (cf. [Lam77, OL82, AAH+85]). The extended constraint languages allow writing such properties; but there is a gap between what a specification can express and what can be formally verified due to both practical limitations concerning the computational complexity and theoretical limitations concerning the decidability of the verification problem for a real-time temporal logic for object-based systems.

We therefore additionally need the ability to test and experimentally verify designs, which is also a precondition for validating complex specifications against the underlying required properties. Likewise, we would like to be able to validate arbitrary agent implementations conforming to all applicable *culture* specifications by monitoring their behavior at runtime. In order to achieve either, we require adequate support for the prototyping of multi-agent systems and code generation based on *culture* specifications.

## 1.3 Approach

The model-driven design approach that is proposed in this thesis is based on two main contributions: A unifying object-oriented conceptual framework for discussing multi-agent systems, provided by the *Culture and Community-based Modeling Approach* (CURCUMA), and a family of visual specification languages for capturing structural and temporal constraints in a formal but accessible manner. Together, they enable the verification and validation activities that constitute the third main subject of this work.

In this introduction, we provide an overview of the proposed approach. We embed this presentation into the discussion of the envisioned design process, which provides the context for the specific concepts and solutions that are presented in detail in the subsequent chapters. We prefix this discussion with a motivating application example that will be used throughout this thesis.

## 1.3 Approach

Figure 1.3.1: The RailCab shuttle system will serve as our running example

**Application example.** The RailCab R&D project[2] is developing a system of autonomous *shuttles* that travel on a conventional railway network using an innovative linear drive (see Figure 1.3.1). The concept strives to combine the advantages of railways and automobiles, providing fast, safe, energy-efficient and convenient individual transportation. In order to achieve significant improvements over existing systems, the project combines traditional mechanical and electrical engineering with software engineering techniques. The project is representative of a new class of advanced mechatronic systems [BSDB00] using sophisticated control and coordination techniques such as reconfiguration, structural adaptation, ad-hoc collaboration, or self-optimization in complex real world situations. The shuttles constitute a multi-agent system which is characterized by both competition, as shuttles compete for resources and lucrative tasks, and cooperation, as shuttles form convoys in order to reduce drag and increase energy efficiency. Each shuttle is itself controlled by a network of agents which are responsible for specific functions or modules such as energy management, the linear drive, or the active suspension and can be reconfigured in accordance with the current situation and priorities.

The system provides a vivid illustration of many of the challenges that software engineers are facing in their design: Decisions need to be made concurrently and in real-time, distributed among many, possibly heterogeneous autonomous agents. These decisions need to be made in the context of changing control structures and based on the state of a complex environment. As they affect moving vehicles, most of them are safety-critical.

Throughout this thesis, we will use examples that are drawn from or inspired by the RailCab project. In previous work, we have already used related examples to demonstrate the compositional verification of real-time coordination patterns [GTB+03], modular system coordination using social structures [GBK+03], and the verification of safety properties that are inductive invariants of the system [BBG+06]. We will revisit and extend some of them, but additionally discuss the large scale logistic coordination of the system and the internal design of the shuttles in later chapters.

---

[2] RailCab project site: http://www.railcab.de

**Process.** The proposed approach does not impose a specific process model or methodology – the CURCUMA framework was designed to reflect concepts from many different agent-oriented approaches, and the constraint languages are general purpose tools. However, the principle of grounding abstract concepts in observable behavior in the environment creates dependencies between the different views of the system that impose certain restrictions on the order in which they can be considered. There are also certain patterns concerning verification, validation, and code generation that are common to most model-driven approaches. Finally, the emergent nature of certain behaviors in multi-agent systems inherently requires an iterative evaluation and refinement based on prototypes when designing these aspects of the system.

The presented process is therefore one possible vision for a model-driven design process built around prototyping and iteration that primarily serves to illustrate how the different parts of the approach interconnect in order to address the overall design problem. As it focuses on the software design, it will need to be embedded into a comprehensive methodology for the design of software-intensive systems such as the process model for the design of self-optimizing mechatronic systems proposed by the Special Research Initiative 614 (cf. [Ste07, Fra06]). The way the contributions of the different disciplines interact in this process and the role of software engineering in particular are discussed in previous work such as [BGM+08, GFG+05].

The process comprises five phases (see Figure 1.3.2):

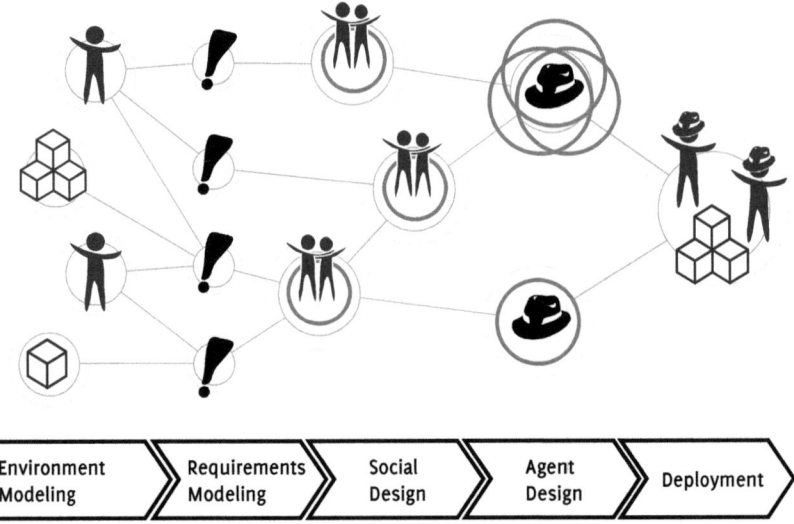

Figure 1.3.2: The development process

## 1.3 Approach

1. In the *environment modeling phase*, a descriptive model of the problem domain is created.
2. In the *requirements modeling phase*, requirements are elicited based on the domain model.
3. In the *social design phase*, the requirements are assigned to social structures; roles and norms fulfilling them are defined; and the required services are added to the environment. Formal verification and experimental validation using rapid prototyping techniques allow the evaluation and step-wise improvement of the design at this early stage.
4. In the *agent design phase*, the agents themselves are designed, respecting all applicable constraints imposed by the social design. The agents can then be evaluated and optimized for performance, again using generated prototypes and a simulated environment. If a complete model of agent behavior is available, they can be formally verified against the social specification.
5. In the *deployment phase*, the agents are tested in their production environment. This requires replacing the implementations of those services, sensors and effectors directly interfacing with the physical environment, but leaves all other aspects of the specification unchanged.

With respect to the different viewpoints used by the Model-Driven Architecture (MDA), the initial analysis phases are concerned with the Computation Independent Model (CIM), which describes the problem domain and the requirements, the third and fourth phase deal with the creation of a Platform Independent Model (PIM), and only the final phase uses a Platform Specific Model (PSM).

Even though each phase deals with clearly defined aspects of the system and builds upon the output of the previous phase, a linear progression through the phases should be seen as an idealization. Within the later phases, prototyping is used to enable iterative improvement of the specification. In practice, it will be necessary to revisit previous phases and make adjustments in this context.

**Environment Modeling Phase.** The analysis of the problem domain starts with the creation of an environment specification. The structure and behavior of the environment are considered as fixed at this stage. Using methods for the identification of classes from traditional object-oriented analysis, the relevant entities from the system's prospective environment can therefore be identified and modeled. Likewise, the behavior of these entities may be observed and modeled through environment processes. If there already is preexisting infrastructure, e.g. some middleware platform, such services as are provided by the environment are also recorded at this time. The result is a domain model of the environment which forms the core of the ontology used in later phases.

As agents (as physical entities), sensors, and effectors are part of the environment specification, they are included in the analysis phase. This is only logical, as any model is, by a common definition, driven by a specific purpose, which in our case is to represent the environment as relevant to the agents. Without at least a basic knowledge of their capabilities, the environment specification could not fulfill this purpose. Nonetheless, it could be argued that the agent types and the sensors and effectors available to them are design decisions that have no place in analysis. While it is true that the addition of new agent types may become necessary in the subsequent social design phase, and the exact capabilities of the sensors and effectors may not be fixed before the agent design phase, we do, however, consider it an important part of analysis to identify prospective classes of agents and establish a general idea of their (potential) capabilities with respect to the environment. Especially when working with (mechanical) agents in physical environments, there are bound to be limitations on the agents and their capabilities that are beyond the scope and control of the design of the multi-agent system. The exact nature of the analysis phase will therefore be shaped by the overall methodology and the input it provides.

**Requirements Modeling Phase.** Based on the domain model created in the first phase, the system requirements can now be specified. Again, established requirements analysis techniques can be used to identify functional and non-functional requirements, as there is nothing inherently agent-specific in the requirements – after all, agent-orientation is supposed to be a solution, not part of the problem. The resulting requirements do not need to be expressed using a specific notation, they can even be informally documented in textual form. If a requirement is to be the subject of formal verification later on, it is however preferable to specify it as a formal constraint that is expressed in terms of the environment specification directly. It is furthermore desirable to structure the requirements by grouping and ranking or weighting them. This will later allow us to apply advanced techniques for judging the quality of a solution with respect to a set of requirements such as our work on selecting the ideal set of configurations for reconfigurable mechatronic systems (cf. [AGKF06]).

**Social Design Phase.** The social design phase begins by taking these requirements, breaking them further down into suitable subsets, and assigning them to agent communities. Each community is then responsible for ensuring that the system meets the requirements in question.

For each set of requirements, a community type which is capable of dealing with this responsibility is then designed. Each community type represents a distinct architectural view that defines a set of roles and norms governing agent behavior. It may delegate specific tasks to subcommunities, which ultimately leads to a hierarchy of community types whose bottom elements are basic interaction patterns dealing with simple, manageable problems. At this time cultures, design patterns that address a specific requirement, can be applied to the system. As cultures may themselves contain more specific subcultures, instantiating a culture may create a whole hierarchy of community types.

When applying cultures or devising new solutions to problems, the designer will need to take the agents' capabilities (as expressed by their sensors and effectors) into account. It is not helpful to require behaviors that agents are unable to enact, or specify norms that depend on something agents cannot sense. If the physical design of the agent is under the designer's control, it is possible to add new capabilities through additional sensors and effectors at this point. Another common way to provide agents with additional capabilities is adding appropriate services that supply them. Finally, as the idea behind communities *is* using interaction in order to achieve goals beyond the reach of the individual agents, communities can themselves provide new capabilities that can be used as a bootstrap by other communities. For example, in order to allow every shuttle in the system to communicate with any other shuttle, one could introduce a network of local access points capable of relaying messages and a community type for managing a distributed directory, instead of upgrading the shuttles' antennas.

Together, the community types need to result in a consistent specification. If the requirements are not

## 1.3 Approach

orthogonal, i.e., the norms of the community types constrain the same effectors or concern the same entities, different community types might be in conflict. For the RailCab system, different concerns such as task execution, efficient routing, or traffic safety quite naturally all affect a shuttle's movement and may suggest quite different ideal behaviors. At this point, we try to spot cases where conforming with all norms is *theoretically* impossible. Other than that, we merely strive to keep dependencies between community types as weak as possible and defer the task of actually reconciling conflicts to the agent design phase.

Once all relevant community types have been specified, the model can be validated. Individual community types can be formally verified: As both their norms and the behavior of the environment can be modeled as a graph transformation system, we can apply the above-mentioned invariant checking techniques [GS04] in order to prove certain required properties, e.g. the absence of accidents or hazards. We can also use a model checker to systematically explore the state space for specific initial configurations up to a certain size. Other aspects such as requirements concerning efficiency and performance or emergent properties of complex systems that cannot be assessed through formal methods require empirical validation by means of a prototype. Still, we are able to generate a monitor from the social design that allows us to automate conformance testing. It is also feasible to emulate the agents at this early stage by non-deterministically applying sensors and effectors that are not explicitly forbidden by some norm and observe the resulting behavior, at least where the norms describe concrete behaviors – when the norms merely state goals, complying with them requires additional strategic reasoning.

**Agent Design Phase.** Once the social specification addresses all pertinent requirements, the actual control logic of the agents can be designed, i.e. specified or implemented. As the environment specification only describes the agents' external interfaces and the social design only operates at the inter-agent level, any internal architecture producing the appropriate behavior is acceptable. It is, however, convenient to use the abstractions used by the social design for guiding the internal design where possible, as this makes the transformation conceptually simpler and facilitates the use of automated techniques.

The agent specification can directly reuse those norms that specify simple reactive behavior, possibly augmenting them with additional strategies for intelligently choosing between the available options where the social design leaves room for non-deterministic choice. Using techniques for controller synthesis, such as our own work in [GKKW05] and [GKB05, GHHK06], it may even be possible to generate a matching controller from norms that encode more complex scenarios. Nonetheless, norms that are declarative in nature, e.g., a requirement to reach a destination by a given deadline, require more elaborate strategies and algorithms that cannot be deduced, but need to be designed explicitly.

Reconciling the requirements of all pertinent community types may not be a trivial task. While it is feasible to automatically compose non-orthogonal concerns (cf. [GV06]) in certain cases, this step generally requires human intervention. While the solutions are often intuitive – e.g. when incorporating the collision avoidance protocol with the controller that moves a shuttle on the shortest path to its destination – the interactions may become arbitrarily complex if the community types are poorly chosen or the problem domain necessarily implies strong dependencies –

e.g. when bidding on tasks, routing, and forming convoys are treated as different concerns but computing the minimal bid for a task nonetheless requires information about the optimal route, which in turn depends on the availability of suitable convoys.

Analyzing the complex interplay between different communities is facilitated by the ability to test prototypes of the agents in a simulation of the environment that is based on the environment specification. By generating behavioral monitors from the social design, we can even automatically check the agents' conformance with the specification. In [ABB+06], we present an integrated prototyping environment for this purpose.

**Deployment Phase.** Once the agent design conforms to the social specification and has proven itself in the simulated environment, it can be moved to its production environment for further testing. An appealing feature of the proposed approach is that this mainly means replacing the simulated parts of the system with their physical counterparts. Provided that it was modeled correctly, the environment specification can simply be dropped. At the service level, the prototyping middleware is replaced by the production middleware. The overall complexity of the software system decreases, as physics, processes and physical constraints (e.g. context) no longer need to be replicated in software; however, the middleware that processes sensor input and interprets effector commands becomes significantly more complex internally.

The model of the actual agents remains unchanged, as their interfaces are unchanged. Depending on the target platform, we may actually be able to reuse the exact same code for simulation and hardware tests [BGK04]. It is nonetheless necessary to perform a sufficient number of tests in order to ensure that there were no errors or oversimplifications in the environment specification that lead to significant discrepancies between simulated and actual behavior (cf.[BN03]).

## 1.4 Contribution

An end-to-end process for the development of complex software systems, with all the required methods and tools, is a rather broad topic. This thesis could not realize its ambitious objective of offering a comprehensive model-driven approach to multi-agent system design without limiting its scope in other directions and building on a wealth of previous work. It is naturally selective in the topics that are treated in depth, devoting most space to the formalization of the visual constraint languages and of the proposed conceptual framework, as this formalization serves as the foundation for all subsequent activities, in particular formal verification. By the nature of our application example, we also restrict the considered application domain to mechatronic systems. While there is no such limitation inherent in the employed concepts or methods, the designs that we present in our case studies do benefit from certain properties of their physical environment, such as the ready availability of a (relatively unambiguous) concept of locality, so that the question whether the approach might be extended to software-intensive systems in general must remain open. Finally, the experimental validation of the approach remains fragmentary. While it is complete in the sense that every major concept, notation, method, or tool has been implemented and tried and tested using isolated examples of varying complexity, there is no real-world

## 1.4 Contribution

problem to which the development process has been applied in its entirety. While we use a real research and development project as our motivating example, none of the presented designs go to a level of detail and comprehensiveness that would be sufficient to empirically confirm the claim that the proposed development process and complexity reduction techniques provide tangible benefits in practice. Our experiences during the work on the case study that was intended for the validation of Intrapid, a large, one year student project, have made it abundantly clear that developing an agent controller, let alone a system of agents, that consistently acts and interacts in a complex and realistic physical environment would deserve a project in its own right.

Among the original contributions we make in this thesis, the CURCUMA framework and the language for temporal properties stand out. The former started out as a descriptive metamodel that attempted to synthesize as many approaches to multi-agent design as were then available into a coherent whole in the fall of 2002. Inspired by the literature on mentalistic concepts (cf. [WJ95b]) and the social system metaphor (cf. [JC97, Cas00]), but also in particular the *criticism* of intentional stance (cf. [VO02]) and the communication semantics derived from it (cf. [Sin98a]) and the confrontation with concepts that flatly deny the usefulness of mentalistic concepts (cf. [Bro91]), the concept of *legal stance* took shape as a defining element of the approach. It is an original idea whose evident tendency to inspire skepticism in the proponents of each of the contributing schools of thought may serve as a testament to its originality and innovative hybrid nature. Combined with evolutionary extensions to the concept of agent organizations, it enables a new level of dynamics in the coordination of agent systems.

The CURCUMA framework then goes beyond mere description and elevates these ideas to design principles. By underpinning them with a rigorous formalization, it firmly embeds them into a systematic software engineering process. The ability to express complex properties in an accessible way was essential for making the step from description to design and putting the framework to practical use. It thus owes a lot to Story-Driven Modeling (cf. [FNTZ98]) and its precursors (cf. [Zün95, SWZ95, SWZ99]).

Our work on structural patterns represents an evolutionary enhancement of this previous work; it focuses on pragmatic and notational aspects and providing a complete and unified semantics for the notations. We nonetheless integrate some powerful, previously unavailable features such as universal quantification and recursion into the languages. Our main innovation lies in the combination of structural patterns and temporal logic, however. While different aspects of the proposed language have been inspired by existing languages and diagrams, the resulting combination of scenarios, graph patterns, and real-time constraints provides an expressive visual notation that is capable of succinctly stating complex combined structural and temporal properties that can only be expressed with difficulty (or not at all) by existing languages.

We only sketch a rough concept for bridging the gap between the discrete, object-graph-based perspective of Story-Driven Modeling and the continuous nature of an embedded system's environment. In this area, we heavily rely on existing or parallel work in the Special Research Initiative 614. The *OCM* [HOG04, OHG04] provides the architectural justification for treating agent coordination as a problem that can be decoupled from questions of hard real-time control, while *Coordination Patterns* [GTB+03] for reliable inter-agent communication and the approach for the safe reconfiguration at the controller level [Bur06] are indispensable for making the implementation of the dynamic agent coordination mechanisms envisioned at the level of the Cognitive Operator at all feasible at the lower levels.

In the same vein, our verification approach builds on the fact that compositional verification is feasible for component designs built around *Coordination Patterns* [GTB+03], allowing us to reduce the verification problem to the question of instantiating the right patterns at the right times, which in turn can be tackled using existing approaches for the verification of graph-based systems [Sch06, BBG+06]. In this area, we mostly apply existing techniques, adding a few refinements where extensions in other places have made them necessary. However, our work on the refinement of graph transformation systems and the monitoring of Timed Story Scenario Diagrams is original.

For supporting the proposed iterative validation approach, significant effort has been invested in the necessary tools, code generation and execution frameworks, and numerous evolutionary or ground-breaking contributions to the Fujaba platform have been made in the process.

## 1.5 Structure

The organization of this thesis does not follow the phases of the design process, but rather proceeds from the theoretical to the pragmatic, starting with the formalization of the employed notations, then introducing the CURCUMA framework as a means of structuring the system specification, and finally moving on to the discussion of verification and validation activities and tool support.

**Notations and semantics.** In order to meet the requirement for accessible but formal notations, all aspects of the system are modeled using extended graphical notations based on the Unified Modeling Language [Obj07]. Formal semantics for the notations, which are required for formal verification and code generation, are provided based on the theory of graph grammars.

The structural aspects of the system are modeled using UML Class Diagrams and UML Component Diagrams. Story-Driven Modeling (SDM) is employed to define system behavior: Story Diagrams [FNTZ98], an extension of UML Activity Diagrams, use Story Patterns, which are graph rules written as extended UML Object Diagrams, as a formal representation of the effects of each activity. Where real-time communication between components is concerned, Real-Time Statecharts [Bur06], an extension of UML State Machines, are used to specify the protocols. These notational and graph-theoretical foundations of our approach are presented in Chapter 2.

In Chapter 3, we introduce the proposed family of visual constraint languages that will allow us to graphically capture *constraints* on component behavior, such as the *norms* set by the *social* specifications. Structural constraints are specified using *Story Decision Diagrams*, which extend Story Patterns with quantification and a concept for modularity. Temporal constraints concerning the structural evolution of the system are specified using *Timed Story Scenario Diagrams*, which combine *Story Decision Diagrams* and temporal logic into an integrated graphical notation. For each notation, we discuss its formal semantics, expressiveness, and relation to the existing notations.

## 1.5 Structure

**Model-driven multi-agent system design.** Building on these foundations, we present our approach for designing the behavior of complex, adaptive systems in Chapter 4. We discuss our notion of a multi-agent system and informally and formally introduce the CURCUMA conceptual framework as a means of integrating agent-oriented concepts with traditional software engineering and decomposing a system into architectural views. We also present concrete examples to show how the proposed notations are used to model norms.

In the subsequent Chapter 5, we follow up with a discussion of the verification and validation activities that can be performed based on the resulting models. We present both what is possible in theory and what is supported by the existing tools, and demonstrate how various types of problems can be identified and resolved.

Practical aspects of using our approach, in particular the available tool support and the application of the new notations and concepts, are discussed in Chapter 6, followed by the conclusion and an outlook on future work in Chapter 7.

# Chapter 2

# Foundations

## 2.1 Introduction

This chapter lays the syntactic and semantic foundations for the remainder of the thesis. We begin by presenting the concept of *Story-Driven Modeling*, which is at the heart of our approach for modeling agent behavior and constraint specifications as it allows us to define formal semantics for UML-based notations. We discuss the existing notations and define their formal semantics as required for the definition of our extended constraint notations and the formal verification of the model. We then look at *Coordination Patterns*, which are underlying the concept of *cultures* used for the decomposition of the system, and give a short overview of the associated notations for component-based modeling and the specification of real-time communication protocols. Finally, we introduce a mapping between the two approaches that will allow us to interrelate message- and state-based coordination behavior and the predominantly rule-based definition of agent behavior.

### 2.1.1 Related Work

**Story-Driven Modeling** is rooted in the theory of *graph grammars* (cf. [Roz97]). Using *graphs* as the central concept, graph grammars provide a very natural way of specifying structures and relationships between entities. Behavior can be expressed by *graph transformation systems*, i.e. transformation systems where each state is represented by a graph. Graph grammars are very useful for defining the syntax and semantics of diagrams and visual programming languages as they allow transferring concepts from the term- and syntax tree-based description of textual languages to the domain of visual modeling (cf. [HE00]).

There is a wealth of published literature on theorems, algorithms, languages, and applications of graph grammars (cf. [EEKR99b, EEKR99a] for an overview). There are also tools such as PROGRES [Zün95, SWZ95, SWZ99] or the Attributed Graph Grammar system (AGG) [AGG, Rud97] that provide environments for specifying and evaluating graph rules.

*Story-Driven Modeling* is the result of merging concepts from PROGRES and the Unified Modeling Language (UML) [Obj07]. By using graph grammars to supply the formal semantics missing in the official specification, the UML thus becomes a formal specification language with operational semantics. Story Patterns [KNNZ00, NSZ03] are an extension of UML Object Diagrams that allow expressing conditions and operations on instance structures. Story Diagrams [FNTZ98] extend UML Activity Diagrams by embedding Story Patterns into activities in order to provide them with operational semantics. The Fujaba Tool Suite[1] implements these notations as part of an open, extensible environment (cf. [BGN+03]).

While the complete operational semantics of both Story Patterns and Story Diagrams have been defined (cf. [Zün01]), there is currently no complete formalization of Story Patterns, let alone Story Diagrams, that is suitable for use in the context of formal verification, e.g. when deriving the input for a model checker. In [Sch06], Story Patterns are used in such a context as part of a formal system specification, but the employed formalization of Story Patterns as graph rules abstracts from many of their advanced features. In this thesis, we extend this formalization by adding support for attributes, inheritance, and cardinalities, thus reenabling the use of several commonly employed elements of the syntax that stem from the UML and differentiate Story Patterns from comparable notations based on graph grammars.

**Coordination patterns** [GTB+03] build on the UML 2.0's notations for component modeling in order to specify the (real-time) coordination and communication behavior of system components. Components communicate via ports that need to conform to the role specifications imposed by the Coordination Pattern in the form of protocol statecharts.

However, the notations for specifying protocol statecharts that are supplied by the UML are insufficient for the comprehensive specification of real-time behavior. In the UML 1.x, real-time properties could only be expressed using the *UML Profile for Schedulability, Performance, and Time Specification* [OMG05]. It allows attaching specific schedulability or quality of service characteristics to classes, but only provides insufficient support for the detailed specification of real-time behavior.

Coordination Patterns therefore employ real-time statecharts (RTSC) [GB03, BGS05, BG03], an extended statechart notation based on the Timed Automata formalism [DMY02]. An important advantage of RTSC over other approaches, such as Statemate [HP98, PMS94], or Timed Automata as used in UPPAAL [LPY97], is that transitions between states are not assumed to be instantaneous, thus making their semantics implementable on an actual physical machine. A detailed comparison of the characteristics of related approaches can be found in a recent comprehensive survey (cf. [GH06]).

In this thesis, we will provide a formalization of Coordination Patterns that allows us to reference their elements in the context of Story-Driven Modeling in a formalized fashion. In order to arrive at such a formalization, we will first need to consolidate two previous formal definitions of Coordination Patterns and RTSC.

---

[1] Fujaba project site: http://www.fujaba.de

## 2.1 Introduction

### 2.1.2 Application Example

In order to present the notations, we use a simplified model of the RailCab system and specify basic shuttle behaviors.

**Structure.** The railway network is modeled as a graph consisting of short track segments, each not much longer than a single shuttle. Tracks are unidirectional, have either one or – in the case of a branching junction – two successors, and are successor to one or – in the case of a joining junction – two tracks. Shuttles are located on track segments, occupying one or – while passing from one segment into another – at most two segments. This model is only intended for the description of higher-level coordination mechanisms and safety properties, whereas it is unsuited to lower-level control engineering problems as it abstracts from the shuttles' exact position on the tracks.

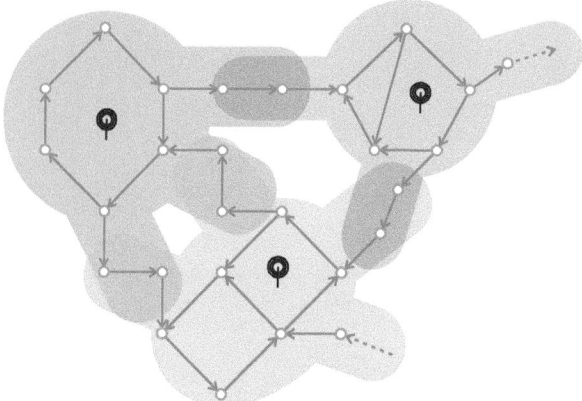

Figure 2.1.1: Base stations with overlapping controlled areas

**Location.** Each track segment is monitored by one or more base stations that are responsible for keeping track of the position of each shuttle within their respective controlled areas. Each shuttle needs to register with the responsible base stations and keep them informed about its exact current position as computed based on GPS navigational data and the shuttle's internal sensor readings. In turn, the shuttle receives updates about the position of all other shuttles in the base stations' controlled areas in regular intervals. The specifics of these interactions are defined by the registration pattern, a real-time Coordination Pattern. As can be seen in the schematic representation of part of such a network in Figure 2.1.1, the controlled areas of different base stations overlap in order to ensure that a shuttle never has to move 'blindly' onto a track segment that is not part of the controlled area of any of its base stations and might already be occupied by another shuttle.

**Coordination.** Another Coordination Pattern, the convoy pattern (cf. [GTB⁺03, BBG⁺06]), ensures that two shuttles in close proximity safely coordinate their behavior. While shuttles must normally not occupy the same track segment at the same time in order to preclude collisions, the convoy pattern provides shuttles with the ability to reduce drag by forming contact-free convoys leaving much smaller gaps between the shuttles. The pattern's task is to ensure that all shuttles in the convoy model their behavior on consistent assumptions so that acceleration and braking maneuvers are properly coordinated – the control algorithms actually performing these maneuvers are out of the pattern's scope. The convoy pattern illustrates the principle that complex behaviors can often be realized by layering higher-level patterns on top of simpler ones. As the pattern can only be implemented correctly if the positions of the other shuttles are known, the registration patterns serve as a bootstrap by guaranteeing that the required information is provided.

## 2.2 Story-Driven Modeling: A Graph-based Approach

The fundamental abstraction that Story-Driven Modeling (SDM) is based upon is the idea of interpreting instance situations of an object-oriented system as graphs. Informally, this seems intuitively plausible, as UML Object Diagrams as a common way of describing instance situations already have a graph-like structure. More specifically, we map each object to a node and each attribute/association to an edge of a labeled graph. The formal semantics that are typically missing from UML-based notations are then provided by the theory of graph transformation systems (cf. [Roz97]), which allows reasoning about states and behavior of object-oriented systems modeled using a visual notation.

### 2.2.1 Notations

#### 2.2.1.1 Class Diagrams

For structural modeling, we use standard UML Class Diagrams (cf. [Obj07, section 7.4]). Class Diagrams are employed at different levels of abstraction: Firstly, they can be used to document the results of an object-oriented analysis (OOA) (cf. [EJW95]), describing notable concepts and entities of the problem domain and their relationships, thus serving as a basic ontology (cf. e.g. [Gru93]). Secondly, they are used at the specification level for formally defining the system entities that interact in the specified constraints and patterns. Finally, at an operational level, they can be used to define the internal structures of individual components.

Figure 2.2.1 presents a specification level diagram of the application example. As this is a basic example, it does not use all available features of Class Diagrams, such as the ability to define subtyping relationships or assign stereotypes.

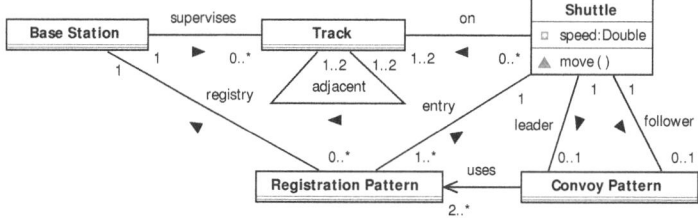

Figure 2.2.1: Central entities and control structures of the application example

Class diagrams do not only define the elements of the system and their relationships, but characterize the set of all possible system states, which is restricted by the specified associations, cardinalities, and attribute types. However, this characterization is rather broad, as there is no way restrict attribute values beyond the type level or place restrictions on combinations of properties, which would be required for defining conditional or instance-level restrictions.

## 2.2.1.2 Story Patterns

UML Object Diagrams (cf. [Obj07, section 7.4]) can be used to depict specific configurations of objects which are valid instances of a given Class Diagram. *Story Patterns* (cf. [KNNZ00, NSZ03]) are an extension of UML Object Diagrams that allows expressing both properties and transformations, in particular structural changes. A Story Pattern consists of two Object Diagrams representing a pre- and a postcondition, the left hand side (LHS) and the right hand side (RHS). At runtime, the LHS is matched against the instance graph representing the current system configuration, and the free elements of the pattern are bound to specific nodes and edges. If a match is found, it is transformed in order to match the RHS by adding, modifying and deleting the appropriate nodes and edges using the Single Push Out strategy (SPO).[2] It is also possible to query and set attribute values in this manner.

**Notation.** When writing a Story Pattern, the RHS and the LHS are integrated into a single diagram in order to obtain a more compact representation. This is achieved by using the stereotypes ≪create≫ for marking elements that are exclusively part of the RHS and need to be created, and the ≪destroy≫ for denoting elements of the LHS which should be deleted as a side-effect of the rule. Figure 2.2.2 shows the definition (Figure 2.2.2a) of a Story Pattern for moving a shuttle from its current track onto the adjacent track and an instance graph representing a small fragment of the system before (Figure 2.2.2b) and after (Figure 2.2.2c) the pattern is applied.

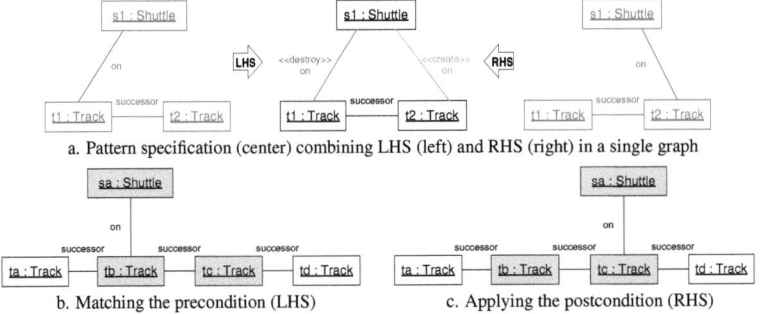

a. Pattern specification (center) combining LHS (left) and RHS (right) in a single graph

b. Matching the precondition (LHS)  c. Applying the postcondition (RHS)

Figure 2.2.2: A shuttle moving to another track

**Negation.** Furthermore, it is possible to indicate forbidden elements in a Story Pattern by crossing them out. Forbidden elements can be employed to specify patterns that are only applied when no match for any *one* of their forbidden elements is found, enabling more differentiated rules. E.g., Figure 2.2.3 encodes the default behavior (used while not running a convoy pattern) that

---

[2] For a thorough discussion of the respective theoretical and practical strengths and weaknesses of the Single Push Out (SPO) and Double Push Out (DPO) strategies see [Roz97], Chapters 3 and 4. While DPO provides a conceptually elegant solutions to problems such as the creation of dangling edges when deleting nodes, using SPO greatly simplifies the operationalization of the graph rules.

## 2.2 Story-Driven Modeling

requires the track that a shuttle is moving into needs to be vacant. However, it is not possible to express that a combination of elements should be absent, as the forbidden elements are interpreted as alternatives, i.e., the pattern application fails as soon as the first forbidden element is found.

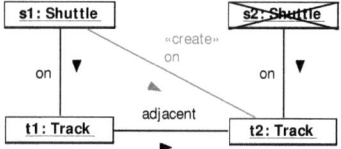

Figure 2.2.3: Forbidden element - default movement is only allowed into vacant tracks

For the same reason, it is not possible to specify forbidden elements that are characterized by multiple associations. This poses a serious practical problem, as such a construct is needed to encode many comparatively simple properties, e.g., 'no convoy pattern exists *between* shuttles *s1* and *s2*'.

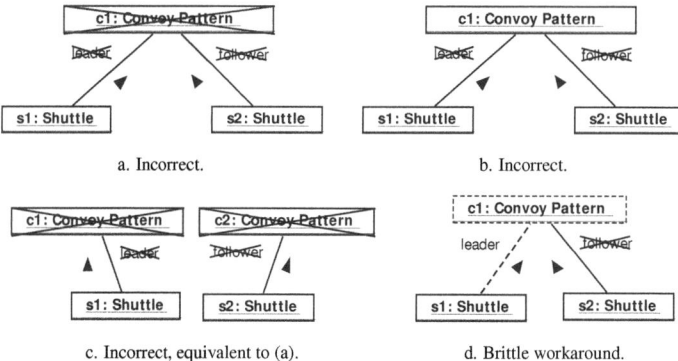

Figure 2.2.4: Attempts to encode that *s1* and *s2* do not already share a pattern.

Figure 2.2.4 presents several common but incorrect approaches to specifying this property. The pattern in Figure 2.2.4a will fail as soon as any of the shuttles has any pattern (false negative). The pattern in Figure 2.2.4b is completely wrong, as it will not only fail to match if there is a pattern belonging to either of the shuttles (false negative), but also if there is no pattern in the system at all (false negative), and additionally also match if there is a pattern that is unrelated to either shuttle, even though the shuttles share a pattern (false positive). Figure 2.2.4c is equivalent to Figure 2.2.4a and thus equally incorrect. Finally, Figure 2.2.4d is a commonly used workaround based on optional elements (read as '*s1* may or may not have a pattern, but if so, then not with *s2*'). While this works as long as *s1* has at most one pattern, the solution is not robust and does not convey the intended semantics. If *s1* has two patterns, the property might hold or not depending on which pattern is bound to *c1*. If the shared element in question is characterized by more than two associations, this problem intensifies.

**Invariant Story Patterns.** When a Story Pattern contains no stereotypes, the LHS and the RHS are identical and the pattern has no side effects. Such Story Patterns describe and allow testing for structural system properties. The Story Pattern in Figure 2.2.5 matches whenever two shuttles (partially) occupy the same segment, i.e. are on the same track. A translation into OCL is provided below the figure.

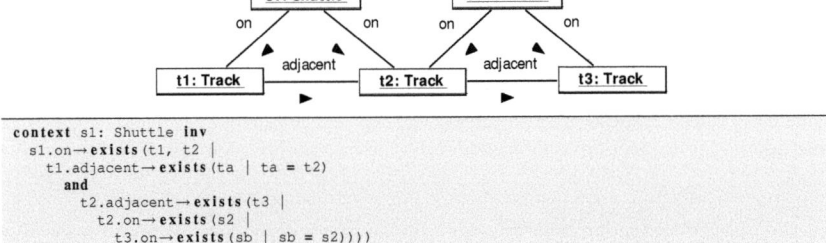

```
context s1: Shuttle inv
  s1.on→exists(t1, t2 |
    t1.adjacent→exists(ta | ta = t2)
    and
      t2.adjacent→exists(t3 |
        t2.on→exists(s2 |
          t3.on→exists(sb | sb = s2))))
```

Figure 2.2.5: Story pattern describing an invariant

For the basic system without convoys, we would like this property to be a negative invariant of the system that never matches for any two shuttles. However, there is no way to make this explicit in the pattern. In [BBG+06], we used Story Patterns to specify invariants of the system that represented forbidden states (accidents, hazards), whose absence could then be formally verified. This required the implicit convention that all patterns represented *negative* invariants of the system, which could not be indicated explicitly. The resulting restriction to negative invariants entailed the use of unintuitive multiple negations, i.e. that a required element of a positive invariant was translated into a forbidden element of a forbidden pattern. Combined with the described limitations concerning negation, this significantly complicated modeling.

#### 2.2.1.3 Story Diagrams

While Story Patterns confer the ability to specify almost arbitrary transformation steps on object graph structures, they provide no facilities for specifying control flow, as is needed for more complex preconditions and transformations. By embedding Story Patterns into UML Activity Diagrams, the former acquire the ability to express complex multi-step transformations, whereas the latter receive the benefit of operational activity semantics. The resulting Story Diagrams [FNTZ98] are in fact expressive enough to represent a Turing-complete programming language.

The Story Patterns interact with the control flow in multiple ways. Most importantly, transitions are selected based on whether a pattern has matched (*success*) or has failed to match (*failure*).

## 2.2 Story-Driven Modeling

It is also possible to indicate that the Story Pattern should not stop after matching the first valid configuration, but actually match a set of objects, which can then be processed in a loop using the *foreach* and *end* transition guards.

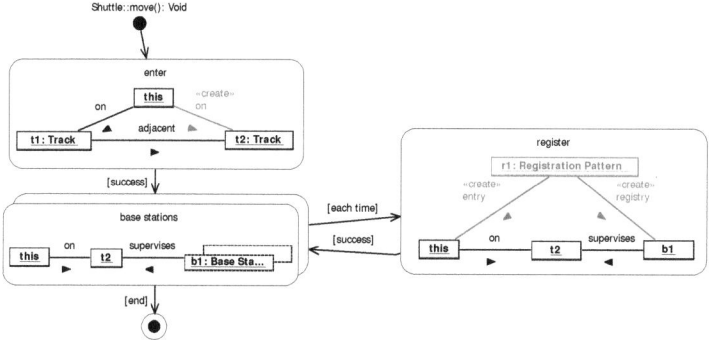

Figure 2.2.6: A shuttle enters a track and registers with all attached base stations.

Figure 2.2.6 shows a Story Diagram implementing one of the move methods of a shuttle. The shuttle (partially) moves onto a track segment and then registers with each base station that supervises it in turn. [3]

While Story Diagrams are instrumental for the detailed design and the subsequent implementation of the system, they only play a marginal role in the proposed analysis, specification and verification activities. We will therefore not discuss their semantics in detail, but refer the reader to the original publications.

### 2.2.2 Formalization

The presented (extended) UML Diagrams provide a visual modeling language for the specification and presentation of systems and their associated constraints which – apart from the mentioned limitations – is expressive and accessible to human users. However, in order to provide them with the formal semantics that UML-based notations are typically lacking, we internally map our notations to a formal graph-based model which, though less suitable for presentation, can subsequently serve as the basis for theoretical analysis, formal verification, and code generation. We first introduce all required concepts and afterwards map the elements of the visual modeling language to them.

---

[3] A realistic implementation would check whether the shuttle was already registered with the base station in question, which is, however, non-trivial because of the syntactic limitations concerning negation discussed above.

#### 2.2.2.1 Graphs

As graphs are the foundation of our modeling language, we start by providing a formal definition and a set of related properties and operators.

**Basic definitions.** Our formalization is based on sets and functions over these sets. In our definitions, we use the following notations:

For a function $f : A \rightarrow B$, we denote by $f|_C$ the function $f'$ with domain $A \cap C$ for which for all $x \in A \cap C$ holds $f'(x) = f(x)$.

We compose two functions $f : A \rightarrow B$ and $g : C \rightarrow A$ using the operator $f \circ g$, resulting in a function $f' : C \rightarrow B$ for which for all $x \in C$ holds $f'(x) = f(g(x))$.

Two functions $f : A \rightarrow B$ and $g : C \rightarrow D$ can be composed using the operator $f \oplus g$ if for all $x \in A \cap C$ holds $f(x) = g(x)$, resulting in a function $h : A \cup C \rightarrow B \cup D$ for which for all $x \in A$ holds $h(x) = f(x)$ and for all $x \in C$ holds $h(x) = g(x)$.

**Labeled graphs.** Following the conventions used in [Roz97], we define a graph $G$ as a directed graph that can accommodate multiple edges between two nodes.

**Definition 2.2.1** *A graph is a tuple $G = (N_G, E_G, src_G, tgt_G)$, where $N_G$ is a finite set of nodes, $E_G$ is finite set of edges, $src : E_G \rightarrow N_G$ is the source function, which assigns a source node to each edge, and $tgt : E_G \rightarrow N_G$ is the target function, which assigns a target node to each edge.*

We can then extend this definition into the definition of a *labeled graph* by adding a pair of labeling functions:

**Definition 2.2.2** *A labeled graph is a pair $(G, L_G)$ of a graph $G = (N_G, E_G, src_G, tgt_G)$ and an appropriate labeling $L_G = (\Omega_G^N, \Omega_G^E, l_G^N, l_G^E)$ where $\Omega_G^N$ is a set of node labels, $\Omega_G^E$ is a set of edge labels, $l_G^N : N \rightarrow \Omega_G^N$ is a node labeling function that assigns a label to each node, and $l_G^E : E \rightarrow \Omega_G^E$ is an edge labeling function that assigns a label to each edge.*

Two graphs $G_1$ and $G_2$ are *label compatible* iff the labelings of both graphs are compatible, i.e., identical for all the elements that are shared by both graphs: $l_{G_1}^N|_{(N_{G_1} \cap N_{G_2})} = l_{G_2}^N|_{(N_{G_1} \cap N_{G_2})}$ and $l_{G_1}^E|_{(E_{G_1} \cap E_{G_2})} = l_{G_2}^E|_{(E_{G_1} \cap E_{G_2})}$.

They are *edge compatible* iff the source and target functions are identical for shared edges that are contained in both graphs: $src_{G_1}|_{(E_{G_1} \cap E_{G_2})} = src_{G_2}|_{(E_{G_1} \cap E_{G_2})}$ and $tgt_{G_1}|_{(E_{G_1} \cap E_{G_2})} = tgt_{G_2}|_{(E_{G_1} \cap E_{G_2})})$.

Two graphs that are both label and edge compatible are called *compatible*.

We use $G_\emptyset$ to denote the empty graph with $N_{G_\emptyset} = E_{G_\emptyset} = \emptyset$.

**Graph Operators.** For compatible graphs, we define the union, intersection and subtraction of the graphs.

Given two compatible graphs $G_1$ and $G_2$, their *union* is built by combining their node and edge sets and combining the labeling, source and target functions: $G' = G_1 \cup G_2$ with $G' :=$

## 2.2 Story-Driven Modeling

$(N', E', src', tgt', \Omega^{N'}, \Omega^{E'}, l^{N'}, l^{E'})$, where $N' := N_{G_1} \cup N_{G_2}$, $E' := E_{G_1} \cup E_{G_2}$, $src' := src_{G_1} \oplus src_{G_2}$, $tgt := tgt_{G_1} \oplus tgt_{G_2}$, $\Omega^{N'} := \Omega^N_{G_1} \cup \Omega^N_{G_2}$, $\Omega^{E'} := \Omega^E_{G_1} \cup \Omega^E_{G_2}$, $l^{N'} := l^N_{G_1} \oplus l^N_{G_2}$ and $l'_E := l^E_{G_1} \oplus l^E_{G_2}$. The union is commutative, $G_1 \cup G_2 = G_2 \cup G_1$ holds.

Their *intersection* of $G_1$ and $G_2$ is built by intersecting the node and edge sets of the two graphs and restricting the labeling, source and target functions to the resulting subgraph: $G' = G_1 \cap G_2$ with $G' := (N', E', src', tgt', \Omega^{N'}, \Omega^{E'}, l^{N'}, l^{E'})$, where $N' := N_{G_1} \cap N_{G_2}$, $E' := E_{G_1} \cap E_{G_2}$, $src' := src_{G_1}|_{(E_{G_1} \cap E_{G_2})}$, $tgt := tgt_{G_1}|_{(E_{G_1} \cap E_{G_2})}$, $\Omega^{N'} := \Omega^N_{G_1} \cap \Omega^N_{G_2}$, $\Omega^{E'} := \Omega^E_{G_1} \cap \Omega^E_{G_2}$, $l^{N'} := l^N_{G_1}|_{(N_{G_1} \cap N_{G_2})}$ and $l'_E := l^E_{G_1}|_{(E_{G_1} \cap E_{G_2})}$. The intersection is commutative, $G_1 \cap G_2 = G_2 \cap G_1$ holds.

The *subtraction* of the two graphs $G_1$ and $G_2$ is similar to intersection. The node and edge sets of a graph are subtracted from the sets of the other graph, and the functions are restricted accordingly: $G' = G_1 \setminus G_2$ with $G' := (N', E', src', tgt', \Omega^{N'}, \Omega^{E'}, l^{N'}, l^{E'})$, where $N' := N_{G_1} \setminus N_{G_2}$, $E' := \{e \in E_{G_1} \setminus E_{G_2} | src_{G_1}(e) \in N' \wedge tgt_{G_1}(e) \in N'\}$, $src' := src_{G_1}|_{E'}$, $tgt := tgt_{G_1}|_{E'}$, $\Omega^{N'} := \Omega^N_{G_1}$, $\Omega^{E'} := \Omega^E_{G_1}$, $l^{N'} := l^N_{G_1}|_{N'}$ and $l'_E := l^E_{G_1}|_{E'}$. For non-empty graphs, subtraction is not commutative, $G_1 \setminus G_2 \neq G_2 \setminus G_1$ holds. The definition of $E'$ results in the implicit deletion of dangling edges, i.e. edges whose source or target node is undefined. Otherwise, the resulting tuple might not represent a graph, as the functions $src_{E'}$ and $tgt_{E'}$ would not necessarily be restricted to $N'$.

**Typed graphs.** We now add the notion of types to our definition of a graph. In a *type system graph* $G_T = (N_T, E_T, src_T, tgt_T, \Omega^N_T, \Omega^E_T, l^N_T, l^E_T)$, nodes represent node types, edges represent edge types, and labels are used to assign type names.

A *typed graph* $G$ is then a labeled graph whose node and edge labels are the nodes and edges of some *type system graph* $G_T$, i.e. $\Omega^N_G = N_T$ and $\Omega^E_G = E_T$.[4] We call $G$ *type conformant* for $G_T$ if the labeling of $G$ is compatible with $G_T$, which means that if there is an edge labeled with $e_1 \in E_T$ between nodes labeled with $n_1 \in N_T$ and $n_2 \in N_T$ in $G$, $e_1$ must be an edge connecting nodes $n_1$ and $n_2$ in $G_T$:

**Definition 2.2.3** *The labeling of a graph* $G = (N_G, E_G, src_G, tgt_G, \Omega^N_G, \Omega^E_G, l^N_G, l^E_G)$ *is type conformant for the type system graph* $G_T = (N_T, E_T, src_T, tgt_T, \Omega^N_T, \Omega^E_T, l^N_T, l^E_T)$ *iff* $\Omega^N_G \subseteq N_T$, $\Omega^E_G \subseteq E_T$ *and* $\forall e \in E_G : (\exists e_T \in E_T : l^E_G(e) = e_T \wedge l^N_G(src_G(e)) = src_T(e_T) \wedge l^N_G(tgt_G(e)) = tgt_T(e_T))$.

We denote the set of all type conformant labeled graphs for a type system graph $G_T$ by $\mathcal{G}[G_T]$.

In order to accommodate subtyping, we need to extend our notion of a type system graph and of type conformity. An *inheritance type system graph* $G_T$ is a type system graph whose edge label alphabet $\Omega^E_T$ contains a special element $isa$. If there is an edge labeled with $isa$ from node $n_{sub}$ to node $n_{super}$, we say that $n_{sub}$ is a *subtype* of $n_{super}$. We define $subtype(n_{sub}, n_{super}) := \exists e \in$

---

[4]Note that we do not assign type names (strings) to objects, which we then would have to (string) compare with the assigned type name of the corresponding type system graph node, but directly use the nodes of the type system graph themselves to label the nodes of the instance graph, which simplifies checking type conformity. The labeling function does not care whether its alphabet is letters or nodes.

$E_T : l_T^N(e) = isa \land n_{sub} = src_T(e) \land n_{super} = tgt_T(e)$. The transitive closure of *subtype* then yields the set $super(n) := \{n' | (n, n') \in subtype^+\}$, while the reflexive-transitive closure yields $types(n) := super(n) \cup n$.

We can now extend our previous definition of type conformity to include subtyping:

**Definition 2.2.4** *The labeling of a graph* $G = (N_G, E_G, src_G, tgt_G, \Omega_G^N, \Omega_G^E, l_G^N, l_G^E)$ *is type conformant for the inheritance type system graph* $G_T = (N_T, E_T, src_T, tgt_T, \Omega_T^N, \Omega_T^E, l_T^N, l_T^E)$ *iff* $\Omega_G^N \subseteq N_T$, $\Omega_G^E \subseteq E_T \setminus isa$ *and* $\forall e \in E_G : (\exists e_T \in E_T : l_G^E(e) = e_T \land src_T(e_T) \in types(l_G^N(src_G(e))) \land tgt_T(e_T) \in types(l_G^N(tgt_G(e))))$.

As for simple type system graphs not containing $isa$ we simply have $types(n) = n$, this definition includes the basic notion of type conformity as specified by definition 2.2.3.

**Attributed graphs.** Finally, we introduce attributed graphs. Following [HKT02], we only allow node attributes, but no edge attributes. Attributes are represented by nodes that are the target of special edges whose source is the attributed node. To abstract from the data types of the attributes, we describe them in terms of an algebra $A$ over a many sorted signature $\Sigma = \langle S_\Sigma, OP_\Sigma \rangle$ consisting of sets of sort symbols $S_\Sigma$ and of operation symbols $OP_\Sigma$.

**Definition 2.2.5** *An* attributed graph *is a pair* $(G, A)$ *of a graph* $G$ *and an algebra* $A$ *over* $\Sigma$, *where for* $|A| := \biguplus_{s \in S_\Sigma} A_s$, *the disjoint union of the carrier sets of* $A$, *we have* $|A| \subseteq N_G$ *and* $\forall e \in E_G : src_G(e) \notin |A|$.

For an attributed graph $G$, we define attribute value nodes $N_G^A := |A|$ and instance nodes $N_G^I := N_G \setminus N_G^A$. We further differentiate between attributes $E_G^A := \{e \in E_G : tgt(e) \in |A|\}$ and links $E_G^I := E_G \setminus E_G^A$.

The notion of type conformance is not affected by this extension. The only additional convention is that when labeling a type system graph $G_T$ (which does not have to be an attributed graph itself), we label nodes that represent attribute types (i.e. are later used to label nodes from $N_G^A$) with the appropriate sort symbol $s \in S_\Sigma$.

#### 2.2.2.2 Graph Patterns

In order to formalize the notion of matching and applying a pattern, we now formalize these notions based on the above definitions.

**Containment.** We formalize the notion of containment of a labeled graph in another labeled graph by comparing their defining functions: For two graphs $SG$ and $G$ we say that $SG$ is a subgraph of G (written as $SG \leq G$) iff $N_{SG} \subseteq N_G$, $E_{SG} \subseteq E_G$, $src_{SG} = src_G|_{E_{SG}}$, $tgt_{SG} = tgt_G|_{E_{SG}}$, $\Omega_{SG}^N \subseteq \Omega_G^N$, $\Omega_{SG}^E \subseteq \Omega_G^E$, $l_{SG}^N = l_G^N|_{N_{SG}}$, and $l_{SG}^E = l_G^E|_{E_{SG}}$. Two graphs are equal iff $SG \leq G$ and $G \leq SG$.

**Pattern matching.** A pattern is supposed to be a generalized way of encoding a recurrent structure. When matching patterns against instance graphs, we only want to compare the graphs w.r.t.

## 2.2 Story-Driven Modeling

their structure, i.e. without considering the identity of the nodes and edges. Instead of the simple subgraph relationship, we therefore need to use the more general concept of graph morphisms (cf. [Roz97]).

**Definition 2.2.6** *A graph morphism $m : G_1 \rightarrow G_2$ is a pair of functions $m := \langle m^N : N_{G_1} \rightarrow N_{G_2}, m^E : E_{G_1} \rightarrow E_{G_2} \rangle$ mapping the nodes and edges of $G_1$ to the elements of $G_2$ while preserving sources, targets, and labels. $m$ thus satisfies the properties $m^N \circ tgt_{G_1} = tgt_{G_2} \circ m^E$, $m^N \circ src_{G_1} = src_{G_2} \circ m^E$, $l_{G_1}^N = l_{G_2}^N \circ m^N$ and $l_{G_1}^E = l_{G_2}^E \circ m^E$. A graph isomorphism $m$ is a graph morphism whose functions $m^N$ and $m^E$ are both bijective.*

This definition can be extended to cover attributed graphs:

**Definition 2.2.7** *An attributed graph morphism $m : (G_1, A_1) \rightarrow (G_2, A_2)$ is a pair of a graph morphism $m_G$ and a $\Sigma$-morphism $m_A : A_1 \rightarrow A_2$ mapping the elements of the carrier sets of $A_1$ to $A_2$ so that $m_A \subseteq m_G^N$.*

If there is a graph isomorphism $m : G_1 \rightarrow G_2$, we write $G_1 =_m G_2$ or $G_1 \approx G_2$ to abstract from the specific morphism $m$. However, as a pattern will typically be smaller than the graph against which we are matching it, the more relevant question is usually whether there is a graph isomorphism from the pattern $G_1$ to a subgraph $SG_2$ of $G_2$, i.e. $m : G_1 \rightarrow SG_2$ with $SG_2 \leq G_2$. If such an isomorphism exists, we write $G_1 \leq_m G_2$, respectively $G_1 \precsim G_2$ to abstract from the morphism.

In the literature on graph theory, graph homomorphisms, i.e., morphisms that are not necessarily bijective, are commonly used instead of isomorphisms. As our definition of $\precsim$ eliminates the surjectivity requirement from the matching process for all practical purposes, the decisive difference is that pattern matching using isomorphisms requires injectivity while matching using homomorphisms does not. We have found that, in most cases, the principle that different pattern elements map to different instances is closer to the intuitive interpretation of a pattern. Consider a pattern encoding that two shuttles $s1$ and $s2$ are on the same track $t1$ (see Figure 3.2.11 in Section 3.2.2.1). For every single shuttle on a track in the system, there is a homomorphism for matching that pattern by simply mapping both shuttles from the pattern to the same shuttle in the system. The pattern then is basically flagging each shuttle as a collision with itself, which hardly reflects the intended meaning. Though this can be prevented by adding an additional constraint $s1 \neq s2$ requiring the two shuttles to be different, this is cumbersome. We therefore prefer using isomorphisms as the default matching strategy and only employ homomorphisms where explicitly indicated.

Based on subgraph isomorphisms, we define simple graph patterns as follows:

**Definition 2.2.8** *A simple graph pattern $[G]$ consists of a graph $G$. If there is a graph $AG$ and an isomorphism $m$ with $G \leq_m AG$, we write $AG, m \vdash [G]$ and say that the graph $AG$ fulfills the pattern.*

**Negative Application Conditions** (NAC) formalize the concept of forbidden elements. The basic idea is that a pattern will only match if a forbidden second pattern does not match as well. The semantics of forbidden elements are thus defined as follows:

**Definition 2.2.9** *A* negative application condition *(NAC) over a graph $G$ is a finite set $\hat{\mathcal{G}}$ of connected graphs with $\forall \hat{G}_i \in \hat{\mathcal{G}} : G \leq \hat{G}_i$, called* constraints. *A constraint $\hat{G}_i$ is fulfilled by a graph $AG$ if $\exists m : G \leq_m AG$ but $\nexists m'$ with $m'|_G = m$ and $\hat{G}_i \leq_{m'} AG$, written $AG, G, m' \vdash \hat{G}_i$. A graph $AG$ and the isomorphism $m$ satisfy a NAC $\hat{\mathcal{G}}$, written $AG, G, m \vdash \hat{\mathcal{G}}$, if it satisfies all constraints $\hat{G}_i \in \hat{\mathcal{G}}$, i.e $\forall \hat{G}_i \in \hat{\mathcal{G}} : AG, G, m \vdash \hat{G}_i$.*

This leads to the general definition of a graph pattern and a match of such a pattern:

**Definition 2.2.10** *A* graph pattern *$[G, \hat{\mathcal{G}}]$ consists of a graph $G$ and a set of NACs $\hat{\mathcal{G}}$ of $G$.[5] It characterizes the set of graphs that contain the graph $G$ but do not contain any extension $\hat{G}_i$ of $G$.*

**Definition 2.2.11** *A* match *$m$ for a graph pattern $[L, \hat{\mathcal{L}}]$ in some graph $G$ with a subgraph $SG \leq G$ is a graph isomorphism $m : L \to SG$ with $G, L, m \vdash \hat{\mathcal{L}}$. We write $G, m \vdash [L, \hat{\mathcal{L}}]$ or $G \vdash [L, \hat{\mathcal{L}}]$.*

#### 2.2.2.3 Graph Transformation Rules

Graph transformation rules describe modifications of a graph by means of two graph patterns, a precondition and a postcondition. We define:

**Definition 2.2.12** *A* graph transformation rule *$[L, \hat{\mathcal{L}}] \to_r [R]$ consists of $r$, the* rule name, *$[L, \hat{\mathcal{L}}]$, the* left hand side (LHS), *a graph pattern encoding the precondition, and $[R]$, the* right hand side (RHS), *a simple graph pattern encoding the postcondition, with $L$, all elements of $\mathcal{L}$, and $R$ compatible and $L \cap R \neq G_\emptyset$.*

A rule is type conformant to a type system graph $G_T$ if all graphs in the rule are type conformant to $G_T$.

When a rule $r$ is applied to a graph $G$, $G$ is called the *application graph* or *source graph*. The resulting graph $G'$ is called the *target graph*.

In order to effect the graph transformation, we use the *Single Pushout Approach* (cf. [Roz97]):

**Definition 2.2.13** *The* Single Pushout Approach *defines the* application *of a graph transformation rule $r$ to an application graph $G$ as a* direct transformation *of the source graph $G$ into a compatible target graph $G'$. Given the rule $[L, \hat{\mathcal{L}}] \to_r [R]$ and a match $m$ for $[L, \hat{\mathcal{L}}]$, such a* direct transformation *is characterized by the occurrence $o$, which is a graph isomorphism $o : L \cup R \to G \cup G'$ with the following properties: $o|_L = m$, i.e. $o$ matches the left hand side in accordance with $m$, $L \leq_o G \land R \leq_o G'$ i.e. the left hand side of $r$ is contained in $G$ and the right hand side of $r$ is contained in $G'$, and $o(L \setminus R) = G \setminus G' \land o(R \setminus L) = G' \setminus G$, i.e. those elements belonging to $L$ but not to $R$ are deleted, while those elements belonging to $R$ but not to $L$ are created. We write $G \Mapsto_{r,o} G'$ to denote such a transformation or $G \Mapsto_r G'$ to abstract from $o$.*

---

[5] A simple graph pattern can be interpreted as a graph pattern with an empty set of NACs.

## 2.2 Story-Driven Modeling

Informally, when $r$ is applied to $G$, all elements (nodes and edges) that are contained in both the left and right hand side are preserved, elements that are only contained in the left hand side are deleted, and elements that are only contained in the right hand side are added, using appropriate morphisms.

If a sequence of direct graph transformations of the form $G_0 \mapsto_{r_0,o_0} G_1 \mapsto_{r_1,o_1} \cdots \mapsto_{r_{n-1},o_{n-1}} G_n$ exists, where $r_0, \ldots, r_{n-1}$ are rules and $o_0, \ldots, o_{n-1}$ their occurrences, so that for $0 \leq i < n$ holds $G_i \mapsto_{r_i} G_{i+1}$, we write $G_0 \mapsto^*_{(r_0,o_0);\ldots;(r_{n-1},o_{n-1})} G_n$, or shorter $G_0 \mapsto^*_{r_0;\ldots;r_{n-1}} G_n$ if the occurrences are unambiguous or irrelevant in the given context. Even more compactly, $G_0 \mapsto^* G_n$ denotes that *some* transformation sequence from $G_0$ to $G_n$ exists.

**Rule composition.** When verifying or monitoring systems, it is often relevant to consider the interactions between individual rules. In the following, we introduce several concepts required for the composition of two rules $r = ([L, \hat{\mathcal{L}}], R)$ and $r' = ([L', \hat{\mathcal{L}}'], R')$ that are not disjoint.

The effect of simultaneously applying two rules to the same graph can be described by a single equivalent rule that results from *joining* the two rules. This equivalent rule is defined as $r'' = \mathsf{join}(r, r') := ([L \cup L', \{\hat{L}_1 \cup L', \ldots, \hat{L}_n \cup L', \hat{L}'_1 \cup L, \ldots, \hat{L}'_n \cup L\}], R \cup R')$, i.e., pre- and postconditions including NACs are combined. If priorities $prio(r)$ are assigned to the rules, we set the priority of the combined rule to the level of the less privileged rule, i.e. $prio(r'') = \max(prio(r), prio(r'))$. For dealing with sets of simultaneously applied rules in a convenient fashion, we extend join on enumerations $r_1, \ldots, r_n$ of rules by defining $\mathsf{setjoin}(r_1, \ldots, r_n) := \mathsf{join}(r_1, \mathsf{join}(\ldots, \mathsf{join}(r_{n-1}, r_n)) \ldots)$.

We are often interested in applying two sets of rules in parallel, e.g. for monitoring rule applications against a specification. Whenever a rule $r$ from the monitored set is applied, the corresponding rule $r'$ in the specification that $r$ is supposed to refine should then equally be enabled. Whenever $r$ can be applied while $r'$ is not enabled, i.e., when $r$ *excluding* $r'$ is enabled, $r$ is in violation of the specification. Such an event can be characterized by the set of graph patterns $\mathsf{exclude}(r, r') := \{[L, \{\hat{L}_1, \ldots, \hat{L}_n, L' \cup L\}], [L \cup L' \cup \hat{L}'_1, \{\hat{L}_1 \cup L' \cup \hat{L}'_1, \ldots, \hat{L}_n \cup L' \cup \hat{L}'_1\}] \ldots [L \cup L' \cup \hat{L}'_m, \{\hat{L}_1 \cup L' \cup \hat{L}'_m, \ldots, \hat{L}_n \cup L' \cup \hat{L}'_m\}]\}$. Basically, this can either occur when the LHS of $r$ is less restrictive than the LHS of $r'$, or when the NACs of $r'$ are triggered by some element that does not affect the NACs of $r$.

Another important question is in which ways two rules $r$ and $r'$ can affect the same subgraph, i.e., how their occurrences can overlap. We can identify such combinations by *intersecting* graph isomorphisms of $r$ into the domain of $r'$ with the rule $r'$ proper, computing all graph isomorphisms $m$ with $m(L \cup R) \cap (L' \cup R') \neq G_\emptyset$. We denote the set of these isomorphisms as $\mathsf{intersect}(r, r')$. We can then define a *merging* (or *overlapping join*) of the first rule with the second rule as $\mathsf{join}(m(r), r')$ for any $m \in \mathsf{intersect}(r, r')$. Consequently, the set $\mathsf{merge}(r, r') := \{\mathsf{join}(m(r), r') | m \in \mathsf{intersect}(r, r')\}$ contains all possible ways to merge the two rules. Denoting the set of all enumerations of the elements of a multi-set or set $\mathfrak{R}$ with $\mathsf{enum}(\mathfrak{R})$, we analogously define all ways to merge a multi-set or set of rules as $\mathsf{setmerge}(\mathfrak{R}) := \bigcup_{r_1,\ldots,r_n \in \mathsf{enum}(\mathfrak{R})} \{\mathsf{setjoin}(m_1(r_1), \ldots, m_n(r_n)) | \forall 1 \leq i < n : m_i \in \mathsf{intersect}(r_i, r_{i+1})\}$.

## 2.2.2.4  Graph Transformation Systems

**GTS.** Using the concepts we have introduced above, we can now define *graph transformation systems* (GTS), a type of state transition system where every state is represented by a graph and every transition is described as a graph rewrite rule:

**Definition 2.2.14** *A typed graph transformation system (GTS) $S$ is a tuple $(\mathcal{T}_S, \mathcal{G}_S^i, \mathcal{R}_S)$ with $\mathcal{T}_S$ a type system graph, $\mathcal{G}_S^i$ the set of all type conformant initial graphs of the system, and $\mathcal{R}_S$ a finite set of type conformant graph transformation rules.*

For each system $S = (\mathcal{T}_S, \mathcal{G}_S^i, \mathcal{R}_S)$ and a graph $G$, the valid applications are denoted by $\models S \Rightarrow_{r,o}$, $\models S \Rightarrow_r$, or $\models S \Rightarrow_w^*$ respectively. We define the – potentially infinite – set of all reachable states as
REACH$(S) := \{G \mid G \in \mathcal{G}[\mathcal{T}_S] \land \exists G_0 \in \mathcal{G}_S^i, w \in \mathcal{R}_S^* : G_0 \models S \Rightarrow_w^* G\}$.

**Extended GTS.** We can extend this definition in various ways:

**Definition 2.2.15** *A GTS $S$ can be extended into a* prioritized graph transformation system *by adding a priority function $prio_S : \mathcal{R}_S \to \mathbb{Z}$ assigning a priority $prio_S(r)$ to every $r \in \mathcal{R}_S$, with lower numerical values having higher precedence.*

For a prioritized system $S = (\mathcal{T}_S, \mathcal{G}_S^i, \mathcal{R}_S, prio_S)$ and a graph $G$, we restrict valid rule applications $G \mapsto_{r,o} G'$ to those cases where no preempting rule application $G \mapsto_{r',o'} G''$ with $prio_S(r') < prio_S(r)$ exists.

**Definition 2.2.16** *A GTS $S$ can be extended into a* constrained graph transformation system $(\mathcal{T}_S, \mathcal{G}_S^i, \mathcal{R}_S, \Phi_S)$ *by specifying a set of forbidden graph patterns $\Phi_S$ which must never match the system state at any time.*

For a constrained system $S = (\mathcal{T}_S, \mathcal{G}_S^i, \mathcal{R}_S, \Phi_S)$ and a graph $G$, we define a *violation* as a rule application $G \mapsto_{r,o} G'$ where $\exists \phi \in \Phi_S : G' \vdash \phi \land \neg G \vdash \phi$.

**Definition 2.2.17** *A GTS $S$ can be extended into a* labeled graph transformation system *with (multiple) rule labels from the label set $\mathcal{B}$ by providing a mapping $l_S : \mathcal{R}_S \to \wp(\mathcal{B})$*

**Parallel composition.** When two graph transformation systems are executed concurrently, the resulting system corresponds to their parallel composition. We define the *parallel composition* $S \| T$ of two graph transformation systems $S = (\mathcal{T}_S, \mathcal{G}_S^i, \mathcal{R}_S)$ and $T = (\mathcal{T}_T, \mathcal{G}_T^i, \mathcal{R}_T)$ as a GTS $U := (\mathcal{T}_U, \mathcal{G}_U^i, \mathcal{R}_U)$ with $\mathcal{T}_U := \mathcal{T}_S \cup \mathcal{T}_T$, $\mathcal{G}_U^i := \mathcal{G}_S^i \cup \mathcal{G}_T^i \cup \{G \cup G' | G \in \mathcal{G}_S^i \land G' \in \mathcal{G}_T^i\}$, and $\mathcal{R}_U := \mathcal{R}_S \cup \mathcal{R}_T$.

For the parallel composition $U := (\mathcal{T}_U, \mathcal{G}_U^i, \mathcal{R}_U, \Phi_U)$ of two constrained graph transformation systems $S = (\mathcal{T}_S, \mathcal{G}_S^i, \mathcal{R}_S, \Phi_S)$ and $T = (\mathcal{T}_T, \mathcal{G}_T^i, \mathcal{R}_T, \Phi_T)$, we additionally define $\Phi_U := \Phi_S \cup \Phi_T$. For prioritized graph transformation systems, we define $prio_U := prio_S \oplus prio_T$. For labeled graph transformation systems, we likewise define $l_U := l_S \oplus l_T$.

## 2.2 Story-Driven Modeling

**Paths.** A path $\pi := G_0 \models S \Rightarrow_{r_1,o_1} G_1 \models S \Rightarrow_{r_2,o_2} G_2 \ldots$ is an alternating sequence of states and valid rule applications connecting these states. We denote the – potentially infinite – length of a path by $l(\pi)$. For $i \in [0, l(\pi))$, we refer to the state graph generated by the $i$-th rule application (i.e., $G_i$) as $\pi[i]$. We use $\pi^i$ to denote the suffix of $\pi$ starting with $\pi[i]$.

The set of all finite or infinite possible paths $\pi$ starting from $G$ is defined as $\mathsf{PATH}(S, G) := \{G_0 \models S \Rightarrow_{r_1,o_1} G_1 \models S \Rightarrow_{r_2,o_2} G_2 \ldots \mid G_0 = G\}$. $\mathsf{PATH}(S)$ denotes all paths that can be generated by $S$ and is defined as the union of all sets $\mathsf{PATH}(S, G)$ with $G \in \mathcal{G}_S^i$. We also write $[\![S]\!]$ for $\mathsf{PATH}(S)$.

When we are considering time, we additionally use a function $T(\pi, i) : [\![S]\!] \times [0, l(\pi)] \rightarrow \mathbb{R}$ to determine the time when each particular state of a path has been reached. Depending on the notion of time that is available in the context where these concepts are applied, we may need to substitute a discrete notion for the continuous notion of time.

#### 2.2.2.5 Properties of Graph Transformation Systems

Using graph patterns as basic propositions, we can derive more complex graph properties. The Computational Tree Logic CTL* (cf. [CGP00]) with its path quantifiers **A** (for all paths) and **E** (for some path) and temporal operators **X** (next), **F** (eventually), **G** (always), **U** (until), and **R** (release) can be used to embed these basic propositions to form an expressive notation for temporal conditions. In [GHK98], it is shown that a sound and complete general propositional temporal calculus remains sound and complete when interpreted on graph transformation systems.

We then have the following syntax for state and path formulae:

- If $\phi$ is a graph pattern or the constant $true$ or $false$, then $\phi$ is a state formula.
- If $\phi$ and $\psi$ are state formulae, then $\neg \phi$, $\phi \vee \psi$, and $\phi \wedge \psi$ are state formulae.
- If $\phi$ is a state formula, then $\phi$ is also a path formula.
- If $p$ is a path formula, then $\mathbf{E}p$ and $\mathbf{A}p$ are state formulae.
- If $p$ and $p'$ are path formulae, then $\neg p, p \vee p', p \wedge p', \mathbf{X}p, \mathbf{F}p, \mathbf{G}p, p\mathbf{U}p'$, and $p\mathbf{R}p'$ are path formulae.

We write $S, G \models \phi$ iff the CTL* formula $\phi$ holds for the state $G$ and $S, \pi \models \phi$ iff the CTL* formula $\phi$ holds for the path $\pi$. We further write $S \models \phi$ to denote that $\forall G \in \mathcal{G}_S^i$ holds $S, G \models \phi$.

The semantics of state and path formulae is then defined as follows for a GTS $S$, a graph $G$, and a trace $\pi$:

- $S, G \models \phi$ iff $\phi$ is a graph pattern and $G \vdash \phi$.
- $S, G \models \neg \phi$ iff $S, G \not\models \phi$.
- $S, G \models \phi \vee \psi$ iff $S, G \models \phi \vee S, G \models \phi$.
- $S, G \models \phi \wedge \psi$ iff $S, G \models \phi \wedge S, G \models \phi$.
- $S, G \models \mathbf{E}\phi$ iff $\exists \pi \in \mathsf{PATH}(S, G) : S, \pi \models \phi$.
- $S, G \models \mathbf{A}\phi$ iff $\forall \pi \in \mathsf{PATH}(S, G) : S, \pi \models \phi$.
- $S, \pi \models \phi$ iff $G = \pi[0] \wedge S, G \models \phi$.

- $S, \pi \models \neg \phi$ iff $S, G \not\models \phi$.
- $S, \pi \models \phi \vee \psi$ iff $S, \pi \models \phi \vee S, \pi \models \phi$.
- $S, \pi \models \phi \wedge \psi$ iff $S, \pi \models \phi \wedge S, \pi \models \phi$.
- $S, \pi \models \mathbf{X}\phi$ iff $S, \pi^1 \models \phi$.
- $S, \pi \models \mathbf{F}\phi$ iff $\exists k, k \geq 0 : S, \pi^k \models \phi$.
- $S, \pi \models \mathbf{G}\phi$ iff $\forall i, i \geq 0 : S, \pi^i \models \phi$.
- $S, \pi \models \phi \mathbf{U} \psi$ iff $\exists k, k \geq 0 : S, \pi^k \models \psi \wedge \forall j, 0 \leq j < k : S, \pi^k \models \phi$
- $S, \pi \models \phi \mathbf{R} \psi$ iff $\forall j, j \geq 0 : (\forall i, i < j : S, \pi^i \not\models \phi) \Rightarrow S, \pi^j \models \psi$

To describe, for example, that a given graph pattern $[P, \hat{\mathcal{P}}]$ should never be matched in any reachable configuration, we can then write:

$$S \models \mathbf{AG}(\neg[P, \hat{\mathcal{P}}]).$$

#### 2.2.2.6 UML Models

We have now defined all the necessary preliminaries that will allow us to formalize the employed visual notations.

**UML Class and Object Diagrams.** A *Class Diagram* can be represented as a *type system graph* $G_T$, where nodes represent classes, edges represent associations, and labels define their names. An inheritance relationship in the diagram translates to an edge labeled with $isa$ from the node representing the subclass to the node representing the superclass.

If the diagram contains attributes, we define a signature $\Sigma$ whose set of sort symbols comprises the required value types, typically $S_\Sigma := \{boolean, integer, real, string, \dots\}$, and add value type nodes labeled with $s \in S_\Sigma$. Attributes are then encoded as edges from class nodes to value type nodes, labeled with the attribute name.

Cardinalities are not incorporated into the type system graph itself, but need to be translated into appropriate constraints, i.e. graph patterns that are negative invariants of the system.

A maximum cardinality of $*$ or $n$ requires no constraint. A maximum cardinality of $k \in I\!N$ can be encoded as a graph pattern containing $k + 1$ copies of the constrained element, which will match any instance situation with $i > k$ instances (see Figure 2.2.7b).

A minimum cardinality of 0 requires no constraint either. A minimum cardinality $k > 0$ can be encoded by adding a pattern containing $i$ copies of the constrained element plus one additional forbidden copy of the element, which will therefore match a configuration containing $i$, but not $i + 1$ copies of the element, for each $0 \leq i < k$. This is not practical for larger minimum cardinalities, but poses no problems for typical values such as 1 (see Figure 2.2.7a) or 2 (see Figures 2.2.8a and 2.2.8b). Note that the necessity to enumerate the undesired configurations (not 0, not 1, not 2, not 3...) is a direct consequence of the restriction to negative invariants, as a single positive invariant – (at least) 4 (or more) – would be sufficient to encode the same minimum cardinality. When we lift this restriction in the following chapter, at most two patterns will be sufficient to encode any cardinality range.

## 2.2 Story-Driven Modeling

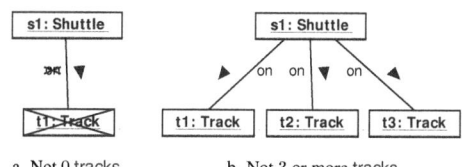

a. Not 0 tracks        b. Not 3 or more tracks

Figure 2.2.7: Shuttle: Encoding the $[1..2]$ cardinality for on

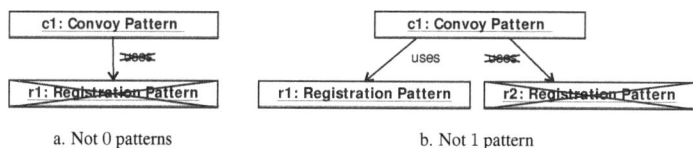

a. Not 0 patterns        b. Not 1 pattern

Figure 2.2.8: Convoy Pattern: Encoding the $[2..*]$ cardinality for uses

An *Object Diagram* can be represented as a *typed graph* $G$ that is *type conformant* for the (*inheritance*) *type system graph* $G_T$ representing the corresponding Class Diagram. Nodes represent objects and edges represent links, each labeled with the respective class or association.

If the Class Diagram defines attributes, the Object Diagram needs to be an *attributed graph*. Objects are then represented by instance nodes $N_G^I$, links are represented by edges from $E_G^I$, attribute value nodes $N_G^A$ represent literals, and the edges $E_G^A$ represent attribute assignments.

**Story Patterns.** Just as the UML Object Diagrams that they extend, Story Patterns can be formally expressed using graphs. Again, objects and attribute values become nodes, while links and attribute assignments become edges.

An *Invariant Story Pattern* without forbidden elements can thus be translated to a *simple graph pattern* consisting of the corresponding graph. In the more general case including negative (forbidden) elements, a given Story Pattern can be translated to a *graph pattern* $[G, \hat{\mathcal{G}}]$ by encoding its positive objects, links and attributes as an attributed typed graph $G$ and building the set of NACs $\hat{\mathcal{G}}$ by adding, for each negated link $l$, a labeled graph $\hat{G}$ consisting of $G$ and the negated link $l$ with its source node $src(l)$ and target node $tgt(l)$. At least one of these nodes already is in $G$ – if $l$ connects two positive nodes, both source and target are in $G$, whereas if $l$ connects to a negative node (as in Figure 2.2.3), that node only is in $\hat{G}$.

Note that the problems with respect to negation that were discussed above are due to limitations of the notation and its established semantics and not inherent in the underlying formalization. It would be possible, instead, to add a NAC $\hat{G}$ (1) for every negative link *between positive objects* and (2) for every *negative object* including *all* its links, thus making Figure 2.2.4a a correct specification with the intended semantics. However, independently of the chosen semantics, the basic problem caused by the decision to integrate the NACs into the positive graph to allow for more compact diagrams remains, namely that the relationships between multiple negated elements (Which ones are alternatives? Which ones need to occur together?) are subtle.

The property encoded by an Invariant Story Pattern thus holds for a configuration represented by an Object Diagram iff the attributed graph $AG$ representing the object diagram fulfills the corresponding graph pattern $[P, \hat{\mathcal{P}}]$: $AG \vdash [P, \hat{\mathcal{P}}]$.

For *Story Patterns* with side effects, we can derive a graph transformation rule $r := [L, \hat{\mathcal{L}}] \rightarrow_r [R]$. We encode the LHS of the Story Pattern, which we obtain by disregarding all elements marked with ≪create≫ and treating those marked with ≪destroy≫ as regular positive elements, as the graph pattern $[L, \hat{\mathcal{L}}]$. The RHS, i.e. the unmarked and newly created elements, are encoded as the simple graph pattern $[R]$.

Applying the Story Pattern to a configuration represented by an Object Diagram $AG$ then corresponds to the rule application $AG \mapsto_{r,o} AG'$.

**System Model.** By means of the above definitions, we can now derive a representation of a complete UML model as a constrained *graph transformation system* by combining the above concepts. The underlying Class Diagram becomes the type system graph $\mathcal{T}_S$, the Story Patterns with side effects become the rule set $\mathcal{R}_S$, the Invariant Story Patterns make up the constraint set $\Phi_S$, and the set of initial graphs $\mathcal{G}_S^i$ is derived from the Object Diagrams representing initial configurations. If there are forbidden patterns encoding the cardinalities of the Class Diagram, these are also added to $\Phi_S$.

## 2.3 Coordination Patterns

For modeling the real-time coordination and communication of a system, we use a component-based approach that is built around the notion of *Coordination Patterns* [GTB+03]. The approach is based on standard UML 2.0 component modeling techniques, but strives for a realistic and implementable semantics by removing certain abstractions and implicit assumptions. For example, communication channel behavior is modeled explicitly in order to provide details such as the associated delay or the available buffer size. In the same vein, the approach replaces all usages of regular UML State Machines with the more expressive Real-Time Statecharts (RTSC) [GB03, BGS05, BG03].

Coordination Patterns suggest a compositional approach to system design where the overall system is created by connecting components using the appropriate patterns. They are also the foundation for the approach to compositional verification presented in [GTB+03], which requires the verification of the individual patterns and the correctness of the composition at the component level, but is then capable of inferring the semantic correctness of the system from the syntactic correctness of the composition. By cleanly encapsulating the externally visible component behavior, Coordination Patterns also provide a suitable abstraction for the discussion and verification of online reconfiguration.

There are extensions of the approach that allow the modeling of continuous and hybrid component behavior by integrating concepts from control engineering and complementing the discrete event-based communication model with a continuous model using continuous ports and communication channels (cf. [Bur06]). The safe online reconfiguration of hybrid components furthermore requires dedicated analysis and implementation techniques in order to ensure stable and valid continuous behavior. As these techniques are seamlessly integrated with the techniques for discrete systems, however, we can safely abstract from these extensions within the context of this thesis. This is desirable from a software engineering point of view because, as a general rule, it would break encapsulation and greatly complicate the design process if low-level continuous behavior featured prominently in the analysis and design of the multi-agent system responsible for the high-level coordination between components.

### 2.3.1 Notations

We will now provide a short overview of the notations employed for the specification of *Coordination Patterns*, i.e., the component model, the behavioral specifications, and the patterns themselves.

#### 2.3.1.1 Components

The concept of a *component* has greatly been refined and extended by the UML 2.0 (cf. [Obj07, section 8.3]) with respect to the UML 1.x, where the use of components was mostly restricted to the modeling of instance-level dependencies. In the UML 2.0, components are *classifiers* and thus closely related to *classes*, but exhibit stronger encapsulation and typically represent larger units of composition. In contrast to classes, all external dependencies of components need to be stated explicitly.

Components define their relationships by means of *required* and *provided* interfaces. The provided interfaces of a component are most commonly represented by circles ('plugs'), whereas the required interfaces are presented as open semicircles ('sockets'), though it is possible to specify them by textually or graphically referencing the interface definitions, using the appropriate stereotypes. As all required interfaces need to be connected to provided interfaces in a consistent manner when composing components into a system, these interface sets constrain the set of valid system configurations.

It is possible to group interfaces that are conceptually related by using *ports*, representing logical interfaces. The assignment of interfaces to ports is non-disjunctive, i.e., it is possible to assign the same interface to multiple ports. By allowing combinations of provided and required interfaces, ports also provide a concept for modeling bidirectional communication. Ports are graphically represented by squares.

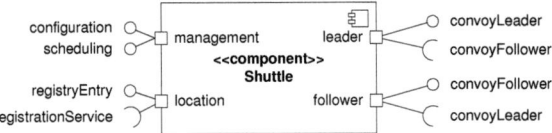

Figure 2.3.1: A basic component

Figure 2.3.1 shows a basic example, an external view on a shuttle with ports for communicating with other shuttles and base stations. Though the emphasis on encapsulation suggests a black box view on components, it is nonetheless possible to adopt a white box view. The internal structure of a component can either be modeled by embedding other components into it or by specifying an object-oriented implementation.

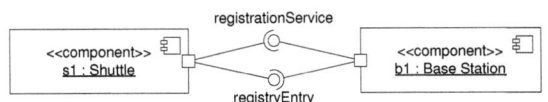

Figure 2.3.2: A system configuration with two interacting components

Components communicate using point-to-point connections between ports. We do not employ multicast transmissions, even when a component such as a base station needs to broadcast an update to many shuttles simultaneously, as we require reliable communication and need to ensure that every single message is actually received. Connections are generally asynchronous and introduce a non-zero delay, as message propagation is never instantaneous. Connections have a buffer that can only store a fixed number of messages and can thus overflow. Connections can also fail altogether.

## 2.3 Coordination Patterns

As with other UML classifiers, components can be used at the instance level in order to illustrate specific deployments or system configurations, as in Figure 2.3.2.

### 2.3.1.2 State Machines

Interface, port, component, and connector behavior is specified using some form of state machine. The externally visible communication behavior is constrained by *protocol state machines*, abstract specifications defining valid sequences of input and output signals but no control logic or side effects. As bidirectional communication necessarily involves at least two interfaces, the corresponding protocols are defined at the port level. The internal implementation of the visible behavior is defined by *behavioral state machines*, which include all required operations and computations.

**UML State Machines.** *UML State Machines* (cf. [Obj07, section 15]) are based on the theory of finite automata, but extend them with additional concepts such as concurrency and hierarchical composite states offering a deep or shallow history. There is rudimentary support for temporal restrictions on behavior by allowing triggers that are relative to a global clock (*when*) or to the entry time into the current state (*after*). The UML Profile for Schedulability, Performance, and Time Specification (SPT) (cf. [OMG05]) provides more refined means of specifying the capabilities of real-time systems by defining deadlines, priorities, worst-case execution times (WCET), and custom clocks, but is not tightly integrated with the behavioral semantics of UML State Machines.

**Real-Time Statecharts.** Due to these limitations with respect to real-time modeling, we use *Real-Time Statecharts* (*RTSC*) as a more expressive replacement for UML State Machines when modeling protocols and behavior. They combine concepts and syntax from UML State Machines (such as composite states and concurrency) and the SPT Profile (such as priorities and deadlines) with formal semantics based on the Timed Automata formalism [DMY02].

RTSC allow the user to explicitly define and reset clocks. Using these clocks, state invariants, transition guards, and deadlines can be defined as simple inequalities comparing clock values with constants. Transitions may additionally be annotated with guard expressions, enabling events, and priorities. Transitions are only enabled when all guards are fulfilled and all required events are available. When multiple transitions are enabled, their priorities determine which one is selected and preempts the others. By default, transitions are *urgent* and *must* fire as soon as they are enabled. However, there is also support for *non-urgent* transitions, which are allowed to delay firing within the specified time constraints.

The most significant feature of RTSC with respect to their implementation by actual systems, however, is the fact that transitions are not instantaneous, but consume time. For each transition, it is therefore mandatory to specify an interval which must allow for the sending of all signals, performing all side effects, and entering the destination state.

**Operations.** It is possible to specify actions that are performed once when entering (*entry*) or leaving (*exit*) a state or, periodically, while in the state (*do*). Actions are typically operations that are invoked on the associated object instance. Here, the component-based perspective interfaces with the story-driven perspective, as these operations and the associated side-effects are specified using Story-Driven Modeling, namely Story Diagrams.

When specifying software that is involved with time-critical control processes that need to respect tight deadlines, the exact worst-case execution time (WCET) of operations becomes important. In order to allow the theoretically sound computation of reliable WCET for Story Diagrams, it becomes necessary to place restrictions on the maximum number of instances for classes and associations as the WCET may otherwise, in theory, become unbounded (cf. [TGS06, BGST05]).

By employing techniques such as the layered architecture of the Operator-Controller-Module (OCM) [HOG04, OHG04], it is possible to decouple the coordination behavior of agents from low-level control processes. Though there are still time constraints at the multi-agent level, it is therefore sufficient to apply less rigorous methods of WCET computation, such as appropriate heuristics, in most cases.

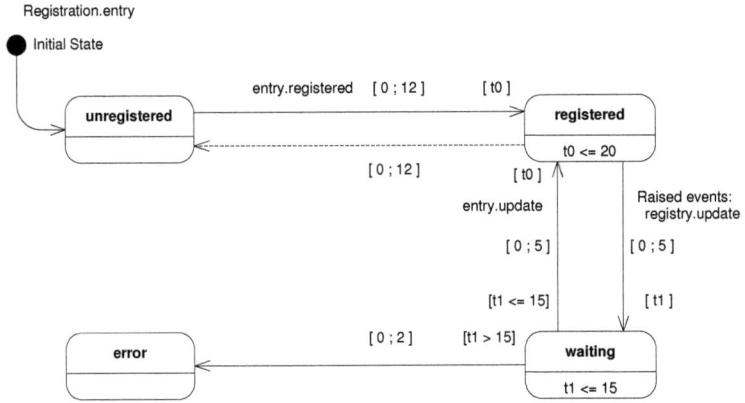

Figure 2.3.3: A Real-Time Statechart

Figure 2.3.3 shows a RTSC specifying a shuttle's communication with a base station.

### 2.3.1.3 Coordination Patterns

*Coordination Patterns* provide an elegant solution for reuse at the component level. A pattern defines a set of *roles*, connectors between them, and a set of protocol state machines modeling their respective required behavior. Additional restrictions may be imposed in the form of *role invariants*. Finally, guarantees for the overall pattern may be stated as *pattern constraints*.

Patterns are applied to a design by assigning pattern roles to ports of components. The state machine of each port must then represent a valid *refinement* of the assigned role, i.e., must operate

## 2.3 Coordination Patterns

within the specified bounds. Refinement typically consists of the reduction of non-determinism, in particular the removal of choices or the tightening of time constraint intervals.

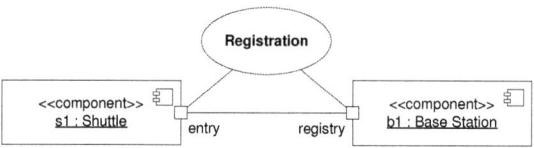

Figure 2.3.4: Representation of a Coordination Pattern

Figure 2.3.4 shows the graphical representation of a Coordination Pattern, the registration pattern, that is applied to two components, shuttle and base station.

The guarantees made by the pattern constraint can be formally verified based on the information that is available in the abstract pattern. As the pattern is restricted to a small number of participants, model checking is feasible with moderate effort. Due to the refinement relation, these guarantees carry over to the concrete component. When a component implements multiple roles, additional – local – checks that preclude detrimental interactions between the different roles are required. A design that has been verified at this level will then, however, remain correct for any syntactically correct combination of such components into a system structure (cf. [GTB[+]03]).

The way the convoy pattern builds upon the data provided by means of the registration pattern in the application example illustrates an important principle: Coordination Patterns can build on the guarantees made by other patterns in order to realize more complex behaviors. This ability to bootstrap advanced behaviors starting from concrete and simple interaction patterns will be of central importance for realizing the high-level coordination between agents below.

### 2.3.2 Formalization

In the following, we will provide a short introduction of the core of the semantics of Coordination Patterns. Due to the focus of this thesis, we will mostly concentrate on those aspects that are relevant for the interaction between the story-driven and component-based perspectives on system behavior.

#### 2.3.2.1 State Machines

A formalization of state machines is required as the foundation of the formal definition of pattern and component behavior. The discussed compositional verification approach presented in [GTB[+]03] uses a class of I/O-automata for this purpose. The concept of *refinement* for these automata is discussed in detail in [Gie03]. Meanwhile, the semantics of Real-Time Statecharts is defined by introducing *Extended Hierarchical Timed Automata* in [GB03]. While both are relevant to Coordination Patterns, the two definitions are, however, incompatible. This situation is remedied by [BGH05], which integrates and extends these definitions for *hybrid automata* that exhibit continuous behavior. However, the integrated definition abstracts from certain aspects such as hierarchical states or propositions, while devoting a significant amount of attention to the continuous aspects, which play a prominent role throughout the formalization.

In the context of this thesis, we are only interested in modeling discrete behavior, but would like to be able to cover all aspects of the notation. Due to this different focus, we choose a complementary approach: We derive a set of definitions that covers both RTSC and refinement in detail, but is restricted to the discrete domain. While related to the definitions for hybrid automata, it is simpler and tailored to the task of providing a consistent terminology for discussing discrete behavior and central points of the semantics.

**Automata.** The concept of a *finite automaton* is fundamental for the discussion of state machines. As we are mostly dealing with reactive behavior, we are more particularly interested in *Mealy automata* whose output depends on both their current state and current input. Using the same modular approach applied to the different flavors of graph transformation systems, we provide a basic definition with a set of possible extensions:

**Definition 2.3.1** *An* automaton $M$ *is defined by a 4-tuple* $(S, S_0, A, T)$, *where $S$ is a finite set of locations with $S_0 \subseteq S$ the subset of initial locations, $A$ is a set of events which most notably includes the set of input events $I$, the set of output events $O$, and the internal event $\tau$, and $T \subseteq S \times \wp(A) \times S$ is a set of transitions connection two locations.*

The important semantic point here is that firing a transition is divided into the phases entry, execution, and exit and may consequently consume as much time as the associated actions. The semantic problems associated with the UML's run-to-completion macro step semantics (cf. [LvdBC00]) are avoided by adopting a simplified semantics that takes advantage of the property that transitions consume time, which makes the restriction to a single executed transaction per cycle conceptually sound.

**Definition 2.3.2** *A* hierarchical automaton $M$ *is an automaton which is extended by a tuple $(rt, \delta, \sigma)$, where $rt \in S$ is the root location, $\delta : S \to \wp(S)$ is a function defining a tree structure of composite locations rooted in $rt$, and $\sigma : S \to TYPE$ is a function assigning types to locations in order to identify special locations such as ENTRY, EXIT, or HISTORY states.*

As hierarchical automata can be flattened into flat automata, they are not more expressive, only more succinct than the simpler formalism. Their importance thus rather lies on the presentation level, not in an enhanced formal analysis.

**Definition 2.3.3** *A* timed automaton $M$ *is an automaton which is extended with a set of clocks $C$, a set of time constraints $C_c$ represented by expressions over clock values, and a set of clock updates $C_u$ setting or resetting clock values. Time constraints can be assigned as state invariants by a function $inv : S \to C_c$ and as transition guards by a function $cg : T \to C_c$. Clock updates can be assigned to states and transitions by a function $cu : S \cup T \to C_u$.*

## 2.3 Coordination Patterns

As stated above, RTSC restrict time constraints to comparisons of elementary clock values and constants. State invariant expressions are naturally restricted to the specification of upper bounds. When encoding RTSC, we additionally need labeling functions $prio$ and $urgent$ for assigning priorities and urgency to transitions.

**Definition 2.3.4** *An extended automaton $M$ is an automaton that includes a data model $D$, for which queries $D_c : D \rightarrow \{true, false\}$ and updates $D_u : D \rightarrow D$ can be formulated. Queries can be assigned to transitions as guards using a function $g : T \rightarrow D_c$. Model updates are primarily used as actions $a_d \in A \cap D_u$ and typically represent $\tau$ steps.*

The data model $D$ may be represented by a GTS $\mathcal{D}$. Query expressions are then finite conjunctions over arbitrary predicates of $\mathcal{D}$, while model updates are transformations of $\mathcal{D}$, which need to be consistent and feasible within the limitations of potential time constraints.

Based on the data model, atomic propositions $P$ can be assigned to locations by means of a labeling function $L : S \rightarrow \wp(P)$. It is then possible to specify system properties as defined in Section 2.2.2.5. By using Clocked Computational Tree Logic (CCTL) [RK99] instead of plain CTL, such properties can even capture real-time aspects of the system.

**Refinement** (cf. [Gie03]) is an important concept for determining the correctness of realizations of state machine specifications. Refinement defines a notion of behavioral equivalence that is stronger than simulation (which is insufficient to exclude undesired additional behavior), but weaker than bisimulation (which is overly restrictive and does not allow narrowing the specification the way an implementation typically does).

**Definition 2.3.5** *An automaton $M = (S, S_0, A, T)$ is a refinement of an automaton $M' = (S', S'_0, A', T')$, denoted by $M \sqsubseteq M'$, iff there is a relation $\Omega \subseteq S \times S'$ mapping locations from $M$ to $M'$ so that $\forall s_0 \in S_0 : (\exists s'_0 \in S'_0 : (s_0, s'_0) \in \Omega), \forall (s_1, s'_1) \in \Omega$ holds $\forall (s_1, A_t, s_2) \in T : (\exists (s'_1, A_t, s'_2) \in T' : (s_2, s'_2) \in \Omega)$ (simulation), and $\forall (s'_1, A'_t, s'_3) \in T' : (\exists (s_1, A'_t, s_3) \in T)$ for some $s_3 \in S, s'_3 \in S'$.*

Several of the described extensions are affected by the concept of refinement. Most importantly, time constraints and clock updates need to be respected in such a way that the refined behavior only restricts the allowed time intervals (which implies not introducing additional clock updates for mapped clocks). While some conditions such as the preservation of labels $L(s_1) = L'(s'_1)$ are straightforward, refinement at the level of the data model, i.e. GTS, is a problem in its own right that is discussed in Chapter 4.

In practice, we are primarily interested in the notion of *restricted refinement* which only considers the subset $A'_t \subseteq A_t \cap A'$, thus allowing the refined automata to introduce arbitrary additional internal actions.

### 2.3.2.2 Coordination Patterns

Following [GTB+03], we can now define a Coordination Pattern as follows:

**Definition 2.3.6** *A Coordination Pattern $CP$ is a 4-tuple $(\mathcal{M}, \Psi, M^C, \phi)$, where $\mathcal{M}$ is a set of automata $M_1, \ldots, M_k$ defining role behaviors with a set $\Psi$ of associated role invariants $\psi_1, \ldots, \psi_k$, $M^C$ is an automaton modeling connector behavior, and $\phi$ is the pattern constraint.*

#### 2.3.2.3 Components

**Definition 2.3.7** *A component definition $C$ is a tuple $(I_p, I_r, P, m)$ where $I_p$ is a set of provided interfaces, $I_r$ is a set of required interfaces, $P$ is a set of ports, and $m : P \to \wp(I_p \cup I_r)$ is a function assigning interfaces to ports. Each port $p$ is characterized by an automaton $r_p$ with the associated set of supported input signals $IS_p$, which must be the union of the input signals $IS$ of each interface in $m(p)$. Additionally, an automaton $r_b$ may be specified which controls the internal synchronization between the component's ports.*

We further characterize the relationship between a component and its internal structure as follows:

**Definition 2.3.8** *A component definition $C$ is implemented by a set of classifiers (i.e. components or classes) $\mathcal{C}$ iff for each $p \in P_C$ there is a $C' \in \mathcal{C}$ for which $\exists p' \in P_{C'}$ that is a restricted refinement of $p$, i.e., $r_{p'} \sqsubseteq r_p$ and $IS_p \subseteq IS_{p'}$. We then write $\mathcal{C} \sqsubseteq C$.*

We finally define how components realize pattern roles:

**Definition 2.3.9** *A component $C$ is a realization of a pattern $CP$ if there is a port $p \in P_C$ whose automaton $r_p$ is a valid restricted refinement of a role behavior $M_i \in \mathcal{M}_{CP}$ and fulfills the associated role invariant $\psi_i \in \Psi_{CP}$.*

### 2.3.3 Integrating Story-Driven Modeling and Coordination Patterns

So far, we have treated Story-Driven Modeling and Coordination Patterns as two mostly independent parallel universes, Coordination Patterns dealing with the external coordination and reactive behavior of components, Story-Driven Modeling describing the structural evolution of the system. While story-driven notations are referenced in the context of pattern definitions and used for the specification of actions, there is a clear separation: Coordination Patterns describe the interaction *between* components, Story Patterns describe internal side effects of operations *within* components.

Previous work has focused on the formal treatment of behavior in the context of existing Coordination Patterns, but has largely ignored the question of their instantiation. When describing reconfiguration behavior, a task for which Story-Driven Modeling is well suited, we would therefore like to be able to apply its techniques at the component or system level in order to model when and how ports, connectors, and Coordination Pattern instances are created, connected, and disconnected. Taking this approach a step farther, we could even model runtime modifications of the state machines themselves. However, applying Story-Driven Modeling at this level requires

## 2.3 Coordination Patterns

the ability to properly reference the core concepts of Coordination Patterns in the context of the employed notations. We therefore introduce a lightweight metamodel and notational templates which allow us to express such references. The basic idea is to derive a class structure from component and state machine specifications and then simply treat the specification elements as instances of this structure, an approach that already is applied in an informal manner in the application example or previous work such as [BBG+06] where Coordination Pattern instances are simply represented by objects.

**Metamodel.** Figure 2.3.5 provides an overview of the metamodel. All elements of the system for which reactive behavior is specified are instances of the abstract class Stateful. Its subclasses are Component, Port, Role, and Connector. Components provide Ports, which in turn are attached to directed input and output Connectors. Ports may also realize Roles.

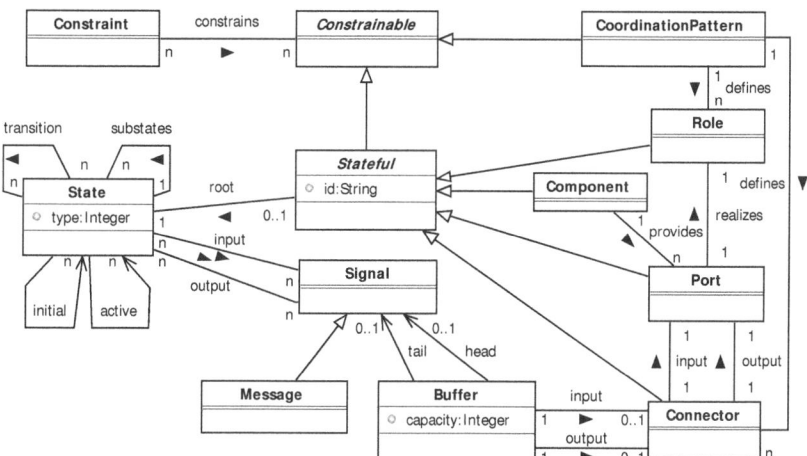

Figure 2.3.5: Coordination Pattern metamodel

State machines are encoded based on the class State, which is used to encode the different types of locations. Each State may be a composition of substates and specifies transitions to possible successor States.[6] In a fashion similar to the state pattern as proposed by [GHJV94], the active substates of a State are indicated by an association. Likewise, initial indicates the set of initial states. A state machine is attached to a Stateful element by assigning it a root State, which is implicitly active. The active States of the state machine are then those with an unbroken path of activation links to the root, which provides a straightforward way of providing deep history

---
[6] For the purposes of this thesis, it is sufficient to model transitions as associations. In a more detailed model, transitions would merit their own class, associated with source and target states.

support. States may specify a method signature that indicates which Signals are accepted while the Stateful element is in this particular State and allows attaching the specified side effects.

Communication across Component boundaries takes place using the Connectors. Each Connector provides an input and an output Buffer with a limited capacity. The Port has access to the head element of the output Buffer of an input Connector and may add a tail element into the input Buffer of an output Connector. By using arbitrarily complex Message objects as Signals, it is possible to provide a detailed object-oriented specifications of the resulting updates to the internal data model.

Finally, Coordination Patterns may define a set of roles and connectors. Both Stateful and Coordination Pattern extend the abstract class Constrainable, which represents entities whose behavior is constrained by a set of Constraints that they need to fulfill.

**Derived class model.** From a given Coordination Pattern specification, a concrete class model can be derived automatically in a direct way, using the introduced metamodel and the formalization of Coordination Patterns presented above.

The class model in Figure 2.3.6 comprises part of the Coordination Pattern from Figure 2.3.4 and the associated Real-Time Statechart from Figure 2.3.3. It represents the central entities of the pattern (component, port, connectors, states) as custom classes and encodes important structural relationships such as the defined transitions as associations. The method signatures of the states are derived from the signals on the transitions in the RTSC, documenting which incoming signals the state will react to.

The concrete classes are marked up with stereotypes that refer to the elements of the metamodel, which is an idiom we will use frequently throughout this thesis. Though technically at different levels of (meta) model abstraction, the concrete classes implicitly 'inherit' the associations and attributes of the metamodel classes, which simplifies modeling and makes the diagrams more compact. For example, a ≪message≫ has the implicit ability to be the ≪head≫ of a ≪buffer≫ without there being an association between, e.g., Update and Queue. Such associations can, however, be made explicit, as is done with the (anonymous) association between Shuttle and Location or with rcv between Waiting and Registered, if this helps to make the model more precise and better convey the intended meaning.

**Applications.** The class model can then be used to reference the elements of the Coordination Pattern in Story Patterns. Firstly, Story Patterns (or Object Diagrams) can be used to model the initial instance situation in detail – i.e., which component, port, and connector instances exist, and which states and transitions they provide.

Secondly, transformations of the internal data model can now make reference to received messages, which may contain complex data structures, in an object-oriented way. Figure 2.3.7 provides a basic example, with the Shuttle consuming the Update and adding the contained Position information to its internal cache of stored shuttle positions, which allows it to reason about the whereabouts of other nearby shuttles.

Finally, Figure 2.3.7 also encodes how the port's ≪state≫ changes from Waiting to Registered due to the received Update, i.e., it reflects the changes in the externally visible state and behavior of

## 2.3 Coordination Patterns

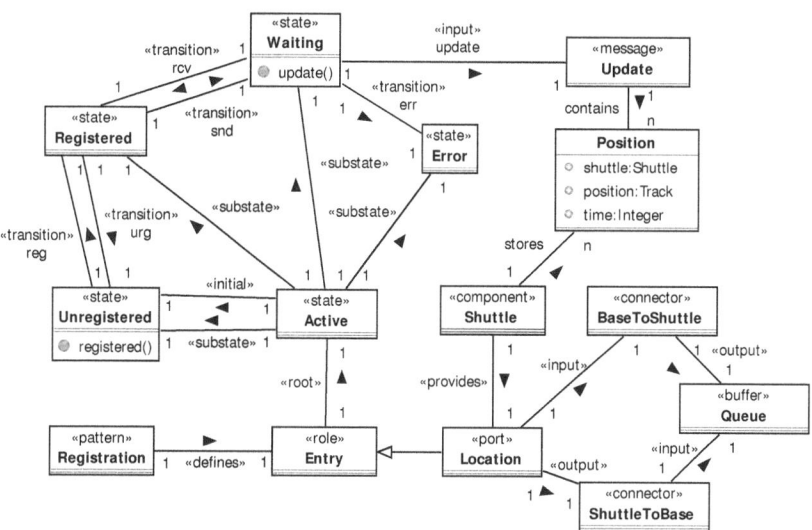

Figure 2.3.6: Partial class model for the shuttle component

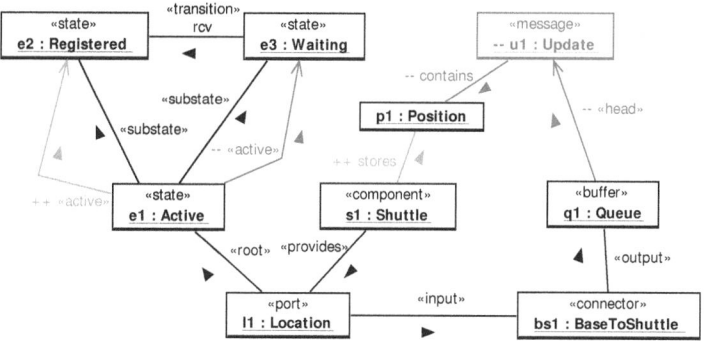

Figure 2.3.7: Processing an update from the base station

the component, not just the internal updates.

In this manner, Story Patterns (or, more appropriately, the extended constraint notations introduced below) could be used to reproduce the complete Coordination Pattern specification in all semantic detail. Story Diagrams, extended with a concept of time, could then be used to implement this specification. The above Story Pattern in Figure 2.3.7 might, for example, become part of the definition of the Waiting state's update operation. While we will not pursue this idea and its implications in more detail in this thesis, it suggests great potential for the specification of advanced reconfiguration techniques featuring compositional adaptation. This could range from the creation of new ports and connectors to the dynamic creation of states and transitions at runtime.

## 2.4 Conclusion

With Story Driven Modeling and Coordination Patterns, we have presented the two fundamental approaches on which this thesis is based in this chapter. We have provided an overview of the employed notations and have laid the formal foundation on which our extended constraint notations and, subsequently, the rigorous specification of multi-agent system behavior will be based. While mostly relying on previously published definitions, we have extended them in scope, e.g. by supporting inheritance in type graphs, and integrated and refined them in many places.

*Story-Driven Modeling* is a very visual and accessible approach that excels at expressing structural properties and structural evolution. However, the current syntax, but also semantics, impose limitations on the expression of more complex properties. Furthermore, there is neither a concept of (real-)time nor an integrated approach for the specification of temporal properties.

*Coordination Patterns* are a powerful approach for the specification of reactive real-time behavior. They enable model-based reuse and the compositional verification of system properties. However, they rely on (intermittently) static structures and provide no inherent support for structural evolution. While actions can be modeled using story-driven notations, these are limited in scope to updates of the internal model, not the pattern.

With the proposed mapping, we provide a way to model reactive behavior, reconfiguration, and structural evolution at the pattern level. Story-driven techniques can then be used to model in detail when and how a pattern is instantiated and how it is implemented, and derive certain structural guarantees. Within this frame, the existing techniques for the compositional verification of real-time behavior can then be applied to a set of static models.

In the following chapter, we shall address the indicated limitations of Story Patterns as a constraint notation and will introduce extended notations for the integrated specification of structural and temporal properties.

# Chapter 3

# Constraints

## 3.1 Introduction

The ability to express constraints is central to the specification of software, from the first elicitation of requirements to the detailed design. Structural or behavioral constraints may merely serve to document desired characteristics of a system, but may also take on the role of a binding and verifiable contract that any acceptable design needs to fulfill. The use of invariants or pre- and postconditions can even be extended down to the implementation level, as the Eiffel Language (cf. [Mey92]) proves.

Constraints are an integral part of the definition of a Coordination Pattern, which defines both role invariants and a pattern constraint. These constraints specify forbidden or required state configurations for different combinations of stateful elements of the system and are expressed using some restricted subset of CTL*. They are typically concerned with the safety of configurations, but may also encode generic liveness properties such as the absence of deadlocks.

Story-Driven Modeling, on the other hand, does not make any provisions for modeling or assigning constraints beyond the mechanism that is underlying Story Patterns, which basically consist of a pre- and a postcondition after all. For all further needs, the approach relies on standard object-oriented techniques as provided by the UML.

The UML's popularity is arguably owed to the accessibility (and broadness) of its basic concepts, which is particularly relevant for its acceptance by industry. In practice, the visual notations for structural modeling remain the most widely used feature of the UML. However, these notations only provide very limited support for constraint modeling, such as the specification of cardinalities in Class Diagrams. For specifying more detailed structural properties, the UML only provides a textual specification language, the OCL [Obj06].

When specifying OCL properties, developers are forced to translate their ideas about required structural properties from the familiar structural view provided by UML Class and Object Diagrams to an intricate textual syntax. Interpreting the resulting OCL specifications involves a complicated and error prone translation in the opposite direction. This mental translation process poses a significant barrier even in most standard software engineering environments where, consequently, OCL is rarely employed. As a result, important structural properties remain undocumented and are easily lost in the course of the development process. Informal natural language descriptions are often seen as the only feasible way of capturing them to some degree.

For temporal logics such as LTL or CTL [CGP00], these problems are even more acute. As reported in [DAC99], developers (even experts) have significant problems handling the intricate nature of these logics. Even in projects with very well trained experts, employing them is often impossible, as the resulting property specifications will usually be unintelligible to domain experts from other disciplines that need to participate in the effort. In the context of software-intensive systems, this problem becomes a serious hindrance. When developing the software for complex mechatronic systems, the software engineers have to work closely with experts in control engineering, mechanical engineering, and electrical engineering.

Apart from the issue of interdisciplinary communication, developing the dynamic software architectures that promise more intelligent, efficient, and flexible systems poses new challenges in its on right. When systems adapt their structure at run-time in response to current needs, their design and validation become much more complex than in the static case. In particular, structural and temporal aspects become much more closely intertwined than before, as real-time behavior can now involve structural adaptations.

**Constraint notations.** With the constraint notations we present in this chapter, we provide a visual language that is capable of capturing constraints on the structural evolution of a system and can facilitate the specification of structural adaptation processes. We have presented preliminary versions of the notations in [GK06b, GK06a], and [GK06c], followed by syntactical refinements and a redefined semantics in [KG07] and [KG06c].

For the modeling of structural properties, we introduce *enhanced Story Patterns* (eSP) and *Story Decision Diagrams* (SDD). While enhanced Story Patterns represent an evolutionary extension of Story Patterns [KNNZ00] and primarily focus on fixing the identified issues concerning their syntax, Story Decision Diagrams extend their scope by introducing several original concepts and expanding the notation into a full-fledged first-order logic for graphs. They combine the concept of structural pattern matching with decision diagrams, which foster the decomposition of complex properties into comprehensible simpler ones. Both notations are full replacements for Story Patterns and may, for example, be used in Story Diagrams. As it is possible to freely mix the two notations, the designer can choose the more appropriate dialect on a case-by-case basis if desired.

Finally, *Timed Story Scenario Diagrams* (TSSD) extend Story Patterns into the temporal domain. They define conditional timed scenarios describing the partial order of specific structural configurations. In this manner, they provide support for the specification of temporal properties that use structural properties as the basic propositions. Their focus is thus on defining a temporal framework into which the structural notations can be embedded. The notation was inspired by various sources, most notably by the Visual Timed Event Scenario (VTS) approach [ABKO04, BKO05] and certain features of Live Sequence Charts (LSC) [HM02] and Story Diagrams [FNTZ98].

## 3.1 Introduction

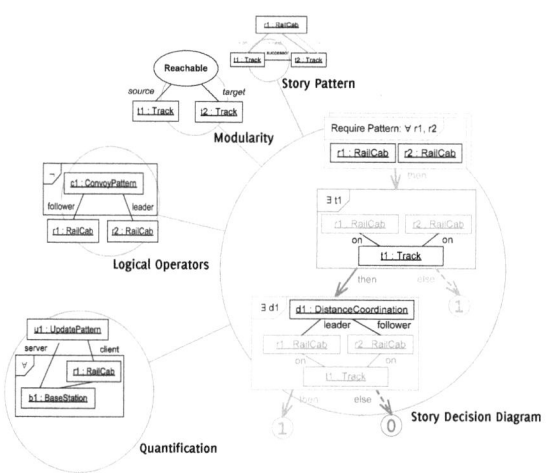

Figure 3.1.1: Key features of *Story Decision Diagrams* (SDD)

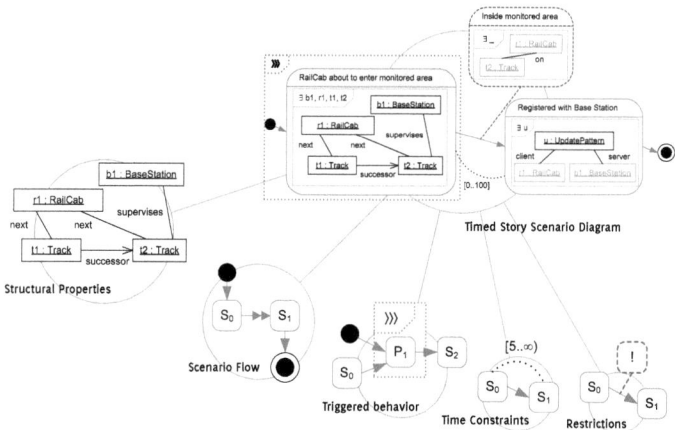

Figure 3.1.2: Key features of *Timed Story Scenario Diagrams* (TSSD)

**Chapter outline.** After reviewing and discussing the state of the art in Subsection 3.1.1, we extend our application example with a number of properties that we would like to encode in Subsection 3.1.2. In the following two main sections, we present the notations. In each section, we first introduce the syntax, along with an informal description of the intended meaning, and then provide a formal semantics definition. We also look into the expressiveness of the languages and their potential uses for validation and verification purposes. Section 3.2 discusses the concepts for modeling structural properties. Section 3.3 embeds the concepts for structural modeling into our approach for modeling temporal properties.

## 3.1.1 Related Work

There is an abundance of formalisms for the specification of properties. Choosing from a plethora of general purpose or task-specific first- or higher-order logics, virtually any relevant property of software-intensive systems can be expressed. Many of them have been thoroughly analyzed so that results concerning their expressiveness, decidability and computational complexity are available. For many, such as $CTL^*$ (cf. [CGP00]) and its various extensions in the area of model checking, there is wide-spread and highly optimized tool support.

While this necessarily is the foundation upon which any formal specification technique must operate, we are mostly interested in the usability of a formalism, i.e., whether it can express a property in a way that can be written, read, and managed by a human user, and how much training is required for using it. As we have already discussed, many formalisms, such as temporal logics, are designed with the requirements of theoretical analysis in mind and fail in this respect. Dedicated specification languages, even though often closely based on some logic, tend to pay much more attention to the users' needs. For example, PSL/Sugar [Ace04], a language that is popular in the telecommunications sector and a future IEEE standard, is closely based on an embedding of predicate logic into a temporal logic, but already provides a much more intuitive way of specifying sequences of events than either. Furthermore, we believe that, for certain classes of properties, visual representations are inherently superior to textual representations as they greatly reduce the effort required for parsing. To us, this seems to be particularly pertinent for the representation of structure, i.e. the relationships between entities.

In our analysis of related work, we therefore restrict our attention to dedicated specification techniques, with a heavy focus on visual formalisms.

**Structural Properties.** Constraint diagrams [KH99] visualize constraints as restrictions on sets using Euler circles, spiders and arrows. To compensate for the decrease in expressive power w.r.t. the OCL, constraint trees [KH02] combine them with the idea of parsing an OCL statement into a tree, replacing only selected constraints with constraint diagrams. The downside of the approach is that while quantification on sets is intuitive, structural constraints quickly result in intricate, visually complex diagrams with little or no relation to the original UML specification.

VisualOCL [BKPPT01] is an approach that focuses on mapping OCL syntax to a visual format as closely as possible, thus facilitating the parsing of complex, nested expressions. As we have seen, Story Patterns (cf. [KNNZ00]) combine an accessible representation with a sound formalization

## 3.1 Introduction

based on graph grammars, but are not expressive enough to fully replace the OCL.

Alloy [Jac02] is a structural modeling language, partially motivated by the desire to overcome the perceived deficiencies of the OCL. It is textual, not visual, and based on first order logic, which makes it amenable to automatic analysis.

**Temporal Properties.** The approaches for the specification of temporal properties are more varied than for the structural domain. However, all visual formalisms for the specification of behavior can be traced either to automata theory or the concept of scenarios. The latter type has the advantage that it is well suited to partial, incomplete specifications of the required behavior.

UML 1.x Sequence Diagrams or message sequence charts have been employed to specify and check timed properties (cf. [LL99]). However, they are usually considered as not expressive enough, as only a set of runs or one specific run of the system, but no conditional properties, can be described. Therefore, the interpretation w.r.t. the system is usually unclear. This limitation has been tackled by a number of approaches such as Live Sequence Charts (LSC) [HM02] or Triggered Message Sequence Charts (TMSCs) [SC02], which add the ability to describe conditional behavior in a sequence diagram style notation. To some extent, these enhancements have found their way into UML 2.0 Sequence Diagrams (cf. [Obj07, section 14.4]).

In the UML 1.x, real-time properties could only be expressed using the *UML Profile for Schedulability, Performance, and Time Specification* [OMG05]. It allows attaching specific schedulability or quality of service characteristics to classes, but only provides rudimentary support for the detailed specification of real-time behavior. UML 2.0 introduces only marginal improvements w.r.t. real-time behavior in Sequence Diagrams.

Other approaches such as the Visual Timed Event Scenario approach [ABKO04, BKO05] focus on scenarios for pure events rather than the interaction of predefined units. Therefore, they provide a more intuitive notion of temporal ordering than Sequence Diagrams, which require specifying a sequence of interactions that enforces this ordering.

In a similar vein, the Process Pattern Specification Language (PPSL) [FESS07, FSES06] extends UML 2.0 Activity Diagrams with stereotypes that allow expressing process constraints. While the specified process patterns constrain the temporal ordering of actions, the language is not designed as a complete visual temporal logic, but rather specifically targets the modeling and verification of business processes.

Specification patterns for temporal properties represent an attempt to alleviate the problem that temporal logics are difficult to apply. As outlined in [DAC99], many useful temporal properties can be constructed using a small set of elementary building blocks. This idea has been extended and applied to real-time systems in [KC05]. However, while applying the patterns may be intuitive, the resulting formulae themselves are no more transparent or readable than hand-written ones. Once the context of the employed patterns is removed, using or updating them might even be more difficult than before.

However, all these approaches focus exclusively on the temporal aspect of behavior, abstracting from its structural aspects. Statements concerning the required temporal behavior of expressive structural properties are not supported.

**Combined Structural and Temporal Properties.** Most approaches which permit combining structural and temporal properties are extensions of the OCL towards the description of dynamics. Through the introduction of additional temporal logic operators into the OCL (e.g., eventually, always, or never), modelers are enabled to specify required behavior by means of temporal restrictions among actions and events (e.g., c.f. [BKS02]). Temporal extensions of the OCL that consider real-time issues have been proposed for events in OCL/RT [CK02] and for states in RT-OCL [FM02]. As temporal logic is already difficult to apply by itself (cf. [DAC99]), integrating the OCL and temporal logic concepts at the textual level yields a sufficiently expressive, but not a sufficiently usable and comprehensible solution.

In [GHK00], an embedding of graph patterns into LTL formulae is proposed in order to allow capturing structural properties. This approach tackles the theoretical aspects of the proposed integration rather than the design of a practical specification language, which would suffer from the intricate nature of the underlying LTL.

Though visually similar to TSSDs, Story Diagrams [FNTZ98] are a programming language rather than a specification language. They are geared towards defining an executable, operational implementation rather than characterizing a set of acceptable behaviors.

The only notation that takes an approach similar to ours is a recent proposal [RS06] for writing temporal graph queries. The approach extends Story Diagrams by annotating unary forward or past operators from LTL with additional explicitly encoded time constraints. It requires the explicit specification of an accepting automaton rather than employing the idea of scenarios. In cases where only partial orders of events or time constraints between partially ordered situations have to be specified, the encoding of the time constraints in the automaton will therefore become rather complex.

### 3.1.2 Application Example

In this chapter, we will flesh out the basic structures we have described in Section 2.1.2 in more detail.

We have already mentioned certain assumptions about the structure of the system, which we can now state formally. Every track needs to be supervised by at least one base station. Additionally, we require that there needs to be a common base station for any three consecutive tracks as the supervised areas have to overlap in order to avoid gaps in the coverage when shuttles pass from one area into another. We would furthermore like to encode that the track graph does not contain any dead ends, which implies that any track is reachable from any other track.

Concerning the evolution of the system, we define both negative and positive invariants. The most important safety property we are considering is the absence of collisions. As the control engineering problems are encapsulated by the Coordination Patterns – at this level, we assume the controller implementation to react correctly provided the input we supply accurately reflects the current environment – we can abstract from the continuous behavior and the associated differential equations and reduce the problem to a discrete one, namely whether the correct Coordination Patterns exist in all specific instance situations. A potential collision, which must never occur,

## 3.1 Introduction

is thus characterized by the fact that two shuttles are in close proximity without running a convoy pattern. As the convoy pattern depends on the registration pattern, we require each shuttle to be registered with all base stations supervising its current tracks at all times.

While structural properties are sufficient for the specification of safety properties, they only allow a reduced, binary view on behavior. For example, a shuttle cannot realistically register instantaneously when entering a track – in order to fulfill the invariant, it will therefore have to instantiate the required registration patterns well before actually reaching the track segment. A scenario with real-time constraints provides a more fine-grained way to specify the desired behavior, indicating exactly when the registration needs to be initiated and when it needs to be completed.

Finally, scenarios can be used to encode liveness properties such as progress, e.g. that a shuttle may not block another shuttle indefinitely. In later chapters, we will also deal with an important class of properties, the making and subsequent fulfillment of commitments, in more detail. When introducing the notation for temporal constraints, we will use trivial examples from the logistic domain to this effect, such as shuttles acquiring tasks and transporting cargo and passengers, in an informal manner.

## 3.2 Structural Properties

In this Section, we will introduce the two available dialects for specifying structural properties. We first present *enhanced Story Patterns*, which are designed to be a simple and compact drop-in replacement for classic *Story Patterns*, and then introduce the more general *Story Decision Diagrams*, which introduce additional concepts such as explicit quantifiers and recursion, enabling them to express complex properties that are beyond the scope of (enhanced) Story Patterns. We will finally discuss their formal semantics.

### 3.2.1 Enhanced Story Patterns

The design goal of *enhanced Story Patterns* (eSP) was to remedy the most immediate shortcomings of the Story Pattern notation while changing it as little as possible. As a result, eSPs are visually closer to Story Patterns than Story Decision Diagrams and should be immediately understandable to anyone familiar with Story-Driven Modeling.

The most important syntactical addition are *insets*, which are UML 2.0 boxes used for the specification of properties for groups of elements in the familiar fashion employed by many UML 2.0 diagrams. An inset qualifies all diagram nodes that lie completely within its bounds, and all diagram edges whose label is completely contained within the inset. The inset may not intersect other nodes or labels - partially overlapped elements are not part of the inset, but might give rise to ambiguous interpretations as there are other intuitively plausible ways of defining when a link is 'inside' an inset.

**Negation.** The most pressing concern is the the negation of complex structures. eSPs solve this problem by using *negation* or *not insets*, which are marked with the ¬ symbol. The inset is required to also qualify all links leading to the enclosed objects in a well-formed pattern as it does not make sense for a required link to be attached to a forbidden element.

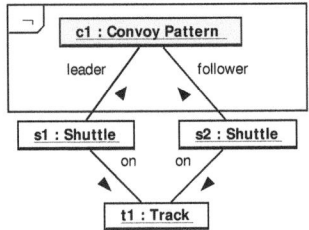

Figure 3.2.1: Complex negation: no common convoy pattern

In a way that is directly analogous to a negative application condition (NAC) for a graph pattern, the pattern will only match if all positive elements are found while the negated structure inside

## 3.2 Structural Properties

the inset is not found. Partial matches for the inset do not affect the validity of the pattern, however.

Figure 3.2.1 therefore correctly captures the property we failed to specify in Figure 2.2.4: The pattern only matches if there are two shuttles on the same track segment who are not engaged in a common convoy pattern. Note that we still need to qualify that such a potential collision is supposed to represent a negative invariant of the system, as this is not obvious from the diagram.

Negation insets could completely supersede negated (i.e. crossed out) elements as the means of expressing negation. For the negation of isolated links, however, the notation is somewhat heavy-handed. We therefore still allow directly negating individual elements, but discourage this in the general case.

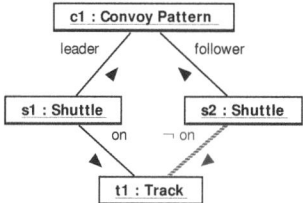

Figure 3.2.2: Direct negation of a link

As crossing out elements drastically reduces the readability of labels, negated elements are marked with ¬ and drawn in a dotted blue line style. In Figure 3.2.2, we describe the situation that the follower in a convoy is not on the same track section as the leader with a negated link.

**Implication.** The second common use case that is not supported by Story Patterns are implications or conditional properties, i.e. patterns that only need to match if another pattern is also found. eSPs allow expressing such conditions by means of *implication* or *if insets*, which are identified by the ∀ symbol. The pattern is fulfilled whenever the qualified elements are *not* found, or if a match for the complete pattern is found for each occurrence of the qualified pattern.

The existing formal semantics can be used to express simple conditional properties by encoding the condition as the graph pattern and the conditional expression as a NAC. The eSP is then fulfilled whenever the graph pattern does *not* match.

The pattern in Figure 3.2.3 encodes the coverage condition, requiring that there is a shared base station for any three adjacent tracks.

**Conjunction and disjunction.** The positive elements of a Story Pattern are all part of a conjunction: they all need to be present for the pattern to match. By again applying the inset concept, eSPs provide a way to mark certain subgraphs as disjunctions by using *disjunction* or *or insets*, identified by the ∨ symbol. The eSP is then fulfilled whenever at least one of the elements of the

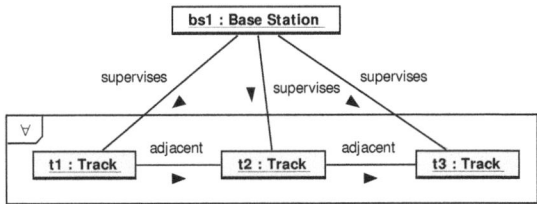

Figure 3.2.3: Implication: consecutive tracks share a base station

inset is matched. The pattern in Figure 3.2.4 matches whenever a registration pattern or a convoy pattern (or both) exists. This can easily be captured at the semantic level by representing the pattern by a set of alternative graph patterns.

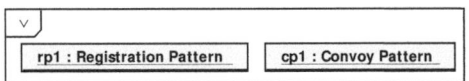

Figure 3.2.4: Disjunction: At least one of the patterns exits

Usability concerns and intuition suggest that when the inset contains only objects, it represents the disjunction over all elements, but that when the inset contains links, it represents the disjunction over just the links. As a link cannot occur without its source and target objects, a link in a mixed inset would otherwise never be evaluated as the connected object would already fulfill the disjunction. The pattern in Figure 3.2.5 thus matches any shuttle that is the leader or the follower of some convoy pattern.

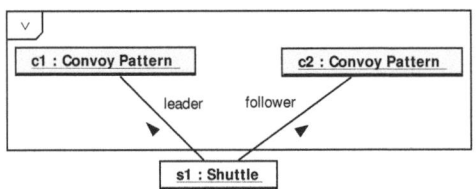

Figure 3.2.5: A shuttle that is involved in some convoy pattern

Alternatives are frequently represented by subgraphs, not individual elements. The *conjunction* or *and inset*, identified by the ∧ symbol, groups elements into a conjunction that can be used like an atomic element inside a disjunction. Figure 3.2.6, which is semantically equivalent to Figure

## 3.2 Structural Properties

3.2.5, is a basic example that makes the fact that the convoy pattern and the leader or follower link need to occur together explicit.

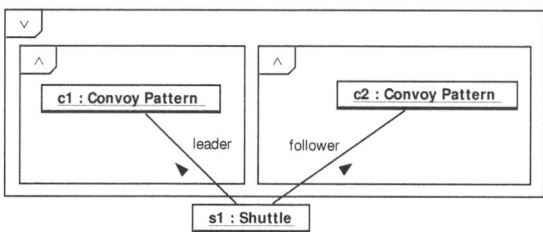

Figure 3.2.6: Conjunction: grouping for alternative subgraphs

This brings up the question of nested insets. There is nothing that precludes arbitrary combinations of negation, implication, disjunction, and conjunction insets – except that, above a certain number of insets, the diagrams may become too visually complex and thus hard to read. For these cases, using Story Decision Diagrams provides a less compact, but more straight-forward alternative approach.

The semantics definition based on plain graph patterns we have used above does not scale to support more complex eSPs. For a complete formalization of eSPs, we will therefore have to rely on the more general semantics we will define for Story Decisions Diagrams. As any eSP can be mapped to an equivalent SDD, we will simply use this relation to provide arbitrary eSPs with a formal semantics.

**Pattern references.** Another useful feature is the ability to reference other patterns in a pattern definition, which provides modularity and a way of hiding complex recurring definitions. eSPs allow such references by means of *pattern references*, which are represented using the UML Pattern syntax, i.e. a dashed ellipse. The eSP may also bind elements of the referenced patterns to its own elements using roles, represented by dashed connectors labeled with the name of the referenced element.

The eSP in Figure 3.2.7 references another pattern called registered, which contains a shuttle called agent and a track called location and encodes that agent is registered with all base stations supervising location. The eSP will then match for any $s1$ and $t1$ that fulfill the registered pattern when used as agent and location.

While simple references merely function as a sort of macro for externalizing parts of a complex pattern, they also allow recursive definitions which greatly expand the expressiveness of the language. As we shall discuss when formally introducing this concept for SDDs, this significantly increases the complexity of the semantics definition as well, though.

**Transformations.** Model transformations are specified in the same way as for Story Patterns by marking elements as part of the LHS or RHS with the appropriate modifiers. eSPs provide

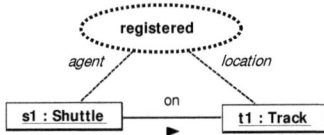

Figure 3.2.7: Reference: a shuttle which is correctly registered

several alternative ways of marking up added and removed elements: Users can choose between using the ≪create≫ and ≪destroy≫ stereotypes as in Story Patterns, using $++$ and $--$, or using $*$ ('constructor') and $\sim$ ('destructor') as the most compact shorthands.

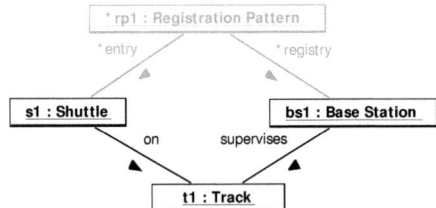

Figure 3.2.8: Adding an element: Instantiation of a convoy pattern

The eSP in Figure 3.2.8 is a (high-level) representation of a shuttle instantiating a registration pattern.

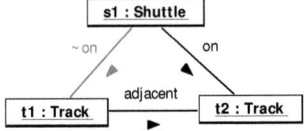

Figure 3.2.9: Removing an element: Leaving a track

In Figure 3.2.9, the shuttle fully moves onto track t2, removing the on link to t1.

### 3.2.2 Story Decision Diagrams

*Story Decision Diagrams (SDD)* take a more radical approach to the extension of Story Patterns. In order to increase the readability of complex properties, SDDs trade off compactness for a clean concept for expressing arbitrary combinations of conjunctions, disjunctions and negations. By making all quantifiers explicit, they also increase the expressiveness of the notation, finally allowing us to include the distinction between positive and negative invariants into the patterns.

## 3.2 Structural Properties

Last but not least, they provide a formalization for modular and even recursive definitions, which make defining transitive properties, such as reachability in graphs, possible. Nonetheless, their visual representation is no more complex or less intuitive than the original notation.

### 3.2.2.1 Basic Principles

An SDD is a directed acyclic graph (DAG). Each node contains a *simple Story Pattern* (*SP*), which basically corresponds to an invariant (enhanced) Story Pattern without forbidden elements, insets, or modifiers. Each SP thus specifies some simple positive property. The SPs on the same path through the SDD share the same variables; i.e., once a pattern element has been bound to an instance, it remains bound in all subsequent nodes.

When evaluating the SDD, the nodes are processed starting from the root node with an empty binding in which all variables are unbound. The progression through the diagram then depends on the result of matching the SP of the current node. Each node in the SDD essentially represents a local if-then-else decision, taken based on the current binding. If a match is found, we extend the binding with the corresponding object and link assignments, thus propagating successfully matched elements to subsequent nodes, and follow the solid then connector; if no match is found, we leave the binding unchanged and follow the dashed else connector.

There are two special *leaf nodes*, (1) signifying *true* and (0) signifying *false*. When a binding reaches a leaf node, it evaluates to true or false, respectively. SDDs are thus similar to decision trees. However, like reduced binary decision diagrams (RBDD), SDDs are not trees, but allow sharing isomorphic subtrees and leaf nodes to reduce diagram size. As in decision diagrams, consecutive conditions correspond to logical conjunction, respectively implication. Both interpretations are equivalent: The intuitive interpretation of the statement if $a$ then $b$ else $c$ is $(a \Rightarrow b) \land (\neg a \Rightarrow c)$, using two implications. Using the definition of implication, this can be reduced to the simpler statement $(a \land b) \lor (\neg a \land c)$, using two conjunctions. Unlike standard decision diagrams, SDDs support alternatives by allowing multiple then or else connectors per node. It is then sufficient for one of the available paths to reach (1) in order to evaluate the whole branch as true.

The SDD in Figure 3.2.10 illustrates these principles. The root node $S$ matches any two shuttles. Node $T$ then checks whether they occupy the same track segment. If they do, then node $P$ verifies whether there is a convoy pattern (yielding (1)) or not (yielding (0)); else there are no further requirements ((1)). The pattern thus encodes our requirement that at all times two shuttles must either not be close to each other or run a convoy pattern if they are.

**Negation.** Observe that there are only positive elements in the patterns. While there is no technical or formal limitation that requires this – in fact, it would be possible to use negative elements or even negation insets in a node – we believe that multiple negations, especially if nested at different levels, tend to make diagrams harder to interpret. We therefore prefer encoding all negations exclusively in the diagram structure.

Unless otherwise specified, a node is interpreted as a positive requirement: matching (then) results in success, i.e. (1), not matching (else) results in failure, i.e. (0). Negation can be expressed

# 3. Constraints

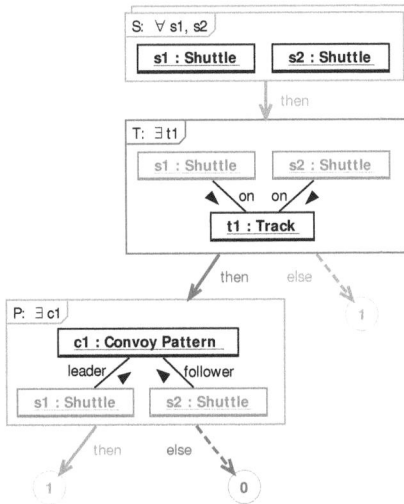

Figure 3.2.10: Basic SDD syntax: when is a convoy pattern required?

by modeling a pattern matching the forbidden instance situation and switching the then and else connectors. Matching then leads to failure, i.e. (0), while the inability to match leads to success, i.e. (1). Figure 3.2.11 illustrates this principle, marking a collision (two shuttles occupying the same *two* tracks would have to be in conflicting physical locations) as a forbidden instance situation. This approach can be used to express arbitrarily complex negative conditions by decomposing them into a sequence of chained nodes.

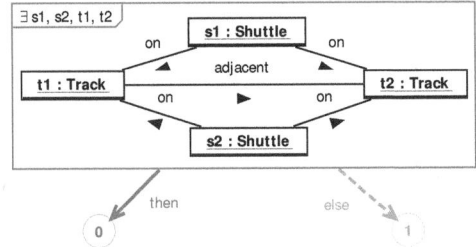

Figure 3.2.11: Negative invariant: collision between two shuttles

As the example shows, the ability to negate entire patterns enables us to adopt the intuitive

## 3.2 Structural Properties

convention that all invariants are positive, i.e. always need to evaluate to true, and still express negative invariants by integrating this information directly into the pattern.

**Presentation.** Syntax highlighting is a standard feature of text editors for programming and specification languages that improves readability and helps to focus the user's attention on relevant details. All of our notations extensively use color for the exact same purpose. The coloring is automatically deduced and thus *never* semantically relevant. Semantically relevant distinctions are, often redundantly, encoded by labels and line styles and are not affected by stripping the colors from a diagram. However, the notations only realize their full potential when used in color, as a restriction to grayscale robs human perception of an entire dimension.

In SDDs, (1) and connectors leading to (1) are green, (0) and connectors leading to (0) are red. A connector's sibling connectors of the opposite type use the inverse color. The remaining then connectors are green, the remaining else connectors are red. Node frames share the color of their then connector as a visual cue that makes negated properties stand out.

In SPs, element definitions are black. Differently from Story Diagrams, we prefer not to omit the type of bound elements because the repeated type information helps in parsing larger diagrams. Previously bound elements are drawn in slate blue instead.

All connector and leaf labels are optional. Leaf nodes can be omitted unless they are semantically required, which is only the case when they are expressing negation.

### 3.2.2.2 Quantification

In Story Patterns, all elements are implicitly existentially quantified. In SDDs, we make all quantifications explicit in order to increase the notation's expressiveness. We therefore differentiate between existential nodes, which require at least one of the bindings they generate to succeed, i.e., reach a (1) leaf node, and universal nodes, which require this of all generated bindings.

**Existential nodes** fall into two categories depending on the contained definitions:

*Existentially quantified nodes* contain free variables, which are bound to objects and links by the node's SP. When a binding reaches it, the node attempts to extend the binding with matches for its free variables that are consistent with its SP definition. If such an extension or several alternative extensions of this kind exist, they are propagated down the then connector. If no such extension exists, the original binding is propagated down the else connector. If the node binds *explicitly* named variables $var_i$ to objects or links, it is marked with $[\exists\, var_i^+]$. If the node only binds *anonymous* variables to links, it is marked with $[\exists\, \_]$.

*Guard nodes* do not contain free variables that could be bound and thus do not extend the bindings that reach them. They merely act as a filter that decides whether a binding should be propagated down the then or else connector, depending on whether it fulfills the node's SP. Guard nodes are marked with [•].

If an existential node only features a then connector, an else connector to (0) is implied. In the less common case that the node only specifies an else connector, a then connector to (1) is implied.

**Universal nodes.** There is only one type of universal node. A *universally quantified* node containing the free variables $var_i$ is marked with $[\forall\ var_i^+]$. It works like an existentially quantified node, except that the extended bindings it generates are not alternatives, but *all* need to succeed. If no extended binding matching the node's SP exists in the first place, the standard semantics of universal quantification requires that the expression evaluate to true – therefore, the node's else connector always implicitly leads to (1).

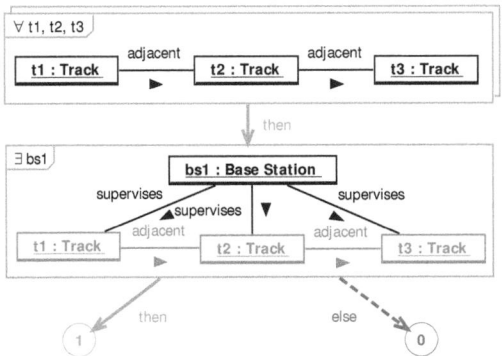

Figure 3.2.12: Connected tracks share a controller

Figure 3.2.12 encodes the coverage requirement that for any three consecutive tracks ($\forall$), there must be a controller ($\exists$) supervising them all. It is thus equivalent to the eSP in Figure 3.2.3.

**Cardinalities.** It is possible to specify *cardinalities* for then connectors. These cardinalities constrain the number of extensions that may be generated for each individual binding that reaches a quantified node. If fewer alternatives than the minimum cardinality or more alternatives than the maximum cardinality are generated from a binding, the extended bindings are discarded and the original binding is propagated down the else connector. It is not possible to specify a cardinality for the else connector as there is always exactly one propagated binding, the original binding, when it is chosen. For the same reason, it does not make sense to place cardinalities on either connector of a guard node, as there will always be one binding on the selected connector.

Figure 3.2.13 encodes one of the cardinalities specified in the underlying Class Diagram (see Figure 2.2.1), namely that each convoy pattern requires at least two registration patterns. SDDs thus eliminate the need to encode cardinalities by means of a set of graph patterns as presented in Section 2.2.2.6. Moreover, SDDs are capable of expressing constraints that cannot be captured by Class Diagrams, e.g., restricting the number of permitted concurrent object instances for each class or imposing conditional cardinalities.

## 3.2 Structural Properties

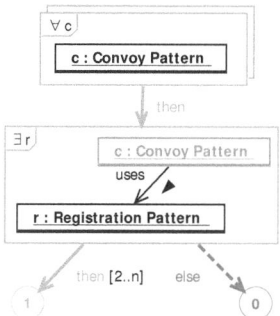

Figure 3.2.13: A convoy pattern depends on at least two registration patterns

### 3.2.2.3 Pattern References

Formal specification languages often allow the composition of complex properties from simpler properties. In the OCL, it is possible to reference more concrete properties in the definition of a property, whereas most visual specification techniques lack this capability. SDDs provide the ability to reference other SDDs as a means of abstracting from arbitrarily complex structural relationships and constraints.

The composition of specifications is accomplished by using *Story Decision Diagram References* (*SDDR*) to *Story Decision Diagram Patterns* (*SDDP*). An SDDP is an SDD encoding some nontrivial property that can be reused in different contexts, while SDDRs are a more refined version of the pattern references we have used in eSPs.

A pattern can explicitly declare a set of free variables, its roles, for which bindings have to be supplied when referencing it. In a node containing a reference, a binding will only match the node if it also fulfills the referenced pattern.

**Basic patterns.** An SDDP specification uses a special type of root node – a $\lambda$ node [$Name$ : $\lambda\, role_1, role_2, \ldots$] – that defines its name and the available roles, i.e., free variables. While node labels are optional for other nodes, the $\lambda$ node's label is mandatory as it is required to identify the pattern. When the SDDP is invoked in a given context, the $\lambda$ node binds the local variables in accordance with the provided context. The evaluation then proceeds based on this binding in the regular way, eventually returning *true* or *false*. The pattern introduces a local scope, which means that the generated bindings are not accessible from the referencing SDD and therefore discarded as soon as a result has been obtained. By extension, any SDD can be used as a pattern, albeit one without assignable roles.

In the host node containing the pattern reference, we again represent the SDDR by using the UML pattern symbol, a dashed circle. Bound elements of the host node are assigned to pattern roles by dashed lines labeled with the respective role name. By default, patterns support optional arguments: If a role is not explicitly bound by the host node, we implicitly add an element definition of the required type to the host node.

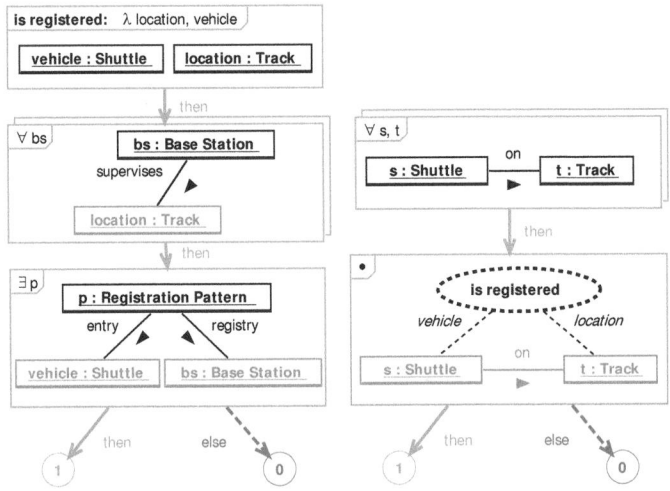

a. Pattern definition: *vehicle* is registered with all supervisors of *location*

b. Pattern reference: All shuttles are properly registered for tracks they are on

Figure 3.2.14: Pattern definition and pattern reference

The pattern in Figure 3.2.14a defines the property that a given shuttle, *vehicle*, is registered with all base stations that supervise a given track, *location*. The SDD in Figure 3.2.14b then requires that this property holds for every shuttles and every track it is on.

**Parametrized patterns.** In addition to the role bindings, it is possible to pass primitive types to patterns as parameters. It is, of course, possible to achieve this based on roles by using object instances representing literals, but this solution is syntactically awkward.

Parameters with their types are declared in the header of the $\lambda$ node: $[Name : \lambda\, parameter_1 : type_1, parameter_2 : type_2, \ldots]$. They can be used wherever using the corresponding primitive type would be allowed, e.g. in constraints on attributes or guard expressions. Numeric parameters can also be employed as cardinalities on then connectors.

**Recursive patterns.** As, like all SDDs, SDDPs may contain pattern references, it is possible to nest definitions. This quite naturally leads to recursively defined patterns. As an example, the pattern in Figure 3.2.15a recursively defines the property that track *to* is reachable from track *from*, used to express that the system is connected in Figure 3.2.15b. The only restriction on recursive definitions is that cardinalities are not allowed for the host node containing the recursive reference as this can lead to logical paradoxa.

## 3.2 Structural Properties

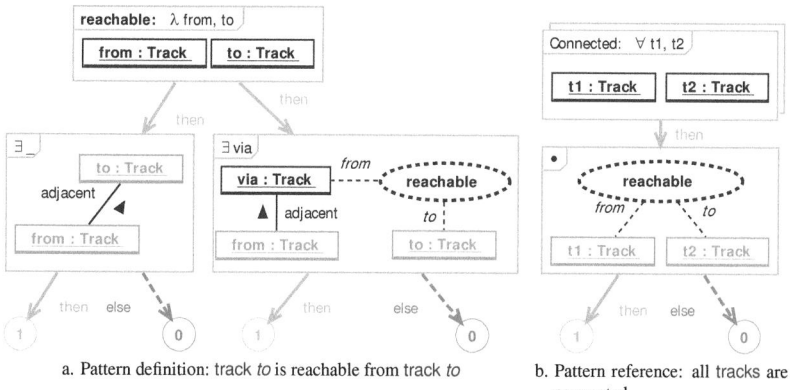

a. Pattern definition: track *to* is reachable from track *to*

b. Pattern reference: all tracks are connected

Figure 3.2.15: Recursive pattern definition

Recursion raises the question of termination. As the only context is provided by the previous application, a pattern could be applied to the same instances infinitely often. For reachable, the evaluation would not terminate for tracks that are not connected if the graph contains at least one cycle. On the other hand, we can assume that any instance graph consists of only a finite number of elements. There is therefore only a finite number of distinct initial bindings that can be passed to a pattern's $\lambda$ node. By adopting the restriction that, in any recursion, each initial binding is evaluated at most once, we can thus guarantee termination.

In practice, invocation parameters can be used to limit the depth of the recursion, e.g. to tracks that are at most $100$ links apart. In theory, parameters complicate proving termination as there may then be infinitely many distinct initial bindings. We then need to prove additional additional termination conditions, e.g. that a parameter is strictly decreasing towards $0$.

**Scoped nodes** are a syntactical feature based on pattern references. A *scoped node*, drawn as a guard node with a bold border, contains a nested SDD, which inherits all the bindings of the host SDD, but itself only creates bindings that have local scope. Internally, the nested SDD is interpreted as a pattern definition, whereas the scoped node is replaced with a guard node containing a reference to this pattern assigning each bound variable of the host SDD to the role of the same name. The mechanism provides a lightweight notation for emulating parentheses. Especially when there are several unrelated $\forall$ quantifiers, scoped nodes can group related nodes, which makes computation more efficient.

#### 3.2.2.4 Transformations

Although the focus of SDDs is on enabling more complex (pre-)conditions (LHS), we do not intend to remove the ability to express postconditions (RHS), i.e. transformations, from the notation. However, as universal and existential nodes employ *simple Story Patterns*, which do not contain any modifiers and therefore by definition never have side effects, such nodes alone can only encode *Invariant Story Patterns*. As we do not want to change the way the LHS is written by abandoning the principle of using simple graph patterns as elementary properties and encoding their relationships in the node structure, we introduce a dedicated node type for encoding the effects of a rule application. We do not adhere to the principle to the point of using dedicated nodes for creating and destroying elements, however, but employ the established modifiers in order to arrive at a more compact and usable solution.

**Transformation nodes.** The RHS of an SDD is specified by dedicated *transformation nodes*. They are marked with $\rightarrow \sim var_i^+$; $* var_i^+$, listing which elements are destroyed ($\sim$) or created ($*$) by the node. All elements of the LHS need to be previously bound; the node only transforms an existing match. Modifiers are specified using the same annotations and colors as in eSPs, i.e., $*$, $++$, or ≪create≫ in green and $\sim$, $--$, or ≪destroy≫ in red.

Transformation nodes replace (1) leaf nodes. When the SDD is fulfilled, the transformations are applied to a *one* set of bindings that fulfills the SDD. For existentially quantified properties, the transformation is simply applied to the first binding to reach the node. Universally quantified transformations are only applied when a binding for each required alternative has reached a transformation (or (1)) node. Note the significant difference between iteration (over existentially quantified properties), e.g., 'iterate over all tasks: if the task is completed, delete the task', and universal quantification, e.g., 'if *all* tasks are completed, delete *all* tasks'.

In the example in Figure 3.2.16, a shuttle instantiates a registration pattern with the supervisor of an adjacent track segment onto which it might move next. Unlike the similar eSP in Figure 3.2.8, however, the SDD verifies whether such a registration pattern exists (implicit then (1)) or not (else transform).

**Ensured conditions.** Conditional transformations are a common idiom, as a pattern without such a guard would generate arbitrarily many new instances in subsequent applications. We therefore introduce a dedicated notation for specifying such a conditional transformation: An *ensure node* guarantees that a given postcondition, such as the existence of a registration pattern, holds. The node will *ensure* that all specified elements are present and only create those that are missing. In a similar manner, the node can be used to ensure the absence of elements, deleting them if they are present but otherwise ignoring them. If there are multiple qualified elements, the check is performed independently for each element.

Ensure nodes are identified by dashed border and a header of the form $\exists var_i^+ \rightarrow \exists crv_i^+, \nexists dlv_i^+$. Internally, the node is expanded in a way that maintains the separation of LHS and RHS. Figure 3.2.17 is thus a more compact equivalent to Figure 3.2.16.

## 3.2 Structural Properties

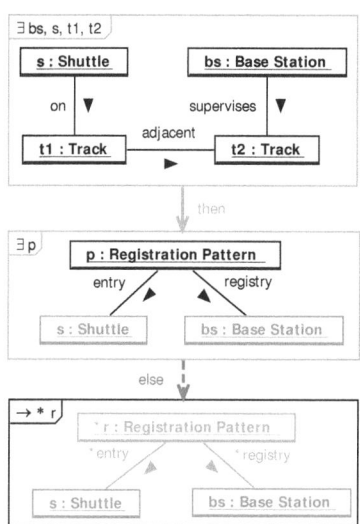

Figure 3.2.16: Creating a registration pattern

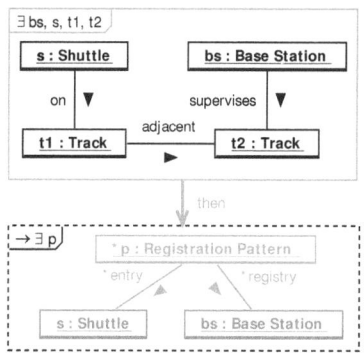

Figure 3.2.17: Ensured transformation: only create the pattern if it does not exist.

#### 3.2.2.5 Annotations

Beside the structural and type constraints expressed in the graph structure, it is possible to annotate the patterns in SDDs and eSPs with additional guards.

# 3. Constraints

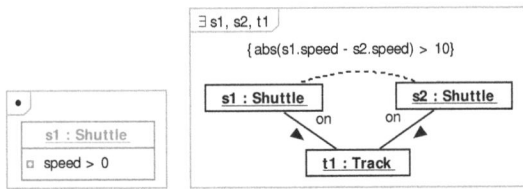

a. Attribute constraint: a moving shuttle

b. Guard expression: speed difference

Figure 3.2.18: Guard expressions involving one or multiple objects

Expressions may contain literals, references to attributes using the *object.attribute* notation, pattern parameters, and calls to queries as defined by the UML (i.e., functions without side effects). Constraints on the attributes of a single object can be specified within the object (see Figure 3.2.18a both for quantified and bound objects. In transformation nodes, new values can be assigned using :=. Constraints that concern multiple objects can be placed freely within the SP (see Figure 3.2.18b).

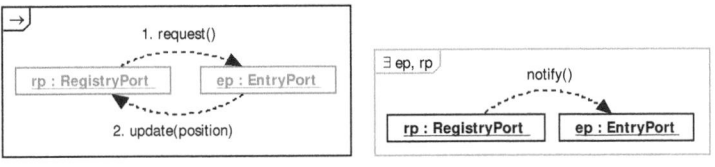

a. Collaboration: sending position updates

b. Signal guard: react to notifications

Figure 3.2.19: Collaboration statements

Collaboration statements appear in transformation nodes and encode a sequence of function calls, just like in UML 1.x Collaboration Diagrams. Collaboration statements are placed on arrows indicating which object is calling the function (see Figure 3.2.19a). When collaboration statements appear in LHS nodes (see Figure 3.2.19b), the pattern will match when the corresponding signal occurs, which is useful for describing temporal behavior.

In accordance with our formalization of Story Patterns, SDDs and eSPs are matched based on graph isomorphisms. While isomorphisms are generally closer to the intuitive interpretation of a pattern (see Section 2.2.2.2), there are cases where it is desirable to allow homomorphism, i.e. different variables that refer to the same instance. Though a set of alternatives can always emulate this using isomorphisms, this may be less intuitive and significantly more verbose. The SDD in Figure 3.2.20, checks whether some *destination* is reachable from a shuttle's current *location*. This is the case when the *destination* is either reachable or simply identical to the *location*. The fact that two instances may be identical is indicated by the special *homomorphism constraint* $\cong$;

## 3.2 Structural Properties

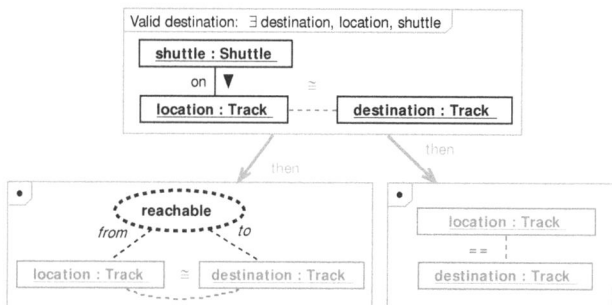

Figure 3.2.20: Explicitly permitted homomorphism

actual identity can then be verified using a guard expression or simply the *identity constraint* $==$ as a shorthand.

### 3.2.2.6 Encoding enhanced Story Patterns

As indicated above, we map eSPs to equivalent SDDs for defining the formal semantics of arbitrarily complex inset structures:

- Basic patterns can be encoded by simply placing the pattern into an existential node. Additional conditions expressed by insets are then chained to the node's then connector.

- *Negation* can be expressed by placing the contents of the negation inset into an existential node with inverted outgoing connectors.

- *Implication* can, as the chosen icon suggests, be expressed using universal nodes. The implication inset becomes a universal node, while the rest of the pattern is placed in a chained existential node (compare Figures 3.2.3 and 3.2.12).

- *Disjunction* is translated by placing each element of the disjunction inset into its own existential node, all chained to the base pattern using alternative then connectors. Conjunction insets are directly turned into existential nodes and chained in the same way.

- *Nested insets* are simply unfolded using the above rules, resulting in a sequence of nodes that are chained using then connectors, except where inversion due to negation insets turns them in to else connectors.

- *Transformations* in patterns with side effects are placed inside a transformation node that replaces all (1) nodes.

- *Pattern references* are simply interpreted as SDD References. Into the λ node of the derived SDD Pattern, we place exactly those roles that are actually used by invocations.

Due to the repeated elements, the resulting SDDs are much less compact, but also easier to evaluate because the sequence of the performed checks is evident from the diagram structure.

### 3.2.3 Formal Semantics

Language definitions that focus on expressiveness and intuitive semantics often run into problems when it comes to defining the formal semantics, which the OCL itself illustrates. On the other hand, languages that are constructed starting from a set of formally motivated operators with precise semantics often suffer in terms of expressiveness and especially practical applicability. We therefore now show that the informal control-flow-oriented semantics we have used to introduce the specification techniques can be mapped to a formal graph-based semantics that allows us to analyze and reason about the matching process. We will then be able to use SDDs for the specification of positive invariants of the system that must hold in every reachable state of the system, i.e., match every graph that is generated by the corresponding GTS. SDDs with side effects can also be used to specify more complex graph transformation rules.

#### 3.2.3.1 Variable Bindings

**Story Pattern Semantics.** For the patterns in each individual node, we can build on our formalization of the semantics of Story Patterns. As the SPs do not contain forbidden elements, each SP can be encoded as a simple graph pattern $[P]$, which can then be matched using standard matching semantics. Likewise, the SPs of transformation nodes can be translated into graph rules $[L] \to_r [R]$, which can also be applied normally – with the exception that the occurrence of the LHS $o(L)$ is already determined by the preceding SDD nodes.

This is where a new aspect comes in: The SPs of an SDD are not independent of each other, but may contain bound objects that have already been matched by preceding nodes. When matching the pattern, we therefore have to respect these previous matchings. The straight-forward way to achieve this would be to take the graph morphism $m$ mapping a pattern $P$ into an instance graph $G$, pass it down to the subsequent pattern $P'$, and merely extend it for the additional elements of $P'$. However, this would introduce the requirement that all SPs in an SDD are compatible, i.e., that the elements of $P$ and $P'$ are actually identical – otherwise, the morphisms for $P$ could not be applied to $P'$. We therefore adopt a similar, but slightly more general solution.

**Bindings.** In order to relate the matches from different patterns in the same diagram to each other, we introduce an additional labeling $l_P^v := (V_S^N, V_S^E, v_P^N, v_P^E)$ for every graph $P$ representing an SP of the SDD $S$. We label each node and edge with the corresponding variable from the set of node variables $V_S^N$ and the set of edge variables $V_S^E$ of $S$. $V_S^N$ consists of all declared object identifiers and $V_S^E$ consists of all declared link identifiers and, as most links are anonymous, generated unique link identifiers. As we are working with attributed graphs, attributes are

## 3.2 Structural Properties

represented by attribute edges – so that $V_S^A \subseteq V_S^E$ – and attribute values are represented by value nodes in $V_S^N$. Finally, SDDP parameters are also represented by node variables $V_S^P \subseteq V_S^N$ that point to value nodes.

Based on this labeling, we can now share matched elements, attributes and parameters between patterns in the same SDD. A variable *binding* $\xi$ for the node and edge variables of $S$ and an attributed instance graph $G$ is then a pair of functions $\xi = (\xi^N, \xi^E)$ with $\xi^N : V^N \to N_G \cup \bot$, $\xi^E : V^E \to E_G \cup \bot$, where $N_G$ is the set of nodes of $G$, $E_G$ is the set of edges of $G$, and $\bot$ is the undefined element. The binding functions are typically partial, as some variables may not be bound yet or, in case of alternative paths through the SDD, may never be bound at the same time. We write $\xi_1 \leq \xi_2 := \forall v \in \mathsf{dom}(\xi_1) : (\xi_1(v) = \xi_2(v)) \lor (\xi_1(v) = \bot)$ if $\xi_2$ is equal to or a more restrictive extension of $\xi_1$. We denote the empty binding that maps all variables to $\bot$ by $\tau$.

**Pattern matching.** We use $var(P)$ to denote the pair of sets of node and edge variables that occur in $P$, i.e. are in the range of the labeling functions $v_P^N$ and $v_P^E$. In order to match the pattern $P$ in the instance graph $G$, we define $P[\xi]$ as the graph which results from substituting all nodes and edges of $P$ with the elements assigned to the corresponding variables by $\xi$, i.e., we replace each $n \in N_P$ with $n_{P[\xi]} := \xi^N(v_P^N(n))$ and each $e \in E_P$ with $e_{P[\xi]} := \xi^E(v_P^E(e))$, provided that $\xi$ is defined for all variables $v \in var(P)$. Together, the variable labeling $l_P^v$ of $P$ and the binding $\xi$ define a graph morphism between $P$ and $P[\xi]$. We call a binding $\xi$ *valid* if $P[\xi]$ is a correct subgraph of $G$, i.e., $P[\xi] \leq G$.

Given a pattern $P$ and a binding $\xi$, we define the set of free variables of $P$ as $free(P, \xi) := \{v \mid v \in var(P) \land \xi(v) = \bot\}$. We then say that the pattern $P$ constrained by the existing binding $\xi$ matches a graph $G$, written as $P|_\xi \precsim G$, if there is a binding $\xi'$ that extends $\xi$ for the variables in $free(P, \xi)$ so that $P[\xi'] \leq G$.

We use $\mathcal{X}_S[G]$ respectively $\mathcal{X}_S[N_G, E_G, V_S^N, V_S^E]$ (for $N_G$ the set of all nodes of $G$, $E_G$ the set of all edges of $G$, and variables $V_S^N$ and $V_S^E$ of $S$) to denote the set of all possible bindings of an SDD $S$ over a graph $G$.

### 3.2.3.2 Witness Sets

**Diagram structure.** For an SDD $S$, we define $\mathcal{N}_S$ as the set of its nodes. For each node $n \in \mathcal{N}_S$, we define $P_n$ as the pattern contained by $n$, $parent(n)$ as the set of parent nodes connected to $n$ by outgoing connectors, with its transitive closure $parent^*(n)$, and $then(n)$ and $else(n)$ as the set of nodes connected to $n$ by then respectively else connectors. Cardinalities are represented by two functions $min : \mathcal{N}_S \times \mathcal{N}_S \to \mathbb{N}$ and $max : \mathcal{N}_S \times \mathcal{N}_S \to \mathbb{N}$, where $min(n, n')$ respectively $max(n, n')$ is the minimum respectively maximum cardinality for the connector from $n$ to $n'$. $\lambda_S$ denotes the unique root node of the SDD $S$ with $parent(\lambda_S) = \emptyset$. The set $\mathsf{true}_S$ contains all (1) and transformation nodes of $S$, $\mathsf{false}_S$ contains all (0) nodes of $S$.

We further define $var(n) := var(P_n)$ as the variables appearing inside $n$ and $free(n, \xi) := free(P_n, \xi)$ as the free variables of $n$ that are not bound, i.e. mapped to $\bot$, by $\xi$.

**Witnesses.** Only a subset of the possible bindings $\mathcal{X}_S$ *satisfies* the SDD $S$, i.e. is valid for a set of patterns $P_n$ on a path to a (1) node. We can immediately discard all those bindings that are not valid for any pattern $P_n$, e.g. because they do not bind all required variables. However, even those bindings that are valid for one pattern $P_n$ might not be valid for some other pattern $P_{n'}$ on the same path. When evaluating an SDD, we therefore need to consider a binding's context, i.e., nodes and their connections.

We define an application $\zeta$ as a pair $(n, \xi)$ of a node $n$ and a binding $\xi$. We call a valid application a *witness*. An application is valid if a path from $\lambda_S$ to $n$ exists so that $\xi$ is valid for all nodes on the path (excluding $n$) but binds no additional variables:

$$\omega(n, \xi) := \exists (n_1, \ldots, n_k) \in \mathcal{N}_S^* :$$
$$(n_1 = \lambda_S \wedge n_k = n \wedge \bigwedge_{i=1..k-1} (n_i \in \mathsf{parent}(n_{i+1}) \wedge P_{n_i}[\xi] \leq G) \wedge$$
$$\forall v : \xi(v) \neq \bot \Rightarrow v \in \bigcup_{i=1..k-1} var(n_i)). \tag{3.2.1}$$

The set of possible witnesses for an SDD $S$ is then

$$\mathcal{Z}_S := \{(n, \xi) \mid n \in \mathcal{N}_S \wedge \xi \in \mathcal{X}_S \wedge \omega(n, \xi)\}. \tag{3.2.2}$$

We further define the truth value $eval(\zeta)$ of a witness $\zeta = (n, \xi)$ as $true$ if $n$ is a (1) or transformation node, $false$ if $n$ is a (0) node, and else $\bot$:

$$eval(\zeta) := \begin{cases} true & \mid n \in \mathsf{true}_S \\ false & \mid n \in \mathsf{false}_S \\ \bot & \mid otherwise. \end{cases} \tag{3.2.3}$$

As the truth value of a witness may thus be undefined, we use the convention that boolean operators ($\wedge$, $\vee$ and $\neg$) applied to $\bot$ also yield $\bot$ in the following. A witness whose truth value is defined is *final*, all other witnesses are *intermediate* and represent unfinished evaluations.

**Candidate sets.** When informally introducing the semantics of SDDs above, we used an operational interpretation where we iteratively propagated individual bindings across the SDD. In order to define the formal semantics using set-based logic, we need to consider sets of bindings.

For a witness $\zeta$ of a universal node $n$, *each* extension of the contained binding that the node generates ultimately needs to satisfy the SDD $S$, or $\zeta$ will not satisfy the SDD. We group the new witnesses that $n$ generates out of $\zeta$ into a *candidate set* of witnesses that need to succeed together. We define such a candidate set as $\mathcal{C} \in \wp(\mathcal{Z}_S)$. $\mathcal{C}$ only satisfies $S$ if all witnesses $\zeta \in \mathcal{C}$ satisfy $S$. The truth value of $\mathcal{C}$ is thus defined as

$$eval(\mathcal{C}) := \bigwedge_{\zeta \in \mathcal{C}} eval(\zeta). \tag{3.2.4}$$

As for witnesses, a candidate set is *final* if its truth value is defined, i.e., it only contains *final* witnesses.

## 3.2 Structural Properties

**Alternative sets.** An existential node or the presence of multiple then or else connectors can create multiple alternative ways to extend the binding $\xi$ of a witness $\zeta$, only one of which needs to satisfy $S$. The new witnesses that the node generates out of $\zeta$ thus form an *alternative set* of witnesses.

**Result sets.** If, starting with a single initial binding for the root node, we naively applied these definitions, we would end up with a nested structure of candidate and alternative sets. If the witness we process is part of some candidate set, we would generate a new candidate set that contains an alternative or candidate set in place of the witness – likewise for witnesses in alternative sets. Such a structure would greatly complicate the formalization. We therefore prefer a flattened structure with only two levels, a set of alternative candidate sets $\mathcal{A} \in \wp(\wp(\mathcal{Z}_S))$. We call such a set of candidate sets a *result set*.

We start the evaluation with a single candidate set containing the initial binding. For the root node $\lambda_S$ of an SDD, we define $\mathcal{A}_\lambda := \{\{(\lambda_S, \tau)\}\}$, i.e. there is one candidate set consisting of the only witness, the empty binding $\tau$ at $\lambda_S$.

Now, whenever a node generates alternatives $\zeta^i$ from a witness $\zeta$, for each $\mathcal{C}$ containing $\zeta$ we add a new candidate set $\mathcal{C}^i$ where $\zeta$ is replaced by $\zeta^i$ to the result set $\mathcal{A}$. As $\mathcal{C}$ is a set of witnesses, each of which may have alternative extensions, the number of new candidate sets $\mathcal{C}^{ijk\cdots}$ generated from $\mathcal{C}$ by a node depends on the Cartesian product of the extensions for each witness in $\mathcal{C}$. Existential nodes thus increase the *number* of candidate sets and thus the size of the result set.

When a universal node generates new interdependent witnesses from a witness $\zeta$, we simply create a new candidate set $\mathcal{C}'$ where $\zeta$ is replaced by the generated witnesses $\zeta^1 \ldots \zeta^k$ in each $\mathcal{C}$ containing $\zeta$. Universal nodes thus increase the *size* of the candidate sets.

As the sets are alternatives, i.e., one valid candidate set is sufficient, the truth value of a result set $\mathcal{A}$ is defined as

$$eval(\mathcal{A}) := \bigvee_{\mathcal{C} \in \mathcal{A}} eval(\mathcal{C}). \qquad (3.2.5)$$

The set of all witnesses occurring in a result set $\mathcal{A}$ is denoted by $\mathcal{W}_\mathcal{A} := \bigcup_{\mathcal{C}_i \in \mathcal{A}} \mathcal{C}_i$. A result set is *final* if all witnesses in $\mathcal{W}_\mathcal{A}$ are *final*.

**Propagation.** We now formalize the computations on result sets that we have described above. For each node $n$, we define the *propagation function*

$$apply_n : \mathcal{G} \times \wp(\wp(\mathcal{Z}_S)) \to \wp(\wp(\mathcal{Z}_S)), \qquad (3.2.6)$$

which basically removes obsolete candidates and adds appropriately extended versions. When computing the updated result set $\mathcal{A}' = apply_n(G, \mathcal{A})$, we initialize $\mathcal{A}' = \mathcal{A}$. For each witness $\zeta = (n_\zeta, \xi_\zeta)$ for $n$ from $\mathcal{W}_{\mathcal{A}'}$ (i.e. $\zeta \in \mathcal{W}_{\mathcal{A}'} \wedge n_\zeta = n$), the following steps are then performed by $apply_n$:

1. The possible extensions of the binding $\xi_\zeta$ are computed. We define

$$\mathcal{X}_\zeta^{(t)} := \{\xi'_\zeta \mid P_n[\xi'_\zeta] \leq G \wedge$$
$$\xi_\zeta \leq \xi'_\zeta \wedge \forall v : \xi'_\zeta(v) \neq \xi_\zeta(v) \Rightarrow v \in free(n, \xi_\zeta)\}, \qquad (3.2.7)$$

i.e., we select those $\xi'_\zeta$ that are valid for $P_n$ and extend $\xi_\zeta$ with the variables introduced by $P_n$. If no such $\xi'_\zeta$ exists, i.e. $\mathcal{X}^{(t)}_\zeta := \emptyset$, we have $\mathcal{X}^{(e)}_\zeta := \{\xi_\zeta\}$, otherwise $\mathcal{X}^{(e)}_\zeta := \emptyset$, i.e.

$$\mathcal{X}^{(e)}_\zeta := \begin{cases} \emptyset & |\ \mathcal{X}^{(t)}_\zeta \neq \emptyset \\ \{\xi_\zeta\} & |\ \mathcal{X}^{(t)}_\zeta = \emptyset. \end{cases} \quad (3.2.8)$$

Note that exactly one of the sets is thus always empty. The definition covers both quantified and guard nodes. As guard nodes do not introduce any new variables, we have the special case that $\xi'_\zeta = \xi_\zeta$ so that $\xi_\zeta$ is either placed in $\mathcal{X}^{(t)}_\zeta$ or $\mathcal{X}^{(e)}_\zeta$ depending on whether $P_n[\xi'_\zeta] \leq G$ holds.

2. The corresponding witnesses are computed, i.e., the generated bindings are propagated along all applicable connectors – which are *either* the then or the else connectors.

   If cardinalities are specified, we first need to verify whether the number of generated extended bindings satisfies the constraints of at least one then connector, i.e. $\exists n' \in \text{then}(n) : min(n, n') \leq \#\mathcal{X}^{(t)}_\zeta \leq max(n, n')$. Otherwise, we need to discard the generated bindings and send the original binding down the else connector by setting $\mathcal{X}^{(t)}_\zeta := \emptyset$ and, accordingly, $\mathcal{X}^{(e)}_\zeta := \{\xi_\zeta\}$.

   We then define the set of generated witnesses as

$$\begin{aligned}\mathcal{W}^+_\zeta := & \{(n', \xi') \mid n' \in \text{then}(n) \land \xi' \in \mathcal{X}^{(t)}_\zeta \\ & \land min(n, n') \leq \#\mathcal{X}^{(t)}_\zeta \leq max(n, n')\} \cup \\ & \{(n', \xi') \mid n' \in \text{else}(n) \land \xi' \in \mathcal{X}^{(e)}_\zeta\}. \end{aligned} \quad (3.2.9)$$

3. The result set $\mathcal{A}'$ is updated. This implicitly removes $\zeta$ from $\mathcal{W}_{\mathcal{A}'}$ and adds the new bindings: $\mathcal{W}_{\mathcal{A}'} := \mathcal{W}_{\mathcal{A}'} \setminus \zeta \cup \mathcal{W}^+_\zeta$.

   (a) If $n$ is universal, we define

$$\begin{aligned}\mathcal{A}'_\forall := \{\mathcal{C}' \mid \exists \mathcal{C} \in \mathcal{A}' : & (\zeta \in \mathcal{C} \land \mathcal{C}' = \mathcal{C} \setminus \zeta \cup \mathcal{W}^+_\zeta) \lor \\ & (\zeta \notin \mathcal{C} \land \mathcal{C}' = \mathcal{C})\}, \end{aligned} \quad (3.2.10)$$

   i.e., we extend each candidate set with the new witnesses.

   (b) If $n$ is existential, we define

$$\begin{aligned}\mathcal{A}'_\exists := \{\mathcal{C}' \mid \exists \mathcal{C} \in \mathcal{A}' : & (\exists \zeta' \in \mathcal{W}^+_\zeta : (\zeta \in \mathcal{C} \land \mathcal{C}' = \mathcal{C} \setminus \zeta \cup \zeta')) \lor \\ & (\zeta \notin \mathcal{C} \land \mathcal{C}' = \mathcal{C})\}, \end{aligned} \quad (3.2.11)$$

   i.e., we add a new alternative candidate set for each new witness.

## 3.2 Structural Properties

### 3.2.3.3 Story Decision Diagram Semantics

In order to evaluate an SDD $S$, we start with a result set $\mathcal{A}$ containing a single candidate (consisting of the initial binding) and successively apply the propagation function of each node of the SDD (using a breadth-first or preorder depth-first traversal) to it, extending and modifying the result set until it is *final*. The evaluation results in a unique final result set that serves to define the semantics of $S$. Note that all nodes actually need to operate on the same instance of $\mathcal{A}$ as candidate sets may contain witnesses for any node in the SDD so that simple recursion down any particular branch could only return results for individual witnesses, but typically not candidate sets.

**Iteration function.** In order to achieve the required evaluation order, i.e. that every node uses the output of the previous node as its input, we define the iteration function

$$iterate(\mathcal{N}, \mathcal{A}) := \begin{cases} [\![n]\!]^G_{iterate(\mathcal{N} \setminus n, \mathcal{A})} \mid n \in \mathcal{N} & | \mathcal{N} \neq \emptyset \\ \mathcal{A} & | \mathcal{N} = \emptyset, \end{cases} \quad (3.2.12)$$

where $[\![n]\!]^G_{\mathcal{A}}$ is the semantics of node $n$ for graph $G$ and set of alternative candidate sets $\mathcal{A}$ as defined below. The iteration function passes the result set $\mathcal{A}$ through every node in the set of sibling nodes $\mathcal{N}$ in turn.[1]

**Semantics definition.** We can now define the semantics of an SDD $S$. For leaf nodes, we have

$$[\![(1)]\!]^G_{\mathcal{A}} := \mathcal{A}, \quad (3.2.13)$$

$$[\![(0)]\!]^G_{\mathcal{A}} := \mathcal{A}, \quad (3.2.14)$$

i.e. they simply return the original result set.

For non-leaf nodes, we define

$$[\![n]\!]^G_{\mathcal{A}} := iterate(\mathsf{then}(n) \cup \mathsf{else}(n), apply_n(G, \mathcal{A})), \quad (3.2.15)$$

i.e. we first apply $n$'s propagation function and then pass the result through all of $n$'s children. Finally, we define for the whole SDD:

$$[\![S]\!]^G := \{\mathcal{C} \mid \mathcal{C} \in [\![\lambda_S]\!]^G_{\{\{(\lambda_S, \tau)\}\}} \wedge eval(\mathcal{C})\}, \quad (3.2.16)$$

i.e. the semantics of the SDD $S$ are defined as the satisfying final candidate sets generated by its root node $\lambda_S$, evaluated for the single candidate set consisting of the empty binding $\tau$ at $\lambda_S$. Note that all candidate sets in $[\![\lambda_S]\!]^G_{\{\{(\lambda_S, \tau)\}\}}$ are *final* so that $eval(\mathcal{C})$ is always defined.

The truth value of an SDD $S$ is then

$$eval(S) := ([\![S]\!]^G \neq \emptyset). \quad (3.2.17)$$

---
[1] Note that *iterate* is in fact a function in spite of the fact that $n$ is chosen non-deterministically. As the nodes in $\mathcal{N}$ are siblings, no node in $\mathcal{N}$ will generate new witnesses for any other node in $\mathcal{N}$. For a fixed set of witnesses, we have $apply_n(G, apply_{n'}(G, \mathcal{A})) = apply_{n'}(G, apply_n(G, \mathcal{A}))$ as the invocations operate on disjunct subsets of the witness set and their effects on the result set are orthogonal.

**Negation.** We define the negation of an invariant SDD $S$, written as $\overline{S}$, as the SDD that is satisfied by all graphs $G$ that do not satisfy $S$. $\overline{S}$ can be derived by inverting all leaf nodes and quantifiers of $S$, i.e. turning all (explicitly specified and implied) (1) leaf nodes of $S$ into (0) leaf nodes and vice versa, and turning all existential quantifiers ($\exists$) in $S$ into universal quantifiers ($\forall$) and vice versa.

**Examples.** We now discuss three examples that illustrate the introduced semantics, especially the relationship between candidate sets and witnesses.

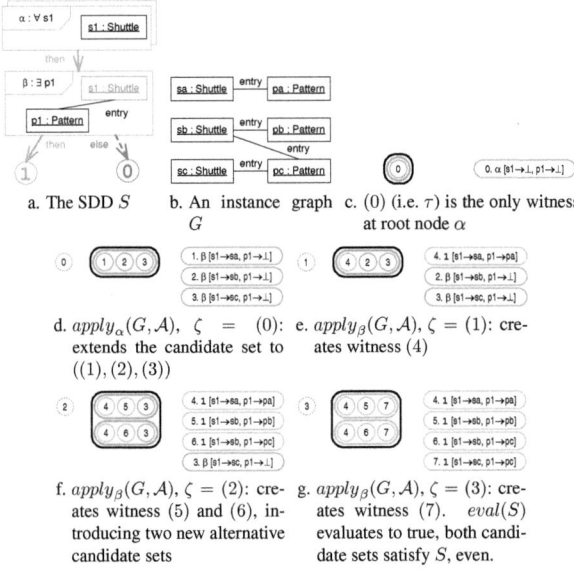

a. The SDD $S$
b. An instance graph $G$
c. (0) (i.e. $\tau$) is the only witness at root node $\alpha$
d. $apply_\alpha(G, \mathcal{A})$, $\zeta = (0)$: extends the candidate set to $((1), (2), (3))$
e. $apply_\beta(G, \mathcal{A})$, $\zeta = (1)$: creates witness (4)
f. $apply_\beta(G, \mathcal{A})$, $\zeta = (2)$: creates witness (5) and (6), introducing two new alternative candidate sets
g. $apply_\beta(G, \mathcal{A})$, $\zeta = (3)$: creates witness (7). $eval(S)$ evaluates to true, both candidate sets satisfy $S$, even.

Figure 3.2.21: Example 1: Successful evaluation of a simple property

In Figure 3.2.21, we present a basic example. The SDD $S$ in Figure 3.2.21a is evaluated on graph $G$ in Figure 3.2.21b. Figures 3.2.21c–g then list the witness $\zeta$ that is currently processed by $apply$, the result set $\mathcal{A}$, and the set of witnesses $\mathcal{W}_\mathcal{A}$ for each iteration of the propagation functions. The result set $\mathcal{A}$ is marked by the outer (black) border, the candidate sets $\mathcal{C}$ in $\mathcal{A}$ are symbolized by the inner (blue) border, and the witnesses are represented by numbers in (orange) circles referencing the corresponding elements of $\mathcal{W}_\mathcal{A}$. Final witnesses and candidate sets are drawn in green or red, according to their truth value.

While the property holds for graph $G$, graph $G'$ in Figure 3.2.22a is not a correct match (as $sc$ is missing a pattern). Evaluation proceeds in an identical fashion to Figure 3.2.21, except for witness (3) in Figure 3.2.22b. As no pattern is found, the witness proceeds to the (0) node.

## 3.2 Structural Properties

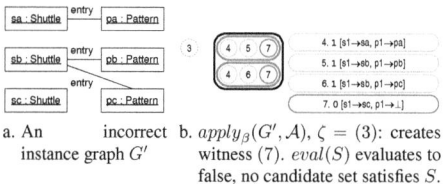

a. An incorrect instance graph $G'$

b. $apply_\beta(G', \mathcal{A})$, $\zeta = (3)$: creates witness (7). $eval(S)$ evaluates to false, no candidate set satisfies $S$.

Figure 3.2.22: Example 1': For the incorrect graph $G'$, the last step differs

The second example in Figure 3.2.23 is more complex. Each A must have a B with a C, or a D. There are multiple (1) nodes, and as $a1$ and $a2$ have a valid B but no D, whereas $a3$ only has a valid D, the successful candidate set unites witnesses that are at different leaf nodes.

The third example is introduced in Figure 3.2.24 and evaluated in Figures 3.2.25 and 3.2.26. The example contains two nested universal quantifiers and serves to illustrate how evaluation is nonetheless based on a flattened data structure. In this example, we not only list the current result set and the currently selected witness, but also which obsolete candidate sets are eliminated in each step.

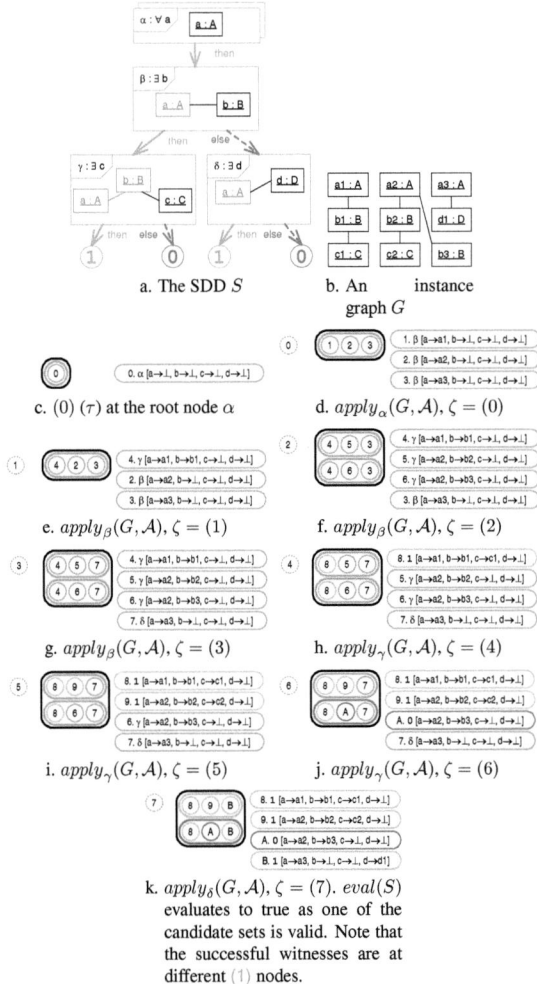

Figure 3.2.23: Example 2: Successful evaluation of a more complex property

## 3.2 Structural Properties

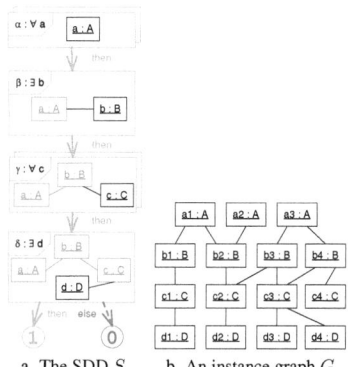

a. The SDD $S$     b. An instance graph $G$

Figure 3.2.24: Example 3: Nested universally quantified nodes

| | | |
|---|---|---|
| 0. α [a→⊥, b→⊥, c→⊥, d→⊥] | | G. 1 [a→a1, b→b1, c→c1, d→d1] |
| 1. β [a→a1, b→⊥, c→⊥, d→⊥] | | H. 1 [a→a1, b→b2, c→c2, d→d2] |
| 2. β [a→a2, b→⊥, c→⊥, d→⊥] | 9. δ [a→a1, b→b1, c→c1, d→⊥] | I. 1 [a→a2, b→b2, c→c2, d→d2] |
| 3. β [a→a3, b→⊥, c→⊥, d→⊥] | A. δ [a→a1, b→b2, c→c2, d→⊥] | J. 1 [a→a3, b→b3, c→c2, d→d2] |
| 4. γ [a→a1, b→b1, c→⊥, d→⊥] | B. δ [a→a2, b→b2, c→c2, d→⊥] | K. 1 [a→a3, b→b3, c→c3, d→d3] |
| 5. γ [a→a1, b→b2, c→⊥, d→⊥] | C. δ [a→a3, b→b3, c→c2, d→⊥] | L. 1 [a→a3, b→b3, c→c3, d→d4] |
| 6. γ [a→a2, b→b2, c→⊥, d→⊥] | D. δ [a→a3, b→b3, c→c3, d→⊥] | M. 1 [a→a3, b→b4, c→c3, d→d3] |
| 7. γ [a→a3, b→b3, c→⊥, d→⊥] | E. δ [a→a3, b→b4, c→c3, d→⊥] | N. 1 [a→a3, b→b4, c→c3, d→d4] |
| 8. γ [a→a3, b→b4, c→⊥, d→⊥] | F. δ [a→a3, b→b4, c→c4, d→⊥] | O. 0 [a→a3, b→b4, c→c4, d→⊥] |

a. Witnesses (0)-(8)    b. Witnesses (9)-(F)    c. Final witness set $\mathcal{W}_\mathcal{A}$

Figure 3.2.25: Example 3: Intermediate and final witnesses

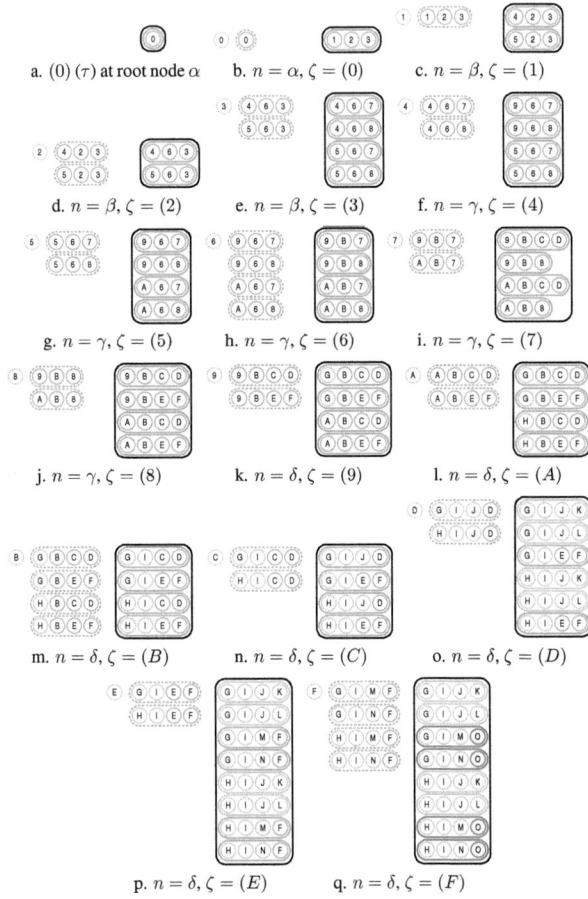

Figure 3.2.26: Example 3: Result sets. Evaluation succeeds

## 3.2 Structural Properties

#### 3.2.3.4 Story Decision Diagram Pattern Semantics

In order to define the semantics of patterns and pattern references, we need to extend the semantics of SDDs in three places: We need to define the way how a pattern's $\lambda$ node binds roles to instances, we need to deal with pattern references in the host nodes containing them, and we need to formalize the semantics of recursive patterns.

$\lambda$ **nodes.** Differently from SDDs, SDDPs typically do not use $\tau$ as their initial binding, but define roles in their $\lambda$ node which are bound externally. The roles are defined as the elements of the pattern $R_\lambda$. For each host node $n$ containing a reference to an SDDP $F$, we define a partial graph isomorphism $m_F$ from $P_n$ to $R_\lambda$, mapping elements of the host SP to roles of $F$ in accordance with the dashed role connectors in the diagram.

The mapping function $\ell_{F_n} : \mathcal{X}_S \to \mathcal{X}_F$ then performs the actual rebinding, binding $F$'s variables in accordance with the binding in the host node. For a binding $\xi_P$ and variable labelings $l_P^v := (V_S^N, V_S^E, v_P^N, v_P^E)$ for $P_n$ and $l_R^v := (V_F^N, V_F^E, v_R^N, v_R^E)$ for $R_\lambda$, we define

$$\ell_{F_n}(\xi_P) := (\xi_F^N, \xi_F^E) \mid \xi_F^N \circ v_R^N \circ m_F^N = \xi_P^N \circ v_P^N \wedge \xi_F^E \circ v_R^E \circ m_F^E = \xi_P^E \circ v_P^E, \quad (3.2.18)$$

i.e. each element of $R_\lambda$ is bound to the same instance as the element of $P$ that is matched onto it by $m_F$.

**Candidate set evolution.** For candidate sets, we define the *evolved from* relation $\mathcal{C} \sqsubseteq \mathcal{C}'$ which indicates that $\mathcal{C}'$ has evolved out of $\mathcal{C}$. We have

$$\mathcal{C} \sqsubseteq \mathcal{C}' := \forall (n, \xi) \in \mathcal{C} : (\exists (n', \xi') \in \mathcal{C}' : \xi \leq \xi' \wedge n \in \mathsf{parent}^*(n')), \quad (3.2.19)$$

i.e. for each witness in $\mathcal{C}'$, there needs to be a witness in $\mathcal{C}$ that is less or equally restrictive at a possible parent node.

We extend this notation to result sets so that for a candidate set $\mathcal{C}$ and a result set $\mathcal{A}'$, we have

$$\mathcal{C} \sqsubseteq \mathcal{A}' := \exists \mathcal{C}' \in \mathcal{A}' : \mathcal{C} \sqsubseteq \mathcal{C}'. \quad (3.2.20)$$

**Pattern references** do not generate new bindings but merely act as an extended form of guard, declaring a binding to be either valid or invalid. Accordingly, they are processed in step (1) of the evaluation of the propagation function.

Let $\mathcal{F}_n$ be the set of SDDPs invoked in the SP of node $n$. When computing $\mathcal{X}_\zeta^{(t)}$, we extend Equation 3.2.7 and additionally require that each $\xi'_\zeta \in \mathcal{X}_\zeta^{(t)}$ fulfills every SDDP $F \in \mathcal{F}_n$, i.e., there needs to be a candidate set in the result set generated by the SDDP that has evolved from the rebound binding $\{\ell_{F_n}(\xi'_\zeta)\}$. For brevity, we use $F(\zeta)$ to denote the witness $(\lambda_F, \ell_{F_n}(\xi))$ with $\zeta = (n, \xi)$. We then have:

$$\mathcal{X}_\zeta^{(t)} := \{\xi'_\zeta \mid P_n[\xi'_\zeta] \leq G \wedge \forall F \in \mathcal{F}_n : \{F((n, \xi'_\zeta))\} \sqsubseteq [\![F]\!]^G \wedge$$
$$\xi_\zeta \leq \xi'_\zeta \wedge \forall v : \xi'_\zeta(v) \neq \xi_\zeta(v) \Rightarrow v \in free(n, \xi_\zeta)\}. \quad (3.2.21)$$

**Non-recursive SDDP Semantics.** Non-recursive SDDPs, i.e. pattern definitions not containing direct or indirect references to themselves, can efficiently be computed like regular SDDs. As the semantics of the SDDP $F$ with $\lambda$ node $\lambda_F$ for a graph $G$ and an initial binding $\xi_P$, we can then define
$$[\![F]\!]^G_{\xi_P} := [\![\lambda_F]\!]^G_{\{\{(\lambda_F, \ell_F(\xi_P))\}\}} \tag{3.2.22}$$
and use the generated result set in place of $[\![F]\!]^G$ in Equation 3.2.21.

**Recursive SDDP Semantics.** We require recursive SDDPs to be *well-formed*. A set of SDDPs is well-formed if it does not contain vacuous cycles, i.e. it cannot recurse infinitely without progressing or reaching a termination node.

In order to define the semantics of a well-formed recursively defined SDDP $F$, we need to compute a fixed point of $F$. If $\mathcal{F}_I$ is a set of interdependent SDDPs $F_i$ that are recursively invoking each other, we need to compute their fixed points together.

The semantics $[\![F_i]\!]^G$ of an SDDP $F_i$ should correspond to a result set containing all valid final candidate sets that can evolve from any initial binding that could be passed to $F_i$ for a given graph $G$. In order to compute this result set, we extend $F_i$ with an auxiliary existential node $\alpha_{F_i}$ quantifying all roles of the SDDP $F_i$, which is added before the $\lambda$ node $\lambda_{F_i}$ and thus becomes the new root node. The existential node will generate all possible combinations of bindings for the roles and pass them on to the $\lambda$ node.

The unconstrained semantics of non-recursive SDDPs can then be computed directly as
$$[\![F_i]\!]^G := [\![\alpha_{F_i}]\!]^G_{\{\{(\alpha_{F_i}, \tau)\}\}}. \tag{3.2.23}$$

However, this will not work for recursive SDDPs, as $[\![F_i]\!]^G$ is required in order to evaluate the propagation function *apply* (see Equation 3.2.21).

We therefore introduce the fixed point operator $\mathcal{F}$, which successively computes the semantics using approximations $[\![f_i^{(j)}]\!]^G$ of $[\![F_i]\!]^G$. Instead of relying on the – undefined – semantics $[\![F_i]\!]^G$, $\mathcal{F}$ substitutes $[\![f_i^{(j)}]\!]^G$ for $[\![F_i]\!]^G$ when computing the extended bindings. Furthermore, as $[\![f_i^{(j)}]\!]^G$ is only an approximation of the final semantics, we cannot just check whether there is a candidate set in $[\![f_i^{(j)}]\!]^G$ that has evolved from a given role binding, but have to differentiate between *unsuccessful* and *undefined* invocations. We therefore do not use Equation 3.2.21, but the original Equation 3.2.7
$$\mathcal{X}'_\zeta := \{\xi'_\zeta \mid P_n[\xi'_\zeta] \leq G \wedge$$
$$\xi_\zeta \leq \xi'_\zeta \wedge \forall v : \xi'_\zeta(v) \neq \xi_\zeta(v) \Rightarrow v \in free(n, \xi_\zeta)\}, \tag{3.2.24}$$
and evaluate the constraints represented by SDDPs in a separate step. We compute the valid extended bindings for which all invocations are successful as
$$\mathcal{X}^{(t)}_\zeta := \{\xi^{(t)}_\zeta \mid \xi^{(t)}_\zeta \in \mathcal{X}'_\zeta \wedge \forall F \in \mathcal{F}_n :$$
$$(\exists \mathcal{C} \in [\![F]\!]^G : eval(\mathcal{C}) \wedge \{F((n, \xi^{(t)}_\zeta))\} \sqsubseteq \mathcal{C})\} \tag{3.2.25}$$

## 3.2 Structural Properties

and the indeterminate bindings that are not valid, but not definitely invalid because there is no invocation that is definitely unsuccessful as

$$\mathcal{X}_\zeta^{(\perp)} := \{\xi_\zeta^{(\perp)} \mid \xi_\zeta^{(\perp)} \in \mathcal{X}_\zeta' \setminus \mathcal{X}_\zeta^{(t)} \wedge \nexists F \in \mathcal{F}_n :$$
$$(\forall \mathcal{C} \in \llbracket F \rrbracket^G \mid \{F((n, \xi_\zeta'))\} \sqsubseteq \mathcal{C} : \neg eval(\mathcal{C}))\}. \quad (3.2.26)$$

Consequently, we only follow the else branch if there are no valid or indeterminate bindings and have

$$\mathcal{X}_\zeta^{(e)} := \begin{cases} \emptyset & \mid (\mathcal{X}_\zeta^{(t)} \cup \mathcal{X}_\zeta^{(\perp)}) \neq \emptyset \\ \{\xi_\zeta\} & \mid (\mathcal{X}_\zeta^{(t)} \cup \mathcal{X}_\zeta^{(\perp)}) = \emptyset. \end{cases} \quad (3.2.27)$$

If one of the SDDPs in $\mathcal{F}_n$ is recursively defined, we ignore the cardinalities and use a modified version of Equation 3.2.9, defining the set of generated witnesses as

$$\mathcal{W}_\zeta^+ := \{(n', \xi') \mid \xi' \in \mathcal{X}_\zeta^{(t)} \wedge n' \in \text{then}(n)\} \cup$$
$$\{(n', \xi') \mid \xi' \in \mathcal{X}_\zeta^{(e)} \wedge n' \in \text{else}(n)\} \cup$$
$$\{(\perp, \xi') \mid \xi' \in \mathcal{X}_\zeta^{(\perp)}\}. \quad (3.2.28)$$

By adding the permanently intermediate witnesses $(\perp, \xi')$, we prevent premature negative results — they basically indicate that $\xi'$ might or might not turn out to be a valid binding.

Starting with the initial result sets $\llbracket f_i^{(0)} \rrbracket^G$, we then apply $\mp$ for all SDDPs $F_i$, in turn, to compute

$$\llbracket f^{(j+1)} \rrbracket^G := \mp(\llbracket f_i^{(j)} \rrbracket^G), \quad (3.2.29)$$

where the actual fixed point operator is defined as

$$\mp(\llbracket f_i^{(j)} \rrbracket^G) := \llbracket \alpha_{F_i} \rrbracket^G_{\{\{(\alpha_{F_i}, \tau)\}\}} \mid \forall F_i \in \mathcal{F}_I : \llbracket F_i \rrbracket^G := \llbracket f_i^{(j)} \rrbracket^G. \quad (3.2.30)$$

$\mp$ is applied until $\mp(\llbracket f_i^{(j)} \rrbracket^G) = \llbracket f_i^{(j)} \rrbracket^G$ for all of the involved SDDPs $F_i$. We have then computed a fixed point $\llbracket f_i \rrbracket^G$ which allows us to define the semantics of the SDDPs $F_i$ as

$$\llbracket F_i \rrbracket^G := \{\mathcal{C} \mid \mathcal{C} \in \llbracket f_i \rrbracket^G \wedge eval(\mathcal{C})\}. \quad (3.2.31)$$

We define two versions of $\mp$, the least fixed point operator $\mp_\mu$ and the greatest fixed point operator $\mp_\nu$. The standard semantics of SDDs are defined by means of $\mp_\mu$, i.e. using least fixed points. The least fixed point operator $\mp_\mu$ starts with empty initial result sets:

$$\forall F_i \in \mathcal{F}_I : \llbracket f_i^{(0)} \rrbracket^G := \emptyset. \quad (3.2.32)$$

The result set is then successively extended with additional valid candidate sets. $\llbracket f_i^{(1)} \rrbracket^G$ contains those candidate sets that succeed without recursive invocations, and $\llbracket f_i^{(j)} \rrbracket^G$ contains those candidate sets that succeed with a recursion depth of at most $j - 1$.

All involved sets (especially the result sets $[\![f_i^{(j)}]\!]^G$) are finite. The intermediate witnesses ($\bot, \xi'$) make sure that $[\![F_i]\!]^G$ grows monotonically, i.e. a candidate set that has been added to $[\![F_i]\!]^G$ is never eliminated in subsequent iterations. $\mathcal{F}_\mu$ can thus only be applied to $[\![f_i^{(j)}]\!]^G$ finitely often before a fixed point is reached.

The greatest fixed point operator $\mathcal{F}_\nu$ starts by assuming that all SDDP invocations are successful. This can be realized by using the set of all possible candidate sets as the initial result set:

$$\forall F_i \in \mathcal{F}_I : [\![f_i^{(0)}]\!]^G := \{\mathcal{C} \mid \mathcal{C} \in \wp(\mathcal{Z}_{F_i})\}. \tag{3.2.33}$$

Successive applications will then eliminate those candidate sets that contain invalid witnesses.

As the fixed point operator $\mathcal{F}_\nu$ only changes $[\![F_i]\!]^G$ by eliminating, never adding, candidate sets, it can again only be applied to $[\![f_i^{(j)}]\!]^G$ finitely often before a fixed point is reached. We can therefore guarantee that the fixed points exist and that their computation terminates for both operators.

The effective difference between the two operators lies in their treatment of cyclic dependencies between recursive invocations. $\mathcal{F}_\mu$ evaluates sets of mutually dependent invocations to *false*, while $\mathcal{F}_\nu$ evaluates them to *true*. An example for such a cycle would be generated by reachable, applied to a circle of tracks that is not connected to the destination tracks. In this case, the standard semantics based on $\mathcal{F}_\mu$ provides the intuitively correct result (*false*). When the recursion is existentially quantified, cycles only occur if $G$ is not acyclic and the evaluation cannot reach a termination condition at all. When the recursion is universally quantified, cycles may occur whenever $G$ is not acyclic. As we have so far encountered no actual practical examples that required greatest fixed point semantics, there currently is no way to specify that $\mathcal{F}_\nu$ should be used in place of $\mathcal{F}_\mu$ in the syntax.

For recursively defined parametrized SDDPs, which can accept and manipulate arbitrary parameters, we can guarantee the existence of a fixed point and termination based on the above definitions if we restrict the domains of the parameters to a finite set represented by value nodes in $G$ and treat the parameters as roles that are bound to the corresponding value node. While the restriction to a finite domain holds on any physical machine, the size of the potential result set would prohibit explicitly computing the fixed point. Unsurprisingly, parametrized SDDPs are thus in the same situation as regular recursive function definitions over infinite domains and subject to conventional recursion theory. In particular, we require that $F$ be *monotonic* as a necessary condition for the existence of a fixed point, following the argument in [KS01].

#### 3.2.3.5 Transformation Semantics

The semantics of transformation nodes are very closely related to standard Story Pattern semantics as they do not contain any quantification or other advanced features, but merely apply are graph rule to a single binding.

**Selection.** In the presence of transformation nodes, we randomly pick a *final* candidate set $\mathcal{C} \in [\![S]\!]^G$ after the SDD $S$ has been successfully matched. For each witness $\zeta = (n, \xi) \in \mathcal{C}$, we then have $n \in \text{true}_S$, i.e. the witness is either at a (1) leaf node or at a transformation node.

## 3.2 Structural Properties

**Application.** If $n$ is a transformation node, we interpret its SP as a graph transformation rule $[L] \to_r [R]$, where bound and destroyed elements make up the LHS and bound and created elements make up the RHS as defined in Section 2.2.2.6.

The rule is then applied using the standard semantics defined in Definition 2.2.13, using the graph morphism from $P_n$ to $P_n[\xi]$ as determined by the binding $\xi$ as the match $m$. However, in order to avoid problems with destroyed elements that are part of several bindings in the selected candidate set, we split the rule application into two parts: We first create the elements in $o(R \setminus L)$ for all witnesses in $\mathcal{C}$ that are at transformation nodes in a first pass, and then delete the elements in $o(L \setminus R)$ in a second pass.

**Ensured conditions** are split into the corresponding existential and transformation nodes. While this is usually trivial, the expansion can be more complex than it may seem at first glance. If the original node is supposed to *ensure* the presence of three elements, one of which is missing, we do not want the transformation to create three elements, but reuse the two existing elements. We therefore need to verify the presence of each element individually and only create the missing ones. This requires either a sequence of conditional transformations ensuring the presence of each single element, or the generation of a dedicated transformation node for each possible combination of missing elements, which may significantly blow up the size of the diagram.

### 3.2.3.6 Expressiveness

**First-order predicate logic** formulae $\varphi$ with $p$ ranging over a finite set of predicates $\mathcal{P}$, sets $X$, and elements $x \in X$, are defined as

$$\varphi ::= p(x) \mid \neg \varphi \mid \varphi \wedge \varphi \mid \varphi \vee \varphi \mid \exists x \in X : \varphi \mid \forall x \in X : \varphi. \tag{3.2.34}$$

**Predicate logic for graphs.** Based on the definitions in Sections 2.2.2.1, we can encode a typed graph by means of predicates $\langle typename \rangle(n)$, $\langle typename \rangle(n, e, n')$, where $n$ and $n'$ are graph nodes, $e$ is a graph edge, and $\langle typename \rangle$ represents some type name from the type system graph. For a given graph $G$, these predicates can be derived based on the labeling, source and target functions.

A predicate logic for graphs over a given graph $G$ can then be derived by using the predicates encoding $G$ as $\mathcal{P}$ and the nodes and edges of $G$ as the domain of the predicates and the quantifiers. Based on Section 3.2.3.1, the set $\mathcal{X}_\mathcal{P}[G]$ of possible bindings becomes the set $X$, and the elements $x$ are bindings $\xi$.

**SDDs and first-order predicate logic.** We can now compare the expressiveness of first-order predicate logic for graphs and SDDs.

**Theorem 3.2.1** *Story Decision Diagrams over a given graph $G$ are at least as expressive as first-order predicate logic for graphs over $G$.*

**Proof.** We prove the theorem by showing that for every first-order predicate logic formula over $G$, there is an equivalent SDD:

- $p(x)$ : If $p$ is a predicate encoding a node and $x$ accordingly is a binding $\xi$ for a node variable, $p(x)$ can be encoded as $P|_\xi \precsim G$ where $P$ is a graph pattern containing a single node with type $p$. If $p$ is a predicate encoding an edge and $x$ accordingly is a binding $\xi$ for an edge and two node variables, $p(x)$ can be encoded as $P|_\xi \precsim G$ where $P$ is a graph pattern containing two nodes connected by an edge with type $p$. The formula can thus be expressed as a guard node containing $P$ as its SP.
- $\neg \varphi$ : If $\varphi$ is encoded by $S$, $\neg \varphi$ is encoded by $S$'s negation $\overline{S}$.
- $\varphi \wedge \varphi$ : If two terms $\varphi_1$ and $\varphi_2$ are encoded by $S_1$ and $S_2$, $\varphi_1 \wedge \varphi_2$ is encoded by two scoped nodes $(S_1)$ then $(S_2)$ then ... (or two regular nodes if the terms have no common variables).
- $\varphi \vee \varphi$ : If two terms $\varphi_1$ and $\varphi_2$ are encoded by $S_1$ and $S_2$, $\varphi_1 \vee \varphi_2$ can be encoded using two scoped nodes as $(S_1)$ then ... else $((S_2)$ then ...$)$, or using two alternative then connectors issuing from a trivially true scoped node $((1))$ then $((S_1)$ then ...$)$ $\vee$ then $((S_2)$ then ...$)$.
- $\exists x \in X : \varphi$ : If $\varphi$ is encoded by $S$, $\exists x \in X : \varphi$ can be encoded using an existential node $n$ containing only the type constraints for $x$ as $n$ then $S$.
- $\forall x \in X : \varphi$ : If $\varphi$ is encoded by $S$, $\forall x \in X : \varphi$ can be encoded using a universal node $n$ containing only the type constraints for $x$ as $n$ then $S$. $\square$

These encodings show that SDDs, though obviously less compact on paper, also are as succinct as first-order predicate logic.

**SDDs and the predicate $\mu$-calculus.** The predicate $\mu$-calculus extends predicate logic with variables $V$, the least fixed point operator $\mu$, and the greatest fixed point operator $\nu$:

$$\varphi ::= p(V) \mid \neg \varphi \mid \varphi \wedge \varphi \mid \varphi \vee \varphi \mid V \mid \mu V(\varphi) \mid \nu V(\varphi). \tag{3.2.35}$$

As SDDs provide recursion by means of SDDPs, formulae of the predicate $\mu$-calculus for graphs can be written as SDDs:

**Theorem 3.2.2** *Story Decision Diagrams over a given graph $G$ are at least as expressive as the predicate $\mu$-calculus for graphs over $G$.*

**Proof.** As we have already shown that any expression of first-order predicate logic can be written as an SDD, we merely need to focus on variables and the $\mu$-operator:

- $V$ : If $V$ is a variable, any expression containing $V$ can be written as an SDDP with role $V$.
- $\mu V(\varphi)$ : If $\varphi$ is a term containing $V$ and $\varphi$ is encoded by the SDDP $F$ defining role $V$, $\mu V(\varphi)$ is equivalent to $[\![F]\!]^G$ using the least fixed point operator $\mathbb{F}_\mu$.
- $\nu V(\varphi)$ : If $\varphi$ is a term containing $V$ and $\varphi$ is encoded by the SDDP $F$ defining role $V$, $\nu V(\varphi)$ is equivalent to $[\![F]\!]^G$ using the greatest fixed point operator $\mathbb{F}_\nu$. $\square$

## 3.2 Structural Properties

### 3.2.4 Discussion

With Story Decision Diagrams and enhanced Story Patterns, we have introduced two expressive notations for the specification of static properties of object-oriented systems. The notations could be seen as two front-ends of a common semantic core, each tailored to different needs, the former focusing on expressiveness, the latter on simplicity. As the notational styles are closely related and can be used interchangeably, it is thus possible to choose the more appropriate one for each property.

In the design process, the notations can serve as a means of documenting requirements and communicating about structural properties of a system. However, they are not merely a conceptual tool but can be used in the formal verification, monitoring, and implementation of a system thanks to their both formal and implementable semantics.

The formal semantics of the notations make the use of formal verification techniques possible, building on existing techniques for the verification of graph transformation systems. These techniques often directly benefit from the increased expressiveness of the language, e.g. in the guise of more intuitive ways of specifying positive invariants, alternatives, recurring patterns, or transitive properties. Depending on the specific formalism that is employed by a technique, it may be necessary to convert the specification to a compatible format first by transforming it into an equivalent, more verbose version, e.g. by splitting one diagram into several simpler ones. While such transformations could be performed automatically and thus be invisible to the user, using complex properties such as transitive relationships will affect performance and increase the effort that is required for verifying a given number of properties, which needs to be considered when already operating at the limit of what is verifiable in practice.

When used at the implementation level, e.g. for defining activities in a Story Diagram, it is possible to generate code which is based on an iterative evaluation strategy from the diagrams. The resulting code is no less efficient than the code generated from Story Patterns, provided that certain extended capabilities of the language such as recursively defined patterns are used judiciously.

## 3.3 Temporal Properties

With the presented notations, we are able to specify arbitrarily complex structural properties. However, they are restricted to the description of static structures (and atomic transformations) and cannot describe the evolution of a system.

Story Decision Diagrams use graph patterns and one basic principle for composing them in order to express complex static properties. It is tempting to apply the same idea to temporal properties and use it to describe the structural evolution of a system.

The behavior of a system can be characterized by a sequence of states. When we model the system as a *graph transformation system* (see Definition 2.2.14), each of these states corresponds to a graph. Between states, the identity of nodes and edges is preserved.

When evaluating temporal properties, it is no longer sufficient to focus on the question whether certain structural properties hold for a single state – we need to consider the duration and temporal ordering of the individual incidences of the properties.

### 3.3.1 Timed Story Scenario Diagrams

The idea behind *Timed Story Scenario Diagrams* (*TSSD*) is to use the ordering of incidences of structural properties in order to specify temporal properties, expressed as sets of valid orderings. The diagrams are thus directed acyclic graphs consisting of nodes, each containing an SDD defining a structural property, and edges, constraining the ordering of incidences.

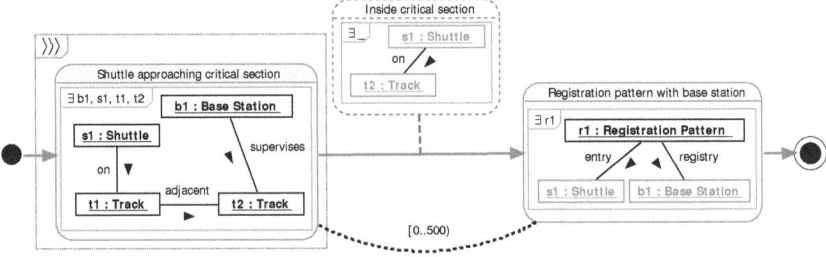

Figure 3.3.1: TSSD: A Shuttle registers with a Registry

Figure 3.3.1 is a basic example presenting the key elements of a TSSD. When a shuttle is approaching a base station's supervised area, they have between 0 and 500 milliseconds to instantiate a registration pattern. In the mean time, the shuttle must not yet have entered the supervised track segment, which is indicated by the (forbidden) state on the transition.

## 3.3 Temporal Properties

### 3.3.1.1 Basic Principles

**Situations.** Each node of a TSSD represents a *situation*, which is characterized by the contained structural property. As the employed properties are patterns, several valid occurrences of a situation may exist in the same system state. Furthermore, the use of patterns reduces the coupling between the different situations, with the effect that a situation may still be incident, i.e. match the system state, independently of the fact that the subsequent situation is already incident as well. Though visually similar, a TSSD is therefore quite unlike a basic statechart, where states are atomic and mutually exclusive. In a TSSD, different occurrences of multiple incident situations can coexist at the same time, which will give rise to a set of concurrent, repeatedly branching execution *traces*. We discuss this behavior in more detail in Section 3.3.1.3 below.

A situation may have a label, which can be used to reference the situation definition. When the SDDs themselves already are quite large, it may be preferable to define the situations separately and then draw the actual TSSD using such situation references – especially if the TSSD itself is complex or the same situation appears multiple times. In general, however, it is preferable to define situations in place in order to benefit from the visual nature of the pattern definitions.

All SDDs that appear on the same path through a TSSD are connected so that bindings are shared between subsequent situations. If a variable is bound by a situation, it cannot be rebound later. If bindings were not retained, it would be difficult to specify simple properties such as 'If a shuttle accepts a task, it needs to complete it.' because any shuttle fulfilling any task would complete the scenario.

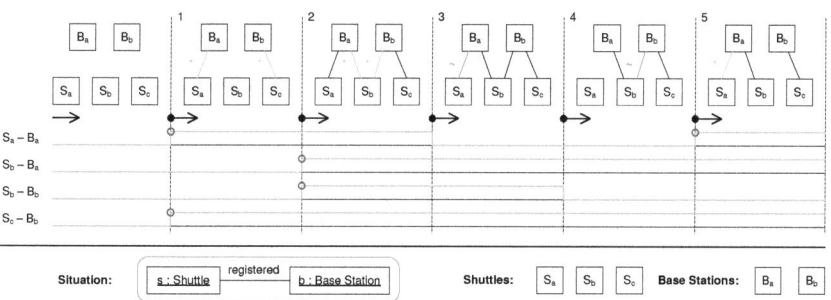

Figure 3.3.2: The relationship between a situation and its observations

When matching a situation at a specific point in time, its SDD generates a result set. Each valid candidate set in the result set is called an *observation* of the situation. However, as the SDD encodes a structural property, whose incidence is typically not limited to a single point in time but spans an interval, the situation could generate infinitely many observations for the same candidate set. An observation is thus made only at the specific time when the concerned structural configuration first occurs, or when it occurs again after being absent. For a given situation encoding a property $p$ and a given candidate set $\mathcal{C}$, an observation is thus generated at every time $t$ where $p(\mathcal{C})$ at $t$ and there is a time $u$ with $u < t$ so that $\neg p(\mathcal{C})$ at all times $v$ with $u \leq v < t$. Figure 3.3.2 illustrates this for a situation encoding that a specific shuttle is registered with a specific base station. As the truth value of this property changes over time for the different pairs, observations (marked by small circles) are only generated where the truth value changes from $false$ to $true$. For the pair $(S_a, B_a)$, two observations are generated, one a time 1 and one at time 5.

**Temporal connectors.** The observations for a TSSD are then placed in relation to each other by means of temporal connectors specifying the temporal ordering of situations.

- The *eventually* connector ($A \longrightarrow B$) denotes that an observation for situation $A$ is made before an observation for situation $B$. Note that this includes the case that the observations for $A$ and $B$ occur simultaneously, i.e. $t(o_A) \leq t(o_B)$. Figure 3.3.3 shows an example of such a connector: A task that is started needs to be completed at some future time.

Figure 3.3.3: Eventually connector: $A \wedge \mathbf{F} B$

- The *until* connector ($A \longrightarrow\!\!\!\blacktriangleright B$) denotes that an observation for situation $A$ is made and that the encoded structural property remains valid until a compatible observation for situation $B$ is made. If no appropriate $B$ is matched before the structural property ceases to be valid, the observation for $A$ is discarded. Figure 3.3.4 shows an example of such a connector: The convoy pattern needs to remain active until the convoy is dissolved.

Figure 3.3.4: Until connector: $A \wedge A \mathbf{U} B$

- The *immediately* connector ($A \longrightarrow\!\!\triangleright B$) denotes that an observation for situation $B$ is made at the same time as the corresponding observation for situation $A$, i.e. in the same state of the system. If no such observation of $B$ exists, the observation for $A$ is also discarded. Figure 3.3.5 provides an example: When an additional task is accepted, the schedule still needs to be consistent.

Figure 3.3.5: Immediately connector: $A \wedge B$

## 3.3 Temporal Properties

Technically, only the eventually connector is actually fundamental. Both the immediately connector, which can be emulated using an eventually connector and a time constraint of 0, and the until connector, which can be emulated using an eventually connector and an appropriate transition guard, are redundant. They are included for convenience, to facilitate the application of optimized evaluation strategies, and to reduce clutter in diagrams.

**Traces.** As situations generate sets of observations and as bindings are retained across situations, the indicated temporal ordering only makes sense when applied to compatible pairs of observations, i.e. if the candidate set of the more recent observation actually evolved from the candidate set of the earlier observation. For example, Figure 3.3.3 constrains the life-cycle of a single task, whereas the behavior of separate tasks is completely independent. Moreover, this same argument applies to multiple observations based on the same candidate set (such as the pair $(S_a, C_a)$ in Figure 3.3.2) as well – a subsequent observation should not be invalidated just because the structure matched by the antecedent reappears. $A \longrightarrow B$ therefore does not imply that all compatible $A$ need to occur before $B$, but rather that a compatible $A$ exists before $B$. Such a sequence of correctly ordered compatible observations is called a *trace*. As there may be multiple antecedent observations with identical candidate sets, a single observation can extend multiple traces. As a candidate set may later be extended in multiple ways, each trace may furthermore be extended by several concurrent observations, resulting in a set of alternative traces.

**Pseudostates.** The evaluation semantics of a TSSD are determined by the graph structure set up by the situations, the connectors, and a set of pseudostates. The latter specify where evaluation should start and terminate and provide a way to encode logical operators.

Evaluation always starts at the initial node ●, which always matches exactly once at the earliest time possible. The descriptive, sequential character of TSSDs implies the assumption that time is bounded in the past so that this point in time is uniquely identified.

The termination node ◉ marks the end of a branch, i.e. sequence of connected situations, of a TSSD. A termination node always matches as late as possible, i.e. the current state during runtime monitoring or the last state of a finite system execution path $\pi$ when analyzing a completed run. When the path $\pi$ is infinite, the termination node technically never matches at all.

A trace is completed once it has reached a termination node, i.e. when it could be extended with an observation for the termination node. A system execution path $\pi$ then fulfills a TSSD if a completed trace to a termination node exists within a prefix of $\pi$.

The basic example in Figure 3.3.6 specifies that sometime during the system execution, a shuttle selects a task and completes it. In conjunction with an $\longrightarrow\!\!\!\blacktriangleright$ connector, a termination node can

Figure 3.3.6: Some task is eventually completed

express that a property, e.g. safety, should hold globally, as illustrated in Figure 3.3.7.

**Branches.** While TSSDs need to be acyclic, each situation may have multiple successors and

Figure 3.3.7: The system is globally safe

predecessors. If the TSSD forks, both branches progress independently and in parallel. Observations are only partially ordered.

By using multiple termination nodes on independent branches, disjunction (logical ∨) can be expressed, as a completed trace at any one of the termination nodes is sufficient. Figure 3.3.8 provides an example: Once a shuttle has acquired a task, it must either complete or delegate it.

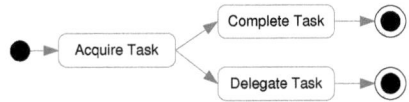

Figure 3.3.8: TSSD containing disjunction

If a situation has multiple incoming temporal ordering edges, observations for all situations directly preceding it need to exist. Multiple incoming connectors thus correspond to conjunction (logical ∧). Figure 3.3.9 provides an example: A shuttle needs to notify the source storage facility and reserve a route before it can pick up the cargo.

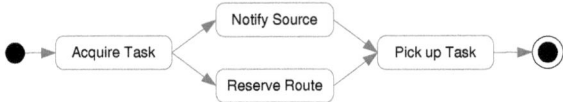

Figure 3.3.9: TSSD containing conjunction

In order to keep the notation based on a limited number of concepts, there are no specific ∧ or ∨ nodes (as exist e.g. in EPCs). This means that it is not trivially possible to ∨-join two branches, which requires the use of scenario situations (see Section 3.3.1.4).[2]

A branch that does not end in a termination node is optional and has no effect on the satisfaction of a TSSD as it can never generate a completed trace. Figure 3.3.10 provides an example: The shuttle may stop for maintenance while executing a task.

More relevantly, it is possible in situations with multiple incoming connectors to have a branch that does not lead back to an initial node in order to make statements about the past. While the *eventually* connector then serves as the *past* operator, *until* can be used to emulate *since* as

---

[2]It could be argued that ∨-joins are contra-intuitive anyway. If a customer can send a complaint by post or email, what if she does both? Both traces continue to be live, and if there are no appropriate procedures in place, the complaint may actually be processed twice. While using *xor* resolves this specific ambiguity, its use can easily introduce subtle semantic issues of its own, as witnessed by EPCs (cf. [Kin06]).

## 3.3 Temporal Properties

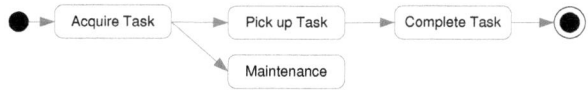

Figure 3.3.10: TSSD with an optional branch

time is assumed to be bounded in the past. In the example in Figure 3.3.11, the shuttle must have been licensed for passenger transport sometime before picking up a passenger. Using references to the past is mostly useful on the conceptual level in order to denote a property as a necessary precondition to, but not an integral part of the specified sequence. Semantically, connecting all branches to the initial node would yield the same result as time is bounded in the past.

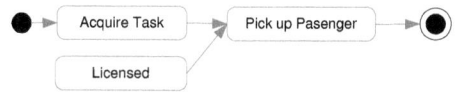

Figure 3.3.11: TSSD containing a reference to past events

**Forbidden scenarios.** As a way of expressing logical ¬ and negating whole scenarios, it is possible to turn branches of a TSSD or the entire diagram into forbidden scenarios. In the style of SDD connectors, required situations and connectors are drawn with solid green lines, while forbidden situations and connectors use dashed red lines. In order to avoid visual confusion with the contained SDDs, TSSDs use darker shades of green and red.

Forbidden scenarios are defined by means of *inhibitors*. Normally, a connector is disabled and becomes enabled when it is reached by an appropriate trace. Inhibitors are enabled and become disabled if a trace reaches them. Inhibitors mark the end of a forbidden scenario and thus are the connectors leading from forbidden to required elements. This can either occur where a forbidden scenario is joined with a required one or at the end of a branch in the termination node, which is considered a required element. Normally, a situation is incident if all inbound connectors are enabled, i.e. a compatible trace for each predecessor exists, and if its structural property can be matched. In the presence of an inhibitor, the subsequent required situation is only enabled if *no* trace completing the forbidden branch exists. The semantics of all other situations and connectors in a forbidden scenario is unchanged.

Figure 3.3.12: A forbidden scenario

The TSSD in Figure 3.3.12 will thus immediately be fulfilled until a shuttle is not properly registered and then collides with another shuttle. As soon as this sequence of events occurs, the TSSD is no longer satisfied.

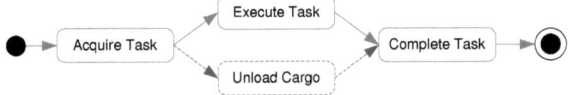

Figure 3.3.13: Forbidden during execution

Figure 3.3.13 encodes that a shuttle may not unload the cargo before the task is completed, i.e. the shuttle has arrived at the proper destination. Complete Task will only match if Unload Cargo has not been observed before.

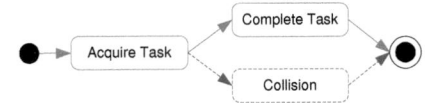

Figure 3.3.14: Forbidden during and after execution

The TSSD in Figure 3.3.14 is similar to the previous example, but as the join only takes place at the termination node which will match as late as possible, any collision, even after the task is completed, will invalidate the scenario.

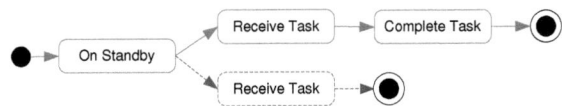

Figure 3.3.15: Forbidden scenario as an alternative

As multiple termination nodes represent alternatives, the example in Figure 3.3.15 is satisfied if the shuttle on standby either receives a task and completes it, or never receives a task at all.

**Parallel composition.** If there are multiple initial nodes in a single diagram, evaluation starts at all initial nodes simultaneously. The TSSD will then only be satisfied if a termination node is reached by a trace from every initial node. In particular, this mechanism can be used to create the parallel composition of multiple TSSDs. If the diagram graph is not connected because the branches have no situations in common, a dotted constraint edge is drawn between the initial nodes in order to indicate that the branches actually constitute a single diagram.

A particularly useful application of this construct is the specification of invariants. In Figure 3.3.16, parallel composition is used to specify that there must be no collision during task execution. The same effect could be achieved by inserting the forbidden scenario between the initial node and both termination nodes of the constrained scenario, which would, however, result in a more complex diagram.

## 3.3 Temporal Properties

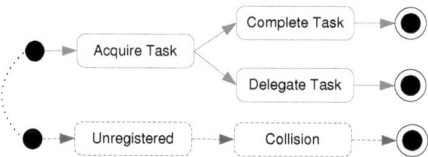

Figure 3.3.16: Parallel composition of scenarios

### 3.3.1.2 Constraints

The valid scenarios recognized by a TSSD can be further restricted by specifying guards that constrain the observations that are admissible between situations and introducing time bounds. The notations we use for specifying constraints are specifically inspired by the Visual Timed Event Scenario approach [ABKO04].

**Constraint Edges.** Constraints can appear directly on the temporal connectors defining the ordering of situations or on dedicated *constraint edges* that may connect any two situations regardless of their relative position in the diagram. Constraint edges are drawn as curved, dotted connectors between situations. They have no direction.

**Guards.** Forbidden scenarios provide a generic notation for prohibiting certain observation sequences between any two situations of a required scenario. However, as subsequent situations may be observed in the same system state, a forbidden scenario forbidding $C$ between $A$ and $B$ requires $A \wedge (\neg C \, \mathbf{U} \, (B \wedge \neg C))$, i.e. $B$ will not match if $C$ is observed at the same time. While it would be possible to prohibit $C$ only strictly before $B$ is observed by placing a non-zero time constraint on the inhibitor leading from $C$ to $B$, this seemed unnecessarily complex, particularly if the forbidden scenario consists of a single situation. In order to directly support the common idiom that a situation is forbidden *between* two situations, we introduce *guards* as a more lightweight notation. By annotating a connector from $A$ to $B$ with a situation $C$, written as $A \xrightarrow{\neg C} B$, we forbid compatible observations for $C$ between two compatible observations for $A$ and $B$, i.e. require $A \wedge (\neg C \, \mathbf{U} \, B)$. Additionally, it is possible to constrain the interval between two observations on concurrent branches of the diagram using a constraint edge $A \cdots \neg C \cdots B$, which cannot be expressed using a single forbidden scenario as this would introduce an implied temporal ordering.

When specifying a guard in a diagram, we link the forbidden situation to the connector with a line. As the situation is forbidden, it is drawn in the style of forbidden scenarios, i.e. dark red and dashed, albeit with a slightly bolder border. See Figure 3.3.17 for an example: While inside the critical section, the shuttle must not be disconnected from the controller.

In Figure 3.3.18, we use a constraint edge in order to specify a constraint spanning multiple situations.

As a natural extension, we also allow specifying required situations $A \xrightarrow{C} B$ that define invariants that always need to hold between the two situations in order to eliminate the need for

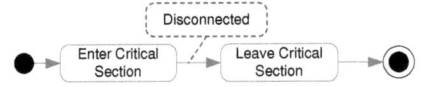

Figure 3.3.17: A forbidden guard

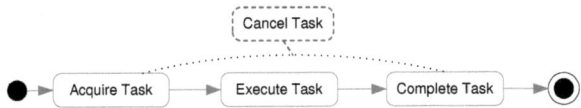

Figure 3.3.18: A forbidden guard spanning multiple situations

unintuitive double negations. Their border is drawn in the style for required elements, i.e. as a dark green solid line. See Figure 3.3.19 for an example: The shuttle needs to be registered with the controller while inside the critical section. As the example suggests, it is easy to convert the two types of guards into each other by negating the contained SDD.

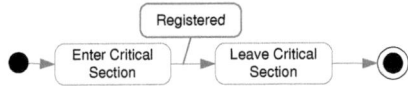

Figure 3.3.19: A required guard

Note that $A \xrightarrow{A} B$ is different from $A \longrightarrow\!\!\!\!\!\rightarrow B$ – the former just requires that at any time between the two observations, some instance of $A$ can be observed, while the latter requires that a specific observation of $A$ remains valid. The example $A \xrightarrow{A} B$ brings up an interesting point: As variables may not be rebound and the same variables may thus not be quantified twice in the same branch, the free variables of a situation reference's contained SDD are implicitly renamed to make their names unique. $A \xrightarrow{A} B$ therefore actually corresponds to $A \xrightarrow{A'} B$, where $A'$ is the situation that is derived from $A$ by renaming $A$'s free variables.

**Strict situations.** There are four commonly used idioms in connection with guards that are supported by a logical extension of the syntax.

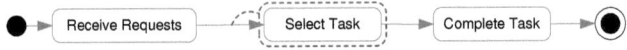

Figure 3.3.20: Strictly next situation

The standard situation semantics only ensure that the same observation cannot be made earlier. However, it is frequently desirable to require that a situation should not have matched at all before it is observed. In the example in Figure 3.3.20, we would like to require that the task that is selected is actually the *first* one to be selected, i.e. that no other task has previously been selected

## 3.3 Temporal Properties

by the same shuttle (this also excludes that the same task is selected again later). Completion of the scenario can thus only be achieved by completing the first selected task – the shuttle may select and complete other tasks, but this is not recognized by the scenario. This effect can be achieved by placing a situation on a connector leading to itself as a forbidden guard. As a more compact notation, it is possible to 'bend' the forbidden guard on top of the situation itself, which is then drawn with an additional slightly bolder dashed dark red border. The situation is then marked as *strictly next*.

Figure 3.3.21: Strictly previous situation

The same concept can be applied in the other direction as well: If a situation is placed on one of its outgoing connections as forbidden guard, the scenario will only accept the *last* observation that is made for the situation. In the example in Figure 3.3.21, requests are superseded by subsequent ones. Such a situation is marked as *strictly previous*. A situation may have multiple guard constraint connectors and be marked strictly previous and strictly next at the same time.

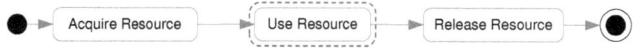

Figure 3.3.22: Strict situation

In LSCs, the message types that appear in a scenario are forbidden where they are not explicitly allowed. This behavior, which is useful to enforce strict orderings between situations, can be emulated by placing a forbidden guard for every situation on every connector within the scenario that is not coming from or leading to a pseudostate. As explicitly specifying this would result in an excessive number of guards, however, it is possible to express this property by simply placing an additional slightly bolder dashed dark red border around the situation without connecting the border to any connectors, which basically says 'required here, forbidden elsewhere'. Such a situation is called *strict*. In the example in Figure 3.3.22, the resource may only be used, exactly once, between acquiring and releasing it (for each acquisition).

Figure 3.3.23: Globally strict situation

Strict situations do not constrain the connectors from and to pseudostates in order to allow the scenario to match repeatedly during the same run of the system, provided that the instances do not overlap. If the intention is to actually express that the scenario appears only once, the scope of a strict situation can be extended to the connectors either coming from initial nodes, leading to termination nodes, or both, by placing the corresponding symbol on the node border. The situation then becomes *globally strict*. Figure 3.3.23 encodes the requirement that the system is initialized exactly once.

An important point to note for any strict situation is that situations are structural properties, not events, and may depend on bindings from previous observations. The guards can therefore only be violated on a connector where all the situation's bound variables are already bound, as these will otherwise be bound to $\bot$ and never match. Implicitly quantifying these variables does not yield the expected behavior, as the guards would then no longer differentiate between traces. In the above example, only the first one among all the users who acquire resources would be allowed to use a resource, which is hardly the intended behavior.

**Time constraints.** While the temporal connectors constrain the temporal ordering of observations, they place no restriction on the elapsed time, making it impossible to prove that a finite trace will not eventually fulfill the scenario. While we can say that a required scenario has not occurred yet, there is no specific point where we can stop waiting for eventual completion. In particular, we lack a means of requiring a practically relevant notion of progress as any finite period of inactivity would be acceptable.

However, by means of *time constraints*, we can specify an interval defining the permitted delay between related observations for two situations $A$ and $B$. The interval is defined by a lower bound $l$ and an upper bound $u$ and may be either open or closed at both ends. A time constraint can either be placed directly on a temporal connector ($A \xrightarrow{[l...u]} B$) or on a dedicated constraint edge ($A \cdots [l \ldots u] \cdots B$). In connection with a constraint edge, the time constraint does not imply an ordering, i.e. that $A$ has to precede $B$ or vice versa – the situations may even be on different branches.

Figure 3.3.24: Basic time constraint

Figure 3.3.24 shows a simple time constraint bounding an eventually connector.

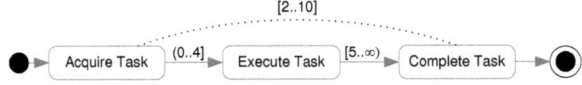

Figure 3.3.25: Multiple time constraint edges

Figure 3.3.25 presents an example with multiple constraints. As all constraints need to hold, the more restrictive bounds dominate the less restrictive ones. Time bounds need to be consistent, i.e. not mutually exclusive and thus contradictory.

In the example in Figure 3.3.26, the maximum delay between two parallel activities is constrained, but the situations do not have to occur in any particular order.

There are two dedicated pseudostates, the *first of* and the *last of* node. The former matches when the first of the attached situations is observed, while the latter matches when the last of the

## 3.3 Temporal Properties

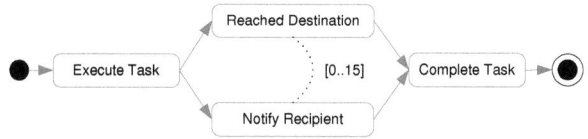

Figure 3.3.26: Constraint across branches

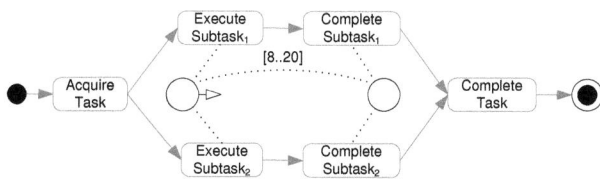

Figure 3.3.27: Constraint on the first/last observation in a set

attached situations is observed. Using these nodes, it is possible to specify a constraint on the time that elapses between the first observation for one set of situations and the last observation for another set of situations. This is typically used on parallel branches indicating a partial order between observations, as illustrated in Figure 3.3.27: The subtasks may not be executed independently of each other, but need to respect a time constraint for the delay between the begin of the first subtask and the end of the last subtask.

**Homomorphism.** If the same situation appears multiple times in the same TSSD by reference, its quantified variables need to be renamed internally in order to avoid binding the same variable twice. As graph isomorphisms are used for matching and different variables are thus not bound to the same graph element, the second situation will not match the same subgraph as the first. While homomorphism for the affected variables can be permitted at the SDD level, this defeats the purpose of using situation references. We therefore allow placing a *situation homomorphism constraint* at the TSSD level as a shortcut for the corresponding expansion at the level of the contained SDDs.

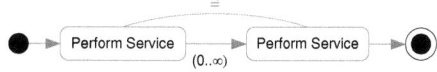

Figure 3.3.28: Allowing homomorphism across multiple instances of a situation

Figure 3.3.28 provides an example: Two different services may be performed, but the same service may also be performed twice (note the time constraint that prevents the second situation from simply matching the same observation as the first).

#### 3.3.1.3 Quantification

TSSDs provide quantification on several different levels, both with respect to structure and time. As observations are generated by SDDs, a situation can be observed as structurally equivalent but distinct instances of the same pattern. This is quite different from typical event- or message-based approaches that do not consider structure and cannot differentiate between multiple (concurrent) instances of the same event.

Consider a scenario encoding a simplified undergraduate program where students are required to sign up for, attend, and eventually complete at least one course, but may sign up for any number of courses. When trying to recognize all conformant sequences, we have to relate the correct observations to each other, i.e. keep track of which student is completing which course, and that he or she had actually signed up for it. The example illustrates why TSSDs are unlike statecharts: We do not only have to keep checking for new students, but also whether a student who is already attending a course has signed up for another one, as we might otherwise miss the one that is actually completed. A situation, once enabled, will keep generating additional observations, which means that a TSSD can 'be' in many states at once as it represents a *set* of traces.

**Situation level quantification.** As we have seen, universal quantifiers in SDDs have made it necessary to introduce candidate sets. Universal quantification can be used in TSSDs, even though it is more common to use existential quantification or restrict universal quantification to local scopes. When evaluating the TSSD, we have to propagate the generated candidate sets and match all subsequent situations based on them, i.e. for every single witness, just like the child nodes of universally quantified nodes in an SDD. Consider the property 'If all tasks are approved (at the same time), then eventually all (these) tasks have to be completed (at the same time)', which could be written by universally quantifying over all approved tasks in the first situation.

**Scenario level quantification.** A more typical requirement would be 'Every *individual* task that is approved eventually needs to be completed'. Here, the involved SDDs are existentially quantified, describing a single task and its states. However, we want this scenario to hold every single time an approved task is observed.

**Triggers.** This is achieved by means of *trigger* blocks. Whenever the sequence within the trigger block has been observed in its entirety,[3] the corresponding trace becomes a *root trace*. The TSSD is then only fulfilled if an extension of every root trace successfully completes the triggered scenario. On the other hand, the TSSD is implicitly fulfilled and places no constraints on the system behavior if the trigger is never completed.

Triggers perform a function similar to precharts in Live Sequence Charts [HM02]. Adopting the corresponding terminology, we distinguish between *universal* TSSDs, which possess a trigger and need to be fulfilled every time it matches, and *existential* TSSDs, which do not have a trigger and need to match just once during the execution of the system. Existential TSSDs can be seen

---

[3] In order to allow branches inside the trigger, the trigger is completed as soon as a situation inside the trigger block that does not have a successor inside the trigger block is observed.

## 3.3 Temporal Properties

as a special case of triggered TSSDs – they are implicitly triggered by their initial node, which matches immediately, but only once.

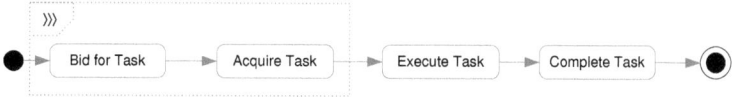

Figure 3.3.29: A complex trigger block

In Figure 3.3.1, we wanted the scenario to be triggered and successfully completed for all cases when a matching shuttle-controller-pair is detected. Here, a trigger consisting of a single situation is sufficient. However, arbitrarily long initial sections of a TSSD can be placed inside a trigger. Figure 3.3.29 provides an example with a non-trivial trigger block containing a sequence of two situations. A root trace is only created once the task is acquired.

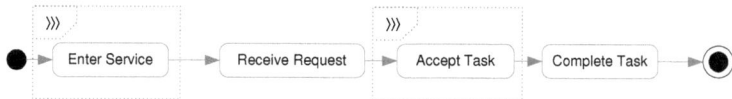

Figure 3.3.30: Multiple trigger blocks

It is possible to have multiple triggers in the same TSSD. In Figure 3.3.30, each shuttle entering service needs to complete every task it accepts. Note that the scenario fails if a shuttle does not accept any task at all because the first trigger has already created a root trace.

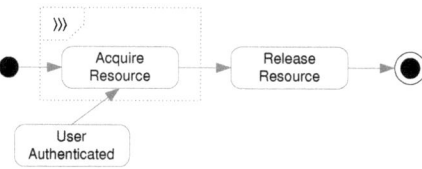

Figure 3.3.31: Antecedent triggered scenario

As a powerful feature, triggers can require the presence of antecedent observations. In Figure 3.3.31, we require that a user acquiring a resource eventually releases it *and* was previously authenticated.

Likewise, the scenario that is defined in Figure 3.3.32 requires that a route was reserved sometime between being planned and actually being used (but only if it is actually used).

The ability to express past and intervening triggered scenarios requires a slight extension of the syntax. Without the trigger block, Acquire Resource would never match without a compatible observation for User Authenticated, nor would Use Route ever match without Reserve Route. A

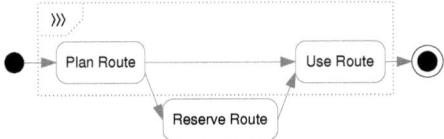

Figure 3.3.32: Intervening triggered scenario

violation would thus not be recognized. We therefore define that when evaluating whether a trigger block is completed, only those previous situations that are directly connected to an initial node are considered as preconditions, not those without predecessors or only with predecessors from the trigger block itself. When defining the formal semantics, we present a way to rewrite past and intervening triggered scenarios in a way that makes this explicit.

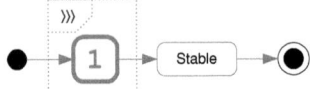

Figure 3.3.33: Globally triggered scenario

A global trigger can be used to express properties that need to hold in every state (i.e. of the form $\mathbf{AG}\,\varphi$) such as fairness (i.e. $\mathbf{AG}(\mathbf{AF}P)$). The example in Figure 3.3.33 expresses the requirement that the system always reaches a stable state *again*, which is expressed by means of a trigger block containing a node marked with 1, which represents a *trivial situation* that is trivially *true* and matches every time compatible traces for all its predecessors are present. The trivially *true* situation thus generates a new root trace in every system state.

**Sequence labels.** We allow attaching labels to a sequence in a TSSD by connecting the first and last element of the sequence with a special dotted blue arrow. This can be used to structure the diagram and may be useful for monitoring, e.g. for listing all currently triggered instances of the sequence. In Figure 3.3.34, the scenario is structured into a selection phase and an execution phase.

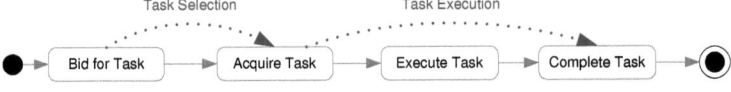

Figure 3.3.34: Sequence labels on a simple scenario

## 3.3 Temporal Properties

#### 3.3.1.4 Subscenarios

Modularity is provided by the ability to invoke a previously defined *subscenario* as part of a TSSD. Subscenarios perform a similar function as pattern references do in SDDs.

**Definition.** A subscenario definition begins with a $\lambda$ situation which, just like an SDDP's $\lambda$ node, binds roles and parameters, but is otherwise a regular TSSD. As in parametrized SDDPs, the parameters in subscenarios may appear anywhere where constants would be allowed. A subscenario may reference other subscenarios, which is the only way to specify loops as TSSDs need to be acyclic. A subscenario can encode an $\lor$-join by encapsulating the alternative branches. In the subscenario in Figure 3.3.35a, a shuttle registers with a base station.

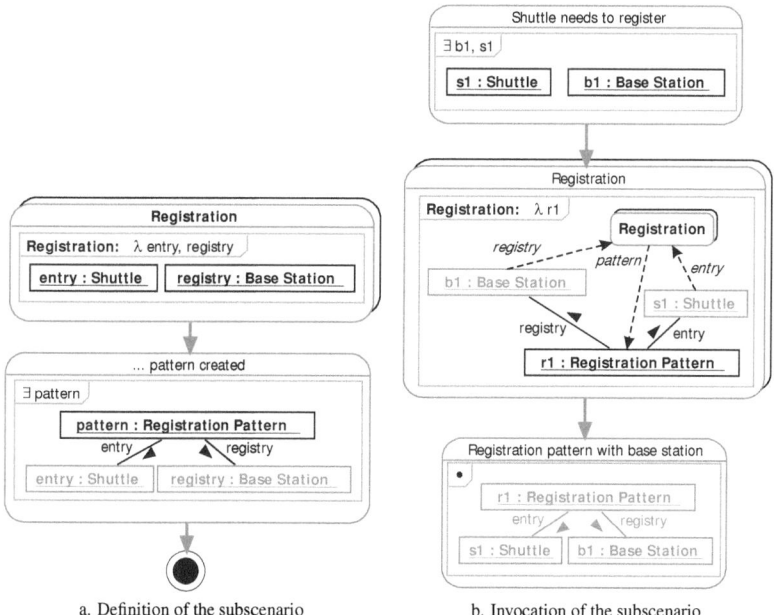

a. Definition of the subscenario    b. Invocation of the subscenario

Figure 3.3.35: Subscenario

**Invocation** works is similar to pattern references, with one notable difference. In the context of scenarios, we will often need to access the bindings that are created by the subscenario in subsequent situations of the invoking scenario. For structural properties, we can simply existentially quantify the free parameter, letting the SDDP filter the invalid bindings. Using this approach for subscenarios would not only be inefficient, but potentially impossible, as the bound element may not yet exist at the time of invocation.

Therefore, the invocation itself takes place inside a $\lambda$-node that allows exporting arbitrary bindings from the subscenario. In Figure 3.3.35b, the registration pattern is created in the subscenario and exported to the main scenario by assigning *pattern* → r1.

**Scenario situations** are the equivalent of scoped nodes in SDDs. They are situations, drawn with a bold border, that may contain a sequence of situations and pseudostates. They again serve as parentheses and can be defined using the existing mechanism for modularity, i.e. subscenarios. A typical example for their use is the explicit ∨-join (see Figure 3.3.36), which allows us to specify the following suffix only once.

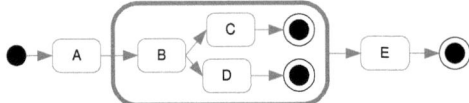

Figure 3.3.36: Explicit ∨-join

The embedded scenario is evaluated in the context set by the surrounding scenario. Its initial node cannot match earlier than any situation preceding the scenario situation in the surrounding scenario, and a termination node may and need not match later than any subsequent situation. Nonetheless, they still match as early respectively late as possible within the given constraints. A 'global' property inside a scenario situation (see Figure 3.3.37) thus constrains exactly the interval between the surrounding situations (e.g. A and C (and is thus equivalent to a required guard). Choosing a different semantics, i.e. interpreting the termination node inside the scenario situation as the end of the surrounding scenario, would break the monotonicity of the scenario interpretation, i.e. a valid observation for C could later be invalidated because B ceases to be valid.

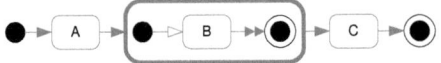

Figure 3.3.37: A globally required property inside a scenario situation is limited to the surrounding interval

**Loops.** For convenience, TSSDs provide a dedicated syntactical construct for specifying loops based on scenario situations. Internally, these loops can be represented as recursively defined subscenarios.

A loop is marked with ↻ or ↻⁺ as in Figure 3.3.38. It needs to be observed at least once, but, as enabled situations keep generating additional traces, also greedily matches any number of iterations of the loop.

## 3.3 Temporal Properties

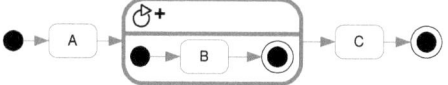

Figure 3.3.38: A loop that needs to match at least once

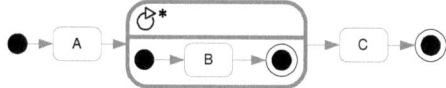

Figure 3.3.39: A loop that is matched zero or more times

An optional loop is marked with ↻* as in Figure 3.3.39. It is equivalent to a regular loop and an additional connector bypassing the loop, i.e. does not need to be observed at all, but may be observed any number of times.

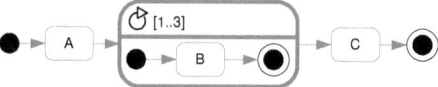

Figure 3.3.40: A loop that is matched a bounded number of times (1 to 3)

Finally, a bounded loop is marked with ↻ $[l..u]$ as in Figure 3.3.40. It needs to be observed at least $l$ and at most $u$ times. ↻$^+$ is thus equivalent to ↻ $[1..\infty]$, while ↻* is equivalent to ↻ $[0..\infty]$. Internally, the bounded loop can simply be unrolled or, more compactly, be represented by a parametrized recursive subscenario that is decreasing the bounds in each iteration.

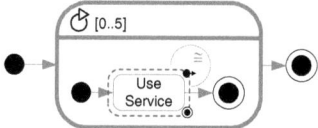

Figure 3.3.41: The user uses services, no more than 5 times altogether

Figure 3.3.41 illustrates two idioms that are relevant in connection with loops: An upper bound is really only meaningful if the TSSD contains guards forbidding 'unobserved' iterations, e.g. by making one situation in the loop (globally) strict. Secondly, if the user does not have to use five different services, but may use the same service several times, we need to include a self-referential homomorphism constraint that is expanded when the loop is unrolled.

## 3.3.2 Formal Semantics

Clear and intuitive semantics are of central to the usability of a temporal logic, as the problems in reading and writing non-trivial properties in LTL or CTL [CGP00] witness. Formalisms with compact semantics based on very few basic operators are easier to implement and analyze, but require large and complex formulae for encoding even simple real-world properties. TSSDs take the opposite approach and sacrifice an elegant formalization for the ability to specify temporal relations such as sequences, partial orders, or triggered reactions in an intuitive way. The notation is not without its subtleties, but these concern the interaction of temporal and structural patterns – a problem that is ignored by other formalisms, which simply treat propositional and temporal logic as orthogonal aspects that need to be integrated by the modeler.

As TSSDs constrain the structural evolution of a system, we are not concerned with individual states, but sequences of states. As the system is represented by a graph transformation system (GTS) as defined in Definition 2.2.14, each state is represented as a graph, and propositions in the form of state and path formula can be specified as discussed in Section 2.2.2.5.

We will first define the semantics of TSSDs, based on the formalization of GTS and of SDDs, and then discuss how they relate to LTL and extensions of LTL with time constraints. In order to facilitate formal analysis, many syntactic features such as the different connector types, required guards, intervening or past triggered scenarios, and situation references are expressed using a more compact semantic kernel.

### 3.3.2.1 Definitions

**System.** The system the TSSD is monitoring or verifying is given as a typed GTS $Y$. While for SDDs, we checked whether a particular state satisfied the specified structural property, we are now interested in the question whether a particular path $\pi$ (as defined in Section 2.2.2.4) that has been generated by $Y$ (or is currently being generated by $Y$) satisfies the TSSD. The states of the path $\pi$ are $\pi[i]$ and occur at time $T(\pi, i)$. Additionally, we define

$$T^{-1}(\pi, t) := i \mid T(\pi, i) \leq t < T(\pi, i+1) \tag{3.3.1}$$

as the inverse of $T$ that returns the index of the current state for a time $t$. We write $\pi^{-1}[t]$ as a shortcut for $\pi[T^{-1}(\pi, t)]$.

**Diagram structure.** A TSSD $D$ consists of a set of situations and pseudostates $\mathcal{U}_D$. A *situation* $U$ is characterized by its SDD $S_U$. We have $var(D) := \bigcup_{U \in \mathcal{U}_D} var(S_U)$ as the free variables of the TSSD. For each situation $U \in \mathcal{U}_D$, we define $\text{pred}_F(U)$, $\text{pred}_I(U)$, and $\text{pred}_U(U)$ as the predecessor situations of $U$ connected to it by **F**, **I**, and **U** connectors. $\text{pred}(U) := \text{pred}_F(U) \cup \text{pred}_I(U) \cup \text{pred}_U(U)$ is then the set of all direct predecessors of $U$. prefix$(U)$ is the transitive closure over pred, i.e. all direct and indirect predecessors. Likewise, we define succ$(U)$ with its subsets $\text{succ}_F(U)$, $\text{succ}_I(U)$, and $\text{succ}_U(U)$ and the transitive closure suffix$(U)$ for the successors of $U$ based on pred$(U)$.

## 3.3 Temporal Properties

The set $\text{init}_D$ contains the initial pseudostates $\alpha_D$ of the TSSD. The set $\text{term}_D$ contains all termination nodes of $D$.

**Trigger Blocks.** We encode trigger blocks by defining $\text{triggers}_D$ as the set of situations that complete a trigger block of the TSSD, i.e. are inside a trigger block but have no successors inside the trigger block. If $D$ is universal, those are the situations $U$ inside a trigger block for which all successors $U' \in \text{succ}(U)$ are not inside the trigger block. If $D$ is existential, we have $\text{triggers}_D := \text{init}_D$.

In order to be able to evaluate past and intervening triggered scenarios without having to change the standard evaluation semantics (situations can only be observed when all predecessors have been observed), such scenarios are internally encoded using additional trivially *true* situations. The trivially *true* situation preceded or followed by an immediately connector represents a neutral element that can be added between any two situations without changing the semantics. This is used to move the references to past or intervening events outside of the trigger.

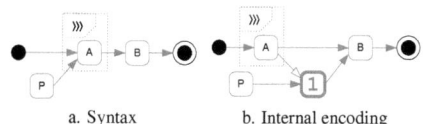

a. Syntax    b. Internal encoding

Figure 3.3.42: Past triggered scenario (end of trigger block)

Figure 3.3.42 illustrates how the past triggered scenario (Figure 3.3.42a) is rewritten (Figure 3.3.42b) so that A can match without P, but the scenario will not complete unless, immediately, a P that was observed before A is found.

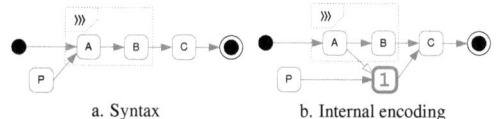

a. Syntax    b. Internal encoding

Figure 3.3.43: Past triggered scenario (inside trigger block)

Figure 3.3.43 illustrates that this also works if the past triggered scenario is connected to an element of the trigger block other than the last.

In Figure 3.3.44, an intervening triggered scenario is encoded. The first trivially *true* node is redundant, but is useful because it provides a simple procedure for encoding any triggered scenario (a sequence of trivially *true* situations, one for every situation inside the trigger block that has outside connections), even if past and intermediate scenarios occur simultaneously as in Figure 3.3.45.

**SDD adaptation.** The SDDs in a TSSD are not independent of each other, but extend the candi-

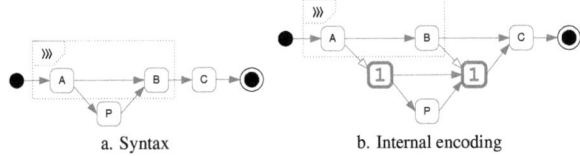

a. Syntax  b. Internal encoding

Figure 3.3.44: Intervening triggered scenario

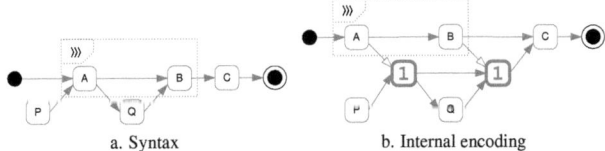

a. Syntax  b. Internal encoding

Figure 3.3.45: Intervening and past triggered scenario

date sets generated by their predecessors. Given an SDD $S$ and its predecessor $S'$, we define

$$\lambda_S[\mathcal{C}_{S'}] := \{(\lambda_S, \xi) \mid \exists (n, \xi) \in \mathcal{C}_{S'} \wedge eval(\mathcal{C}_{S'})\} \tag{3.3.2}$$

which takes the bindings of a valid final candidate set $\mathcal{C}_{S'}$ for $S'$ and creates a corresponding candidate set at the initial node $\lambda_S$ of $S$.

$$\lambda_S[\mathcal{A}_{S'}] := \{\lambda_S[\mathcal{C}_{S'}] \mid \mathcal{C}_{S'} \in \mathcal{A}_{S'}\} \tag{3.3.3}$$

performs this for a whole result set. We accordingly extend parent$(n)$ so that the $\lambda$ node of $S_U$ has all the (1) (and transformation) nodes of the SDDs of all situations in pred$(U)$ as parents in order to make the *evolved from* relation $\mathcal{C} \sqsubseteq \mathcal{C}'$ applicable across situations.

Situation references allow reusing the same situation definition and, in particular, the same contained SDD. In order to make sure that all quantified variable names are unique, we define a relabeling function $\ell_U$ which, when applied to the SDD $S_U$, relabels all variables in $free(S_U)$ with globally unique variable names. $\ell_U$ is then also applied to the SDDs of all situations in suffix$(U)$ so that variable names on the same branch are consistent.

While this allows multiple references to the same situation definition to appear on the same branch, the graph isomorphisms used for matching ensure that the subsequent instances will never generate observations of an identical structure, even if the structure becomes invalid and valid again and the first situation generates a new observation. If a different behavior is desired, this has to be made explicit by using homomorphism constraints. Internally, this will add the original variables to the SDD definitions of the subsequent situations and connect them to their renamed counterparts with homomorphism links.

**Forbidden Scenarios.** Basically, there is no such thing as a forbidden scenario at the semantical level, only *inhibitors*. Inhibitors are connectors that keep the situation they point to from

## 3.3 Temporal Properties

matching when they are enabled, whereas regular connectors need to be enabled in order to allow their target to match. For every situation $U$, we identify the inhibitors by means of the set inhibit$(U) \subseteq$ pred$(U)$, consisting of the situations $U'$ connected to $U$ by inhibitors. Only the last connector in a forbidden scenario is an inhibitor; all other situations and connectors of the forbidden scenario are just normal elements of $\mathcal{U}_D$. The TSSD in Figure 3.3.46a is thus internally represented as Figure 3.3.46b. Only for convenience, situations from which all paths to a termination node lead across an inhibitor, and the connectors leading to them, are displayed as forbidden elements to make the undesirable parts of the scenario stand out.[4]

Given a situation $U$, $U_I \in$ inhibit$(U)$, and $U_T$ as the last node in prefix$(U_I)$ that is not part of the forbidden scenario, or $\alpha_D$, we add $U_T$ to pred$_F(U)$, i.e. a connector as shown in Figure 3.3.46c.[5]

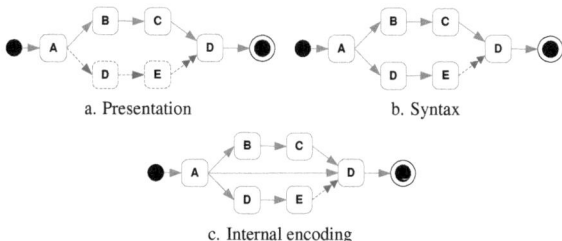

a. Presentation  b. Syntax

c. Internal encoding

Figure 3.3.46: Encoding a forbidden scenario

This expansion eliminates the need for a special treatment of TSSDs that only consist of forbidden elements. While the intended semantics are not obvious from Figure 3.3.47a respectively 3.3.47b, the expanded version in Figure 3.3.47c directly ensures that the TSSD succeeds unless an $A$ is found.

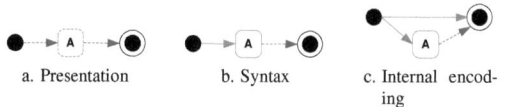

a. Presentation  b. Syntax  c. Internal encoding

Figure 3.3.47: Encoding of a forbidden property

**SDD restriction.** In order to verify the requirement imposed on a situation $U$ with SDD $S_U$ by a U connector, we need to derive an SDD $S'_U$ that verifies for a valid candidate set $\mathcal{C}$ generated by

---

[4]In the – rather theoretical – case that we explicitly want to specify a forbidden scenario within a forbidden scenario, the tool will automatically turn the coloring off so that the actual inhibitors can be identified.

[5]As an optimization to accelerate matching, we can also choose to add a trivially *true* situation $U_1$ as padding between $U_I$ and $U$ as part of pred$_I(U)$ and transfer all guards and constraints between $U_I$ and $U$ to the connector between $U_I$ and $U_1$, as this will speed up evaluation of Equation 3.3.18.

$S_U$ whether it continues to be valid in the present state. $S'_U$ can be obtained by eliminating the quantifiers for the free variables in $free(S_U)$ from $S_U$.

We introduce $S|_\mathcal{V}$ as notation for the SDD $S'$ that removes the quantifiers for all variables $V \in \mathcal{V}$ from $S$ but is otherwise identical to $S$. We define

$$S|_\mathcal{V} := S' \mid \mathcal{N}_{S'} = \mathcal{N}_S \land free(S') = free(S) \setminus \mathcal{V} \qquad (3.3.4)$$
$$S|_{S'} := S|_\mathcal{V} \mid \mathcal{V} = free(S') \qquad (3.3.5)$$
$$S|_\mathcal{C} := S|_\mathcal{V} \mid \mathcal{V} = \{V \mid \exists \xi \mid (n,\xi) \in \mathcal{C} : \xi(V) \neq \bot\}. \qquad (3.3.6)$$

We can then define $S'_U := S_U|_{S_U}$.

**Guards** and strictness conditions are stored in a function $guard : \mathcal{U}_D \times \mathcal{U}_D \to \wp(\mathcal{U}_D)$, mapping pairs of situations to a set of situations that are forbidden between them. A required situation $U$ with SDD $S_U$ is treated as a forbidden situation with guard $\overline{S_U}$, the negation of the SDD, so that all guards represent forbidden situations. No guard for a pair of situations may thus match for any state between the observations for the pair (but may match in conjunction with the second observation).

U connectors are reduced to **F** connectors with an additional guard ensuring that the generated candidate set has not ceased to satisfy the structural constraint. We require that

$$\forall U' \in \text{pred}_U(U) : \exists U_G \in guard(U', U) : S_{U_G} := \overline{S_{U'}}|_{S_{U'}}). \qquad (3.3.7)$$

**Time constraints** are encoded by a function

$$delay : \wp(\mathcal{U}_D) \times \wp(\mathcal{U}_D) \to I, \qquad (3.3.8)$$

where $I$ is the set of all intervals $[l, u]$, $(l, u]$, $[l, u)$, and $(l, u)$ with $l \in \mathbb{R}$ and $u \in \mathbb{R} \cup \infty$. $delay$ assigns an interval constraining the permitted delay between the earliest element of the first and latest element of the second set. The function is total: Unless defined otherwise, $delay$ returns $[0, \infty)$. For simple time constraints, the two sets contain a single element. We further require that

$$\forall U' \in \text{pred}_I(U) : delay(\{U'\}, \{U\}) = [0, 0], \qquad (3.3.9)$$

thus reducing the **I** connectors to **F** connectors with time constraints.

**Observations.** Provided a TSSD $D$ and a path $\pi$, we define an *observation* $o$ as a tuple $(U, \mathcal{C}, t)$ of a situation $U$, a candidate set $\mathcal{C}$, and a time $t$. Note that this implies an extension of the codomain of the binding functions $\xi$ contained in $\mathcal{C}$ from the nodes and edges of a single graph $G$ to the nodes and edges of all type conformant graphs $\mathcal{G}[\mathcal{T}_Y]$ for $Y$'s type system graph $\mathcal{T}_Y$. We use $\mathcal{O}_D(\pi)$ to denote the set of all possible observations for $D$ and $\pi$ with

$$\mathcal{O}_D(\pi) := \{o = (U, \mathcal{C}, t) \mid \mathcal{C} \in [\![S_U]\!]^{\pi^{-1}[t]}\}. \qquad (3.3.10)$$

**Traces.** A *trace* $\rho \in \mathcal{O}_D(\pi)^*$ is a valid sequence of observations. The question whether or not a sequence of observations is valid is central to the semantics of TSSDs and discussed in the next

## 3.3 Temporal Properties

subsection. Note the difference between a path and a trace: as the scenario defined by a TSSD can occur multiple times during the same run of the system, i.e. in the same path, there can be many traces within a single path.

In an analogous manner to our definitions for a path $\pi$, we define $\rho[i]$ as the $i^{th}$ observation, $T(\rho, i) := t \mid \exists U, \mathcal{C} : (U, \mathcal{C}, t) = \rho[i]$ as the time of the $i^{th}$ observation, $\rho^{-1}[t]$ as the last observation before time $t$, and $l(\rho)$ as the length of $\rho$. The set of all observations on a trace $\rho$ is denoted by $\mathcal{O}_\rho$. We write $\rho[U] := (o = (U_o, \mathcal{C}_o, t_o) \in \mathcal{O}_\rho \mid U_o = U)$ for the unique observation for $U$ in $\rho$.

For observations on a trace $\rho$, we define

$$\text{pred}(o) := \{o' \mid o = (U, \mathcal{C}, t) \in \mathcal{O}_\rho \land$$
$$o' = (U', \mathcal{C}', t') \in \mathcal{O}_\rho \land U' \in \text{pred}(U)\} \quad (3.3.11)$$

and, analogously, prefix($o$), succ($o$), and suffix($o$).

For two traces $\rho$ and $\rho'$, we write $\rho \sqsubseteq \rho'$ if $\rho$ is a prefix of $\rho'$.

**Trace trees.** The set of traces generated by a TSSD $D$ for path $\pi$ is stored in a *trace tree* $\mathcal{R}$. Each tree node represents an observation, every path from the root node represents a trace. The tree is simply built from the set by reusing common prefixes; all set operations are thus defined for the tree. The set of all observations in $\mathcal{R}$ is denoted by $\mathcal{O}_\mathcal{R}$. If there are multiple initial nodes due to a parallel composition, the trace tree becomes a trace forest.

The trace tree is a tree rather than a DAG because when the two branches of a TSSD reunite in an $\land$-join, we combine the traces for the branches into a new single trace. For that purpose, we define the notion of *observation compatible* traces. We define

$$\rho_1 \Uparrow \rho_2 := (\exists \rho' : \rho' \sqsubseteq \rho_1 \land \rho' \sqsubseteq \rho_2 \land \forall (U_1, \mathcal{C}_1, t_1) \in \mathcal{O}_{\rho_1} \setminus \mathcal{O}_{\rho'},$$
$$(U_2, \mathcal{C}_2, t_2) \in \mathcal{O}_{\rho_2} \setminus \mathcal{O}_{\rho'} : U_1 \neq U_2), \quad (3.3.12)$$

i.e. the two traces have a common prefix and afterwards contain no competing observations for the same situation. We then define the combination of two compatible traces

$$\rho_1 \cup \rho_2 := \rho' \mid \mathcal{O}_{\rho'} = \mathcal{O}_{\rho_1} \cup \mathcal{O}_{\rho_2} \land$$
$$\forall i \mid 0 < i < l(\rho') : T(\rho', i-1) \leq T(\rho', i). \quad (3.3.13)$$

Comparing SDDs and TSSDs, an observation can be likened to a binding, whereas a trace corresponds to a witness. There is a small difference, however — a witness is a binding that has *arrived* at a node, whereas a trace ends at the last situation that has already been *matched*. Trace trees play the role of result sets.

### 3.3.2.2 Situation Semantics

We can now proceed to define the semantics $[\![U]\!]_t^\pi$ of a situation $U$ at time $t$ as the trace tree generated by $U$ until $t$, containing the *valid* traces. We can exploit the fact that a TSSD is a directed acyclic graph to recursively derive this trace tree. A situation's semantics depend on the semantics of all previous situations that – both structurally and temporally – came before it, i.e. $\forall t', U' : t' < t, U' \in \mathsf{prefix}(U)$.

As we use a continuous notion of time, there would be infinitely many points in time $t'$ for which we would have to compute the semantics. However, as the states generated by a GTS are discrete and there is only a finite number, namely $i$, of states that have occurred before $\pi[i]$, we can restrict our attention to a finite number of observation points in time. We therefore define $[\![U]\!]_t^\pi := [\![U]\!]_{T^{-1}(\pi,t)}^\pi$, i.e. the semantics for the last state of $\pi$ reached before $t$.

The semantics $[\![U]\!]_i^\pi$ are computed using a four step process:

1. Identify the sets of traces that satisfy all preconditions for $U$ (structural recursion)
2. Match $U$ for the candidate sets generated by those traces and compute a result set
3. Verify which elements of the result set represent original observations for state $\pi[i]$ (temporal recursion)
4. Generate the appropriate extended traces using the new observations.

**Computing valid prefixes.** Determining the sets of traces that satisfy all preconditions is the most complex step as most syntactical features (connectors, guards, time constraints, forbidden scenarios) are treated at this point.

In the following, we treat $D$, $U$, $\pi$, $i$, and $t = T(\pi, i)$ as given. In order to be able to match $U$, there first of all needs to be a set of compatible traces containing a valid trace for every situation $U' \in \mathsf{pred}(U) \setminus \mathsf{inhibit}(U)$. We combine each such set into a new combined trace. The unfiltered set (I) of these combined traces is then

$$\mathcal{R}_{(I)}^{U,i} := \{\rho \mid (\rho = \bigcup_{\rho_j \in \mathcal{R}'} \rho_j) \wedge \mathcal{R}' \in \{\{\rho_1, \ldots, \rho_m\} \mid (\forall 1 \leq j, k \leq m : \rho_j \mathbin{\Uparrow} \rho_k)$$
$$\wedge \forall U' \in \mathsf{pred}(U) \setminus \mathsf{inhibit}(U) : (\exists l : \rho_l \in [\![U']\!]_i^\pi)\}\}. \qquad (3.3.14)$$

We first validate the time constraints of the TSSD. We consider the observations in the traces $\rho$, plus the observation $(U, \emptyset, t)$ serving as a placeholder for any new observation we might make for $U$ at time $t$ to ensure that time constraints for the current situations are also considered. We then require that the maximum time difference between any two subsets of this observation set observes the bounds set by the *delay* function. The time-filtered set (II) is then

$$\mathcal{R}_{(II)}^{U,i} := \{\rho \mid \rho \in \mathcal{R}_{(I)}^{U,i} \wedge \forall \mathcal{O}_1, \mathcal{O}_2 \in \wp(\mathcal{O}_\rho \cup (U, \emptyset, t)) : \Delta t \in delay(\mathcal{U}_{\mathcal{O}_1}, \mathcal{U}_{\mathcal{O}_2})|$$
$$\Delta t := |max(\{t|(U, \mathcal{C}, t) \in \mathcal{O}_2\}) - min(\{t|(U, \mathcal{C}, t) \in \mathcal{O}_1\})|\}. \qquad (3.3.15)$$

We then check whether the traces respect all guards. First of all, we need to check whether any guards involving $U$ and any other $U_o$ in the trace have matched before $\pi[i]$:

$$\mathcal{R}_{(IIIa)}^{U,i} := \{\rho \mid \rho \in \mathcal{R}_{(II)}^{U,i} \wedge$$
$$\forall (U_o, \mathcal{C}_o, t_o) \in \mathcal{O}_\rho : (\forall U_G \in guard(U_o, U) :$$
$$(\forall j \mid T^{-1}(\pi, t_o) \leq j < i : [\![S_{U_G}]\!]_{\lambda_{U_G}[\mathcal{C}_o]}^{\pi[j]} = \emptyset))\}. \qquad (3.3.16)$$

## 3.3 Temporal Properties

The guards for any two observations in the trace that are on the same branch have already been verified earlier, before the second observation was generated. However, we need to check the guards for observations that originate from separate branches that are joined at $U$, because these have not previously been verified. The guard-filtered set (III) is then

$$\mathcal{R}_{(III)}^{U,i} := \{\rho \mid \rho \in \mathcal{R}_{(IIIa)}^{U,i} \land \forall (U_1, \mathcal{C}_1, t_1), (U_2, \mathcal{C}_2, t_2) \in \mathcal{O}_\rho \mid$$
$$(\text{suffix}(U_1) \cap \text{suffix}(U_2) \cap \text{prefix}(U) = \emptyset) :$$
$$(\forall U_G \in guard(U_1, U_2) : (\forall j \mid T^{-1}(\pi, min(t_1, t_2)) \leq j$$
$$< T^{-1}(\pi, max(t_1, t_2)) : [\![S_{U_G}]\!]_{\lambda_{U_G}[C_o]}^{\pi[j]} = \emptyset))\}. \quad (3.3.17)$$

Finally, we have check for fulfilled forbidden scenarios that could inhibit new observations. If $inhibit(U) \neq \emptyset$, we define $\hat{U} := U$ but set $inhibit(\hat{U}) := \emptyset$ and compute $\mathcal{R}_{(III)}^{\hat{U},i}$ using Equations 3.3.14–3.3.17. As we are not excluding the inhibitors this time, the traces in $\mathcal{R}_{(III)}^{\hat{U},i}$ also need to extend the forbidden scenarios. If a trace is valid for $\hat{U}$, it therefore contains a forbidden trace. The corresponding trace in $\mathcal{R}_{(III)}^{U,i}$, which is the trace for $\hat{U}$ without the observations for the forbidden scenarios, is then not valid for $U$. The inhibition-filtered set (IV) is then

$$\mathcal{R}_{(IV)}^{U,i} := \{\rho \mid \rho \in \mathcal{R}_{(III)}^{U,i} \land \nexists \hat{\rho} \in \mathcal{R}_{(III)}^{\hat{U},i} : \mathcal{O}_\rho \subseteq \mathcal{O}_{\hat{\rho}}\}. \quad (3.3.18)$$

We then have $\mathcal{R}_\lambda^{U,i} := \mathcal{R}_{(IV)}^{U,i}$ as the set of valid prefixes, i.e. traces for which an observation for $U$ and the $i^{th}$ state at time $t$ might exist that is a valid extension of the trace.

**Generating candidate sets.** We now need to compute the observations for $U$ in the $i^{th}$ state. Each valid prefix $\rho \in \mathcal{R}_\lambda^{U,i}$ defines a candidate set that an observation for $U$ could extend. If $U$ has only one predecessor, this candidate set is just the candidate set of the latest observation in $\rho$. However, if $U$ is at an $\land$-join, there are multiple observations with multiple candidate sets that we need to combine. As we have already ensured that the traces for the different branches are compatible, we already know that these candidate sets do not contain conflicting bindings. If the situations in the branches contain only existential quantifiers, there is also just one candidate set as there is just one way to combine the different extensions of each original witness into a new witness (if $\{(a_1), (a_2)\}$ was extended into $\{(a_1, b_3), (a_2, b_4)\}$ and $\{(a_1, c_8), (a_2, c_9)\}$, the only combination is $\{(a_1, b_3, c_8), (a_2, b_4, c_9)\}$). If there are universal quantifiers, the result is a set of several alternatives that merely need to contain each required witness at least once in some combination (if $\{(a_1)\}$ was extended into $\{(a_1, d_1), (a_1, d_2), (a_1, d_3)\}$ and $\{(a_1, e_1), (a_1, e_2)\}$, one possibility would be $\{(a_1, d_1, e_2), (a_1, d_2, e_1), (a_1, d_3, e_1)\}$). We define the set of these combinations as

$$combine^+(\rho, U) := \{\mathcal{C} \mid \forall U_i \in \text{pred}(U) : ((U_i, \mathcal{C}_i, t_i) = \rho[U_i] \land$$
$$(\forall (n, \xi) \in \mathcal{C} : \exists (n_i, \xi_i) \in \mathcal{C}_i : \xi_i \leq \xi) \land$$
$$(\forall (n_i, \xi_i) \in \mathcal{C}_i : \exists (n, \xi) \in \mathcal{C} : \xi_i \leq \xi))\}. \quad (3.3.19)$$

This definition includes unnecessarily restrictive candidate sets (e.g. $\{(a_1, d_1, e_2), (a_1, d_2, e_1), (a_1, d_3, e_1), (a_1, d_3, e_2)\}$ containing a fourth required witness where three would be sufficient).

We thus remove those candidate sets for which there already is a less restrictive equivalent and define

$$combine(\rho, U) := \{\mathcal{C} \mid \mathcal{C} \in combine^+(\rho, U) \land$$
$$\nexists \mathcal{C}' \in combine^+(\rho, U) : \mathcal{C}' \subset \mathcal{C}\}. \quad (3.3.20)$$

We can now define the set of valid input candidate sets as

$$\mathcal{A}_\lambda^{U,i} := \bigcup_{\rho \in \mathcal{R}_\lambda^{U,i}} combine(\rho, U). \quad (3.3.21)$$

We can then evaluate the SDD $S_U$ and have

$$\mathcal{A}_i^U := \{\mathcal{C} \mid \mathcal{C} \in [\![S_U]\!]_{\mathcal{A}_\lambda^{U,i}}^{\pi[i]}\} \quad (3.3.22)$$

as the result set containing those candidate sets that match $U$ in $\pi[i]$.

**Generating observations.** Classic events (like messages) occur at a particular time. Situations, however, may have a duration that spans multiple states, which means that the same instance of a situation could be observed multiple times. If we kept generating observations, this would defeat the purpose of time constraints. We therefore use the convention that we generate only one observation per distinct match and do so at the earliest possible time. Two matches are either distinct if they are characterized by different candidate sets or if they first occurred at different times — i.e., if a situation (e.g., constraining some attribute) matches, does not match, and matches again, we generate a second observation. We therefore require that a candidate set matches $U$ in $\pi[i]$, but did not match $U$ in $\pi[i-1]$:

$$\mathcal{A}_i^{U+} := \mathcal{A}_i^U \setminus \mathcal{A}_{i-1}^U. \quad (3.3.23)$$

In state $\pi[0]$, there can be no previous matches; we therefore define $\mathcal{A}_{-1}^U := \emptyset$.
The generated observations are then

$$\mathcal{O}_i^{U+} := \{(U, \mathcal{C}, t) \mid \mathcal{C} \in \mathcal{A}_i^{U+}\}. \quad (3.3.24)$$

**Generating traces.** We finally need to extend the prefix traces in $\mathcal{R}_\lambda^{U,i}$ with the appropriate new observations. As we treated all prefix traces together in the previous step (which was required to be able to properly compare $\mathcal{A}_i^U$ and $\mathcal{A}_{i-1}^U$), we now need to pick those observations for each prefix trace which actually evolved from it. We thus have

$$\mathcal{R}_i^{U+} := \{\rho.o \mid \rho \in \mathcal{R}_\lambda^{U,i} \land o = (U, \mathcal{C}^+, t) \in \mathcal{O}_i^{U+} \land$$
$$\exists \mathcal{C} \in combine(\rho, U) : \mathcal{C} \sqsubseteq \mathcal{C}^+\} \quad (3.3.25)$$

as the new traces generated by $U$ in $\pi[i]$. As the semantics of the situation, we can now define the trace tree of all traces generated by $U$ until $T(\pi, i)$, which is

$$[\![U]\!]_i^\pi := [\![U]\!]_{i-1}^\pi \cup \mathcal{R}_i^{U+}. \quad (3.3.26)$$

## 3.3 Temporal Properties

We define $[\![U]\!]^\pi_{-1} := \emptyset$ so that $[\![U]\!]^\pi_0$ is properly computed.

**Special situations.** Initial nodes match once and immediately and thus do not require complex computations. As the semantics of an initial node $\alpha_D$ of $D$, we define

$$[\![\alpha_D]\!]^\pi_i := ((\alpha_D, \{\{((1), \tau)\}\}, 0)) \qquad (3.3.27)$$

for any $i$.

For a termination node $\Omega$, the result set $\mathcal{A}^\Omega_i$ computed in step (2) simply contains all candidate sets $\mathcal{A}^{\Omega,i}_\lambda$ generated in step (1). termination nodes are special because they match as late as possible, which means that they maintain no history and discard previously generated traces as no longer pertinent. This entails two significant changes: The set of generated candidate sets is not filtered for termination nodes so that

$$\mathcal{A}^{\Omega+}_i := \mathcal{A}^\Omega_i, \qquad (3.3.28)$$

and the semantics of a termination node are defined as the freshly generated traces *only*:

$$[\![\Omega]\!]^\pi_i := \mathcal{R}^{\Omega+}_i. \qquad (3.3.29)$$

Unlike the semantics $[\![U]\!]^\pi_i$ of regular situations, the semantics $[\![\Omega]\!]^\pi_i$ of a termination node can thus shrink, e.g. because a forbidden scenario is completed or a guard is violated.

The trivially true situation is similar to termination nodes in that the result set contains all candidate sets in $\mathcal{A}^{1,i}_\lambda$ and that the result set is not filtered against the result set for the previous state, i.e. the trivially true matches in every state where its preconditions are fulfilled. For the trivially false situation, $[\![0]\!]^\pi_i$ is always empty.

### 3.3.2.3 Scenario Semantics

**TSSD semantics.** In SDDs, witnesses from the same candidate set can end up at different leaf nodes. In TSSDs, there is no analogon to a candidate set, and the validity of each trace can be decided independently.

As the semantics of a TSSD $D$, we can therefore simply define the union of the trace trees for all situations of $D$, i.e.

$$[\![D]\!]^\pi_i := \bigcup_{U \in \mathcal{U}_D} [\![U]\!]^\pi_i. \qquad (3.3.30)$$

**Completeness and uniqueness.** The semantics of a TSSD is defined for arbitrary finite prefixes of any given path $\pi$. As the diagram only contains a finite number of nodes and thus the suffix of any initial node is finite (suffix$(\alpha_D) \subset \mathcal{U}_D$), and as the number of states in the considered prefix of $\pi$ is, by definition, finite, the recursive definition of the semantics always has a natural end point, both in the structural (at some $\alpha_D$) and temporal (at state $i = 0$) domain.

The semantics is also unambiguous and unique as there are no non-deterministic choices in the definition. All possible alternative observations are explicitly considered and represented by separate traces.

**Root traces.** Whenever we extend a trace with an observation for a situation in triggers$_D$, i.e. a situation that completes a trigger block of $D$, we add the extended trace to the set of *root traces* $\mathcal{R}_i^{rt[D]}$. We can thus define the set of root traces as

$$\mathcal{R}_i^{rt[D]} := \bigcup_{U \in \text{triggers}_D} [\![U]\!]_i^\pi.$$

**TSSD satisfaction.** We can now finally define *satisfaction* of a TSSD. A TSSD $D$ is satisfied by a path $\pi$ at time $t$, i.e., we have $eval(D, \pi, t) = true$ if

$$\forall \rho^{rt} \in \mathcal{R}_i^{rt[D]} : (\exists \rho_s \in [\![D]\!]_i^\pi : (\rho^{rt} \sqsubseteq \rho_s \wedge \rho_s^{-1}[t] = (U_s, \mathcal{C}_s, t_s) \wedge U_s \in \text{term}_D)),$$

i.e. for each trace in the set of root traces, there needs to be an extension reaching a termination node. This definition covers both existential and universal TSSDs. For existential TSSDs, there will only be one root trace – the root of the trace tree, generated by the initial pseudostate. For universal TSSDs, there will be a root trace for every time a trigger block was completed.

Evaluation is focused on a specific state: When the satisfaction condition is not fulfilled, we have $eval(D, \pi, t) = false$ even if there are traces that still might be completed to satisfaction in the future. When monitoring the ongoing execution of a system, this view is too pessimistic and will lead to an overwhelming number of false positives. On the other hand, $eval(D, \pi, t) = true$ does not imply that the property cannot be invalidated in the next state. For model checking, it may thus be too optimistic.

Using the satisfaction levels for finite-length traces as defined by PSL/Sugar [Ace04, Section 4.4.5], we can differentiate between *holds strongly* (i.e. now and forever), *holds* (now), *pending* and *fails*. The result is *pending* if $eval$ returns $false$ but all root traces are still live and might be completed; it only *fails* if there is at least one root trace for which there can be no further valid extensions, e.g. because of a violated guard, time constraint, or invalidated binding. The result *holds strongly* if there are no guards and no inhibitors on the connectors leading to the relevant termination nodes, which is decidable based on the structure of the TSSD, *and* no new root traces can be generated, which can only be decided based on an analysis of the underlying GTS. For monitoring purposes, we therefore focus on the distinction between *holds* ($true$), *pending* ($\bot$) and *fails* ($false$).

**Negation.** The negation $\overline{D}$ of a TSSD $D$ can be computed by inverting (1) all triggers, (2) all inhibitors, and (3) conjunction and disjunction. In order to deal with triggers (1), two preliminary expansion steps are necessary: We have to add a new termination node, connect it directly to an initial node, and add an inhibitor from each situation completing a trigger to pointing it. This makes the semantics that the scenario is satisfied if no trigger is ever completed explicit. We also need to add all trivial trigger blocks, which consist of (a) trigger blocks containing only a single

## 3.3 Temporal Properties

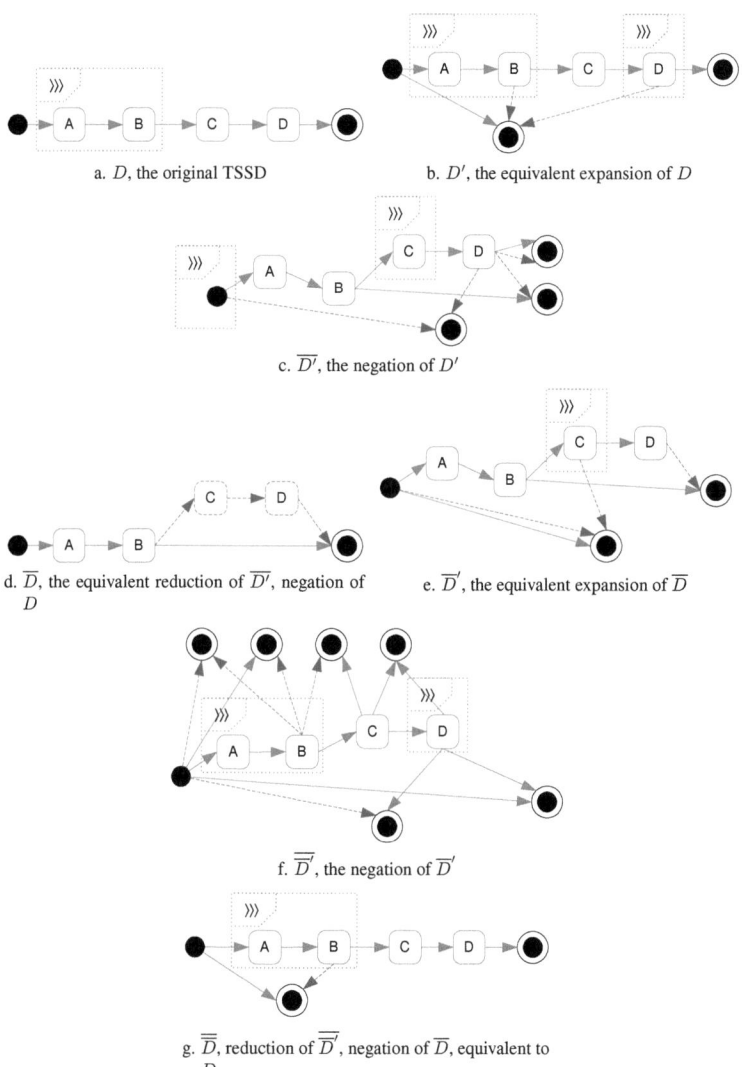

Figure 3.3.48: Double negation of a universal TSSD

situation for which all $U' \in \text{succ}(U)$ are termination nodes and (b) trigger blocks containing all elements of a forbidden scenario except those that actually have outgoing inhibitors, to the diagram. We can then simply invert the triggers by placing each consecutive sequence that is not inside a trigger block into a trigger block and deleting the existing triggers.

Inverting the inhibitors (2) is effected by simply turning all regular connectors leading to termination nodes into inhibitors and all inhibitors into regular connectors. Note that this has to be performed on the internal, expanded representation.

To achieve (3), all termination nodes of the diagram are joined into a single node. All $\wedge$ join points are then split up by duplicating the suffix, creating new alternatives.

This algorithm for negation does not produce the minimal TSSD for expressing the negated property. The negated scenario contains gratuitous trivial triggers, termination nodes connected to an initial state by an inhibitor which can never match, and tautological statements, which can be removed. Figure 3.3.48 iterates through an example.

Negation can also trivially be expressed by placing the whole scenario into a single forbidden scenario node.

**Example.** We now present a small example that illustrates the idea of traces, trace trees, and root traces. Figure 3.3.49 specifies the property that any process that is *ready*, i.e. not *waiting* for any external resources, must eventually be *running* until it is *terminated*. To keep the candidate sets simple, there are no quantifiers in the SDDs — the bindings generated by the trigger block never change, while the state is encoded as an attribute.

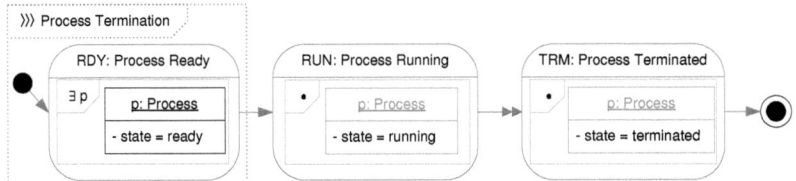

Figure 3.3.49: Example 1: The TSSD $D$

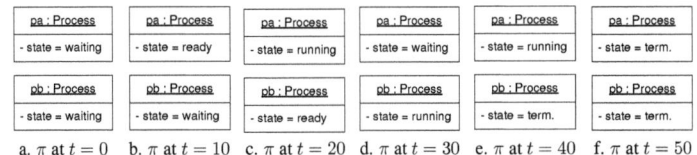

a. $\pi$ at $t = 0$    b. $\pi$ at $t = 10$    c. $\pi$ at $t = 20$    d. $\pi$ at $t = 30$    e. $\pi$ at $t = 40$    f. $\pi$ at $t = 50$

Figure 3.3.50: Example 1: The path $\pi$

Figure 3.3.50 shows the states of a path representing a run of the system that we would like to analyze. As is apparent in state $\pi[5]$, both processes eventually terminate. Figure 3.3.51 illustrates

## 3.3 Temporal Properties

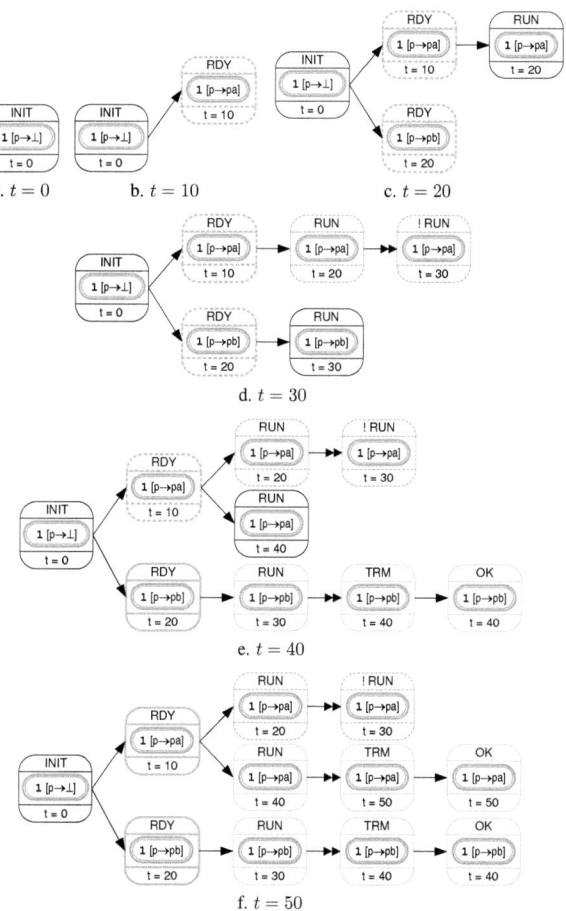

Figure 3.3.51: Example 1: The trace trees generated by $D$ over $\pi$

the trace trees $\mathcal{R}_t$ generated by $D$ when evaluated on $\pi$. The nodes represent observations, a trace is a path from the tree root to an observation. The root traces are marked by a bold border around the triggering observation. Their border is drawn dotted and orange while they are *pending*, solid green once they are satisfied (*holds*), and dashed red once they have *failed*. In the tree at $t = 30$, the dashed red border indicates that this particular trace will never be extended again because the UNTIL requirement was violated as $p_a$ had stopped running. Eventually, an extension of each root trace reaches the termination node so that the TSSD whole is satisfied (*holds*).

#### 3.3.2.4 Subscenario Semantics

Even though they play a similar role, *subscenarios* are conceptually simpler than SDDPs. The three main differences are that trace trees are propagated in a linear fashion *through* the subscenario, that TSSDs already have a mechanism for moving candidate sets between situations, and that termination is not a practical issue.

**Invoking a subscenario.** As a subscenario may export generated bindings, its invocation in the host scenario $D$ occurs in a specific $\lambda$ situation $U_D$. A subscenario $B$ can basically be seen as a macro that adds its situations between $U_D$ and its predecessors $\text{pred}(U_D)$. The subscenario's $\lambda$ situation $U_B$ than extends the witnesses in the candidate sets $\mathcal{A}_\lambda^{U_B,i}$ arriving at $U_B$ with bindings for the roles of $B$. These bindings are generated from the existing bindings in accordance with the specification of $U_D$ using a rebinding function $\ell_B$ (from $var(D)$ to $var(B)$), which works exactly like the rebinding function of the $\lambda$ node of an SDDP. Likewise, subscenario parameters are added to the bindings and can be used in constraint expressions.

**Returning from a subscenario.** The extended candidate sets then progress through $B$ normally. When they complete the subscenario and reach $U_D$, another rebinding function $\ell_D$ (from $var(B)$ to $var(D)$) is used to extend the witnesses in the candidate sets in $\mathcal{A}_\lambda^{U_D,i}$ with the new bindings that are exported from the subscenario. $\ell_D$ also erases the bindings for all variables $v \in var(B)$ from the candidate sets, i.e. resets them to $\bot$.

**Subscenario instances.** When a subscenario is inserted into a TSSD, its situations and roles are qualified with a unique identifier so that multiple instances of the same subscenario are distinct. Qualifying the situations is necessary to ensure that there are no multiple observations for the same situation in the same trace, and to avoid attempts to rebind variables. Qualifying the roles allows a subscenario $B$ to contain recursive references to itself. Recursive definitions can, of course, not be expanded statically, but need to be expanded on the fly as required.

**Loops,** which represent the most frequent application of recursive subscenarios, can be expressed as tail recursions. The termination node of an iteration is merged with the first situation of the next iteration, while the initial node of a subsequent iteration is merged with the last situation of the previous iteration. As a consequence, the guards on both corresponding connectors need to hold between the two situations. Bounded loops can be realized by explicitly unrolling them (for sufficiently small bounds) or by means of parameters that are decreased during each iteration and used as guards in the appropriate situations.

### 3.3 Temporal Properties

**Completeness and uniqueness.** On any finite prefix of a given path $\pi$, the semantics of a TSSD containing invocations of non-recursive subscenarios are uniquely defined as the number of contained situations is guaranteed to be finite. The semantics of a TSSD containing an invocation of a recursively defined subscenario are equally uniquely defined if the subscenario encodes any kind of progress, i.e., if the definition requires a state change (e.g. because two of its situations are mutually exclusive) or includes a time constraint with a non-zero lower bound, as the subscenario can only be observed a finite number of times on a finite prefix of $\pi$. In order to ensure that the semantics definition still holds for a subscenario definition that contains no such constraints and could thus endlessly match the same state (e.g. by defining only a single non-$\lambda$ situation), we have to automatically insert such a non-zero time constraint between iterations that will prevent the recursive definition of the semantics from evaluating the same state more than once. This does not reduce the expressiveness of the notation, as the specified property is actually structural if no progress is required and can therefore be specified using a single situation containing an invocation of a recursive SDDP, for which we guarantee termination.

While such a semantics could be defined, we do not define a semantics for infinite paths on which a recursive subscenario loops forever as the corresponding situations are actually observed over and over infinitely often.[6] As a trace is currently only considered valid if it has reached a termination node, only finitely many iterations of any subscenario are possible in a valid trace. As a consequence, a well-formed subscenario needs to contain at least one branch without a recursive invocation to ensure that termination is at all possible.

#### 3.3.2.5 Expressiveness

In Section 2.2.2.5, we have discussed how temporal properties of graph transformation systems can be specified based on CTL*. The discussion in [GHK98] proves that it is possible to define a sound propositional calculus whose elementary propositions are based on graph patterns. However, in order to discuss the expressiveness of TSSDs, we additionally need a calculus that includes a concept of time and, in particular, intervals.

**Linear Temporal Logic (LTL).** Linear Temporal Logic (LTL) is a subset of CTL* that is restricted to a single path quantifier, an implied initial **A**. Given a GTS $Y$, a set of graph patterns $\mathcal{P}$ and a set of possible bindings $\mathcal{X}_\mathcal{P}[\mathcal{G}[\mathcal{T}_Y]]$, with pattern $P \in \mathcal{P}$, binding $\xi \in \mathcal{X}_\mathcal{P}[\mathcal{G}[\mathcal{T}_Y]]$, and $G \in \mathcal{G}[\mathcal{T}_Y]$, we define LTL for GTS as follows:

- A graph predicate $P|_\xi \precsim G$ and the constants $true$ and $false$ are valid LTL formulae,
- if $\varphi$ is a valid LTL formula, so is $\neg \varphi$,
- for two valid LTL formulae $\varphi$ and $\varphi'$, $\varphi \wedge \varphi'$ is a valid LTL formula,
- for a valid LTL formula $\varphi$, **X** $\varphi$ is a valid LTL formula,
- for two valid LTL formulae $\varphi$ and $\varphi'$, $\varphi$ **U** $\varphi'$ is a valid LTL formula.
- For convenience, the derived operators **F**, **G**, and **R** are also provided so that for two valid LTL formulae $\varphi$ and $\varphi'$, **F** $\varphi$, **G** $\varphi$, and $\varphi$ **R** $\varphi'$ are valid LTL formulas.

---
[6]Note, however, that it is nonetheless possible to specify that some finite scenario should occur infinitely often using appropriate triggers.

The semantics of LTL for GTS are then defined as:

- $Y, G \models \varphi$ iff $\varphi$ is $true$.
- $Y, G \models \varphi$ iff $\varphi$ is a graph predicate and $P|_\xi \precsim G$.
- $Y, G \models \neg\varphi$ iff $Y, G \not\models \varphi$.
- $Y, G \models \varphi \vee \psi$ iff $Y, G \models \varphi \vee Y, G \models \varphi$.
- $Y, G \models \varphi \wedge \psi$ iff $Y, G \models \varphi \wedge Y, G \models \varphi$.
- $Y, \pi \models \varphi$ iff $G = \pi[0] \wedge Y, G \models \varphi$.
- $Y, \pi \models \neg\varphi$ iff $Y, G \not\models \varphi$.
- $Y, \pi \models \varphi \vee \psi$ iff $Y, \pi \models \varphi \vee Y, \pi \models \varphi$.
- $Y, \pi \models \varphi \wedge \psi$ iff $Y, \pi \models \varphi \wedge Y, \pi \models \varphi$.
- $Y, \pi \models \mathbf{X}\varphi$ iff $Y, \pi^1 \models \varphi$.
- $Y, \pi \models \varphi \mathbf{U} \psi$ iff $\exists k \mid k \geq 0 : Y, \pi^k \models \psi \wedge \forall j \mid 0 \leq j < k : Y, \pi^k \models \varphi$
- $Y, \pi \models \mathbf{F}\varphi$ iff $Y, \pi \models true\mathbf{U}\varphi$.
- $Y, \pi \models \mathbf{G}\varphi$ iff $\neg Y, \pi \models \mathbf{F}\neg\varphi$.
- $Y, \pi \models \varphi \mathbf{R} \psi$ iff $\neg Y, \pi \models \neg\varphi \mathbf{U} \neg\psi$.

**TSSDs and LTL.** We can now compare the expressiveness of LTL for GTS and TSSDs. [7]

**Theorem 3.3.1** *Timed Story Scenario Diagrams over a given path $\pi$ are at least as expressive as Linear Temporal Logic for GTS over $\pi$.*

**Proof.** We again prove this constructively by showing that for any LTL formula, there exists an equivalent TSSD. This construction is mostly trivial, as there is an equivalent for each of the fundamental concepts of LTL in TSSDs, with the exception of the **X** operator. As TSSDs are based on a dense time model, for which the concept of a *next* state is not applicable, such properties are only meaningful in conjunction with time constraints.

- $P|_\xi \precsim G$: As any graph predicate can be encoded by means of an SDD, $P|_\xi \precsim G$, $true$, or $false$ can be encoded as a situation containing the corresponding SDD.
- $\neg\varphi$: If $\varphi$ is encoded by $D$, $\neg\varphi$ is encoded by $\overline{D}$.
- $\varphi \wedge \varphi'$: If $\varphi_1$ and $\varphi_2$ are encoded by $D_1$ and $D_2$, $\varphi_1 \wedge \varphi_2$ can be written using two scenario situations containing $D_1$ and $D_2$ that are connected to the same termination node.
- **X** $\varphi$: As the temporal operators are expressed as connectors in TSSDs, there are no unary operators. However, if $\varphi$ is encoded by $D$, **X** $\varphi$ can be expressed by connecting a *strictly previous* trivially *true* situation that serves as the first operand to $D$ using an *eventually* connector (which yields the classic encoding of **X** as $false$ **U** $\varphi$).

---
[7] As various theorems proving that any LTL formula can be expressed by first-order logic exist, we could conjecture based on Section 3.2.3.6 that any LTL formula could already be expressed by a single SDD. However, this is not possible because an SDD is limited to a single graph $G$ as its argument, i.e. all nodes are implicitly evaluated on the same graph. To overcome this, we could, for each state graph of a path, add an attribute indicating the corresponding state to each node and join the state graphs into a single graph. However, such an abuse of notation would forfeit all claims to intuitiveness.

## 3.3 Temporal Properties

- $\varphi \, \mathbf{U} \, \varphi'$: If $\varphi_1$ and $\varphi_2$ are encoded by $D_1$ and $D_2$, $\varphi_1 \, \mathbf{U} \, \varphi_2$ can be written using two scenario situations containing $D_1$ and $D_2$ that are connected by an *until* connector.
- $\mathbf{F} \, \varphi$, $\mathbf{G} \, \varphi$, and $\varphi \, \mathbf{R} \, \varphi'$: Using the above definitions, the derived operators can be defined in the same way as for LTL. $\mathbf{F} \, \varphi$ does not need to be derived, as it is supported directly by means of the *eventually* connector. $\mathbf{G} \, \varphi$ can also be written as ⟶▷ $\varphi$ ⟶▶▶ ⊙ . □

**Metric Temporal Logic (MTL).** An extension of LTL that allows time constraints in the form of intervals for temporal operators is MTL (cf. [Koy90, AH93]). All temporal operators in MTL are defined in terms of the U operator. The X operator is subsumed by the F operator as the concept of a next state is not meaningful on dense time domains. MTL is very expressive and, e.g., allows encoding the halting problem. Satisfiability of MTL formula is undecidable.

**TSSDs and MTL.** Any valid MTL formula can be written as an equivalent TSSD:

**Theorem 3.3.2** *Timed Story Scenario Diagrams over a given path $\pi$ are at least as expressive as Metric Temporal Logic for GTS over $\pi$.*

**Proof.** As any LTL formula can be written as a TSSD, we only need to show that the extensions introduced by MTL, namely time constraints on operators, can be expressed using TSSDs. As TSSDs directly support time constraints on the temporal connectors that encode the temporal operators, this is trivial. □

**Time Point Temporal Logic (TPTL).** Another extension of LTL with time constraints is TPTL (cf. [AH94]). TPTL introduces the concept of clocks which, in a given state, can be defined (and set to 0) or compared with the a given interval. TPTL is strictly more expressive than MTL (cf. [BCM05]).

**TSSDs and TPTL.** Any valid TPTL formula can be written as an equivalent TSSD:

**Theorem 3.3.3** *Timed Story Scenario Diagrams over a given path $\pi$ are at least as expressive as Time Point Temporal Logic for GTS over $\pi$.*

**Proof.** Again, we only need to show that the extensions introduced by TPTL can be expressed using TSSDs. TPTL can only compare times for temporally ordered states, which corresponds to situations on the same branch in a TSSD. Defining a clock in a state can then be represented by attaching one end of a constraint edge to the corresponding situation, while a reference to the clock in a subsequent situation is encoded by attaching the other end of the constraint edge to it. The interval for comparison is than placed on the constraint edge as a time constraint. □

**Conclusion.** We have shown that TSSDs are very expressive in the temporal domain. They also meet the criteria for a temporal logic for real-time system specification proposed in [BMN00]: They are based on first-order logic, prohibit quantification on time variables, have a metric for time, use the interval as the fundamental time entity, support a time model that is based on relative time (though absolute time is also available as the time relative to the initial node), and provide a limited number of basic operators that can be composed into reusable specialized building blocks by means of subscenarios.

Finally, with their integrated support for structural properties and their quantification, TSSDs go beyond the scope of other existing temporal logics in this respect.

### 3.3.3 Discussion

With Timed Story Scenario Diagrams, we have presented a notation that is very expressive in the temporal domain, with the added benefit of integrated support for structural properties. Thanks to the fact that the basic propositions are patterns, the notation can describe and differentiate between multiple instances of the same event or configuration and even deal with dynamic systems with a previously unknown, unbounded number of instances. While this can be emulated in other logics, there is no inherent support and users will have to devise often cumbersome auxiliary constructions by themselves. Especially in the context of Story-Driven Modeling, the notation is a natural extension for the specification of behavioral constraints. Again, the notation is useful both for the documentation and communication of requirements that could only be captured informally before, and as part of a model-driven design process.

Unlike SDDs, TSSDs are not an implementation level formalism. While it would be possible to generate operational behavior satisfying a TSSD from a sufficiently detailed specification, the focus of the notation is on *what* should be achieved, not *how* it should be achieved. However, a TSSD can provide a good starting point for deriving Story Diagrams that 'fill in the blanks'.

When using TSSDs for formal verification, we have to be aware of the theoretical limitations concerning the verification of time constraints over dense domains and triggered behavior. As there are undecidability results for formalisms such as Metric Temporal Logic (MTL), which we have shown to be less expressive than TSSDs, or some of the related advanced features of Visual Time Event Systems (VTS), it is obvious that many properties that can be specified using TSSDs will not be decidable. Given the complexity that can result from the inclusion of (dynamic) structural aspects, even fewer properties will be verifiable in practice. Nonetheless, there are subsets of the language that are useful while being decidable. For diagrams that are restricted to the subset of the TSSD syntax that can be mapped to LTL, it would be an option to transform the specification to the input format of existing LTL model checkers, although this is complicated by the fact that the atomic propositions in TSSDs are graph patterns, a concept which is not natively supported by standard tools.

Graph patterns make it simple to describe systems with large or even infinite state spaces. The support for dense time domains further increases the size of the search space. Instead of a single path consisting of a countable number of discrete states as for runtime monitoring, verification needs to account for infinitely many possible different timings for the same sequence of states unless some discretized approximation is employed. On the other hand, time constraints help to limit the size of the problem. While an unconstrained enabled situation or subscenario may keep generating infinitely many new alternative observations, time constraints can define a limit

## 3.3 Temporal Properties

after which no new observations are possible. Certain problems, such as progress, only become decidable using finite resources when the scenario is bounded in such a way.

While a complete verification of TSSDs is therefore often not possible, we always have the option of generating *behavioral monitors* that verify the correctness of a specific execution trace. Their implementation can build closely on the formal semantics definition, but needs to introduce suitable optimizations to make the evaluation efficient, especially if online monitoring is required.

## 3.4 Conclusion

In this chapter, we have presented a novel visual approach for the specification of temporal and structural properties. We have shown how UML Object Diagrams as a widely accepted type of visual diagram can be extended into Story Decision Diagrams for the description of complex structural conditions. We have also presented enhanced Story Patterns as a lightweight notation that can act as a replacement for Story Patterns in the context of Story-Driven Modeling. Story Decision Diagrams have moreover been employed in the context of Timed Story Scenario Diagrams, timed scenarios which provide a natural way of specifying temporal orderings of states and events as sequences of observations. The presented constraint notations thus support both the specification of detailed structural properties and of requirements concerning structural dynamics in a coherent visual notation.

We have defined formal semantics for all notations, which confirms their theoretical soundness and provides the required solid foundation for their use in a model-driven design process. We have compared the notations to related formalisms and have shown that they are very expressive in their respective domains. In spite of their expressive power, applying them is comparatively straight-forward. This aspect is studied in more detail in Chapter 6, where we also present the available tool support. While some of their advanced features necessarily place limits on their decidability, the notations are nonetheless a suitable foundation for model-driven verification and validation activities. We discuss the relevant methods in more detail in Chapter 5.

# Chapter 4
# System Design

## 4.1 Introduction

In the preceding chapters, we have presented and integrated techniques for the specification of component behavior, structural adaptation, and real-time communication protocols and have introduced powerful notations for expressing constraints on all of these aspects. We now turn to the discussion of the conceptual and architectural principles that will allow us to apply these techniques to the problem of designing adaptive behaviors for software-intensive systems situated in complex dynamic environments.

Software-intensive systems are typically distributed with multiple loci of control. Particularly when the interacting components are heterogeneous or represent independent entities (e.g. companies), it is therefore plausible to view the different components as autonomous actors whose behavior is only partially known and cannot be deterministically predicted. This is especially true of *self-optimizing* systems (cf. [FGK$^+$04, p.22]), which are capable of reflecting on their own objectives and evolving their strategies and behaviors in response to their environment.

**Agents.** It is consequently a common interpretation to view the components as *agents*. While a universally accepted definition of this term has been the subject of much debate (e.g. cf. [Kle03] for an exhaustive discussion), we believe that it is helpful to apply the label to any independent component pursuing some form of objectives. This broad definition is compatible with the prevalent view in pragmatic approaches to agent-oriented software engineering, which is based on a *weak notion of agency* [WJ95a, Woo00] which requires autonomy, proactivity, reactivity, and interaction, but no artificial intelligence.

Because agent-oriented abstractions are designed to describe loosely coupled interactions between autonomous entities, they are a good fit for describing the considered class of software-intensive systems. While agents are often styled as a revolutionary paradigm shift, they should rather be seen as an evolutionary extension that can build on a wealth of experience concerning the design of distributed information systems. After all, the adoption of agents can only hide some of the complexity arising from distribution and concurrency, not eliminate it.

**Coordination.** Most methodologies for multi-agent system design focus on the specification of complex agent interactions using a social system metaphor, which is intuitive to apply but difficult to formalize. From a software engineering point of view, the key challenge is to constrain and coordinate these interactions in accordance with the given requirements.

Traditional approaches for the design of safety-critical systems impose tight restrictions in order to achieve a maximum degree of predictability. This is apparently at odds with concepts such as autonomous agents or self-optimization, which necessarily make a system less predictable – an effect which is multiplied in networks of such systems. Suppressing or overly restricting these effects would be self-defeating, however, because much of the power of networked systems stems from the interactions of their elements and the complex behaviors that emerge from them.

The fact that seemingly chaotic interactions can yield purposeful large scale behavior is harnessed in different fields: Swarm intelligence (cf. [KE01]) uses random interactions based on sets of basic rules in order to solve complex optimization and coordination problems. Probabilistic protocols (cf. [Gup04]) achieve significant increases in efficiency for the price of only a slight reduction in reliability. In [KT06], we even use swarms of selfish agents to actually increase the reliability of a system. While there are established patterns that can be reused for solving specific problems, the overall design process for emergent behaviors is driven by experimentation resulting in iterative refinements, which leads to less predictable results than conventional analytical approaches.

In order to reconcile these perspectives, we build on our work towards a separation of concerns in multi-agent systems (cf. [KG05]). By introducing dedicated architectural views for different aspects of the system, we can, to some extent, study each concern in isolation and reduce the complexity of the design. We can moreover target the use of more restrictive techniques for safety-critical systems to the affected views only. Conflicts that arise between views are resolved locally in each agent, which can be achieved by building on the compositional techniques for component design that were discussed in Section 2.3. Layered architectures like the Operator-Controller-Module that cleanly separate critical control and coordination processes from advanced functionality can moreover help to prevent many conflicts by default.

**Environment.** For software-intensive systems, the context in which they are situated is of central importance. While agents are often defined relative to some environment they sense and act on,[1] the environment per se has traditionally received little attention. Most approaches focus on agent design and treat the environment as a mere stage for the agents' behavior which can be delegated to the realm of agent frameworks, middleware, and other implementation level constructs. They abstract from the environment by defining interfaces through which it can be perceived and manipulated.

We believe that building on an environment specification with expressive semantics is instrumental in designing situated agents that are capable of flexible and complex interactions with their surroundings. By applying object-oriented specification techniques, in particular Story-Driven

---

[1]Wooldridge and Jennings, for example, propose the following as the most basic definition of an agent: 'An agent is a computer system that is *situated* in some *environment*, and that is capable of *autonomous action* in this environment in order to meet its design objectives.' (emphasis theirs) [WJ95b].

## 4.1 Introduction

Modeling, at this level, we can create a detailed and seamless model of the interactions between an agent and its environment.

**Design.** For structuring the design of multi-agent systems, we propose CURCUMA, the *Culture and Community-based Modeling Approach*. A central contribution of this approach is the ability to describe the concrete aspects of a multi-agent system, i.e. sensing and acting in physical and virtual environments, and its conceptual aspects, i.e. communication, coordination and social structure, within a single coherent conceptual framework. By grounding all concepts in the observable behavior of agents, we can consistently apply our specification techniques to all aspects of the system and provide a unified model for analysis and verification.

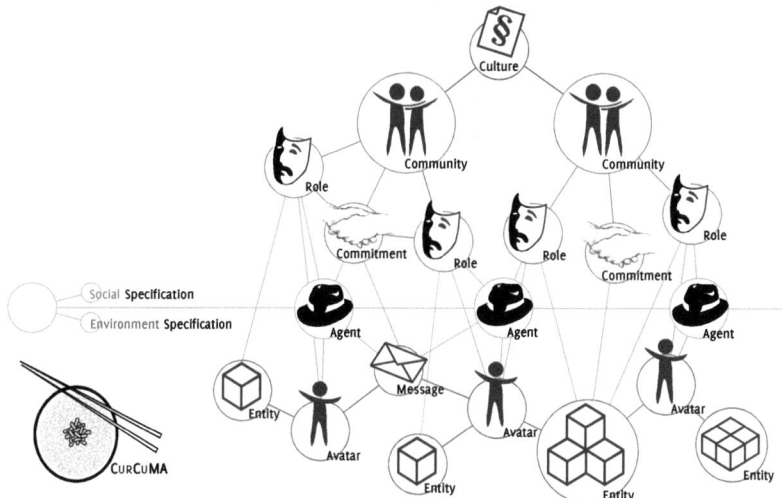

Figure 4.1.1: Overview of central CURCUMA concepts

We distinguish between the environment specification and the social specification. The former defines an essentially object-oriented model of the entities with which the agents can interact through sensors and effectors and the services that the environment provides to agents. The latter is a set of models defining social structures and coordination mechanisms. The different concerns are handled through a separation into agent communities, whose behavior is governed by cultures, high-level patterns encoding permitted or required behavior.

By introducing the concept of legal stance, which enables reasoning about an agent's intentions based on shared conventions for the interpretation of observed behavior, we ensure that social rules are both realizable and enforceable. This grounded approach allows the seamless integration of otherwise abstract concepts such as objectives or commitments into the concrete, object-oriented model of the system.

**Chapter outline.** In the following subsection, we further develop our running example and introduce additional requirements.

In Section 4.2, we present the elements of our conceptual model, extending our previous work on the analysis and design of multi-agent systems (cf. [KG05, KG06a, KG06b]).

In order to make them amenable to formal analysis, we provide a rigorous formalization of all employed concepts in Section 4.3. Employing our proposed constraint notations allows the formalization to go significantly beyond a previously published version (cf. [GK07]), which was limited by its reliance on plain Story Patterns.

Section 4.4 concludes the chapter with an overview of related work and a discussion.

### 4.1.1 Application Example

In this chapter, we extend and refine our running example in two directions. Firstly, we organize the previously discussed coordination behaviors that are responsible for ensuring the *safety* of the system, i.e. the registration and convoy patterns, into a coherent model which will allow us to define and verify important safety properties. In particular, this requires a complete set of rules controlling their instantiation.

Secondly, we consider an additional aspect of the system that is more closely related to its primary purpose. The shuttles are meant to provide on-demand, point-to-point transportation for passengers and cargo. In order to achieve this, we need mechanisms for distributing tasks among shuttles, controlling access to scarce resources like terminals, and optimizing the large scale logistics. We also need rules that control the orderly execution and completion of tasks and a scheme for compensating the carriers. We have documented a selection of these problems, which has been used as a case study in various contexts, in [GK05].

A guiding principle of the design philosophy that we apply to the application example is the reliance on decentralized structures and distributed control. Another recurrent theme is the use of market mechanisms for the allocation of resources. Combining these principles, we introduce dedicated agents for controlling scarce resources that auction off their services to the interested shuttle agents. Following the laws of supply and demand, the price for using a specific resource will then be dependent on its utilization, which may make it rational to avoid certain spots even if this requires taking a detour or foregoing an attractive task. Shuttles that already have accepted one task headed for a popular terminal will be able to offer more competitive prices for other tasks with the same destination than other shuttles due to the resulting synergies, which favors the bundling of related tasks and has the desired effect of reducing the saturation of the terminal.

Resource agents and shuttle agents enter into a binding contract concerning the use of a resource. If a shuttle agent fails to use a resource within the agreed time frame, a penalty that progresses with the size of the deviation becomes due. Beyond a certain window, the shuttle is no longer entitled to using the resource at all. Conversely, the resource agent has to pay a very steep penalty to its client if it fails to deliver on its promise in order to discourage overbooking.

Transportation tasks are assigned in a similar manner. Figure 4.1.2 illustrates how passengers

## 4.1 Introduction

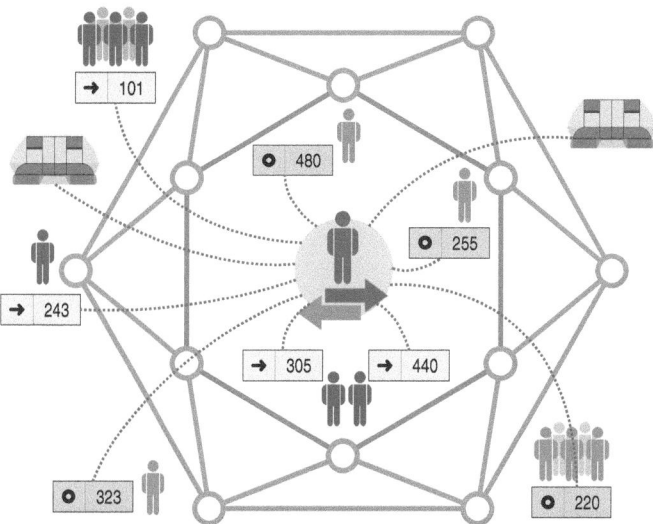

Figure 4.1.2: Broker agent matching up requests and shuttles

can indicate when and where they would like to depart (black icons/labels) and arrive (blue icons/labels) to a broker agent, which will then relay this information to the available shuttles. The shuttles may then decide to bid on certain tasks or bundles of tasks. The broker matches the bids with the requests and assigns tasks to the winning bidders, forming a binding contract.

There are broker agents, as opposed to only resource agents for each task, in order to enable more sophisticated auctioning strategies involving task bundles. There also needs to be some sort of directory that allows shuttle agents to browse through the open tasks. However, there may be multiple local broker agents, each of which is responsible for assigning the tasks under its responsibility. A task will nonetheless be listed by all brokers whose area is touched by the prospective route(s) in order to avoid the overhead that would result if every shuttle had to query every broker individually.

In the following sections, we focus on the problem of strategically coordinating the movement of the shuttles in a way that promotes the creation of energy-efficient convoys. This new concern is separate from, but not completely independent of the safety-related parts of the system, as both affect the shuttles' movements. Again, we apply a similar concept that does without a central coordinator.

The formation of convoys is of central importance for the economics of the shuttle concept and cannot be left to chance. In a typical sparsely populated system where shuttles travel with similar velocities, it is even quite unlikely that two shuttles will ever meet outside of a terminal. A viable solution for the logistics problem therefore needs two ingredients: An incentive that provides a motivation for forming convoys, and an infrastructure that enables shuttles to actually do so.

The former is provided by another system of monetary exchange where shuttles are paid for socially desirable behavior. Contrary to intuition, it is not necessarily the leading shuttle that needs to expend the most energy in a convoy due to the complexity of the involved air flows and the idiosyncrasies of the shuttles' linear motor and energy supply, which needs to be factored into the formula for computing the transfer payments. There are also other aspects that need to be considered, e.g. whether the shuttle with the tightest deadline might not choose to pay the preceding shuttles in the convoy to speed up. The resulting requirements are bundled and handled by the convoy arbitration culture.

The latter is provided by the positioning culture, which forces shuttles to publish their projected routes in order to give other shuttles the chance to plan their routes based on this information. This is accomplished in a decentralized manner by means of virtual markers with the estimated arrival time (or time interval) that are placed at the respective track segments.

In Figure 4.1.3, we see two situations: At time $t = 848$, shuttle 1 is traveling slowly and will pass the intersection well behind the other shuttles. Shuttle 2 has come from the same direction as shuttle 1, but has made a left turn at the intersection. Shuttle 3, arriving on the other branch at high speed, will go straight across the intersection and catch up with shuttle 2 at time $t = 878$. The deadlines marked in green are in the past and have already been met successfully.

Shuttle 2 realizes that it will block shuttle 3 and has entered into negotiations to work out an agreement concerning the speed of the future convoy, as proscribed by the convoy arbitration culture. At time $t = 850$, shuttle 2 has updated its plan (marked in yellow) by accelerating slightly, which will allow it to match shuttle 3's current speed by the time the two join up.

Again, shuttles are penalized for deviating from their announced plans, depending on the size of the deviation and how much advance notice they provide. On the other hand, the above example already shows that a certain amount of flexibility is indispensable for achieving the desired effects. The culture therefore needs to strike a balance between the reliability of predictions and the overall efficiency of the system.

## 4.1 Introduction

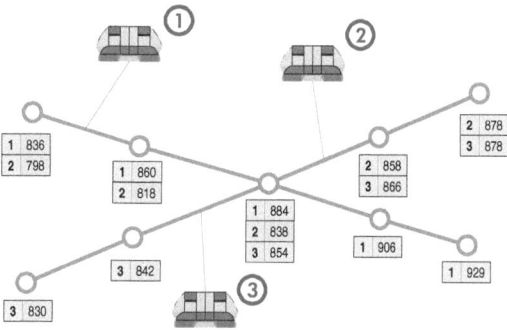

a. Situation at time $t = 848$

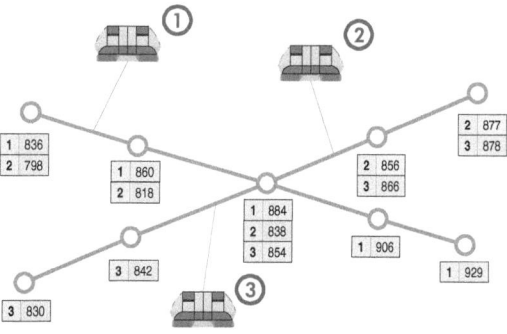

b. Situation at time $t = 850$

Figure 4.1.3: Shuttles marking their projected routes with estimated arrival times.

## 4.2 Conceptual Framework

In this section, we present the principles that shape CURCUMA, the conceptual framework we use for designing agent coordination, along with informal descriptions of its elements. We also provide an overview of the associated design process.

### 4.2.1 Approach

Our modeling approach mixes established concepts from agent research with model-driven and pattern-based software engineering techniques. The result is a conceptual framework that, on the one hand, is intentionally sufficiently generic so that many existing approaches could be mapped to it. On the other hand, it has quite specific semantics and design principles. Where conceptual differences warrant it, we therefore consider it justified to define proprietary terminology in order to avoid confusion with similar but distinct existing concepts.

**Concept.** The notion of agents interacting with an environment through sensors and effectors is fundamental to our approach. However, this should not be interpreted as a limitation to mechanical systems, but rather as a design philosophy: Environments may be simulated or purely digital, and sensors and effectors may be function calls. Nonetheless, it is this attention to the system around an agent that makes the approach relevant to software-intensive systems and allows us to apply software-engineering techniques to social system specifications.

There is consequently a clear distinction between concrete entities that agents can perceive and manipulate directly and conceptual entities that only exist virtually. Conceptual entities have to be explicitly derived from concrete entities by means of conventions. The concrete part of the model is predominantly descriptive in nature. Of course, design decisions do have a profound impact on the model, as the choice of sensors and effectors provided to the agents constrains what can be expressed. However, agents in the implemented system can immediately interact with concrete entities, even in heterogeneous open systems. The conceptual part of the model, on the other hand, is engineered deliberately, with the system's design objectives in mind. The way that conceptual entities are grounded in the concrete entities is *not* immediately visible to the agents. In order to allow an agent to interact with the system, this knowledge needs to be made explicitly available to the agents or implied in their implementation. This problem is also touched on by [WPM+04], who distinguish between *natural* and *arbitrary* protocols and observe that the more natural protocols are, the easier ensuring interoperability becomes.

**Structure.** Based on this distinction, the conceptual framework is divided into two parts that are layered on top of each other.

The environment specification defines the (physical or virtual) environment, containing agents that use sensors and effectors to interact with the entities surrounding them. Services describe the infrastructure that the environment provides to the agents. The level of abstraction of the specification is chosen according to the requirements of the envisioned coordination design. Besides, services can be employed to perform further discretization and abstraction steps on top of the basic model.

## 4.2 Conceptual Framework

The design of the coordination mechanisms is contained in the social specifications: The culture specification defines cultures, generic organization and interaction patterns employing such social system concepts as roles and intentions. They abstract from the domain of a concrete environment by means of template types. By mapping the template types of a culture to the elements of an environment in a community specification, we obtain a concrete community type.

The organization and coordination in the system is managed by instances of such community types. Communities are dynamically formed groups of agents. They frequently overlap, i.e. an agent can be a member of several communities simultaneously. Agents in the same community are able to interact in meaningful ways because they share the same rules governing valid role behavior and the same conventions for deriving a socially agreed interpretation of an action or message. The ability to attribute intentions to agents based on observable behavior is essential for reasoning about the agents' behavior while abstracting from their implementation.

**Process.** In the requirements engineering phase, we decompose complex systems into simpler architectural views by assigning requirements to dedicated communities. The complete system specification is therefore the composition of all relevant communities.

In the end, concrete agent designs that implement the system specification have to be derived. Role behavior can be refined and may allow non-deterministic choice; but ultimately, the agent needs to stay within the boundaries set by the culture specification. We believe that even though a top down approach to agent design is necessary in order to obtain predictable and verifiable results, it is nonetheless possible to design systems supporting flexible ad-hoc interaction, adaptation and emergent behavior in this way.

**At a glance.** Figure 4.2.1 gives a rough impression of the development process and positions the most important concepts.

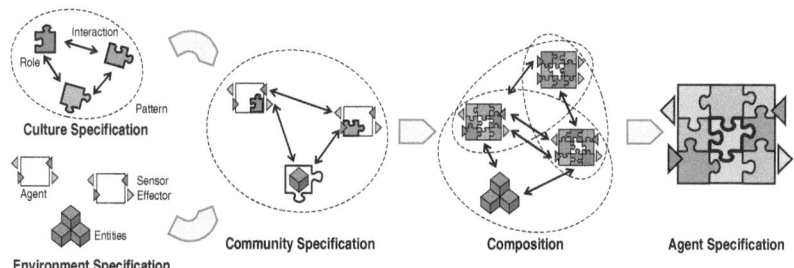

Figure 4.2.1: Overview of the approach

In our case study, the environment specification defines passive entities such as railroad tracks and active agent entities such as shuttles and base stations. As the case study focuses on agent coordination, it is sufficient to use a rough approximation of the system's actual physics, abstracting from the exact shapes and differential equations. Shuttles and base stations possess effectors and sensors, e.g. radio transmitters that allow them to send and receive messages. In order to simplify the agent designs, we define services for handling the details of transmissions or calculating shuttle positions.

The culture specification captures and structures the requirements of the system, such as safety, timeliness, or efficiency. Each culture defines roles, e.g. client and server, and requires certain interactions, e.g. that clients have to publish their position on the available servers, that are sufficient to ensure the assigned subset of these requirements.

In the community specification, agents and roles are matched up, in this case by designating the shuttles as the clients and the base stations as the servers.

The agent specifications are then derived from the composition of the community specifications representing different concerns such as positioning, convoy coordination, or task assignment. As these concerns may be non-orthogonal, it is necessary to carefully reconcile the imposed constraints within each agent. For example, a shuttle needs to strike a balance between timeliness and safety, as these goals call for quite contrary strategies.

The final product of this process is a set of agent controller specifications which, when implemented and run together, will interact in such a way as to fulfill all of the stated requirements. As the resulting system operates in a highly decentralized manner, without a central location of control, the underlying culture and community specifications are only implicitly relevant at runtime.

## 4.2.2 Environment Specification

In the environment specification, we want to describe all concrete entities, environment processes, and infrastructure services as they are relevant to the agents.

**Entity specification.** However, we try to model the entities as 'objectively' as possible, i.e. as they are, not as the different agents perceive them. Concrete entities can be physical – these entities need to be simulated while prototyping and are later provided by the physical environment – or digital – which means they need to be implemented in software both in the prototypes and the production system.

Each agent is itself an entity that interacts with other entities through its sensors and effectors. A passive entity, i.e. one that is not an agent, is called an item.

Both sensors and effectors can only be applied to a specific context, i.e. the subset of all entities that is, e.g., of the right type and physically close enough to the agent.

A sensor transforms concrete entities into perceptions. When generating perceptions, the sensor usually only retains a subset of an entity's attributes, may transform and aggregate them, may introduce random errors with a specific probability distribution, or may even fail to produce a perception with a given failure probability.

An effector creates, manipulates, or destroys entities, their attributes and associations. Unlike typical AI-centric agent specifications that provide an agent with a set of named actions or performatives, the semantics of the effector actions we specify are fully transparent both for the agent and any formal method we would like to employ at the agent level; i.e. we can seamlessly integrate

## 4.2 Conceptual Framework

the environment into our analysis of an agent's behavior. When using story-driven techniques for the effector specifications, we are capable of specifying any conceivable state transition of the specified environment and thus the effects of any effector, no matter how complex.

**Process specification.** It is a common practice to require all activity and change in the system to be attributable to some agent, in particular in many formal approaches. For applications that are situated in a complex environment, this solution is not viable and leads to both methodological and conceptual problems. We therefore introduce environment processes as a way of capturing behavior that is not attributable to an agent. They describe laws of nature (e.g. gravity), the behavior of simple machines (e.g. a conveyor belt) or components, and non-deterministic external influences on the system (e.g. an entity arriving in the environment). They are useful both for simulating the system and reasoning about its expected behavior at the agent level. Processes can be specified using the same story-driven techniques as for effectors.

Obviously, the specified effects need to stay within the limits of what is reasonable and physically possible in order to obtain a valid model. Generally, the validity of any results obtained by means of simulation and formal verification of the model largely depends on the quality of the environment specification, i.e., whether it is a correct and appropriate representation of the production system. This is less of a problem for digital entities, as – due to the reliance on proven object oriented formalisms – they can be represented by their actual design. It is somewhat more problematic for physical entities, where we can only strive to provide as good an approximation as possible. As software engineering techniques are designed for use with discrete models, our approach is better suited to describing structural modifications than continuous changes. Difference equations can provide an approximation of continuous processes that is sufficient for most purposes because of the agents' layered architecture that separates direct control functions from higher-level functions. If an in-depth treatment of the mechanical engineering aspects of the system is essential, it is possible to additionally apply techniques for the design of hybrid systems [Bur06].

**Service specification.** As we have already suggested with the introduction of environment processes, entities are not limited to being inert, monolithic objects, even if entities in the environment specification are limited to rather simple behavior. In principle, entities may be complex and have extensive internal machinery that performs complex actions. The essential distinction is that item entities are never autonomous and do not possess internal motivation, i.e. they are passive unless activated by an agent or an environment process.

The service specification basically describes the infrastructure used by the agents. This infrastructure is implemented as a set of services that may be provided through dedicated entities called facilities. Services can fall into various classes, e.g. life cycle management, resource allocation, scheduling, communication, directory services, persistence, access control, authentication, or application-specific functions. They can reach a high level of sophistication, e.g. a distributed blackboard with consistency management.

Services represent functionality that is traditionally associated with middleware. Indeed, services will often be implemented using some type of middleware. We can differentiate between production middleware that will be present in the final system, providing lookup, messaging and other higher level functions, and prototyping middleware that is concerned with emulating the production environment, providing services that will later be implicitly performed by the physical environment (e.g. computation of the available physical context) or the production hardware (e.g. scheduling of multiple agents). While the service model thus generally becomes less complex when moving to the production environment, there are also services that perform tasks that are trivial in a simulation but complex in a physical environment. This is especially true of services whose purpose is to provide agents with a virtual discretized representation of the environment, i.e. make it appear more like a simulation, such as the virtual spaces used in [WSHL05].

As services are specified in terms of entities, we can apply the same object-oriented modeling techniques as for entity behavior and effectors. As services can be standardized to some degree, they offer obvious potential for reuse. Specifying the same services from scratch over and over again would be tedious and inefficient. Templates encoding recurring design patterns for reuse offer a solution to this problem. Such templates may range from simple patterns describing the functionality of a single facility to complex systems of connected facilities representing a whole agent platform, component framework or distributed computing library. This means that after a service description for a particular solution has been modeled once, it can be reused, adapted and combined with other building blocks in a modular manner.

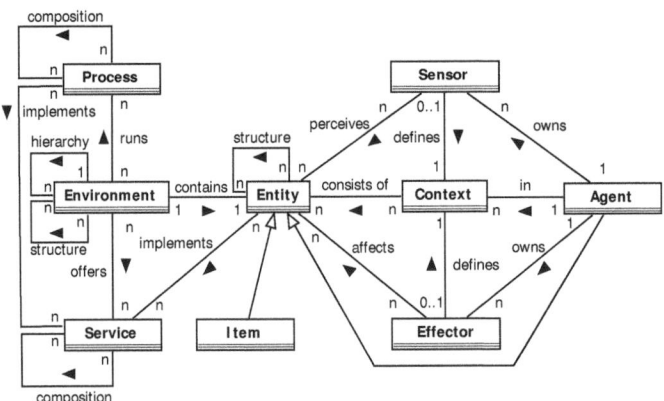

Figure 4.2.2: Key elements of the environment specification

Figure 4.2.2 provides an overview of the introduced elements and their relationships. The overall environment specification is a complete specification of the environment, encompassing type system, behavior, and constraints. If story-driven techniques are employed, this specification corresponds to a constrained graph transformation system. The type system is made up of instances of all classes of the metamodel, whereas only certain classes such as sensors, effectors, processes, and services contribute behavior and constraints.

## 4.2.3 Social Specification

What about agents, organizations, roles, and communication languages? Frequently, agent-oriented methodologies that closely build on object-oriented software engineering techniques are criticized for focusing on the technical aspects of multi-agent systems and neglecting advanced agent-oriented abstractions, thus providing poor support for the coordination of multi-agent systems and essentially limiting their scope to simple reactive agents. We, however, believe that such abstractions can in fact be supported based on an object-oriented design.

Mentalistic concepts have proven useful for reasoning about autonomous, cognitive agents. It is mainstream in agent-oriented research to assume that agents have intentional stance, assigning beliefs, goals and intentions to them [RG95]. Despite its unquestionable appeal, formalisms based on intentional stance face some well-documented problems, notably when used in the context of agent communication and communication languages. Such formalisms often assume a specific implementation of the agents' internals, which severely limits their applicability to real-world scenarios. As the semantics of messages depend on the state of an agent's mind, they may not be decidable from an outside perspective (cf. [Sin98a]). Besides, the resulting specifications are notoriously complex, and proving the conformance of an implementation may be impossible (cf. [Woo98]). One solution that was proposed to solve these problem is to model agents as *observable sources* that expose a well-defined part of their internals in order to allow other agents to reason about their beliefs and intentions (cf. [VO02]).

**Legal Stance.** We propose using the environment to a similar effect, thus providing a generic mechanism that is completely independent of the agents' implementations. Instead of reasoning about what an agent actually intends or believes, we base our specifications on what an external observer, or more specifically other agents in the system, can know or reasonably assume the other agent to believe or intend. It is inspired by the way human interaction, or more specifically human laws, work. Courts frequently infer beliefs and intentions from situations, acts, and speech. Legal codes (in the continental tradition) devote significant effort to fixing the exact modalities of how and when a person can profess an intention. In criminal codes, intent is a defining characteristic of various crimes, and the punishment of attempted crimes hinges on establishing the intention (e.g., an unauthorized person breaking into and hot-wiring a car could clearly be supposed to intend to steal it). In civil law, what a person should have known (e.g. caveat emptor) and seems to have intended based on the given evidence is a common question. We therefore call this view that is concerned with the professed intentions (and professed beliefs) that can be deduced from the environment legal stance.

Conventions for interpreting the environment can be attached to any entity type. This specifically includes messages, allowing the specification of agent communication languages, the predominant kind of social convention in current multi-agent systems. The implied professed intentions can be used to reason about the system at a higher level of abstraction. Concepts such as assertions for professing beliefs, directives, permissions, and interdictions as a means of soliciting, allowing, and forbidding specific behavior, or commitments for making behavioral guarantees (cf. [Sin98b]) help to structure and guide agent behavior.

Just like laws, professed intentions are artificial constructs that are only valid in a specific social context. A group of agents needs to agree on a set of conventions before it can become useful for governing their interactions. In the context of such an agreement, however, professed intentions become as real as concrete entities and can be referred to in subsequent rules and constraints.

**Community specification.** The required social context is provided by communities, which are – possibly overlapping – groups of agents sharing the same conventions. Research into agent organizations has shown that social structure is essential for designing complex, heterogeneous systems (cf. [FG98]). While our ideas are conceptually close to established work on organizations, we chose the term *community* in order to avoid confusion because we felt that *organization* suggests a greater degree of institutionalization, persistence, and complexity than exhibited by many of the communities we have in mind, and, on the other hand, we did not want to try to change established concepts by making additions that are specific to our modeling approach to them.

The conventions used by a community are set down in the corresponding community type. The specification of a community type again encompasses the aspects type system, behavior, and constraints. Their description requires no more esoteric concepts than used in the specification of the environment above. When story-driven techniques are used, the employed objects and links are merely marked up with stereotypes in order to indicate their specific semantics. It is then possible to describe a community type as a graph transformation system which can be seamlessly integrated with the graph transformation system of the environment specification to yield a comprehensive specification of the system's physical and social behavior.

The specific type system of a community type consists of its roles and professed intentions. Its behavior is controlled by a set of rules, which are organized according to their scope as different types of norms. Invariants are used to express additional constraints. Both norms and invariants are expressed in terms of observable physical and social entities.

In detail, a community type defines the following:

- a set of roles that can be assumed by agents,
- a set of professed intentions that can be attributed to agents,
- a set of existential norms, which create social structures by instantiating community instances (instantiation norm) and control how agents join and leave the community or assume and relinquish roles (affiliation norm),
- a set of social norms, which govern the interactions inside communities by defining social conventions for generating professed intentions from observations (conventional norm) and specifying allowed or required behavior (behavioral norm),
- a set of invariants that document properties that are guaranteed to hold for the community at all times, and
- a set of community types that can be used to form subcommunities contained in the community.

Community types can specify complex organizations, but may as well describe the ad-hoc interaction between a pair of agents. In general, a community type deals with a particular problem, which usually grows in complexity in proportion to the community type's position in the hierarchy.

## 4.2 Conceptual Framework

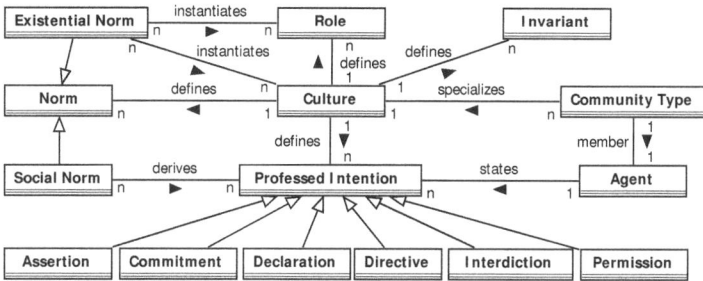

Figure 4.2.3: Key elements of the social specification

Figure 4.2.3 provides a summary of the discussed main elements of a community specification, but also introduces a new concept: a culture.

**Culture specification.** As there may be commonly recurring subproblems (e.g., collision avoidance, job assignment, coordinating distributed problem solving), we propose the use of templates or design patterns. We call these patterns cultures. Cultures extract the essence of a community type by abstracting from the concrete environment. This is done by replacing the concrete agent and entity types used in norms (e.g. 'motorist', 'car salesman', 'car') with more generic agent ('buyer', 'seller') and item ('merchandise') template types. The culture otherwise has exactly the same elements as a community type, i.e. roles, professed intentions, norms, invariants, and subtypes, which are called subcultures.

The culture can then be reused in future systems, deriving new community types from it simply by assigning appropriate concrete types or sets of types from the system's environment specification to its abstract template types. The new community types are said to *specialize* the culture.

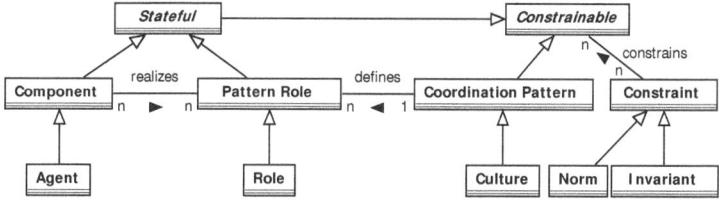

Figure 4.2.4: Relating cultures to coordination patterns

Cultures can be interpreted as an extension of *Coordination Patterns* as introduced in Section 2.3. Figure 4.2.4 relates concepts from both, showing how agents, roles, and norms can be seen as extensions of components, pattern roles, and constraints.

Among other advantages, this allows us to build on or even directly reuse the results concerning the verification of *Coordination Patterns* (cf. [GTB+03]) and apply similar compositional techniques to the verification of cultures. In practice, this means that once it has been proven by formal verification that a culture satisfies a given set of requirements and correctly solves a problem, all correctly derived community types inherit these properties.

When describing community and culture specifications, we primarily use a story-driven approach and the associated notations. However, it is possible to refer to the elements of a *Coordination Pattern* in norms based on the mapping presented in Section 2.3.3. It is also possible to directly reuse existing *Coordination Patterns* as subcultures.

**Agent specification.** Even though community types impose requirements and limitations on the capabilities and behavior of agents, they do not restrict the specifics of the implementation of agents in any way, making the approach agnostic with respect to their internal architecture. As the specification is only concerned with observable behavior, correctly implementing it comes down to behaving correctly in the environment.

The legal stance is not to be confused with a purely behavioral perspective: achieving correct behavior may require a limited theory of mind, i.e. keeping track of other agents' intentions as professed in accordance with the pertinent conventions, as the correct reaction may depend on the (social) state of the interacting agents. Nonetheless, as all mentalistic notions are only attributed to agents in the context of a community, there is no requirement that these correspond to an agent's internal model (or current state) in any way. It is generally easier to use an internal model that is roughly compatible with the socially attributed model, even more so if the requirements imposed by the specification are intricate so that finding an equivalent alternative representation may be non-trivial.

## 4.3 Formal model

We now formalize the presented conceptual framework of CURCUMA and show how it can be used for the specification of coordination behavior. We also discuss how the presented specification languages and notations can be applied to its various elements.

While we use numerous specific concepts that allow writing expressive, high-level specifications, all elements of the model are described using story-driven techniques that ultimately map down to plain graphs or graph rules. The fact that the specification can be reduced to a GTS allows us to apply generic analysis and verification techniques.

### 4.3.1 Environment Specification

**Entities.** On the level of the environment, the entity specification specifies the types of observable entities that make up the environment. Entities can either be passive items or the physical manifestation of agents. Agents may have a set of sensors and effectors that they can use to interact with their environment, i.e. manipulate entities or communicate with other agents.

## 4.3 Formal model

**Definition 4.3.1** *An* entity specification $O$ *consist of a type system graph* $\mathcal{T}_O$. *The types of the type system graph can be classified into disjoint subsets so that* $N_{\mathcal{T}_O} = A_O \cup S_O \cup E_O \cup I_O$ *with agent types* $A_O$, *sensor types* $S_O$, *effector types* $E_O$, *and item types* $I_O$. *The entity types* $N_O$ *are* $A_O \cup I_O$.

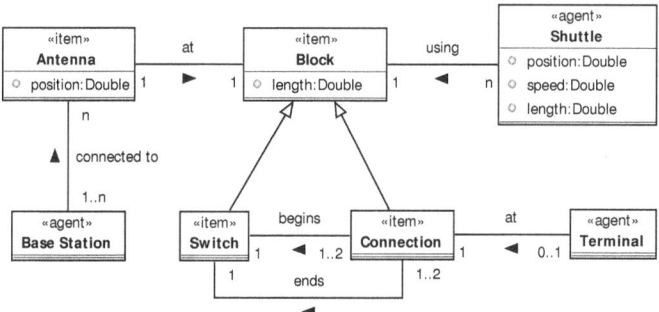

Figure 4.3.1: Entities of the application example

The entity model provides the basic ontology of the system. As discussed in previous chapters, it can be modeled using Class Diagrams. Figure 4.3.1 presents a basic entity model for the application example: The track network is modeled as a graph consisting of switches connected by connections. There are also terminals for unloading passengers and cargo, and antennas that are placed alongside the tracks in order to provide wireless communication with the base stations. Finally, there are the shuttles, with an exact relative position on the block they are currently using. Obviously, this model is not particularly detailed, e.g. presenting shuttles as monolithic entities, but it is accurate and sufficient for our purposes. In comparison with the model used in the previous chapters, we have eliminated the patterns, which are virtual, and the track segments, which are logical, not physical units.

**Sensors and effectors.** A sensor or effector specification specifies which types can be part of a sensor's perceptive or an effector's operative context, i.e. which entity types it can perceive or act on. A set of rules describes the effects of using an effector or which entities and attributes can be perceived, optionally indicating details like delay, precision and accuracy. Additionally, constraints on the simultaneous application of these rules are imposed.

**Definition 4.3.2** *A sensor specification* $S$ *is a tuple* $(s_S, a_S, \mathcal{T}_S, \mathcal{R}_S, \mathbb{R}_S)$ *where* $s_S \in S_O$ *is a sensor type,* $a_S \in A_O$ *an agent type,* $\mathcal{T}_S$ *a type system graph,* $\mathcal{R}_S$ *a set of rules determining effects containing exactly one sensor node of type* $s_S$, *and* $\mathbb{R}_S$ *a set of multi-sets over* $\mathcal{R}_S$ *denoting how many instances of the rules are applicable in parallel.*

**Definition 4.3.3** *An effector specification $E$ is a tuple $(e_E, a_E, T_E, \mathcal{R}_E, \mathcal{IR}_E)$ where $e_E \in E_O$ is an effector type, $a_E \in A_O$ an agent type, $T_E$ a type system graph, $\mathcal{R}_E$ a set of rules determining effects containing exactly one effector node of type $e_E$, and $\mathcal{IR}_E$ a set of multi-sets over $\mathcal{R}_E$ denoting how many instances of the rules are applicable in parallel.*

For specifying effector and sensor rules, we have multiple options. Most sensors and many effectors can be specified using a single eSP/SDD, which facilitates translation into a plain GTS for subsequent analysis. If effectors perform more complex operations that consist of more than one transformation, we can use Story Diagrams, which may make model checking more complicated, but nonetheless allow the direct generation of prototypes. Finally, if timing is relevant for the operation, the behavior of an effector may by constrained by a TSSD. Executing a prototype then requires first deriving a concrete realization of this specification.

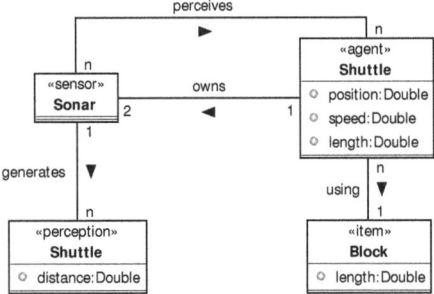

Figure 4.3.2: Sensor-specific type system

The specific type system graph contains the sensor, the agent, the relevant entities, and types representing the perceptions that can be generated by the sensor. In the example, shuttles have a short range sensor that allows them to measure the distance to the preceding shuttle. In Figure 4.3.2, we present the corresponding type system. The perceived shuttle – the class is defined in a dedicated internal package and thus distinct from the shuttle entity – only has a distance attribute, indicating that the original attributes speed, length, and position are not available to the perceiving agent (at least not directly, in the last case).

In Figure 4.3.3, we specify how the sensor generates a perception. We would need additional rules (or use an SDD) in order to support the case where the shuttles are on adjacent blocks, e.g. when one of the shuttles is passing a switch.

For effectors, there is typically no need to introduce additional classes (such as perceptions). In the example, we are mostly interested in the shuttles' linear motor, which allows them to accelerate and decelerate (see Figure 4.3.4). As the ability to compose and break up convoys on-the-fly requires a new system of passive switches where the vehicles can actively control onto which branch they want to proceed, the shuttles also have an effector for determining which connection they will be

## 4.3 Formal model

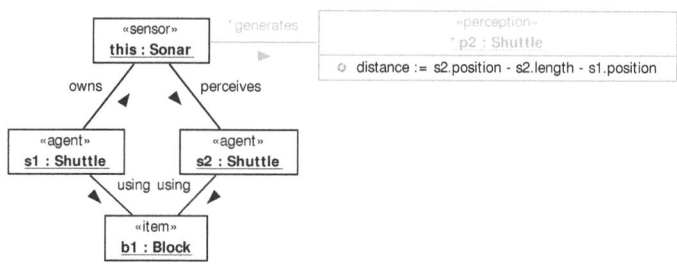

Figure 4.3.3: Sensor for measuring the distance to a preceding shuttle

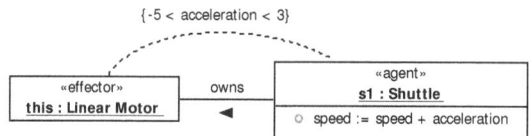

Figure 4.3.4: Specifying the effects of the linear motor

using next. Finally, shuttles have an effector for wirelessly transmitting information to antennas that are sufficiently close.

As there may be multiple rules for the same sensor and effector, there are restrictions on which ones may be applied in parallel. While the sonar can perceive any number of shuttles in various positions in parallel, the linear motor can only be applied once and either accelerate or decelerate at any one time.

**Processes.** The process specification describes changes in environment that are not caused by agents, e.g. by laws of nature or external influences. The model consists of a set of processes, but additionally allows specifying invariants of the environment.

Processes can be used to describe laws of nature, mechanical reactive behavior (which is merely a more complex form of applying the laws of nature), or non-deterministic changes in the system. In their effects, they are thus similar to effectors, meaning that they can be specified using a set of eSP/SDDs, Story Diagrams or TSSDs.

Unlike effectors, which are applied deliberately, processes run continuously, i.e. the rules are applied in every time step as the system is only quasi-continuous. This is particularly true of processes representing laws of nature. While process rules are always evaluated, they may contain activation conditions so that certain effects are only produced if the corresponding trigger is matched.

Processes that describe external influences on the environment are special because they are supposed to be inherently non-deterministic, at least to some degree. They can either be specified by means of eSP/SDDs or Story Diagrams that are applied at random or, if more specific information about the frequency of the external process is available, TSSDs that encode the expected intervals between occurrences.

The process model may impose certain structural and behavioral constraints on the environment and limit its possible states. In physical environments, these may be implied by the laws of nature, but they may also represent fundamental restrictions of a virtual environment (e.g. only a single active thread per processor core). These restrictions are encoded by invariants that are guaranteed to hold at all times.

**Definition 4.3.4** *A process specification $P$ is a tuple $(\mathcal{T}_P, \mathcal{R}_P^E, \Phi_P)$ where $\mathcal{T}_P$ is a type system graph, $\mathcal{R}_P$ a set of rules determining the effects of processes, and $\Phi_P$ a set of constraints representing invariants of the environment.*

In the example, shuttles are moved by a process (simulating inertia) in accordance with their current speed. This is more realistic than providing shuttles with an effector for explicitly moving the shuttle and also provides a more convincing model for explaining why two shuttles might collide.

External processes are very useful for abstracting from parts of the system. For example, we could define a process that is spawning transportation tasks at random terminals based on some statistical model if we were only interested in the way the shuttles deal with a certain task distribution, not the tasks themselves.[2]

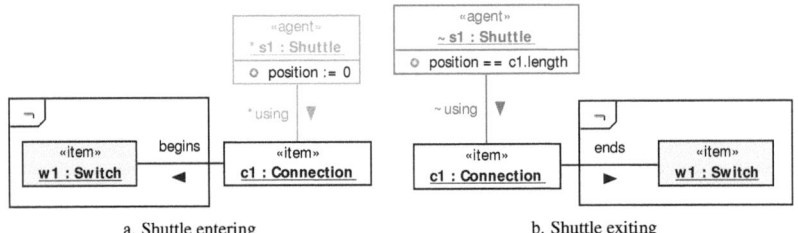

a. Shuttle entering          b. Shuttle exiting

Figure 4.3.5: Modeling a part of the network as an open system

This is not merely useful for hiding aspects of the system entirely, but also for restricting the size of the system we have to analyze. Instead of considering the whole track network at once, we could focus on a limited section which we treat as an open system that shuttles can enter (see Figure 4.3.5a) and leave (see Figure 4.3.5b). As we shall discuss below for the purpose of verification, an advanced idea that is based on this technique would be to use a carefully controlled

---

[2]This was, in fact, used in a student project, where a central process generated tasks based on a combined exponential (controlling frequency) and multinomial (controlling endpoints) distribution.

## 4.3 Formal model

process which *moves* the considered section along with an agent, generating and destroying its relevant context as it moves through the environment.

Invariants of the environment include the fact that two shuttles can never be in the exact same position on a block and, by extension, that no shuttle can pass another shuttle on the same block. It is also a law of nature that a collision occurs whenever the positions of two shuttles are too physically close to each other.

**Services.** The service specification introduces additional entities and processes into the environment, but no fundamentally new concepts. Formally, each service specification is equivalent to an additional process specification and can be treated as such.

In the example, there are two primary production level services. The first one is a messaging service that provides communication protocols. Using the antenna infrastructure and the shuttles' effector for communicating with it as the physical link layer, it allows shuttles to send message entities to other shuttles or base stations asynchronously. The exact behavior of the communication channels, such as the introduced delays, the available buffer sizes, and the probability of failure are all modeled as rules using a class model that is based on the model we used for connections in Section 2.3.3.

Like all services, this service depends on the underlying facilities, i.e. the entities that implement it. Here, these are primarily the antennas and the shuttles (respectively their unspecified communications hardware). When either of these elements fail, the service (partially) fails as well, which is why the design should provide a certain amount of redundancy.

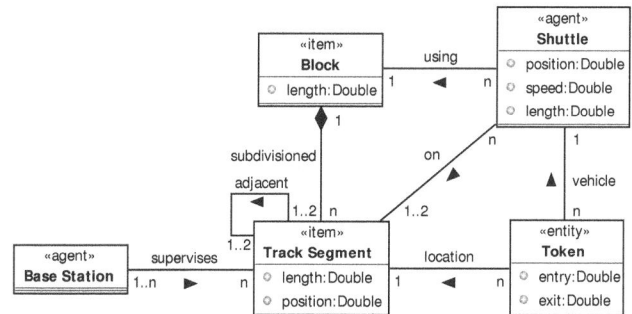

Figure 4.3.6: Location services provide track segments and tokens

Secondly, we define a discretization service that makes abstract reasoning about the shuttles' current and future positions easier and which is similar in function to the above-mentioned virtual environment from [WSHL05]. It provides the logical segmentation of track blocks into track segments (see Figure 4.3.6) that we used in previous chapters without explaining where the information encoded by the on links actually came from. The service does not only define a normative segmentation scheme that is identical for all agents, but also computes the on links from the shuttles' physical position on the respective block and makes this information available to the agents. Within the limits of a specified maximum delay that is required for updating the model, the service will ensure that the discrete model of the system is synchronized with and thus a reliable and accurate representation of the (physical) reality of the environment.

Additionally, the same service allows placing tokens at the (virtual) track segments, which document a shuttle's projected position at some (future) point in time. The service ensures that all shuttles can perceive the tokens and that the token model is kept consistent and up-to-date. For its implementation, the service relies on the messaging service as the means of sending updates to the shuttles. The base stations serve as the facilities managing the model. The service therefore (partially) fails if either of the required entities breaks down.

**Environment specifications** combine such partial specifications into a consistent overall specification. Completed by a set of instance graphs representing the initial state of the system, these specifications form a GTS that models the possible behavior of the physical environment. In the example, the initial state consists of a topology, i.e. the track and infrastructure layout, and the configuration and initial states of the agents, i.e. the shuttles. As the number of conceivable different topologies is infinite, we characterize the initial state set by means of a generating GTS instead. In the example, it contains rules for generating correct track layouts by appending switches and connections to existing ones, and rules concerning shuttle placement.

**Definition 4.3.5** *A environment specification $W$ is a tuple $(S_T, O, S, \mathcal{E}, \mathcal{P})$ with $S_T$ a GTS generating all valid initial states, $O$ an entity specification, $S$ a set of sensor specifications, $\mathcal{E}$ a set of effector specifications, and $\mathcal{P}$ a set of process specifications.*

For a given specification, we can then derive a GTS describing the behavior of the entire environment. In order to achieve the desired result, we need to use prioritized, constrained GTS (see Section 2.2.2.4). The prioritization of the rules is essential for achieving realistic behavior - otherwise, it would, for example, be possible to keep applying an effector ('move forward') an arbitrary number of times without also applying the effects of the relevant processes ('gravity'), yielding distorted results (unless the objective is to actually simulate the classic 'cartoon character walking off a cliff' behavior). To each of the defined rules, we therefore assign a priority, with processes preempting sensor and effector applications.

While priorities solve the theoretical problem, additional considerations are necessary to make the GTS, which does not have an inherent concept of time, conform to reality, which does. In practice, it is not only relevant which rule is applied next, but also when. In practice, the idea of a preempting rule can only reasonably be interpreted as meaning that this rule is activated first, implying immediately – as opposed to all agents consciously suspending all effector use and waiting for some enabled preempting rule to be actually applied. On the other hand, sensor and effector use is supposed to be deliberate, not compulsory: The agents are not only free to choose *which* effector they intend to use, but also *when* they intend to use it. Immediately applying one of the enabled rules does not properly reflect this freedom.

We therefore adopt the convention that negative priorities signal urgent rules which have to be applied immediately, while 0 marks a rule as discretionary or non-urgent. It is feasible to assign

### 4.3 Formal model

positive priorities to rules, but this may only be used as a means of indicating the precedence of different discretionary choices of the same agent – not preemption across entities! – and needs to be recognized as such by the employed tools and methods.

In the environment specification, we assign a priority of 0 to rules describing sensor and effector effects, and priorities from the highest priority group $V$, e.g. ranging from $-1024$ to $-768$, to the rules describing processes. This brings us back to a previous point: The rules defining the effects of continuous processes need to contain provisions that ensure that they are only applied once per discrete time step in order to preclude the equally undesired inverse effect that an enabled effector is infinitely preempted by a process.

When deriving the GTS, we can either consider the closed system behavior, which only includes processes and services, or the open system behavior, which includes the behavior of the agents as manifested in their sensor and effector applications, which is non-deterministic from the point of view of the environment.

Given an environment specification $W = (S_T, O, S, \mathcal{E}, \mathcal{P})$, the corresponding *open environment behavior* $M^{OW}$ (i.e. the behavior of the environment including agents) is specified by the constrained GTS $(\mathcal{T}_{OW}, \mathcal{G}^i_{OW}, \mathcal{R}_{OW}, \Phi_{OW})$ as follows:

- $\mathcal{T}_{OW} = \mathcal{T}_O \cup \bigcup_{S \in \mathcal{S}} \mathcal{T}_S \cup \bigcup_{E \in \mathcal{E}} \mathcal{T}_E \cup \bigcup_{P \in \mathcal{P}} \mathcal{T}_P$,
- $\mathcal{G}^i_{OW} = \mathsf{REACH}(S_T)$,
- $\mathcal{R}_{OW} = \bigcup_{S \in \mathcal{S}} \mathcal{R}_S \cup \bigcup_{E \in \mathcal{E}} \mathcal{R}_E \cup \bigcup_{P \in \mathcal{P}} \mathcal{R}_P$, and
- $\Phi_{OW} = \bigcup_{P \in \mathcal{P}} \Phi_P$.

Analogously, the corresponding *closed environment behavior* $M^{CW}$ (i.e. the behavior excluding agents) is defined by the constrained GTS $(\mathcal{T}_{CW}, \mathcal{G}^i_{CW}, \mathcal{R}_{CW}, \Phi_{CW})$ as follows:

- $\mathcal{T}_{CW} = \mathcal{T}_O \cup \bigcup_{S \in \mathcal{S}} \mathcal{T}_S \cup \bigcup_{E \in \mathcal{E}} \mathcal{T}_E \cup \bigcup_{P \in \mathcal{P}} \mathcal{T}_P$,
- $\mathcal{G}^i_{CW} = \mathsf{REACH}(S_T)$,
- $\mathcal{R}_{CW} = \bigcup_{P \in \mathcal{P}} \mathcal{R}_P$, and
- $\Phi_{CW} = \bigcup_{P \in \mathcal{P}} \Phi_P$.

In the example, the closed system is fairly static (unless shuttles are moving initially) as almost all activities in the system are triggered by agents. In the open system, shuttles will accelerate and move around, but will do so without purpose and cause many collisions. In order to achieve behavior that is both meaningful and safe, it will be necessary to add appropriate coordination mechanisms.

#### 4.3.2 Culture Specification

We begin our discussion of social level specifications with cultures as the more fundamental concept from which community types are derived.

**Culture.** Coordination mechanisms are encoded by reusable patterns that govern the interaction between agents and their environment and form a hierarchy of cultures. Each culture specifies a type system consisting of a set of template types, a set of roles, and a set of professed intentions, a set of norms, partitioned into existential norms and social norms, and a set of subcultures.

**Definition 4.3.6** *A culture $U$ is a tuple $(\mathcal{T}_U, \mathcal{N}_U^X, \mathcal{N}_U^S, \mathcal{C}_U)$ where $\mathcal{T}_U$ is a type system graph defining template types, roles and professed intentions, $\mathcal{N}_U^X$ a set of existential norms, $\mathcal{N}_U^S$ a set of social norms, $\Phi_U^S$ a set of invariants, and $\mathcal{C}_U$ a set of (sub)cultures.*

Any well-formed culture needs at least one template type and one existential norm, whereas roles, professed intentions, social norms and subcultures are optional. A culture that does not either define social norms or subcultures will have no effect on the system, though.

In the example, there is a variety of cultures: Starting from the positioning culture, via the traffic safety and the traffic routing culture, down to the update and distance coordination cultures, which encode only simple interaction patterns that correspond to the registration and convoy patterns from previous chapters.

**Type system.** A culture defines roles that help reasoning about an agent's status and responsibilities, and professed intentions, which allow reasoning about an agent's intentions from an external, social perspective. Besides these entities representing social system concepts, the culture's rules also need to refer to physical entities. To enable reuse in different environments, the culture abstracts from concrete entity types by means of template types, i.e. an abstract type system that is specific to the culture.

**Definition 4.3.7** *Given a culture $U$ with type system graph $\mathcal{T}_U$, $N_{\mathcal{T}_U} = T_U \cup R_U \cup P_U$ where $T_U$ is a set of template types (consisting of $T_U^A$, the set of agent template types, and $T_U^I$, the set of item template types), $R_U$ is a set of roles, and $P_U$ is a set of professed intentions, all of them disjoint.*

The type system for the positioning culture of the application example is displayed in Figure 4.3.7. When comparing this diagram with the location service model in Figure 4.3.6, there is a striking similarity between the subsets shuttle, base station, track segment, and token and vehicle, registry, location, and marker. As the latter are in fact the template types of the culture's type system, this similarity is intentional – it will later allow us to directly substitute the corresponding types.

Designing for reuse is a deliberate decision and requires additional thought and effort. As long as a culture is only used in one place in a single environment (as in our application example), there is no benefit to be gained from inventing a new, more abstract type system. It is perfectly acceptable to simply use the existing entity types such as shuttle at the culture level in this case. While this does not technically reduce the reusability of the culture, applying the pattern to a related domain, e.g. automobiles crossing an intersection, would become more difficult and less intuitive. Stripping unnecessary detail from the model also makes formal verification simpler and faster.

Apart from the template types and the culture itself, there are two roles and a professed intention (a commitment) in the example. There is a static and a dynamic aspect to a role: On the one hand, a

## 4.3 Formal model

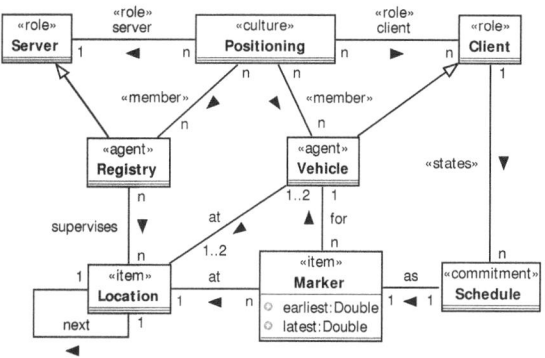

Figure 4.3.7: Type system of the positioning culture

role is like an interface that defines certain relationships, attributes, and possibly behaviors that an agent that wants to assume this role needs to support, which explains why the relationship between the agent and the role is modeled as a generalization. On the other hand, there is the dynamic aspect concerning the roles an agent currently has in a given community (in the context of some culture), which is represented by an association between the agent (respectively the role it implements) and the community.

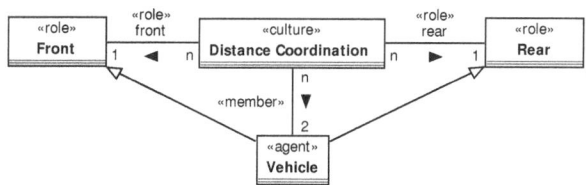

Figure 4.3.8: Type system of the distance coordination culture

The type system can be simple. Figure 4.3.8 shows the type system of the distance coordination culture, which is little more than a plain *Coordination Pattern*.

**Norms.** The norms and invariants of a culture are again encoded as graph rules. While invariants and many of the simpler norms can be encoded using eSP/SDDs, the modeling of social norms greatly benefits from the advanced capabilities that are provided by TSSDs.

**Existential norms** control the creation of social structures, i.e. community instantiation (instantiation norms) and community membership and role assignment (affiliation norms). The instantiation norms and affiliation norms of a culture need not be disjunct sets. Especially when a community is created dynamically in reaction to the interaction of two agents, separating these two aspects would be unnatural.

Instantiation norms define when and how a community should be instantiated. At the culture level, the culture class and its instances serve as a placeholder representing the community (type) – when a concrete community type is derived, these are replaced by the community type, along with the template types. As a culture is abstract, it is never actually instantiated at runtime.

Affiliation norms create and destroy associations between agents, communities, and roles. They allow agents to dynamically join and leave communities and, at the same time, assume and resign roles. As mentioned above, the ability to assume a role is a static property that depends on whether the agent implements the associated interfaces and protocols. Assuming a role is modeled by creating the appropriate link between the agent and the community. An agent may play the same role multiple times, also in different communities.

Different types of communities may have different life cycles. A community may be tied to a specific persistent entity, or may even be singleton that exists *a priori*. However, a community may also be short-lived and only exist while a specific entity configuration occurs.

In the application example, the positioning cultures are persistent, as they depend on the registries, which are in turn part of the static infrastructure. They are thus created only once, during initialization, as defined by the existential norm in Figure 4.3.9. In this context, SDD *ensure* nodes will be used frequently to ensure the correct cardinality. The distance coordination culture, on the other hand, is created in an ad-hoc fashion whenever two vehicles come close (as defined by the existential norm in Figure 4.3.10) and dissolved once they move apart. As in this case the community is characterized by the two participating agents and the roles they assume, it would not make sense to separate the instantiation and affiliation aspects of the norm.

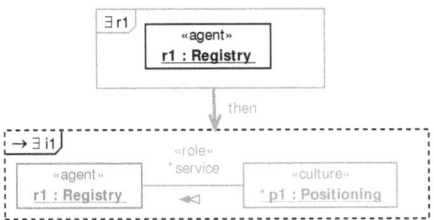

Figure 4.3.9: Instantiating an positioning culture

For roles, the situation is similar. Often, an agent assumes a role upon joining a community and never resigns it again until the agent leaves the community or the community is dissolved. While there is a ≪member≫ association between matching community and agent types in the type system, there is often no need to use it in norms, as it is immediately superseded by a more specific role (as in Figure 4.3.10). Only in the opposite case, when an agent joins a community and then successively assumes and resigns various roles, it may be better to explicitly create the membership link.

## 4.3 Formal model

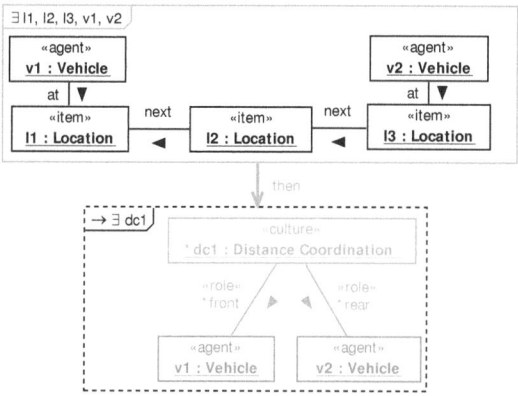

Figure 4.3.10: Instantiating a distance coordination culture

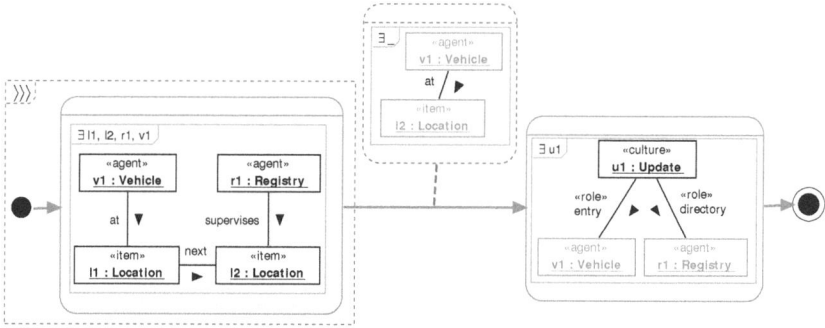

Figure 4.3.11: Joining an update culture

When using TSSDs, such as for the existential norm in Figure 4.3.11, we can not only describe what triggers the instantiation and how it is performed in more detail, but also describe the whole life cycle of a role or community in a single norm.

**Social norms** govern the interactions within the created social structures. For each role, they define acceptable behavior (behavioral norms) and socially agreed interpretations of behavior (conventional norms). Again, the two subtypes are not mutually exclusive: a behavioral norm may additionally contain conventions as it is often convenient to specify the physical and social consequences of an action together.

Conventional norms encode conventions defining how agents can affect the state of the social system, i.e. manipulate conceptual entities such as roles and professed intentions. Most importantly, they generate and revoke professed intentions, which represent socially agreed assumptions about an agent's intentions. By providing a normative interpretation of observable behavior, conventions allow agents using the same culture to react to each other's actions and messages (as any language is based on conventions) in an adequate way.

In order to allow more expressive conventions, we distinguish different types of professed intentions (based on the categorization of speech acts proposed in [Sin98a]), most importantly assertion, encoding a factual statement that was explicitly or implicitly made by an agent, commitment, a promise concerning future behavior, permission, directive and interdiction, allowing, ordering or disallowing a particular behavior, and declaration, a classic speech act of the 'I now declare...' kind.

These categories are only defined informally – every professed intention could be modeled as an assertion, which would however go against the original motivation for introducing the categories, namely providing a more differentiated view on agent interactions. The formal semantics of a professed intention depend only on the structure of the graph rules encoding the corresponding norms. A required permission becomes a precondition, while an interdiction inhibiting a certain behavior becomes a negative application condition. A directive may appear as a precondition, in particular in the trigger of a TSSD. A commitment may be similar in effect to the above (e.g. correspond to an interdiction an agent places on itself if it is a commitment to abstain from some action). However, the typical commitment promises to bring about a certain configuration in the future. Encoding this using structural patterns requires at least two conventional norms: One for creating the commitment (e.g. when an agent enters into a contract), a second one for removing it once the promise has been fulfilled (e.g. when the agent has paid). TSSDs are very helpful in this context, as they allow encoding the entire life cycle of a commitment in a single norm.

In the example in Figure 4.3.12, the vehicle commits to not occupying its current location indefinitely, but eventually moving on.

Formally, this meaning is only supplied by the second conventional norm in Figure 4.3.13, which removes the commitment after the vehicle has moved.

Behavioral norms restrict or require certain agent behavior. They primarily deal with modifications of template entities representing physical entities. However, they may be constrained by the state of the social system and, e.g., require the presence of a directive or the absence of a particular interdiction as part of their precondition.

When they are modeled using the structural notations, they only describe a single transformation step and proscribe which sensors or effectors an agent may or must use in a given situation. Typically, such a behavioral norm extends a single effector rule with additional (physical or social) pre- and postconditions. The communities, roles, and professed intentions that are created by existential respectively conventional norms in reaction to the defined behaviors are the only way of relating different behavioral norms to each other. When encoding a complex scenario in this manner, it is thus split up into a large number of norms, which has proved to be not very intuitive and may make maintaining consistency between the norms a daunting task. Nonetheless, the approach

## 4.3 Formal model

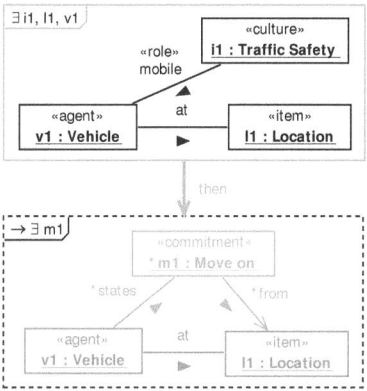

Figure 4.3.12: Making a commitment

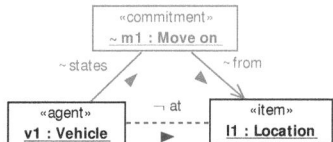

Figure 4.3.13: Fulfilling a commitment

has its merits, as it allows the direct application of existing formal verification techniques such as the discussed invariant checking approach, which relies on single step semantics.

From the point of view of both usability and expressiveness, however, behavioral norms are the domain of TSSDs, whose creation was initially motivated by this very use case. When using the temporal notation, the norms may encode a complex sequence of events and describe the interaction between multiple agents and the environment. They are also the only way of capturing time constraints without the aid of auxiliary constructs. As a TSSD is declarative, the norm can describe either a concrete sequence of effector applications or merely a broad requirement which needs to be implemented by the agents. While there need not be a direct mapping to effector applications, a norm is only implementable if its required effects can be brought about in the allowed time frame by a combination of the available effectors and environment processes.

In the application example, many parts of the system depend on the requirement that the vehicles declare which locations they will move to in the future. In the short term, this is used to avoid collisions and manage convoys. In the longer term, this is the basis for achieving efficient routing.

Vehicles publish their plans by means of markers which are attached to specific locations and specify an earliest entry and a latest exit time for the vehicle (In the concrete system, this is realized by the distributed token infrastructure that is provided by the location service). There is a conventional norm that interprets each marker as a commitment to a specific schedule (as defined by the type system in Figure 4.3.7).

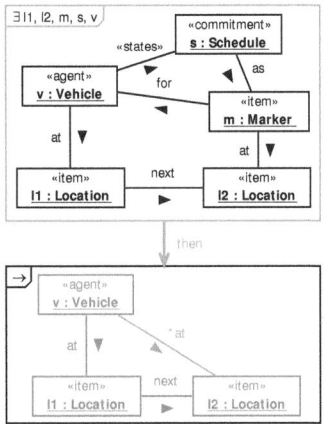

Figure 4.3.14: Only authorized movement is allowed

The most fundamental norm is that no unannounced movement is allowed (see Figure 4.3.14): There needs to be a marker that is currently valid for the vehicle in question.

Unless the vehicles have additional arrangements (such as a convoy of shuttles), there may only be one vehicle per location at the same time. There is therefore a norm that enforces that vehicles must not make conflicting announcements.

The norm in Figure 4.3.16 finally illustrates the life cycle of a schedule commitment, from its creation to its fulfillment.

In order to promote socially desirable behavior and yet allow a certain flexibility, there is a system of 'monetary' incentives in place that promotes timely, concise and reliable announcements. If a marker is placed early and the specified interval is small, the agent is rewarded, if the interval is large and the marker is placed on short notice, the agent is punished. If an agent updates the marker with more concise bounds, it is rewarded; if it moves or expands the interval, it is punished. However, an agent is punished even more severely if it fails to fulfill the commitment altogether and forfeits its reservation.

Invariants can be specified for specific roles or the whole culture. They are used for representing design goals of the culture, e.g. important safety properties that may never be violated. Invariants may be concerned with the state of the environment or the violation of professed intentions, e.g. an agent making conflicting commitments. In the example, we can guarantee that all vehicles are properly registered with a registry at all times based on the corresponding instantiation norms.

## 4.3 Formal model

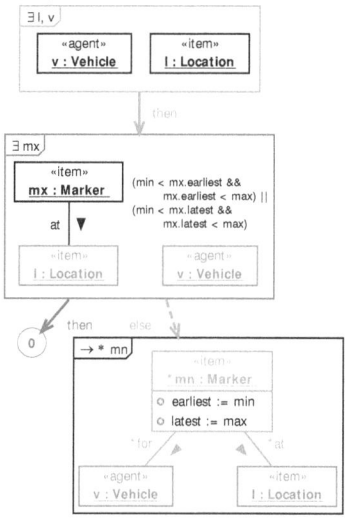

Figure 4.3.15: Schedules need to be compatible

**Norm system.** For any culture $U = (\mathcal{T}_U, \mathcal{N}_U^X, \mathcal{N}_U^S, \mathcal{C}_U)$, we distinguish the norms $\mathcal{N}_U^X = \mathcal{N}_U^I \cup \mathcal{N}_U^A$ where $\mathcal{N}_U^I$ are instantiation norms and $\mathcal{N}_U^A$ are affiliation norms, $\mathcal{N}_U^S = \cup_{R \in R_U} \mathcal{N}_U^{B,R} \cup \mathcal{N}_U^C \cup \Phi_U^S$ where $\mathcal{N}_U^C$ are conventional norms, $\mathcal{N}_U^{B,R}$ are the behavioral norms of role $R \in R_U$, and $\Phi_U^S$ are invariants. Every norm $N \in \mathcal{N}_U^X \cup \mathcal{N}_U^S$ is based on the type system graph $\mathcal{T}_U$.

When implementing a culture, we can break the specification down according to the affected entities and roles. Social norms typically only affect those specific roles that appear in the corresponding graph rules, and even then, these may not be actively involved in the required behavior. For structural patterns that refer to a single effector application, the active agent is easy to identify, which may not be the case in complex scenarios, though.

When reasoning about norm systems, we need to consider the dependencies between the different norms. All norms depend on the existence of a specific community that provides their context, but furthermore, some may also depend on the presence of additional roles and professed intentions. The norms are therefore dependent on the set of those norms that are capable of creating the required social entities. This can be statically analyzed by checking which types are instantiated or referenced by a norm. The result is a dependency graph that organizes the norms into a hierarchy. As the analysis takes place at the type level, the graph does not necessarily have to be acyclic in order to represent a consistent system. However, it is safest to strive to avoid cyclic dependencies. This can be achieved easily by assigning a level to each professed intention and requiring that it may only depend on professed intentions with lower levels.

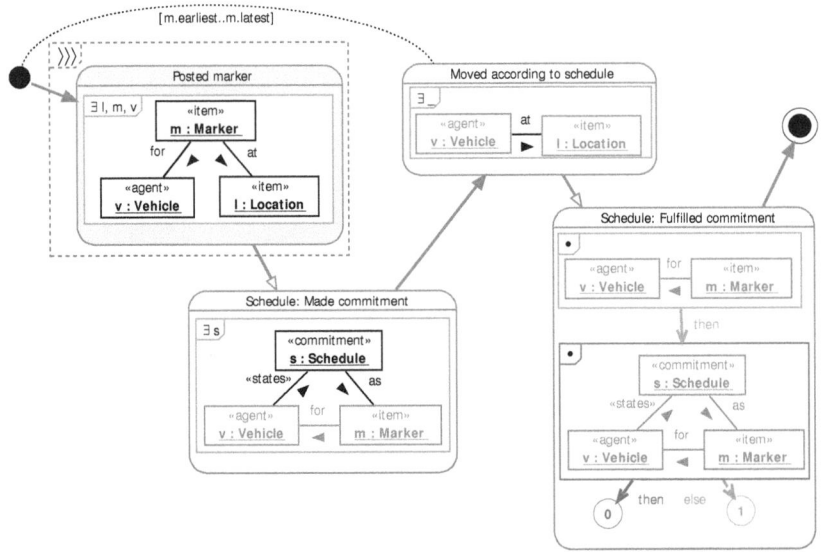

Figure 4.3.16: Markers as commitments: TSSD combining two conventional norms and a behavioral norm.

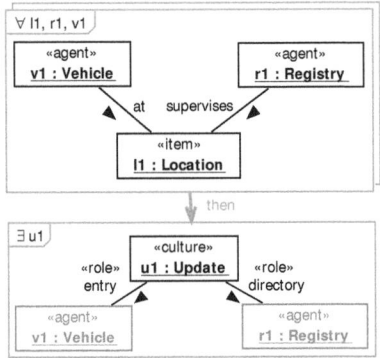

Figure 4.3.17: Invariant: all vehicles are properly registered.

This also has an impact on the assigned priorities, which are crucial for correctness of the norm system. Instantiation norms (priority group $IV$) preempt affiliation norms (priority group $III$), which

## 4.3 Formal model

are processed before conventional norms ($II$) and behavioral norms ($I$ / 0), with number ranges for the individual groups chosen as needed, provided that $V < IV < III < II < I < 0$. A combined existential norm is treated as an instantiation norm, whereas a combined social norm is ranked as a behavioral norm. While the other norm types are always urgent, behavioral norms can either be urgent or discretionary. The priority serves to indicate whether the described behavior is required ($I$) or merely permitted (0), which cannot be expressed in the graph rule itself.

**Subcultures.** A culture may contain subcultures that extend and depend on it. By definition, a culture's norms only apply to its members. This means that it cannot instantiate itself – there needs to be a superculture whose members agree to respect its instantiation norms. Likewise, an agent can only join a culture if it is already member of a superculture where the corresponding affiliation norms are accepted. There is therefore a connected hierarchy of cultures. At the top of this hierarchy, the global *default* culture implicitly contains all agents and serves a the parent of all cultures without an explicitly defined superculture. In order to be able to bootstrap the system starting from the *default* culture, each superculture incorporates the existential norms of its immediate subcultures. As membership is transitive, agents implementing a subculture are bound by all norms of all supercultures containing it, but not vice versa.

**Definition 4.3.8** *For a culture $C$ and its subculture $S$ with $S \in \mathcal{C}_C$, we have $\mathcal{T}_C^R \subseteq \mathcal{T}_S^R$, $\mathcal{N}_C^X \subseteq \mathcal{N}_S^X$, $\mathcal{N}_C^S \subseteq \mathcal{N}_S^S$ (subcultures import their superculture), and $\mathcal{N}_S^{IX} \subseteq \mathcal{N}_C^X$ (subcultures export $\mathcal{N}_S^{IX}$, their original existential norms).*

In this context, a coordination pattern can be seen as a special restricted type of culture that may not define its own existential norms, professed intentions or subcultures.

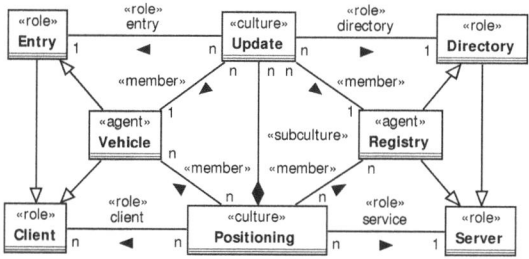

Figure 4.3.18: Culture and subculture

In the application example, most cultures are subcultures of the positioning culture. In Figure 4.3.18, we define the type system of the update culture and its relationship to its superculture. Often, only agents that already have a specific role in the superculture can join the subculture in certain capacities, which is why the new entry and directory roles inherit from the client and server roles.

**GTS.** For a given culture $U_i = (\mathcal{T}_U, \mathcal{N}_U^X, \mathcal{N}_U^S, \mathcal{C}_U)$ with $\mathcal{N}_S^X = \cup_{R \in R_U} \mathcal{N}_U^{B,R} \cup \mathcal{N}_U^C \cup \Phi_U^S$ where $\mathcal{N}_U^{B,R}$ are the behavioral norms of the role $R \in R_U$, $\mathcal{N}_U^C$ are conventional norms, and $\Phi_U^S$ are invariants, we can derive the constrained GTS $M_i^S = (\mathcal{T}_{S_i}, \mathcal{G}_{S_i}^i, \mathcal{R}_{S_i}, \Phi_{S_i})$ with

- $\mathcal{T}_{S_i} = \mathcal{T}_U$,
- $\mathcal{G}_{S_i}^i = \emptyset$,
- $\mathcal{R}_{S_i} = \mathcal{N}_U^X \cup (\cup_{R \in R_U} \mathcal{N}_U^{B,R}) \cup \mathcal{N}_U^C$, and
- $\Phi_{S_i} = \Phi_U^S$.

The GTS provides a complete model of the culture. It is at the a level of abstraction that is comparable to typical formal agent specification techniques. We can therefore derive certain invariants and verify the internal consistency of the norm system. However, as there is no model of the environment and all transformations originate from the confines of the culture's norms, this model is only an incomplete representation of the actual system and therefore insufficient for a complete validation of the design.

### 4.3.3 Community Specification

**Community type.** Before we can actually instantiate a culture, we need to derive a concrete realization that is adapted to a specific environment. Such a community type needs to map all template types to entity types from the environment specification. This mapping is more than a simple renaming of types, associations and attributes, but an actual model transformation that is expressed by graph rules. For one, a single template type instance may be replaced by a structure consisting of multiple entities where the environment specification is more detailed. However, we currently do not allow mapping multiple template types to the same entity type as this might lead to the invalidation of analysis results from the culture level.

For the included agent types, the community type needs to specify which sensor and effector types are constrained by the culture's roles and mark them as implementations of the pertinent social norms. This results in a modified type system graph and transformed norms using the types of the concrete underlying entity specification.

As the transformed social norms are now expressed in terms of physical entities, every agent type that is constrained by a norm requires a sensor capable of perceiving these entities or will be unable to evaluate it. Likewise, the agent types need effectors which are capable of producing the required effects, i.e. the postcondition of effector's graph rule must satisfy the (physical) postcondition of the behavioral norm. If a norm specifies a scenario, this mapping is non-trivial and may also depend on the chosen implementation.

A social norm constrains the effectors used to implement it. A role constrains all effectors that are constrained by any of its social norms, plus all that are explicitly declared constrained. If an effector is not constrained, an agent assuming the role may use it at will.

## 4.3 Formal model

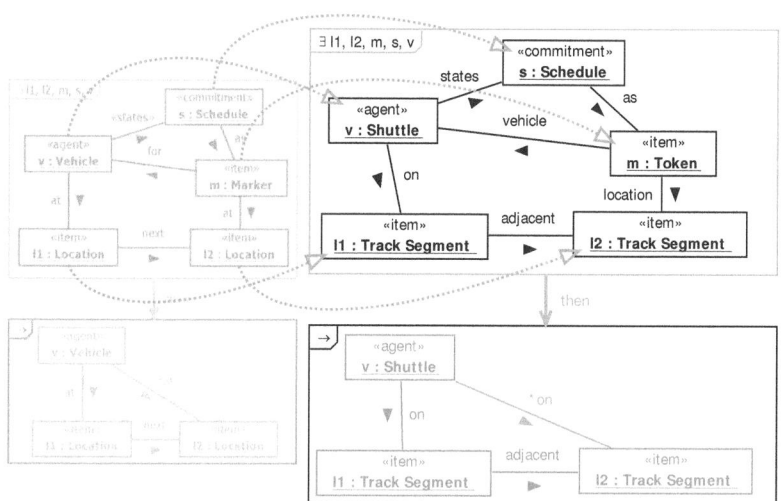

Figure 4.3.19: Transforming a behavioral norm

In the application example, there are indirect restrictions on the way shuttles may accelerate using their motor effector. In Figure 4.3.19, we map the behavioral norm from Figure 4.3.14 from the domain of the positioning culture to the concrete environment of the shuttle system.

**Definition 4.3.9** *A community type $C$ is a tuple $(W_C, U_C, \text{MAP}_C, cnst_C, C_C)$ consisting of an environment specification $W_C = (S_W^T, O_W, S_W, \mathcal{E}_W, \mathcal{P}_W)$, a culture $U_C = (\mathcal{T}_U, \mathcal{N}_U^X, \mathcal{N}_U^S, \mathcal{C}_U)$ defining roles and professed intentions $R_U, P_U \subset N_{\mathcal{T}_U}$, a set of graph isomorphisms $\text{MAP}_C : \mathcal{T}_U \to \mathcal{T}_{O_W} \cup \mathcal{T}_U$ that replace template types and associations with (sets of) entity types and associations, a mapping function $cnst_C : (R_U \times A_{O_W}) \mapsto \wp(E_W \cup S_W)$ that assigns the permitted sensors and effectors to each valid pair of a role and agent, and a set of community types $C_C$ that are compatible realizations of the subcultures from $\mathcal{C}_U$.*

*The mapping in $cnst_C$ must only assign sets of sensors and effectors that are available to the agent and sufficient for implementing all applicable norms. Formally, this means that for all roles $R \in R_U$ and for every agent $a \in A_{O_W}$ assigned to a template type by $\text{MAP}_C$ holds that only sensors and effectors for the corresponding agent are assigned:*

$$\forall (t_1, a_1, \mathcal{T}_1, \mathcal{R}_1, \mathcal{R}_1) \in cnst_C(R, a) : a = a_1.$$

*Furthermore, for every role $R \in R_U$ with norms $n \in \mathcal{N}_U^{B,R}$ and all agent types $a \in A_{O_W}$ that $\text{MAP}_C$ assigns to a template type attached to $R$ holds that the physical part of each behavioral norm $n$ can be constructed as a combination of the available sensors and effectors $cnst_C(R, a) =$*

$\{(t_1, a_1, \mathcal{T}_1, \mathcal{R}_1, I\!\!R_1), \ldots, (t_m, a_m, \mathcal{T}_m, \mathcal{R}_m, I\!\!R_m)\}$. There must exist a $\mathfrak{R} \in (I\!\!R_1 \otimes \cdots \otimes I\!\!R_m)$ (for $X \otimes Y := \{x \cup y | x \in X \wedge y \in Y\}$) and $r_1, \ldots, r_n \in \text{enum}(\mathfrak{R})$ with:

$$\exists r \in \text{setmerge}(r_1, \ldots, r_n) : r = n|_{\mathcal{T}_O}.$$

**Communities** are instances of community types, created in accordance with instantiation norms. They are a conceptual representation of a culture and the group of agents realizing it. Constrained by the limits of the (sub)culture hierarchy, communities can overlap or be subsets of each other. There is an implicit *default* community containing all agents that implements the *default* culture.

As discussed, communities can be persistent, e.g. when tied to a persistent entity, but may also be short-lived and created in an ad-hoc fashion, which is common for communities implementing coordination patterns.

**GTS.** Given a community type $C = (W_C, U_C, \text{MAP}_C, cnst_C, \mathcal{C}_C)$ with environment specification $W_C = (S_W^T, O_W, \mathcal{S}_W, \mathcal{E}_W, \mathcal{P}_W)$ and culture $U_C = (\mathcal{T}_U, \mathcal{N}_U^X, \mathcal{N}_U^S, \mathcal{C}_U)$ with GTS $M^S = (\mathcal{T}_S, \mathcal{G}_S^i, \mathcal{R}_S, \Phi_S)$, we can derive the corresponding constrained GTS $M^C = (\mathcal{T}_C, \mathcal{G}_C^i, \mathcal{R}_C, \Phi_C)$ with

- $\mathcal{T}_C = \mathcal{T}_{O_W} \cup \bigcup_{m \in \text{MAP}_C} m(\mathcal{T}_U)$,
- $\mathcal{G}_C^i = \emptyset$,
- $\mathcal{R}_C = \{m(r) | r \in \mathcal{R}_S, m \in \text{MAP}_C\}$, and
- $\Phi_C = \{m(\phi) | \phi \in \Phi_S, m \in \text{MAP}_C\}$.

### 4.3.4 Agent Specification

**Agent.** Ultimately, cultures need to be implemented by agents. An agent may have an internal state, which is expressed as an instance graph that it is free to define and modify as it sees fit, but can only interact with the environment using its defined sensors and effectors. As we have ensured that, in principle, agents are capable of the required actions and perceptions when deriving the concrete community types, an agent should be able to conform to the cultures' norms, provided they are internally consistent. However, an agent may be a member of multiple communities (possibly of different types) at once and thus needs to reconcile their various requirements. This corresponds to the problem of role composition as discussed in [GV06].

**Definition 4.3.10** *An agent specification $A$ is a tuple $(a_A, W_A, \mathcal{C}_A, \mathcal{T}_A, \mathcal{R}_A^I, \mathcal{R}_A^E, map_A)$ where $a_A$ is an agent type, $W_A = (S_W^T, O_W, \mathcal{S}_W, \mathcal{E}_W, \mathcal{P}_W)$ is an environment specification, $\mathcal{C}_A$ the set of community types which assign roles to $a_A$, $\mathcal{T}_A$ is a type system graph defining the agent's internal type system, $\mathcal{R}_A^I$ is set of rules that describe internal state transitions, $\mathcal{R}_A^E$ is set of rules that describe transitions with external effects, and $map_A : \mathcal{R}_A^E \mapsto \wp(\bigcup_{C \in \mathcal{C}_A} \mathcal{N}_C^B)$ maps external transitions to social norms of different communities. We require $\mathcal{T}_A \cap \mathcal{T}_{O_W} = a_A$, that $\forall r \in \mathcal{R}_A^I$ holds that $r$ is type conformant w.r.t. $\mathcal{T}_A$, and that $\forall r' \in \mathcal{R}_A^E$ holds that $r'$ is type conformant w.r.t. $\mathcal{T}_{O_W} \cup \mathcal{T}_A$.*

## 4.3 Formal model

An agent is expected to be able to bootstrap its internal state starting from just an instance of the agent type using only rules in $\mathcal{R}_A^I$. Internal and external transitions are typically discretionary (priority 0), but may also be urgent (priority group $I$). The external transitions of an agent may freely use sensors and effectors not constrained by a role and refine available social norms of the assigned roles. For any $r \in \mathcal{R}_A^E$ and an enumeration of available sensor and effector rules $r_1, \ldots, r_n$ with permitted multiple occurrences must hold:

$$\exists r' \in \mathsf{setmerge}(r_1, \ldots, r_n) : r|_{\mathcal{T}_O} = r'|_{\mathcal{T}_O}.$$

**GTS.** Given an agent specification $A_j = (a_A, W_A, \mathcal{C}_A, \mathcal{T}_A, \mathcal{R}_A^I, \mathcal{R}_A^E, map_A)$ with an environment specification $W_A = (S_W^T, O_W, \mathcal{S}_W, \mathcal{E}_W, \mathcal{P}_W)$, and a set of community types $C_k = (W_{C_k}, U_{C_k}, \mathsf{MAP}_{C_k}, cnst_{C_k}, \mathcal{C}_{C_k})$ with GTS $M_k^C = (\mathcal{T}_{C_k}, \mathcal{G}_{C_k}^i, \mathcal{R}_{C_k}, \Phi_{C_k})$, we can derive the corresponding constrained GTS $M_j^A = (\mathcal{T}_{A_j}, \mathcal{G}_{A_j}^i, \mathcal{R}_{A_j}, \Phi_{A_j})$ with

- $\mathcal{T}_{A_j} = \mathcal{T}_{O_W} \cup \bigcup_{C_k \in \mathcal{C}_A} \mathcal{T}_{C_k} \cup \mathcal{T}_A$,
- $\mathcal{G}_{A_j}^i = \emptyset$,
- $\mathcal{R}_{A_j} = \mathcal{R}_A^I \cup \mathcal{R}_A^E$, and
- $\Phi_{A_j} = \emptyset$.

The formal model emphasizes what was discussed informally in the previous section: Agents do not need to keep an explicit internal representation of the social system state as long as their behavior is consistent with their role obligations. This raises another related issue: How can we formalize the concept of consistent behavior? This question leads us back to the problem of *GTS refinement*, which was already hinted at during our discussion of *refinement* for automata in Chapter 2.

**GTS Refinement.** When defining behavioral refinement, be it for automata [Gie03] or objects [Sek94], the central idea is the same: Allow only behavior that is allowed by the specification, remove ambiguities, do not eliminate any required behavior. Adopting this view, a GTS is a refinement of another GTS if it contains all of its required but none of its forbidden transitions. One of the desirable properties of this definition is that it preserves important characteristics of the original GTS: If it guarantees certain invariants, these will hold for every refinement. After all, each refinement can only remove reachable states from the domain of the defining GTS, i.e. the relevant part of the state space.

Unfortunately, comparing two GTS is more difficult than comparing two automata. For one, their states are only defined implicitly, which means that there may be an infinite number of them. This also entails that what appears as two distinct states to one GTS may be indistinguishable from the point of view of another, leading to different sets of enabled transitions and divergent behavior. Furthermore, the transitions with which the definition is concerned are also only defined implicitly by means of graph rules. Refinement is therefore not limited to simply eliminating graph rules, but may change the definitions of the rules themselves. The most fundamental question is therefore how we can recognize corresponding transitions when the rule sets are not identical.

**Corresponding transitions** can only be identified by looking at the underlying graph rules, which means that the fundamental problem is actually the analysis of graph rule correspondence: Which rules are enabled at the same time and have comparable effects? In order to determine this, we need to analyze the pre- and postconditions that define the rules, ergo consider graph patterns again.

When comparing patterns, we only need to compare their structure, i.e. check for isomorphisms between them, as the relevant rule applications abstract from the identities of elements of the patterns anyway. This leads to the following notion of equivalence between graph patterns:

**Definition 4.3.11** *Two graph patterns* $\mathcal{P} := [P, \hat{\mathcal{P}}]$ *and* $\mathcal{Q} := [Q, \hat{\mathcal{Q}}]$ *are* equivalent, *written as* $\mathcal{P} \cong \mathcal{Q}$, *iff* $P \approx Q$, $\forall \hat{P} \in \hat{\mathcal{P}} : \exists \hat{Q} \in \hat{\mathcal{Q}}$ *so that* $\hat{P} \approx \hat{Q}$, *and, vice versa,* $\forall \hat{Q} \in \hat{\mathcal{Q}} : \exists \hat{P} \in \hat{\mathcal{P}}$ *so that* $\hat{P} \approx \hat{Q}$.

Given a graph rule $[L, \hat{\mathcal{L}}] \to_r [R]$, let $\mathcal{L}$ be $[L, \hat{\mathcal{L}}]$ and $\mathcal{R}$ be $[R, \hat{\mathcal{R}}]$, where each $\hat{R} \in \mathcal{R}$ results from adding an element from $L \setminus R$, i.e. the set of elements deleted by the rule application, to $R$. $\mathcal{R}$ thus makes the deletions an explicit part of the postcondition. Using Definition 4.3.11, we then define:

**Definition 4.3.12** *Two graph rules* $[L, \hat{\mathcal{L}}] \to_r [R, \hat{\mathcal{R}}]$ *and* $[L', \hat{\mathcal{L}}'] \to_{r'} [R', \hat{\mathcal{R}}']$ *are* equivalent, *written as* $r \cong r'$, *iff* $\mathcal{L} \cong \mathcal{L}'$ *and* $\mathcal{R} \cong \mathcal{R}'$.

For each individual rule, extending the postcondition into $\mathcal{R}$ does not result in additional constraints, as $\mathcal{R}$ holds by definition after $r$ has been applied using standard graph rule semantics. The difference is, however, relevant when comparing distinct graph rules that represent variations of each other. As a refinement relation may be the result of additional restrictions at the pattern level, we need criteria for deciding when a graph pattern is a restriction or relaxation of another pattern.

A pattern $\mathcal{Q}$ is a restriction of a pattern $\mathcal{P}$ if $\mathcal{P}$ matches whenever $\mathcal{Q}$ matches. This entails two requirements: Naturally, $P$, the positive part of $\mathcal{P}$, needs to be less specific, i.e. contained in $Q$, so that a match for $Q$ guarantees a match for $P$. But at the same time, any one of the negative application conditions (NACs) $\hat{P}$ needs to be *more* specific, i.e. contain at least one NAC of $\mathcal{Q}$, in order to ensure that a forbidden pattern preventing $\mathcal{P}$ from matching will also prevent $\mathcal{Q}$. We define:

**Definition 4.3.13** *Let* $\mathcal{P} := [P, \hat{\mathcal{P}}]$ *and* $\mathcal{Q} := [Q, \hat{\mathcal{Q}}]$ *be two graph patterns.* $\mathcal{P}$ *is then called a* subpattern *of* $\mathcal{Q}$, *written as* $\mathcal{P} \subseteq \mathcal{Q}$, *iff* $P \precsim Q$ *and* $\forall \hat{Q} \in \hat{\mathcal{Q}} : \exists \hat{P} \in \hat{\mathcal{P}}$ *so that* $\hat{Q} \precsim \hat{P}$.

If $\mathcal{P} \subseteq \mathcal{Q}$, we can say that $\mathcal{P}$ is a relaxation of $\mathcal{Q}$, or that $\mathcal{Q}$ is a restriction of $\mathcal{P}$.

Let us now consider a GTS $S$ and its refinement $S'$, written as $S' \sqsubseteq S$. For every rule $r'$ of $S'$, there needs to be a rule $r$ in $S$ *allowing* it. This implies that $\mathcal{L} \subseteq \mathcal{L}'$, as the precondition

## 4.3 Formal model

of $r'$ needs to be at least as restrictive as the precondition of $r$ to prevent the former from being enabled when the latter is not. For the postcondition, the inverse is true: We require that $\mathcal{R}' \subseteq \mathcal{R}$ (ignoring the elements in $L' \setminus L$) so that $r'$ deletes nothing not deleted by $r$ and adds nothing not added by $r$. This *permissive interpretation* is, however, too weak in those cases where only partially applying a transformation leads to an inconsistent state, which are rather the norm than the exception. If $r$ only describes a valid transition if all of its effects are applied, we need to use a *strict interpretation* requiring $\mathcal{R}'$ to be equivalent to $\mathcal{R}$, except for the elements in $L' \setminus L$ that are not and must not be affected by the transformation and thus also appear in $R'$. This means that both rule applications only differ w.r.t. their preconditions but have exactly identical effects.

For every *required* (i.e., urgent) rule $q$ of $S$, there needs to be some (urgent) rule $q'$ of $S'$ implementing it. This entails that $\mathcal{L}' \subseteq \mathcal{L}$ so that $q'$ has the less specific precondition and is therefore enabled whenever $q$ is enabled. The effects of the refining rule need to at least include the effects of the original defining rule, leading to the *permissive interpretation* $\mathcal{R} \subseteq \mathcal{R}'$. Whether doing more than required is acceptable cannot be encoded as part of the defining rule and depends on the specific context, which might again make the *strict interpretation* of $\mathcal{R} \cong \mathcal{R}'$ the preferable and more natural choice.

The symmetry between the two cases is not accidental: In order to be *allowed*, a rule from $S'$ requires a corresponding rule in S, making these relationships dual. This symmetry is, however, broken by the fact that any rule $q'$ implementing a *required* rule $q$ nonetheless needs to be *allowed* as well. Consequently, we have both $\mathcal{L} \subseteq \mathcal{L}' \wedge \mathcal{L}' \subseteq \mathcal{L}$ and $\mathcal{R}' \subseteq \mathcal{R} \wedge \mathcal{R} \subseteq \mathcal{R}'$, resulting in $q' \cong q$, for urgent rules of $S$.

Taken together, this yields the following definition of corresponding rules:

**Definition 4.3.14** *Given two GTS $S$ and $S'$, we call a rule $[L, \hat{\mathcal{L}}] \rightarrow_q [R, \hat{\mathcal{R}}] \in S$ and a refining rule $[L', \hat{\mathcal{L}'}] \rightarrow_{q'} [R', \hat{\mathcal{R}'}] \in S'$ corresponding, written as $q \equiv q'$, iff $prio(q) < 0$ (urgent) and $q \cong q'$ or $prio(q) \geq 0$ (discretionary) and $\mathcal{L} \subseteq \mathcal{L}' \wedge \mathcal{R}' \setminus (L' \setminus L) \cong \mathcal{R}$.*

Based on this definition, we can then define the refinement relationship for GTS as follows:

**Definition 4.3.15** *A GTS $S'$ is a refinement of a GTS $S$, denoted by $S' \sqsubseteq S$, iff $\forall r \in S | prio(r) < 0$ (urgent) $: \forall G : \exists r' \in S' : r' \equiv r \wedge G \vdash r \Rightarrow G \vdash r'$ and $\forall r' \in S' : \forall G : \exists r \in S : r' \equiv r \wedge G \vdash r' \Rightarrow G \vdash r$.*

Simply put, this means that whenever an urgent rule in $S$ is enabled for some graph $G$, some corresponding rule in $S'$ needs to be enabled, and whenever any rule in $S'$ is enabled for some $G$, some corresponding rule in $S$ needs to be enabled.

An advantage of this definition is that it can be verified statically by comparing and matching up the two sets of graph rules, which can be done very efficiently. $S' \sqsubseteq S$ under a *strict interpretation* means that $S'$ contains all urgent rules of $S$, and otherwise only contains rules that are derived from discretionary rules of $S$ by, optionally, restricting their preconditions. Under a *permissive interpretation*, $S'$ might additionally relax the postconditions of discretionary rules. If the necessary rules are present in either GTS, the refinement relationship holds by definition.

The definition's downside is that it is too limiting for our purposes. Ultimately, we are interested in comparing community types, whose norms include social entities, with agent definitions, whose rules are likely to contain references to the agents' internal state, but are only interested in their effects on a common core that is represented by the environment. We therefore introduce the concept of *restricted GTS refinement*.

**Restricted GTS refinement** restricts the refinement relationship to a common domain that is shared by both GTS, allowing them to perform modifications in their private domains without restrictions. While these domains could be defined using arbitrary graph patterns (e.g. defining the internal state space of each individual agent as private), the simplest way to do this is at the type level by explicitly defining the common type system $\mathcal{T}_C$. For two GTS $S$ and $S'$, we typically define $\mathcal{T}_C := \mathcal{T}_S \cap \mathcal{T}_{S'}$ as the intersection of the two type systems.

We then modify the above definition of refinement by replacing all involved graph patterns with their respective restricted versions $\mathcal{L}|_{\mathcal{T}_C}$ and $\mathcal{R}|_{\mathcal{T}_C}$ when computing the sets of corresponding rules. Using $r \equiv |_{\mathcal{T}_C} r'$ as a shorthand for $r|_{\mathcal{T}_C} \equiv r'|_{\mathcal{T}_C}$, we define:

**Definition 4.3.16** *A GTS $S'$ is the* restricted refinement *of a GTS $S$ for the shared domain $\mathcal{T}_C$, written as $S' \sqsubseteq |_{\mathcal{T}_C} S$, iff $\forall r \in S \mid prio(r) < 0$ (urgent) : $\forall G : \exists r' \in S' : r' \equiv |_{\mathcal{T}_C} r \wedge G \vdash r \Rightarrow G \vdash r'$ and $\forall r' \in S' : \forall G : \exists r \in S : r' \equiv |_{\mathcal{T}_C} r \wedge G \vdash r' \Rightarrow G \vdash r$.*

Effectively, this means that $S'$ and $S$ act like two GTS $S'|_{\mathcal{T}_C} \sqsubseteq S|_{\mathcal{T}_C}$ as far as the shared domain $\mathcal{T}_C$ is concerned. Nonetheless, they still affect and are affected by their private domains. As the correspondence between rules is computed based on their restricted versions whereas rule applications are computed using the original versions, we can now no longer statically guarantee that corresponding rules are always enabled together. Due to the influence of the private domains, the refinement relationship can no longer be verified without considering the context of the rule application – we may even have to consult the entire previous execution path in order to determine whether a corresponding rule would be enabled.

While this definition exactly captures the desired relationship by allowing us to define refinement based on the observable behavior in the environment, it significantly complicates analysis. As long as an agent is only concerned with community types that are independent of each other, finding a valid refinement is trivial because it is sufficient to simply imitate their GTS definitions and apply the available discretionary rules at random. Once the agent starts constraining the original GTS in order to make its behavior goal-directed or to reconcile multiple community types, however, a more sophisticated verification approach is required, as required behavior may now be blocked by internal constraints that are not obvious to an outside observer.

### 4.3.5 System Specification

We now combine the elements we have defined into the overall system. Figure 4.3.20 provides an overview: The environment, the community types and, indirectly, the cultures specify the desired system behavior, the agent designs need to respect the boundaries set by this specification.

## 4.4 Conclusion

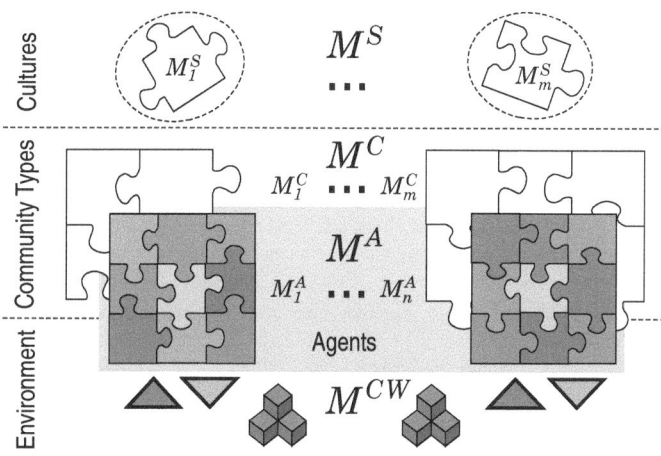

Figure 4.3.20: The integrated specification

**Definition 4.3.17** *A consistent* system specification $Y$ *is a tuple* $(W_Y, \mathcal{C}_Y, \mathcal{A}_Y)$ *where* $W_Y$ *is an environment specification,* $\mathcal{C}_Y$ *is a set of community types using* $W_Y$, *and* $\mathcal{A}_Y$ *is a set of agent specifications using* $W_Y$ *where holds* $\forall A \in \mathcal{A}_Y : \mathcal{C}_A \subseteq \mathcal{C}_Y$.

The corresponding GTS $M$ is then the parallel composition of the agents described by the GTS $M_1^A, \ldots, M_n^A$, and the closed behavior of the physical world, described by the GTS $M^{CW}$.

$$M := (M_1^A \| \ldots M_n^A \| M^{CW}). \tag{4.3.1}$$

The system model now provides a complete representation of both the environment and the coordination architecture. Within the limits of the quality and precision of the employed model, it is therefore a suitable foundation for both verification and validation activities.

## 4.4 Conclusion

Now that we have presented our concept in more detail, we can compare it to related approaches before summing up the discussion.

### 4.4.1 Related Work

**Separation of concerns.** The principle of *separation of concerns* [Par72, Dij76] has recently come back into focus due to new approaches inspired by aspect-oriented programming (AOP)

[KLM+97] and its support for crosscutting concerns. Similar ideas have been put forward as subject-oriented programming (SOP) [HO93] or, more abstractly, a viewpoint framework using multiple perspectives on the same engineering artifacts [NF92]. Their common principle is the separation into aspects or views on the system which can be considered in isolation and only be composed into a coherent design or implementation at the end of the process. Development efforts can then focus on specific problems, and the individual parts of the solution become easier to analyze. Cross-cutting concerns like persistence, logging or error handling are frequently presented as suitable targets for this type of treatment. However, most approaches assume that concerns are orthogonal and start to break down when the number of interactions between views increases. In contrast, we also consider the systematic composition of non-orthogonal functional concerns as discussed by [GV06].

Our approach uses model-based composition that is performed at the specification level, whereas aspect composition usually operates at the source code level. Notable exceptions include *subject-oriented design* [CHOT99], which synthesizes object-oriented design models from individual *design subjects*, or *role-based modeling* [RWL96]. In [MGF02], a tool for aspect weaving based on UML role models annotated with OCL constraints is sketched, combining the idea of aspects at the design level with role modeling. However, these approaches focus on the composition of structural features and method bodies, not on the behavioral composition of reactive behavior.

In the context of multi-agent systems, current proposals focus on exploiting the principle of separation of concerns within individual agents as an implementation technique (cf. [GSCL02]), whereas we apply it at the system level to design the overall coordination behavior.

**Environment.** For software-intensive systems and agents alike, the concept of situatedness is very important. The system's context is relevant both at the physical and the knowledge or social level [Jen00]. While most approaches are based on a strict separation between physical and metaphysical context (cf. [BBB01]), our conceptual framework provides a unifying view on both.

Context has been studied intensely in the field of Artificial Intelligence: [SB04] compares the two dominant formal theories of context, Propositional Logic of Context [BBM95] and Local Models Semantics [GG01]. While these provide important insights on the epistemological aspects and theoretical limitations of context, they have gained, as [Edm02] notes, little practical relevance for the design of multi-agent systems. In the vein of [SBG99], various more pragmatic context classification schemata have been proposed (see [KO04] for a survey), often geared towards a specific aspect like human interaction or tied to a particular middleware or implementation technique.

Research in the area of reactive agents follows the quite different philosophy that 'the world is its own best model' [Bro91], which basically places an agent's environment outside the scope of explicit modeling. While this approach emphasizes the close relationship between agent and environment and provides a pragmatic way to design how agents perceive and affect it, it deliberately rejects cognition and explicitly reasoning about the environment.

Viewing the environment as a first-order abstraction [WPM+04] has only recently begun to gain acceptance in the agent community, notably after work on stigmergy [Bon99, FKR95, PBS05]

## 4.4 Conclusion

had drawn attention to the environment's potential for the efficient coordination and control of multi-agent systems. As our approach prominently uses the grounding of social interactions in the observable environment, there are parallels with other research in this domain:

Weyns et al. [WPM+04] discuss several functions of environments that are also important to our approach, namely structuring the system, providing a shared state, providing service support, enabling coordination, and acting as a regulating entity. We support the systematic model-driven development of these aspects.

Recent work by Omicini et al. [ORV+04] proposes *artifacts* as a general way to structure the interaction between agents and the environment. While this is similar to the way the environment provides services, our approach is rooted in software engineering practices and can furnish complete behavioral specifications, whereas artifacts come from an AI background and only provide abstract message-based interfaces, which makes analysis of the provided services harder.

**Agent coordination.** The concept of social structure was established by Ferber's organizational models [FG98]. We see strong relationships between the concept of communities and current work on organization-centered multi-agent systems (OCMAS) based on the agent, group, role (AGR) model [FGM03]. Common points include the predominance of inter-agent aspects and the abstraction from agents' cognitive abilities. However, we apply dynamic, intersecting groups as a more general, implementation-agnostic modeling concept.

Bridging the gap between the social and the individual perspective is a problem that all methodologies that begin designing at the social level (e.g. MESSAGE [CCG+02]) face. The idea of the legal stance is both related to work on intentional stance (cf. [WJ95b]), the social level [JC97] and social order [Cas00]. It was inspired by Viroli and Omicini's idea of agents as *observable sources* [VO02], but goes beyond it by basing observations on the environment model. This provides a more flexible, general mechanism, at the cost of diminishing the ability to formally reason about the observations from an AI perspective.

Law-governed interaction [MU00], though similar in name, takes a fundamentally different approach. Instead of checking the observed behavior against a specification, it works by restricting an agent's interactions with the system in such a way that, a priori, only socially acceptable actions are possible.

**Agent modeling.** In the field of agent-oriented software engineering, there are numerous approaches that use UML dialects which extend the standard with agent-specific concepts (cf. [BM03] for a survey). In contrast, our approach is based on powerful general purpose notations which allow modeling multi-agent system concepts, but are not limited to a specific view. As certain notations suggest themselves for specific tasks, there are superficial similarities to other approaches: [KG97] uses class diagrams for ontology modeling, object diagrams to describe system states, and state charts for control structures. [BO05] discusses a component-based model of agent interactions. None of them offers the expressiveness and complete formalization our notations provide, however.

While the approach presented in [KK07a, KKK02] does not propose a general purpose modeling language per se, it is notable for its use of graph transformations for the description of the actions of autonomous agents in their environment.

The TROPOS methodology focuses on the initial analysis of requirements (cf. [BGG+04]). The proposed notation for modeling dependencies between agents, tasks, goals, and soft goals is intentionally informal. The resulting diagrams are visually complex due to a lack of structuring elements and provide only limited guidance for the subsequent design process.

The Agent Modeling Language (AML) [CT07], a UML-based modeling language, is the result of a promising initiative that has tried to distill a common core from a selection of popular methodologies. Our own research (cf. [Kle03]) that laid the groundwork for the CURCUMA framework had followed a comparable objective based on a similar set of methodologies. It is thus quite informative to note the parallels and dissimilarities between our independently derived results. While the AML metamodel seems like a sound compromise, we nonetheless detect the exact same issues that motivated our move away from the smallest common denominator and the adoption of behavioral semantics based on Story-Driven Modeling, the principle of physical grounding, the legal stance, and the dynamic organization into communities in CURCUMA.

### 4.4.2 Discussion

In this chapter, we have presented an approach for designing a coordination architecture for complex software-intensive systems. We have motivated the use of the multi-agent paradigm and shown how 'soft' agent-oriented abstractions can be integrated into an object-oriented design approach using our CURCUMAframework. The framework also provides the unique ability to use these abstractions in a way that is fully rooted in the environment. We have also provided a rigorous formalization of the framework.

We have also discussed how cultures and communities seamlessly integrate with existing concepts such as *Coordination Patterns*. In previous publications, we have already successfully applied the community concept in order to explain and formalize the dynamic instantiation of such patterns.

In the next chapter, we will explore how this approach integrates into the overall design process for software-intensive systems and supports the verification and validation of the design.

# Chapter 5
# Verification and Validation

## 5.1 Introduction

There is no such thing as a flawless design. A system can at best strive to faithfully implement its specification, which in turn is based on an approximation of the real requirements and assumptions about the expected environment and operation conditions. However, it is not realistic to expect the first iteration of a design to achieve even this limited level of perfection.

Verification and validation activities, and by extension iteration, must therefore be part of any systematic software engineering process. In some domains, there even are legal requirements that mandate certain verification techniques for safety-critical technical systems. Practical experience shows that activities such as debugging, testing, and verification consume significant amounts of time and account for up to three quarters of the total cost of development in a typical commercial development organization (cf. [HS02]).

The terms *verification* and *validation* carry a certain ambiguity – they are not used consistently throughout the literature, sometimes even interchangeably. In this work, we use the common distinction that *validation* is concerned with the question whether the system meets customer needs and expectations (building the right system), whereas *verification* answers the question whether the system is correct with respect to some specification (building the system right). The former is based on the original requirements, the latter typically refers to the result of a previous phase of the development process.

The techniques that are employed for verification and validation range from various forms of testing with different subjects, scopes, and levels of detail, automation, coverage, and formality to formal methods such as model checking or theorem proving [CW96]. When discussing verification in this work, we are primarily concerned with *formal verification*, i.e. the formal proof that a model is correct with respect to a formal specification [Int95]. However, as our approach as discussed in the previous chapter yields specifications of agent behavior that are both rigorous and comprehensive, we are able to provide support for an appropriate blend of formal verification and conformance testing in a simulation of the environment according to each application's needs and requirements.

**Multi-agent system verification.** Most well-known approaches to multi-agent system development (cf. [BDKJT97, WJK99, WD01, BG02, BM03]) focus on the design phase and do not provide specific support for verification. Verifying multi-agent coordination and flexible interaction is notoriously difficult due to their concurrent nature, the agents' autonomy, and the effects of learning and adaptation. Those approaches that do exist focus on the verification of interaction protocols, ignoring structural adaptation or interactions with the environment. They usually yield incomplete results, achieving a level of coverage that is far below what is common for traditional technical systems.

The CURCUMA framework allows us to describe multi-agent systems that use the social system metaphor for coordinating and structuring interactions and are embedded in and interacting with a complex environment in a way that can support both formal and empirical verification techniques. This allows us to consider the verification problem starting from the early phases of the development process. The importance of the principle of explicit grounding cannot be overemphasized in this context: As all instances of abstract concepts such as communities or commitments can be traced back to entities from the system's environment model, it is possible to observe and thus reason about all aspects of the system from an external perspective. Due to our use of *legal stance*, the focus on concrete elements of the system that can be expressed using standard software engineering techniques does not impair our ability to include the agents' beliefs and intentions in our considerations.

As both the environment and the social interactions between agents are typically complex even by themselves, the resulting state space of the overall system tends to be huge. As Graph Transformation Systems give us the ability to describe open systems, the state space may even be infinite. It is therefore indispensable to apply complexity reduction techniques, such as the separation of the specification into more tractable subsets. The decomposition into architectural views that was used to attack the design problem again proves useful in the context of verification, as it lends itself to the application of compositional verification techniques.

Our formal verification efforts therefore focus on the community as a useful unit of consideration that is limited in both size and scope. As discussed, its member agents need to respect the behavioral specification that is provided by the community type, but are free to implement it in any way that represents a valid refinement. This leads to two different verification problems: Is the specification internally consistent and sufficient for guaranteeing the desired properties? And does the implementation conform to the specification?

The first question concerns the culture or community type in question and its system of roles, norms and professed intentions. As there is no fundamental difference between the verification of cultures and community types, except perhaps concerning their degree of specificity and level of detail, we will focus on the verification of cultures in our discussion.

The second question concerns the agent themselves. In order to answer it, we need to extend our concept of refinement from automata to GTS. As the agents need to conform to all relevant cultures at once, this is also the point where conflicts between different views are identified and resolved, which may cause repercussions for the social design if two cultures are found to be mutually exclusive. The consistency of the employed ontologies that is achieved by basing ev-

## 5.1 Introduction

erything on the environment helps when identifying potential conflicts between different views, as it makes it easier to spot where their domains overlap.

Where possible, we try to answer both questions using formal verification. As the semantics of our specification is based on GTS and *Coordination Patterns*, we are able to apply the existing techniques and optimizations. Still, there are limits to what can be formally verified, even when dealing with a single culture. Brute-force model checking will only work for select properties of specifications of moderate size. The approach for invariant checking [BBG+06] is only designed to deal with safety properties and not applicable to liveness properties. Finally, chaotic behavior of the environment is completely beyond the reach of verification techniques. Understanding emergent properties of a physical system would require detailed differential and probabilistic analysis. What we strive for is hence the complete formal verification of those properties that are relevant to the safety of the system, while falling back on less reliable means of verification if necessary where only the efficiency of the system is concerned. This will allow us to prove that the system is never unsafe and can reasonably be expected to perform well in the general case.

**Multi-agent system validation.** In an ideal process, validation would only need to establish that the documented requirements are concise, complete, and correct, and everything else would verifiably follow from there. In the real world however, neither the requirements nor the process should be expected to achieve such perfection. The requirements are bound to be incomplete and may use inappropriate or oversimplifying abstractions. Non-functional requirements often prove difficult to formalize. The specifications that are created in later phases may amplify the inaccuracies in the underlying specifications or introduce errors of their own.

We can therefore follow two avenues towards a better approximation of an ideal process, which are both rooted in Model-Driven Engineering: We can improve the process and reduce human error by automating transformation steps; and we can improve the requirements and subsequent specifications by subjecting them to validation as early as possible. Both approaches benefit from techniques such as behavioral synthesis, model transformations, and code generation, which eliminate menial tasks and greatly facilitate the creation of simulations or prototypes which can be used to check whether the current specification remains true to the original intent.

It is again thanks to the CURCUMA framework and its emphasis on concrete entities that we are able to apply model-driven techniques to the system in its entirety and enable the rapid prototyping and iterative refinement of multi-agent system specifications. As all elements of the specification are testable, i.e. can be evaluated on the environment model, and most of them are even executable due to the operational semantics that exists for the employed formalisms, it is possible to put all key elements of a design to the test directly. Experimental validation can therefore be used even for partial specifications, such as cultures or community types. In later phases, increasingly detailed environment models can be used to test agent designs and, ultimately, the overall system. As emergent behavior, i.e. order resulting from seemingly random interactions, can usually only be observed at the system level, the ability to generate, try, and tweak prototypes is invaluable for its design.

A rapid prototyping approach with rapid cycles of experimental evaluation and subsequent refinement of the design specification does not only require appropriate tool support for the above-mentioned model-driven techniques, but also an infrastructure for executing, monitoring, testing, and evaluating the prototypes. Basic services that are used by the agents themselves, such as communication or persistence, also need to be made available. While it is conceivable to generate these services from the *service model*, the more common approach is to rely on existing runtime libraries and only model their interfaces or appropriate adapters explicitly. Finally, if the agents are embedded and a detailed simulation of the environment is required that goes beyond the discrete approximation that is provided by the *environment model*, a dedicated simulation kernel needs to be used. The challenge in this context is to integrate these components in a manner that is sufficiently generic to support a wide range of applications.

The systematic experimental exploration of a design is greatly facilitated if appropriate direct feedback is provided by the system. Again, the concise and operational nature of the specification proves useful, as it allows us to generate behavioral monitors from the specified constraint diagrams that are able to observe the behavior of a simulation or, with proper instrumentation, even the production system. Structural constraints (based on eSP/SDDs) can be used to flag violations of invariants or warn if the required preconditions for an action are not fulfilled (e.g. when an effector application is physically possible but the agent ignores that it is not permitted at the social level). Temporal constraints (based on TSSDs) describe entire scenarios and can be used to ascertain that required behavior actually occurs. The monitors can also be used to generate and store partial traces, which can then be used to display counterexamples at the model level. Likewise, the collected information can be used to provide a high level overview of the current state of the system, e.g. a list of open commitments.

**Chapter outline.** In this chapter, we do not expand our example in scope, but only add detail as required. We begin the following Section 5.2 with a discussion of the formal verification techniques that can be applied to the specification. We then delve into the question to which aspects and which properties of the system these techniques can be applied in theory and in practice. In Section 5.3, we look at the support for prototyping and experimental validation. The available tool support for both verification and validation is discussed separately in the following chapter. Related work is discussed in the concluding Section 5.4.

## 5.2 Verification

Every verification problem has the same basic structure: A *model*, a formal description of the behavior of a *system* that makes it amenable to analysis by representing it at a more abstract level, is checked against a *specification*, a set of requirements constraining that behavior. However, there is a large spectrum of formalisms for expressing models and specifications and, by extension, of verification techniques that can be applied to them.

Formal verification is a hard problem; it is complex and computationally expensive. In order to enable it for non-trivial cases, it is important to select the right abstractions for describing a particular system – and still, highly optimized implementations will be required for making verification feasible in practice. Popular model checkers such as SPIN (cf. [Hol97, Hol03]),

## 5.2 Verification

NuSMV (cf. [CCGR99]), or Bogor (cf. [RDH03]) therefore use dedicated modeling languages and contain many optimizations and heuristics that are tailored to certain types of models or even specific use cases. While there are attempts to achieve greater standardization in order to reduce the lock-in to a specific tool, such as the framework for integrating different model checkers that is proposed in [Kat06], it remains to be seen whether such a solution will gain general acceptance. Researchers often work at the limits of current technology and may therefore resent the inevitable loss in features and performance, whereas more widespread use outside of academia is likely to go hand in hand with a push for greater standardization.

There is no model checker that is dedicated to the presented modeling and specification approach, in particular not to the constraint specification languages that are proposed in Chapter 3. Fortunately, there is previous work that covers significant parts of the approach such as *Coordination Patterns* (cf. [Hir04]) or aspects of *Story-Driven Modeling* (cf. [BBG$^+$06, Sch06]). Even though there is a great variety of tools and languages, there is only a limited number of basic classes of models and specifications so that it is often possible to transform a specification and map it to the input format of an existing tool of the appropriate class or, with greater conceptual effort, a related class. We therefore provide an overview of common formalisms and methods before discussing several solutions that are suited for use with our approach in more detail.

**Models.** The elementary mathematical model underlying most formalisms is the *Labeled Transition System* (LTS), consisting of states, transitions, and labeling functions for either transitions or states. Many common types of deterministic and non-deterministic *finite automata* can be interpreted as LTS with transition labels, such as the *Mealy automata* used to define state machine behavior in Definition 2.3.1 in Section 2.3.2.1 or *Büchi automata*, the extension of finite automata to input words of infinite length. Kripke structures, minimalist LTS whose states are labeled with sets of valid propositions, are commonly used as the basic structure for model checking the behavior of reactive systems.

More expressive formalisms extend LTS with concepts such as real time or probabilistic behavior. *Timed Automata* (cf. [AD94, Yov96, BY03]) introduce the concept of clocks, which are used to define constraints on transitions. In turn, they form the basis of *Hierarchical Timed Automata* (cf. [DMY02]) and the *Extended Automaton* of Definition 2.3.4. *Stochastic Timed Automata* [BDHK06] use probability distributions in order to compute minimum time bounds for each transition, thus making it subject to chance which one is actually triggered first. In a similar vein, models based on *Markov Chains* (cf. [ASSB00]) use a memoryless probability distribution in order to compute the subsequent state.

*Petri Nets* (cf. [Pet62, Rei85]) are an alternative approach for the description of event-driven, parallel behavior. Their mathematical foundation permits the direct analysis of many interesting properties such as reachability, liveness, and absence of deadlocks [Mur89, RR98]. They are bipartite directed graphs, typically consisting of place and transition nodes, and a set of tokens marking places in order to indicate the active state. As for automata, there are extensions for handling time (*Timed Petri Nets*) and probability (*Stochastic Petri Nets*).

In Chapter 2, we have already introduced *Graph Transformation Systems* (see Definitions 2.2.14 through 2.2.17 in Section 2.2.2.4) as transition systems whose states are graphs. GTS are different from other types of transition systems because they describe the system at the meta-level, defining only classes of valid states (by means of the type system) and transitions (by means of graph patterns) (cf. [RSV04]). An important effect of this characteristic is that a GTS may have infinitely many states, and, more importantly, infinitely many *reachable* states, as graph rules are capable of generating new graph elements.

Of these formalisms, *Timed Automata*, which were used to define the *Real-Time Statechart* semantics, and GTS, which are the formal foundation of all story-driven modeling techniques, have the highest direct relevance for our approach. However, most model checking tools are not based on the mathematical formalism directly, but use custom input languages that sacrifice conceptual simplicity but provide better scalability through higher level abstractions (such as classes, processes or channels), e.g. Promela (SPIN) [Hol97, Hol03], NuSMV (NuSMV) [CCGR99], and the Bandera intermediate language (Bogor) [RDH03] for the above-mentioned model checkers. Unfortunately, the semantics of user-oriented specification languages tend to be complex, an observation of which Chapter 3 bears ample proof. It is therefore non-trivial to export a given model to a specific tool, even if both are rooted in the same formalism.

**Specifications.** The basic building block of a specification is the *atomic proposition*. Any property whose truth value is well-defined for each state of the system can be used as such. In some formalisms such as *Kripke structures*, states are explicitly labeled with the propositions that hold in them. In the context of GTS, we use *graph patterns* for defining elementary properties (see Section 2.2.2.5). In our extended automaton (see Definition 2.3.4 in Section 2.3.2.1), atomic propositions are elementary queries on the data model, which is represented by a GTS.

An *invariant* of a model is a formula of propositional logic, i.e. an expression combining atomic propositions and logical operators, that is required to hold for every state. Invariants are sufficient to express the important safety property that some proposition $p$ is always false ($\neg p$ holds), e.g. that a certain hazard never occurs. They are an integral part of our approach, down to the definition of *constrained GTS* (see Definition 2.2.16). In the specification of processes (see Definition 4.3.4) and cultures (see Definition 4.3.6), we use invariants to express constraints and requirements. These are typically written as SDDs, which allow expressing negation explicitly and remove the restriction to implicitly negative invariants. For *Coordination Patterns*, we allow defining role invariants (see Definition 2.3.6).

However, invariants are unable to deal with more complex properties connected to a system's dynamics as they do not distinguish between states and indiscriminately apply to the entire system. In order to describe dynamic properties, we need to use temporal logic. In the context of verification, most popular temporal logics are in some way related to the *Computational Tree Logic* CTL* (see Section 2.2.2.5). Its two most important subsets are CTL, which is restricted to state formulae, and LTL, which is restricted to path formulae. CTL allows making statements about all possible execution paths of a system (branching time), whereas LTL focuses on a single execution path at a time (linear time).

For both variants, there are timed extensions available: Clocked Computational Tree Logic (CCTL) [RK99] extends CTL, Metric Temporal Logic (MTL) [Koy90, AH93] and Time Point Temporal Logic (TPTL) [AH94], which were discussed in Section 3.3.2.5, extend LTL. As for

## 5.2 Verification

models, there also are several probabilistic extensions: *Probabilistic CTL* (PCTL) only replaces the standard quantifiers with probabilistic quantifiers, while the *Continuous Stochastic Logic* (CSL, for use with Markov models) and the *Probabilistic Timed CTL* (PTCTL, for use with *Probabilistic Timed Automata*) additionally support continuous time (cf. [Kwi03]).

In our approach, the primary means of expressing temporal constraints are TSSDs. As we have shown in Section 3.3.2.5, they are related to temporal logics such as LTL, MTL, and TPTL. However, mapping TSSDs to temporal logic is non-trivial. TSSDs are also much more succinct when in comes to describing certain aspects of a process, e.g. partially ordered parallel sequences. On the other hand, TSSDs are restricted to a single execution path, i.e. linear time, and do not allow encoding arbitrary CTL formulae. For some purposes, e.g. when defining pattern constraints for *Coordination Patterns*, we directly use temporal logic formulae as well.

**Methods.** The applicable methods depend both on the model and the specification. The specified properties in particular determine how we can verify them and how complex this will be. *Safety properties* are defined as properties that can be disproven by a finite counterexample. For a transition system with a finite number of states, verifying *safety* and its dual *reachability* is therefore straight-forward. *Liveness properties* such as progress or fairness (cf. [Lam77, OL82, AAH+85]) cannot be decided on a finite path because future states could always, potentially, fulfill or invalidate them – a problem we have already encountered when discussing the semantics of TSSDs. Verifying liveness properties is significantly more complex, which has even prompted attempts to reduce this problem to the checking of safety properties for certain cases [Sch05].

The most elegant way to verify a property is to prove that it can be deduced directly from the model. However, this task requires specialized skills and, e.g. when proving an invariant using some formal calculus, demands a significant effort. Most importantly, it is near impossible to automate for the general case. It can be useful in specific cases, however, e.g. when dealing with certain properties of Petri nets for which general proofs exist.

Quite contrary to this, model checking is all about automation. It is essentially a brute force approach that verifies properties by means of an exhaustive search of the state space. For state formulae, as in CTL, this can be done quite efficiently. For path formulae, as in LTL or CTL*, it is not sufficient to merely consider every possible state, but necessary to consider every possible *sequence* of states, which requires more elaborate procedures. The key problem in both cases is the size of the search space.

The two basic approaches are explicit state model checking and symbolic model checking. *Explicit state* model checkers represent and process every state explicitly, using optimized algorithms to improve performance. *Symbolic* model checkers focus on finding an optimized encoding of the state space, typically based on reduced ordered binary decision diagrams (ROBDDs). This makes it feasible to apply less elaborate algorithms because the representation makes computations more efficient and allows applying operations to sets of states.

Model checking real-time systems requires dedicated methods and tools, such as the model checker UPPAAL (cf. [LPY97]). The introduction of clocks further blows up the state space, even though time constraints introduce bounds that may make it possible to decide liveness properties on a finite trace. The additional complexity of the model therefore entails further restrictions for the types of properties that may be verified. Probabilistic models, which likewise require specific probabilistic model checking techniques, suffer a similar fate.

**Approach.** Settling on a single comprehensive solution is indeed desirable when dealing with a specific problem, and alluring in its clarity and elegance. However, the theoretical and practical problems that we are dealing with are too hard and varied to allow such simplicity.

A toolkit deserves to be as diverse as the problems it solves. We can distinguish three main dimensions for classifying these problems in our case: The *subject* progresses from cultures, community types (i.e. cultures with an environment), and agents (i.e. a composition of community types) to the overall system (i.e. the combination of multiple agents), each more extensive and complex than the last. The *properties* that are of interest are expressed by specifications that range from invariants to real-time temporal logic. Finally, the *result* that we strive to achieve can lie between a complete verification, i.e. ensuring the absence of errors, and exploration, for which stumbling upon a single counterexample might be sufficient. The latter points are closely related as the significance of the obtainable results generally decreases the more expressive the employed formalisms become.

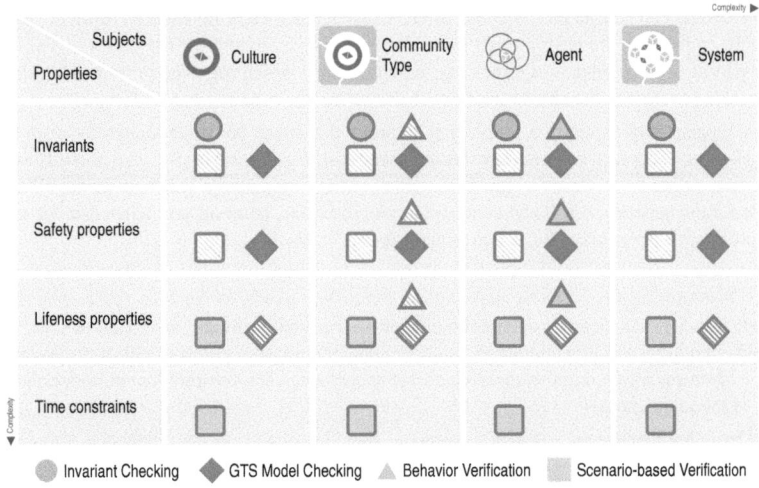

Figure 5.2.1: Overview of the employed verification techniques

Figure 5.2.1 provides an overview of the techniques we employ below. The table indicates for which types of problems the different approaches are recommended (solid icons) or applicable in theory (hatched icons).

*GTS model checking* can be employed for all subjects and a wide range of properties, for which it provides complete verification. In practice, it is often relegated to the early phases by the size and

## 5.2 Verification

complexity of the overall system. In this work, we adapt the existing approaches to our notations and methodology.

*Invariant checking* is restricted to inductive invariants, which allows it to provide complete verification for all subjects regardless of the size of the system. We adapt the approach to our notations and methodology and additionally propose optimizations for increasing the relevance and reliability of the generated counterexamples.

*Behavior verification* uses an original approach that is closely related to the concept of GTS refinement. Its specific focus is the conformance between the behavior of an agent and the norms to which it is required to adhere. The verification is efficient, but not guaranteed to be complete.

*Scenario-based verification* is proposed as a way to bring the full expressive power of TSSDs to bear. The approach is applicable to all subjects, but most at home in later phases of the process. The ability to discuss properties of execution paths and real-time constraints make it powerful, but also make complete verification impossible.

The different methods are bound together by the use of graphs as a common formal foundation. Besides, the CURCUMA framework serves as a unifying principle. As the approach promotes a clean decomposition into specialized communities, it invites the use of compositional verification techniques to keep the size of the analyzed models small. It even makes it possible to use different approaches for different communities, according to their specific purpose.

### 5.2.1 Model Checking

When modeling the system, we have stressed the conceptual and architectural separation between the state-based perspective of *Coordination Patterns* and the graph-based perspective of *Story-Driven Modeling*; the former dealing with real-time and continuous behavior, the latter using the provided abstractions and focusing on reconfiguration and compositional adaptation. This clear separation also serves us when verifying the system.

Model checking *Coordination Patterns* is well understood. The underlying real-time statecharts can be exported as Hierarchical Timed Automata, which can then be flattened into plain Timed Automata that can be processed by the model checker UPPAAL (cf. [LPY97]). The tool is then able to verify certain important properties of a protocol, for instance its freedom from deadlock (see [Hir04]). If the pattern contains continuous or hybrid components [Bur06, BGH05], its verification poses additional challenges that are the object of current research activities.

The operative aspect is, however, that for our purposes the *Coordination Pattern* can be seen as an atomic element whose correctness can be established independently from the rest of the system in either case. A compositional approach like this does not miraculously eliminate complexity, but relies on the additional requirement that, within each agent, the composition of the patterns preserves the role protocols and invariants of each of them, which may be non-trivial if the patterns are interdependent or affect intersecting sets of entities. Yet from the point of view of the multi-agent system, this means that the verification problem can be reduced to the question whether each required pattern is present at the right times.

#### 5.2.1.1 GTS model checking

The model describing the structural evolution of the system and the norms governing the instantiation of communities and, as a special case thereof, coordination patterns are both graph-based. In this context, the mapping that was presented in Section 2.3.3 allows us to seamlessly integrate *Coordination Patterns* into the graph-based structural model of the system, instantiating, destroying, or manipulating (e.g. disabling as a consequence of a failure) the patterns and their elements such as ports or communication channels just as any other graph node. The verification problem can thus be represented as a *constrained GTS*.

There are two prominent tools for the verification of GTS, CheckVMS (cf. [Var02, Var04, Var03, SV03]) and GROOVE (cf. [Ren03]). In [RSV04], the two authors provide a comparison of their respective approaches.

GROOVE implements a custom kernel, which is specifically designed for efficiently handling graphs, and provides explicit state CTL model checking with a focus on reachability. The kernel itself is written in Java and not highly optimized, but contains specific optimizations for recognizing and capitalizing on symmetries in the graph, which are capable of reducing both space and time requirements drastically.

CheckVMS, on the other hand, translates the specification to a Promela specification and relies on the symbolic model checker SPIN for performing the actual model checking. Consequently, the focus is on LTL model checking. As SPIN is highly optimized, this gives CheckVMS an edge in certain scenarios, but precludes most graph-specific optimizations. Most importantly, SPIN runs afoul of a defining characteristic of GTS, their ability to generate new elements and thus new states. In order to simulate this effect, CheckVMS explicitly captures those elements that might be dynamically created or destroyed, at the cost of greatly increasing the size and complexity of the specification. Object-based Graph Grammars [DFRdS03], a superficially related graph-based approach, likewise use SPIN for verification, but focus on message interchanges between objects instead of structural adaptation and therefore avoid this problem.

**GROOVE.** Due to the nature of the considered models and properties, GROOVE is the obvious choice for the verification of safety-related properties of our model. However, differences concerning syntax, semantics, and supported features make several transformations necessary before either the model or the specification can be exported to the tool.

Firstly, GROOVE matches graph patterns based on graph homomorphisms, meaning that all pattern elements of the same type might be matched to the same instance. In order to suppress this behavior, it is necessary to specify isomorphism constraints between nodes, forcing the matching algorithm to map them to distinct instances. The chosen approach is diametrically opposed to the one used by *Story Driven Modeling*, where all instances are implicitly assumed to be distinct unless this restriction is lifted by a homomorphism constraint. When exporting patterns to GROOVE, it is therefore necessary to add inequality constraints between all pairs of nodes of the same type to reproduce the original semantics. As the necessary number of constraints grows quadratically with the number of nodes for each type, the resulting graph patterns may quickly become very unwieldy for larger patterns.

## 5.2 Verification

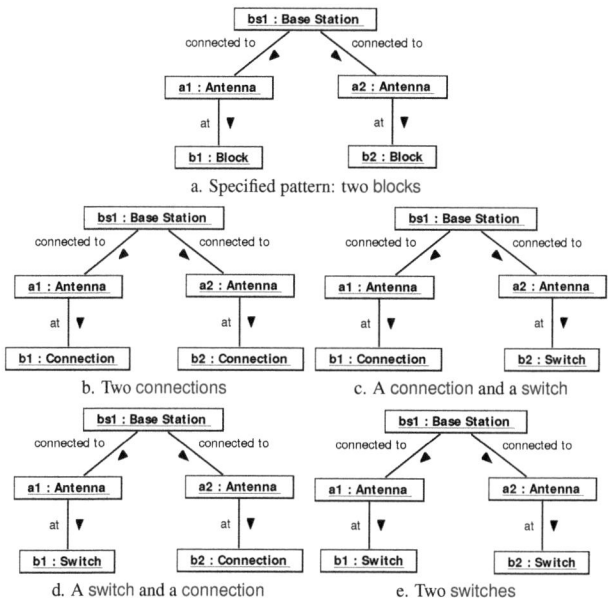

Figure 5.2.2: Expanding a pattern containing abstract types to simulate inheritance

Secondly, GROOVE does not provide support for the additional features that we have introduced in Chapter 2 in order to enable a more direct mapping from the employed UML-based notations to our formalization of GTS. Most importantly, there is no support for inheritance (see Definition 2.2.3). As GROOVE does not use a type system at all, there is no straight-forward way to add such a concept to the engine either. In order to emulate the effect of inheritance, it is therefore necessary to generate sets of alternative patterns where each instance of a type is in turn replaced with each concrete subtype. Figure 5.2.2 illustrates this for a pattern encoding that two blocks are connected to the same base station. As block is abstract, we only need to check for switches and connections here. As the expansion results in $j^n$ different type combinations for a pattern with $n$ nodes of a type with $j-1$ subtypes, combinatorial explosion quickly becomes a problem when the patterns or type hierarchies are large or abstract base types are used frequently. This is partially counteracted by the fact that GROOVE does not distinguish instance names, which means that symmetrical expansions such as Figures 5.2.2c and 5.2.2d are treated as one. If the patterns mostly operate on concrete types, this approach is viable, though. In a similar manner, cardinalities have to be encoded as a set of forbidden pattern as described in Section 2.2.2.6, which is less problematic as one to three patterns are sufficient to encode most common cardinalities.

Finally, there is quite naturally no support for the proposed extended constraint languages. As GROOVE relies on forbidden elements instead of *negative application conditions* for negation and does not provide explicit quantification, matching an SDD (or even eSP) requires a more elaborate approach that splits a single diagram into a sequence of interlocking graph rule applications.

In [KG06c], we provide a detailed presentation of an algorithm for generating a set of graph rules that are able to determine whether an SDD holds for a given instance situation. This rule set consists of specific pattern rules that encode the graph patterns of the SDD and a carefully orchestrated set of generic auxiliary rules that emulate the effects of quantification, then and else connectors, and (1) and (0) nodes. The rules generate a tree of auxiliary *marker* nodes that double both as a means of guiding the control flow of the rule applications and of storing the generated bindings. By means of their relative position in the marker tree structure, they indicate which nodes have already been processed, while appropriately named edges from the marker to the corresponding nodes indicate which instances are part of a binding. The rules heavily rely on GROOVE's ability to assign rule priorities in order to ensure that all patterns are matched in the right order, the result is propagated back to the root marker, and all markers are cleaned up afterwards.

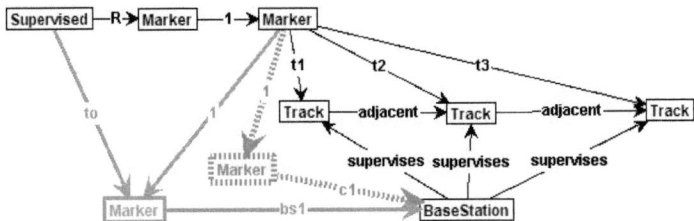

Figure 5.2.3: Graph rule encoding the implication

Figure 5.2.3 provides an example of a pattern rule encoding the second part of the supervised property as defined in Figure 3.2.12. For three consecutive tracks, the pattern tries to identify a base station *bs1* that is supervising them. Figure 5.2.4 shows an augmented instance graph during evaluation. The marker structure indicates that the property has just been confirmed for the first three tracks. A binding's validity is undetermined by default, but it is marked as either success or failure using a result node once it is completed. While all of the paths from the root marker to a leaf marker represent bindings, only this particular binding is final in the example.

While the required number of auxiliary rules is high – in the dozens for a typical SDD – evaluation is nonetheless efficient because the individual rules are small and their priorities ensure that only a subset of them is applicable at any one time. Checking a set of static properties of an instance situation is therefore no problem. However, a sequence of rule applications is necessarily less efficient than a single rule application, which means that the size of the most complex systems that can realistically be verified using GROOVE is significantly reduced by the use of elaborate SDDs.

## 5.2 Verification

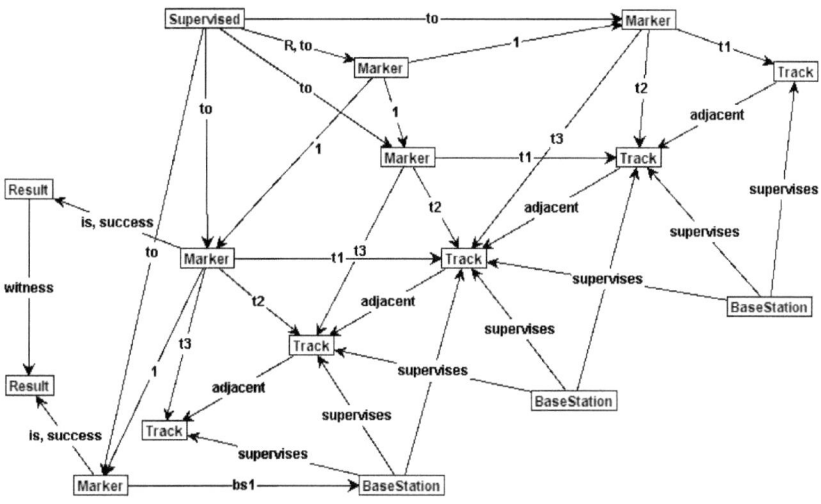

Figure 5.2.4: Markers while processing

In theory, it is possible to extend the marker concept to the temporal domain and use it to guide the evaluation of TSSDs, an idea that is also sketched in [KG06c]. At the cost of further increasing the computational complexity, it is in fact suitable for monitoring a single execution trace. Unfortunately, it is not only inefficient but conceptually impossible to perform model checking based on TSSDs with GROOVE. TSSDs encode path formulae and therefore do not merely consider the current state, but rely on history information about previous states which would have to be encoded by markers. GROOVE, on the other hand, is built for checking reachability. While only considering states, it is consequently concerned with computing all possible successors of a state. As states that would be indistinguishable from GROOVE's point of view suddenly become distinct due to the additional history information, the state space explodes and the tool's fundamental approach for recognizing and unifying recurring states is defeated.

**CheckVMS.** As the comparative analysis in Section 3.3.2.5 already suggests, an LTL model checker is thus indispensable for the verification of TSSDs. Putting aside the above-mentioned scalability problems, CheckVMS could be used for the verification of the subset of TSSDs whose temporal structure can be expressed as an LTL formula. Regrettably, typical scenarios combine non-trivial graph patterns with inherently dynamic models, often containing significant structural adaptation or the potential for unbounded instance creation, thus touching upon the weak spots of the approach. A complete formal verification of even restricted TSSD specifications is therefore not feasible in the foreseeable future.

### 5.2.1.2 Usage

Which aspects of the designed component behavior can be checked using GTS model checking? As cultures, community types, the environment, and agent coordination are all specified using graph patterns, we can apply the technique to a variety of subjects – basically, any one of the constrained GTS we have defined in the previous chapter's formalization could provide a suitable model and specification.

We first turn our attention to the verification of cultures, encoded as GTS $M_i^S$. The abstraction from a specific domain that cultures introduce was motivated by reuse, but is also helpful for stripping away unnecessary details during verification. Furthermore, each culture is normally limited in size. For initially developing and improving a social design, they are therefore well suited.

**Cultures.** When using GTS model checking on an isolated culture, we can establish whether it is internally consistent, i.e. whether its norms taken by themselves do not allow violations of the specified invariants. As this is a necessary condition for a culture's usefulness, negative results at this point are very helpful for the iterative improvement of the design. The verification is comparatively cheap and quite transparent, especially when using GROOVE's visualization component for stepping through the counterexamples. However, positive results are not indicative for the overall system. For cultures focusing on agent communication and coordination, the results may be directly applicable to concrete communities implementing them, but for cultures involving physical entities, this requires including the environment into the consideration.

**Environment.** Verifying the environment by itself is typically trivial. If the closed environment behavior $M^{CW}$, i.e. just the processes without agents, is capable of violating the environment's invariants, or rather the laws of nature, this is indicative of a modeling error. The open environment behavior $M^{OW}$, on the other hand, allows arbitrary agent behavior and is almost certain to yield chaotic, undesirable results.

**Communities.** We therefore need to look at the community type $M^C$ that results from mapping a culture to a specific environment and combine it with the behavior of the environment in order to verify that the specified norms lead to the desired result in a concrete environment as well. If we use the closed environment behavior $M^{CW}$, the GTS will resemble the previously checked system for the culture, but additionally include the effects of environment processes. However, the behavior of agents that are not a member of a community of the studied type may also have an effect, which points us to the open environment behavior $M^{OW}$ additionally including all available sensors and effectors. However, as the very idea of a community type is to restrict behavior, we need to keep in mind that roles of $M^C$ restrict the use of the concerned effectors, which we make explicit in the restricted environment behavior $M^{RW}$ by extending the effector definitions of $M^{OW}$ as to require the absence of all applicable roles as a precondition.

An important point, which we touched upon when discussing sensors and effectors, is the difference between the intended and actual effects of an action, which cannot be expected to be identical in a complex environment. If our model is too abstract, we might conclude that no invariants are violated because the agents do not intend to violate them. In our case study in the

## 5.2 Verification

previous chapter, shuttles use their effectors to accelerate and decelerate, not for explicitly moving to the next block, which provides a more realistic view on the limited control physical bodies have over their movement.

The concrete effect this has on the correctness of cultures and community types can be seen in an example that we have presented in detail in [GK07]. Two semaphores control the exclusive access to an intersection. Only one semaphore may be open at a time, and vehicles may only pass open semaphores. Finally, a closed semaphore may only open when there is currently no vehicle in the intersection. When only studying the involved cultures (one controlling vehicle movement, one coordinating the semaphores) and using an abstract, or perhaps naive, model of intentional movement, the system seems safe. However, when including the environment and using a model of implicit inertial movement, the model checker (GROOVE) finds a counterexample: Two vehicles approach the intersection. The first one ensures that its semaphore is open and decides to enter the intersection, but has not passed the semaphore yet when it closes. As the intersection is empty, the second semaphore is now allowed to open immediately. If the second vehicle now decides to also keep going and pass it, both vehicles collide in the intersection. While common sense might have been enough to spot this specific problem – after all, the traffic lights at an intersection do not all change simultaneously either, and there is a yellow phase to account for the fact that vehicles have inertia and may not be able to stop anymore – it is easy enough to get caught up in the perspective of the employed model, especially if it is more complex, and lose track of the underlying assumptions, which underlines the importance of verifying and validating a model in a way that is actually pertinent.

**Composition.** Checking individual cultures or community types is convenient, but may not be sufficient. As an agent may be the member of multiple communities dealing with non-orthogonal concerns, there may be undesired interaction effects that we have to consider. The global properties of the system may be different from the sum of the local properties, which rules out a purely compositional approach.

However, compositional verification is possible if we include an abstraction of the relevant effects of other communities into the model as another external process (cf. [EDK89]). Where another community type merely affects the same entities, we can nondeterministically apply its respective behavioral norms as an overapproximation of its possible effects. If both types constrain the same effector, each use must be sanctioned by both. In a manner similar to the previously mentioned approach for the compositional verification of component behavior (see [GTB$^+$03]), we delegate this reconciliation problem to the level of the agent, as only the agent is aware of all relevant rule sets. We can, however, statically determine whether it is possible for the communities to contain contradictory norms, simultaneously requiring and forbidding the use of the same effector. While this approach works for the verification of safety properties, it is unable to deal with complex interdependencies, such as a shuttle missing a deadline in one community because of restrictive traffic laws in another. Such issues can only be recognized at the system level, and resolving them may require fine tuning all involved community types. Mostly, however, we are able to simply layer the different community behaviors on top of each other, with safety-related communities typically not affecting goal-driven behavior but vetoing unsafe actions where necessary – not unlike the classic subsumption architecture (cf. [Bro91]), where higher-level strategies (drive-to-destination) are temporarily overruled by lower-level strategies (avoid-obstacle).

**System.** By studying $M$, the parallel composition of the agent GTS $M_1^A, \ldots, M_n^A$ and the environment GTS $M^{CW}$, we can finally verify the overall system behavior against our original requirements. This verification problem may, however, become arbitrarily large.

The more comprehensive our perspective gets, the more meaningful the results become. Unfortunately, these results also become harder and harder to obtain. One aspect that has a strong influence on the problem size is the start graph on which we base the evaluation. In the environment specification $W$ in the previous chapter, we used a GTS $S_T$ that characterized all possible start graphs. While this is very useful in theory because it allows us to actually let GROOVE check all imaginable systems at once, $S_T$ can be expected to generate infinitely many different start graphs, making the problem intractable before we have even begun to consider agent behavior.

Selecting suitable, representative start graphs is therefore important. A technique that we have successfully used for limiting the required size of the graph was focusing on a section of the instance graph, hiding its interactions with the rest of the system, which only occur at specific interface points, behind processes emulating their effects. In this way, we could for example treat a part of a closed system as an open system that agents leave and enter. When we are more interested in the evolution and behavior of a specific agent, we can turn this idea around and dynamically generate the environment around the agent as it is relevant to it. This requires defining a new process that is based on rules from the GTS $S_T$. How much environment should be generated is primarily dependent on the agent's sensors, as these provide a first approximation of what could have an effect on the agent's decisions. Additionally, we need to consider the defined physical and social invariants and norms to ensure that the process only creates consistent extensions. Basically, this approach allows verifying that an agent behaves correctly in the face of an arbitrary correct environment.

**Case Study.** Of the cultures in our case study in the previous chapter, we are able to verify the positioning and traffic safety cultures with their update and distance coordination subcultures. The latter exclusively deal with communication between agents and can therefore be verified at the culture level. The former are also verified at the community type level because they are more tightly coupled with the physical environment. Due to the described limitations, we can only verify them for a small number of shuttles on a selection of track layouts that we consider characteristic.

The main limitation of this approach is that the cultures whose focus is on the fulfillment of commitments cannot be verified as the corresponding LTL properties are not supported by GROOVE. We can obtain limited results, e.g. by creating a start graph containing a commitment and checking if it is fulfilled in the future, which represents a reachability problem again, but this is insufficient for obtaining a definite confirmation.

## 5.2.2 Invariant Checking

As discussed, invariants are an important element of our specification, used to describe structural and safety requirements. While they are more limited than generic temporal logic properties, their simpler structure makes it possible to apply efficient algorithms that allow us to check systems that would be too large or complex to handle for a GTS model checker.

*Constrained GTS* (see Definition 2.2.16) define a set of constraints that represent *operational invariants* of the system. This means that, starting from the set of initial states, there is no sequence of rule applications that leads to a state where one of the invariants is violated. The required computations for the verification of this property basically correspond to the reachability analysis that is performed by GROOVE, with all the associated limitations.

In order to overcome these restrictions, the approach presented in [Sch06, GS04] relies on *inductive invariants* instead. In principle, inductive invariants are stronger than operational invariants because they require that in any valid state there are only transitions leading to other valid states, which implies the corresponding operational invariant – provided the initial states are valid – but also extends to states which may not be reachable from the set of initial states at all.

However, instead of dealing with the state space of the GTS directly, it is possible to treat the problem at the pattern level, i.e. reason about classes of states containing occurrences of the same graph pattern. While each class may represent infinitely many states, there is only a finite number of relevant classes. In particular, it is possible to characterize all states where an invariant has just been invalidated due to a rule application by means of a set of patterns. The central idea is that an invariant can only become invalid because either a forbidden element has been added or a required element has been deleted in the instance graph. As all invariants are represented by graph patterns of finite size, there is only a finite number of (partial) mappings from the elements of each graph rule to corresponding elements of the invariant and consequently only a finite number of different rule applications that might create or delete the critical elements. For each such mapping or *target graph pattern*, the algorithm then has to compute the *source graph pattern* characterizing the preceding states by reverting the effects of the rule application. If the computed source pattern does not itself violate an invariant and no preempting transformation rules with higher priority are enabled in it, the mapping represents a (class of) counterexample(s), i.e. an enabled transition from a valid to an invalid state. An important detail will be of interest below: As the source graph $SGP$ is a pattern representing a class of instances, a forbidden pattern or a precondition of a preempting rule $P$ is only relevant if it matches all possible instances of the pattern, which is only the case if $P$ is less restrictive than $SGP$. This means that $P$ needs to be a subpattern of $SGP$ ($P \subseteq SGP$) as defined in Definition 4.3.13, i.e. have a less strict positive part but stricter negative application conditions (NACs).

Figure 5.2.5 presents an almost minimal example: Two shuttles may not share the same track (collision in Figure 5.2.5a), but can move forward freely (unchecked move in Figure 5.2.5b). In the generated target graph pattern (see Figure 5.2.5c), *s1-sa* has (just) crashed into *s2*, which is an invalid state. As the corresponding source graph pattern (see Figure 5.2.5d) is valid, this is a counterexample, proving that, unsurprisingly, the system is not safe.

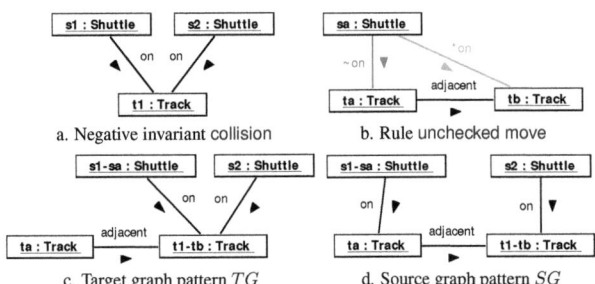

Figure 5.2.5: Example generating a counterexample

**Strengths and limitations.** The main advantage of the method is that it is capable of dealing with systems with an infinite state space because it combines model checking with an additional abstraction step. The effort for enumerating and checking all mappings using a brute force approach only depends on the number of ways to combine rules and invariants, which is in turn determined by their size and number. For heterogeneous patterns that contain many different types but only a few elements, this number is typically small. However, for patterns with homogeneous type structures containing $n$ and $k$ elements of the same type, there may be up to $\binom{n}{k}$ distinct mappings for these elements alone, which may result in a prohibitive number of relevant cases. The limiting factor for the method is therefore not the size of the state space, but the size of the specified graph rules and invariants.

In [BBG+06], we have presented a concept for using the relational calculator CrocoPat [BNL05] for performing the checks. While this approach incurs a certain overhead that may outweigh its benefits when applied to smaller patterns, the symbolic encoding can help to reduce the impact of larger patterns that generate a large number of mappings when processed using explicit enumeration.

A drawback of the method is that it tends to produce a potentially large number of false negatives because it overapproximates the original operational invariant. In practice, many of the generated counterexamples do not correspond to feasible topologies and violate explicit or implicit assumptions about the system structure. A related problem is that the employed subpattern check is actually too strong (whereas a simple isomorphism check would be too weak): There are source graph patterns for which no valid instance exists even though none of the forbidden patterns is a subpattern. The corresponding counterexamples are thus false negatives.

#### 5.2.2.1 Constraint languages

The desire to be able to express positive invariants in order to avoid the need for double negations first arose when working with the invariant checking method. As it was one of the motivating use cases for the extension of the existing constraint languages, it is unsurprising that eSPs and

## 5.2 Verification

SDDs can be used in conjunction with it. As TSSDs go far beyond invariants, they are out of the scope of the method by design.

When using the two structural languages for invariant and rule specification, some restrictions and considerations apply, however. As we have chosen to use positive or required invariants to improve usability whereas the invariant checking approach is based on negative or forbidden invariants, we need to *internally* convert all specified invariants to implicitly negative invariants by simply negating the respective SDDs. $p$ and $\neg q$ thus become $\neg p$ and $\neg\neg q$, respectively $q$.

The most significant restrictions stem from the central assumption that the changes that affect an invariant are always local, i.e. operate on elements that are directly matched by the corresponding pattern. Universal quantification and the generated candidate sets violate the locality assumption because the size of a candidate set is not bounded a priori and may comprise the entire instance graph. It is therefore necessary to *internally* replace the universal quantifier with its dual, the existential quantifier, i.e. converting $\forall x : P(x)$ to $\neg \exists x : \neg P(x)$.

While SDD References to SDD Patterns are not a problem per se – although they directly contribute to the size of the graph pattern – it is not possible to use recursively defined SDDPs. Transitive properties such as reachability might be invalidated by changes anywhere in the instance graph, which completely breaks the locality assumption.

As SDDs allow expressing complex properties consisting of a hierarchy of nested required and forbidden patterns, the algorithm that is used for performing the actual pattern matching needs to be upgraded from plain graph patterns, which is straight-forward due to the applied transformations and imposed restrictions. The crucial question, however, is whether the algorithms for computing the target graph pattern and the backwards step still work. Fortunately, the restriction to existential quantification entails that every SDD produces only candidate sets consisting of a single binding (or no candidate sets at all). Therefore, though a diagram may produce a wide range of candidate sets due to the quantification or possible alternative branches, each individual binding results from a unique sequence of successful or unsuccessful attempts to match the various patterns of the nodes of the SDD. By merging the matching patterns $P_n^+$ into a pattern $P^+$ and collecting the failed patterns $P_n^-$ in a set $\mathcal{P}^-$ for each alternative, we can derive graph patterns $[P^+, \mathcal{P}^-]$ representing the different alternatives which can then be used for the computation of target and source graph patterns in the usual fashion. In a manner of speaking, the SDD is expanded into a set of alternative graph patterns which are then processed in its place.

The inclusion of attributes into rules or invariants is not problematic for discrete models. In [Bec07], the approach is even extended towards hybrid models that support continuously changing attributes, although this requires significant extensions to the underlying model.

In Figure 5.2.6, the invariant collision is expressed as a positive invariant using an SDD. Internally, it is converted to the negative invariant in Figure 5.2.5a above. The invariant connected states that each track must have a predecessor and a successor. It is given as a positive invariant using universal quantification in Figure 5.2.6b. Internally, it is converted to a negative invariant containing a NAC, expressing the requirement by means of a double negation (see Figure 5.2.6c).

# 5. Verification and Validation

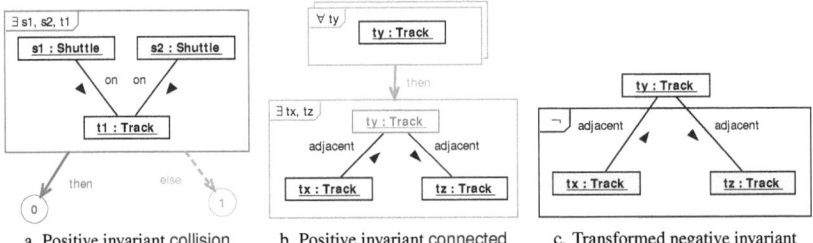

Figure 5.2.6: Converting positive and negative invariants

### 5.2.2.2 Optimizations

Thanks to the described transformations, the algorithms for target graph pattern generation, backwards application of rules, and handling the dangling edge problem that were presented in [GS04] and [Sch06] can be applied without modifications when using SDDs as part of the specification. However, the greater number of relevant invariants, combined with the negations introduced by the conversion into negative invariants and the removal of the universal quantifiers, lead to an increased number of interrelated rules and invariants with NACs, which acerbates the discussed problem of false negatives. In order to improve the method's usability in the context of our modeling approach, we therefore propose several refinements that help to reduce the number of false negatives.

A measure that is simple but essential for the verification of non-trivial specifications is the inclusion of additional soundness conditions in the set of considered invariants. Based on the scheme presented in Chapter 2 that was also used for exporting the specification to GROOVE, the cardinalities of the type system can automatically be translated into invariants, which is indispensable for eliminating a multitude of obviously false counterexamples. Furthermore, it is also advisable to encode relevant assumptions about the structure of the system that go beyond simple cardinalities. For example, two track segments (see Figure 4.3.6 in the previous chapter) will never form a cycle in any sane initial graph, which will be true for any instance graph as the structure is never modified by subsequent rule applications. As the invariant checking algorithm does not consider initial graph structures, this particular pattern might however occur in hundreds of purely theoretical counterexamples. To mark these cases as irrelevant a priori, such a structure should be encoded as an explicitly forbidden pattern.

It is furthermore possible to reduce the number of generated false negatives by modifying the employed algorithm itself. By deriving additional implied forbidden patterns that can be derived as logical consequences of combinations of the explicitly specified patterns[1] before computing counterexamples, we can eliminate further false negatives at comparatively little cost. For counterexamples where a forbidden pattern matches the source graph pattern but is not a subpattern of

---

[1] If $a$ implies $b$, and $b$ is incompatible with $c$, then we can conclude that $a$ and $c$ are likewise incompatible.

## 5.2 Verification

it, it is sometimes possible to show by construction that there is no valid way to extend the source graph pattern in a way that actually completes one of the forbidden pattern's NACs, making the source graph pattern effectively invalid. While this latter extension can be computationally expensive, it seems greatly preferable to performing a corresponding analysis manually.

#### 5.2.2.3 Usage

Most of the points that were made above for GTS model checking also apply to the use of invariant checking, as both have a similar scope. We are again able to check the positioning and traffic safety cultures, as all relevant properties are specified as invariants. With respect to professed intentions, the restriction to invariants only allows asserting static consistency properties (no contradictory statements) and completely removes temporal aspects such as the fulfillment of commitments from the scope.

Now, however, we are not just able to guarantee safety for a limited number of shuttles on specific track layouts, but obtain a universal result applying to any valid topology. Concerning the proposed optimizations, we turn to the environment specification in order to obtain the relevant cardinalities and structural assumptions, which can be deduced from the generating GTS $S_T$.

In [BBG+06], we have published benchmarks for checking a system consisting of 8 rules and 19 invariants of small to medium size that was quite similar to the traffic safety culture. Verification of the overall system took around 5 minutes, a figure that has since been further reduced by optimizations in the employed algorithms.

### 5.2.3 Behavior Verification

The previously presented techniques focus on the reachability of forbidden states, which is sufficient to prove many important properties of a system, in particular concerning its safety. However, other aspects of the modeling approach from the previous chapter that rather have a temporal character, such as the fulfillment of commitments, are not covered by them. By focusing on forbidden states, we have largely ignored the behavioral dimension of the model so far. After all, cultures do not only state *what* an agent should (or should not) achieve, but may also suggest or require *how* it should or should not go about this in more detail. Their behavioral norms shift the focus to actions, or behaviors corresponding to sequences of actions.

A basic behavioral norm simply forbids or requires specific effector applications. On the GTS level, this boosts the importance of transitions because it is now possible to have forbidden transitions connecting two states each of which is valid taken by itself: If, for example, we introduce traffic lights with the goal of excluding collisions, running a red light is still forbidden (for good reasons!) even when the intersection is empty.

As we shall see, adding transitions to the equation does have benefits in other areas, both with respect to expressiveness and state-space reduction, although it makes things more complex conceptually. After all, we can now detect illegal behavior immediately instead of recognizing it only indirectly by deducing it from subsequent constraint violations.

But how can we verify this type of property? This question is closely related to the concept of *restricted GTS refinement*, which we have defined in Definition 4.3.16 in the preceding chapter.

#### 5.2.3.1 Refinement Verification

The main challenge that is posed by the verification of a restricted refinement relation between two GTS lies in the restriction to a shared domain that is also its main motivation. Because the private domains are invisible to the other GTS, their effects on the selection of the applied rules are intransparent and the problem that apparently identical states result in different behavior is intensified. As both GTS basically are black boxes to each other whose future behavior might depend on the complete history in some unknown way, the only way to determine whether the refining GTS will act in accordance with the defining GTS is to actually execute the two GTS in parallel.

Formal conformance checking nonetheless requires dynamically testing the same conditions that can be used for static analysis in the unrestricted case: Is the transition in the refined GTS allowed? And is every required transition present? As the refining GTS takes the lead in deciding which discretionary rules it applies, whereas the defining GTS sets the standard for urgent rules, the GTS cannot simply be run side by side. Ideally, the 'leading' GTS would announce the next transition, and the 'reflecting' GTS would check whether it could match it. In the absence of such an announcement, the 'reflecting' GTS would have to perform this check after the fact, which would require caching the previous state for precondition checks. The best solution is therefore to combine the two systems into a single GTS that implicitly performs the desired checks.

In the combined GTS, we have to ensure that the leading (i.e. refining respectively required) rule is never executed without its reflecting (i.e. allowing respectively implementing) rule. A static analysis of the rule sets allows us to identify these rule pairs and mark them with an identical label. When using restricted refinement, the structural mapping between the rules is merely a necessary, but no longer a sufficient condition, meaning that we can only obtain negative results from static analysis, e.g. whether an agent is lacking or never using an effector that is needed to implement some urgent behavioral norm of a community type.

For defining the synchronous execution of the two rules, we can finally put our elaborations on rule composition from Section 2.2.2.3 to use: The combination of a leading rule $r$ with its reflecting rule $r'$ can be defined as the joining of the rules join$(r, r')$. Simply replacing all rules with their joined counterparts would merely block all non-conforming behavior, however. We explicitly need to retain the option of executing a leading rule $r$ although the reflecting rule $r'$ is *not* enabled where it was present in the original rules. Formally, these cases are characterized by the composition exclude$(r, r')$, characterizing a set of forbidden states where a violation is about to occur. Using these definitions, we can arrive at a first approximation of the desired GTS:

**Definition 5.2.1** *The* labeled parallel composition *of two constrained, labeled GTS* $S := (\mathcal{T}_S, \mathcal{G}_S^i, \mathcal{R}_S, \Phi_S, l_S)$ *and* $T := (\mathcal{T}_T, \mathcal{G}_T^i, \mathcal{R}_T, \Phi_T, l_T)$ *is defined as the GTS* $U := (\mathcal{T}_U, \mathcal{G}_U^i, \mathcal{R}_U, \Phi_U, l_U)$, *where* $\mathcal{T}_U := \mathcal{T}_S \cup \mathcal{T}_T$, $\mathcal{G}_U^i := \mathcal{G}_S^i \cup \mathcal{G}_T^i \cup \{G \cup G' | G \in \mathcal{G}_S^i \wedge G' \in \mathcal{G}_T^i\}$, $\mathcal{R}_U := \mathcal{R}_S \cup \mathcal{R}_T \cup \{\text{join}(r, r') | r \in \mathcal{R}_S \wedge r' \in \mathcal{R}_T \wedge l_S(r) \cap l_T(r') \neq \emptyset\}$, *the constraint set* $\Phi_U$ *consists of*

## 5.2 Verification

$\Phi_S \cup \Phi_T \cup \{v | r \in \mathcal{R}_S \wedge r' \in \mathcal{R}_T \wedge l_S(r) \cap l_T(r') \neq \emptyset \wedge v \in \text{exclude}(r, r')\}$, and $\forall r \in \mathcal{R}_S$ holds $l_U(r) = l_S(r)$, $\forall r \in \mathcal{R}_T$ holds $l_U(r) = l_T(r)$, and if $r \in \text{join}(r', r'')$ with $r' \in \mathcal{R}_S$ and $r'' \in \mathcal{R}_T$, we have $l_U(r) = (l_S(r') \setminus l_T(r'')) \cup (l_T(r'') \setminus l_S(r'))$ or $\tau$ if this set is empty.

The *labeled parallel composition* of two GTS is denoted by $S \|_l T$.

As a final preliminary, we define the *restriction* of a constrained, labeled GTS $U := (\mathcal{T}_U, \mathcal{G}_U^i, \mathcal{R}_U, \Phi_U, l_U)$ to a label set $\mathcal{B}$, denoted by $U|_\mathcal{B}$, as the GTS $(\mathcal{T}_U, \mathcal{G}_U^i, \{r \in \mathcal{R}_U | l_U(r) \subseteq \mathcal{B}\}, \Phi_U, l_U)$.

The desired combined GTS can then be defined as *labeled parallel composition* of the two original GTS $S$ and $T$, *restricted* to $(\mathcal{B}_S \cup \mathcal{B}_T) \setminus (\mathcal{B}_S \cap \mathcal{B}_T)$ so that all original rule pairs are eliminated and only the joined versions remain. The resulting GTS can then be used either as the basis for graph model checking or testing the system.

Even if the number of possible execution paths was finite or at least reducible to a finite number due to symmetries, the cost of checking every possible execution path can be expected to be forbidding. In practice, this means that we will have to content ourselves with verifying a selection of representative execution paths, e.g. by simulating the system and verifying the exhibited behavior.

#### 5.2.3.2 Usage

Cultures are supposed to set boundaries that restrict agent behavior enough to meet the assigned requirements, but without unduly limiting the agents' autonomy. Once a culture, respectively community type, has been shown to be correct, this should be sufficient to ensure the correctness of any conformant agent implementation.

**Conformance.** Given a verified community type and an agent specification, the question is therefore whether the agent actually conforms to the community type. If the agent specification is available as a GTS, we could apply the same techniques that were applied to the community type to prove the desired properties again, but this would neither prove conformance at the behavioral level (as different sets of norms can guarantee the same invariants), nor be efficient due to the the greater complexity of the agent specifications.

We therefore employ the concept of *restricted GTS refinement* to ensure that the externally visible behavior of an agent conforms to the behavior specified by a community type. In this case, the common domain is the environment, whereas the internal data structures of the agent are inaccessible from the outside and all social entities are private to the community type.

The structural checks ensure that the agent possesses all the effectors that are required by an urgent behavioral norm. But we can go beyond that: Does the agent have sufficient sensors for perceiving all entities appearing in norms that affect it? This may not be a hard criterion in all cases, as the agent may be able to compensate for a missing sensor by behaving defensively, but always indicates a point that deserves special attention. If we can show that certain inevitable commitments can only be fulfilled in a certain way, there may also be effectors that are indispensable for conforming even though they are not required by a urgent behavioral norm.

For performing the dynamic part of the conformance checks, we need to construct the *labeled parallel composition* of the agent behavior and the community type behavior. As a result of the static analysis, we have already labeled all norms of the GTS $M^C$ and the corresponding rules of the GTS $M^A$ with the scoped name of the norm. The rules describing the agent's internal processes are labeled with $\tau$. The environment is represented by $M^{RW}$, consisting of processes and those agent behaviors that remain unrestricted, all labeled with $\tau$. The resulting labeled GTS are denoted by $\tilde{M}^C$, $\tilde{M}^A$, and $\tilde{M}^{RW}$.

This can also be performed for multiple community types $M_1^C, \ldots, M_m^C$ or agents $M_1^A, \ldots, M_n^A$ at once. As the individual community types are independent of each other, as are the individual agents, we use plain parallel composition to construct $\tilde{M}^C = \tilde{M}_1^C \| \ldots \| \tilde{M}_m^C$ and $\tilde{M}^A = \tilde{M}_1^A \| \ldots \| \tilde{M}_n^A$ in this case.

The overall model $\tilde{M}$ is then derived by combining $\tilde{M}^C$ and $\tilde{M}^A$ with $\tilde{M}^{RW}$ using labeled parallel composition and restricting the result to $\tau$ in order to eliminate the original rules and norms:

$$\tilde{M} := (\tilde{M}^A \|_l \tilde{M}^C \|_l \tilde{M}^{RW})|_{\{\tau\}}. \tag{5.2.1}$$

Based on $\tilde{M}$, we can then detect violations of norms by checking whether any of the invariants in $\Phi^{\tilde{M}}$ does not hold. As the original invariants $\Phi^W$ and $\Phi_i^C$ are also included in $\tilde{M}$, we can also detect violations of the original requirements, which should not occur however if the community types themselves are correct.

**Commitments.** Professed intentions, and in particular commitments and their fulfillment, are important for the more complex coordination mechanisms of a multi-agent system. Apart from urgent norms that can require reactive behaviors, social rules compelling agents to achieve some long term goal are the only way to force an agent, which is supposed to have a certain degree of autonomy, to do anything at all. However, this aspect can usually not be treated abstractly at the level of community types or cultures without considering the concrete agent specifications: While safety properties can be ensured by simply restricting certain behaviors, designing the norms in such a way that the fulfillment of all commitments is guaranteed would typically result in a specification that is much more restrictive than a culture is expected to be. After all, there are usually multiple strategies to fulfill a commitment, and the specification should not unduly exclude any of them. A comprehensive specification that nonetheless enforced a step by step fulfillment would correspond to a characterization of all possible strategies at a detailed level, which is not feasible in general.

Most cultures only state that a commitment has to be fulfilled, but make no or only limited prescriptions as to how exactly this should be done. We can therefore only detect in certain cases if the culture itself makes it impossible to fulfill a commitment. In general, we can observe that an agent has fulfilled its commitments, thus proving that the culture allows this, but we cannot draw conclusions about the validity of the culture from the fact that the agent has failed, as this might merely be due to the fact that the strategy implemented by the agent was insufficient.

When formally verifying the fulfillment of commitments, we need a precise definition of what exactly we require of the agents. The strongest property that could be hold for a commitment $c_i$ would be that every time it is made and the corresponding professed intention is created ($c_i^+$), it is

## 5.2 Verification

also eventually fulfilled and removed ($c^\sim_i$), regardless of the behavior of the agent's environment, i.e. $\mathbf{AG}(c_i^+ \Rightarrow (\mathbf{AF}c^\sim_i)$. This *unconditional* or *strong* notion of commitment is too strong for most practical purposes, as it is only realistic if the agent has complete control over all aspects of the commitment. At the other end of the spectrum, the *cooperative* or *weak* notion of commitment $\mathbf{AG}(c_i^+ \Rightarrow (\mathbf{EF}c^\sim_i)$ only requires that there is at least one path where the agent fulfills its commitment, which may however depend on the correct behavior of the environment and require the goodwill of other agents, as well as the agent itself.

The most realistic option is to require agents to fulfill all their commitments provided that all other agents behave correctly and fulfill their commitments as well. The dependency graph relating the different norms of a culture to each other helps us determine which commitment depends on others and accordingly assign levels $lv(c_i)$ to them. If multiple commitments are not fulfilled, we can determine which ones of them were dependent on other unfulfilled commitments and place the blame at the agent with the lowest-level commitment in each group of unfulfilled commitments. Using $c_i$ to denote $\mathbf{G}(c_i^+ \Rightarrow (\mathbf{F}c^\sim_i)$, the *social* notion of commitment then corresponds to

$$\tilde{M} \models \mathbf{A}((\wedge_{i:lv(c_i)<lv(c_n)} c_i) \Rightarrow c_n). \tag{5.2.2}$$

As the above conditions cannot be translated to either CTL or invariants, using GROOVE or *invariant checking* is out of the question for theoretical reasons, whereas using CheckVML is likely to be impossible in practice due to the size of the problem. By running simulations based on $\tilde{M}$, we can verify each generated execution path and ascertain that correct behavior is possible or generate counterexamples, which are important insights, but we cannot decide that no correct behavior exists or that no incorrect behavior is possible.

### 5.2.4 Scenario-based Verification

Thinking in individual rule applications is well suited to many problems, in particular those concerning safety. Allowing, forbidding, or requiring specific actions based on the current context offers a natural way of achieving behavior that is adapted to the immediate requirements of a situation. It is less helpful when considering goal-directed, strategic behavior in the longer term or complex interactions between agents.

Scenarios allow thinking in larger, logical arcs encompassing multiple steps of a process. TSSDs, the supplied scenario language, describe sequences of actions rather than individual actions. While they are defined using sequences of states, the intended focus is on the flow, just as movies are made up by static frames. TSSDs therefore conserve the ability to fail immediately due to a forbidden action that was touted in the previous section. Unfortunately, they also more than match previous methods in computational complexity. As we have discussed, exhaustive formal verification is only feasible for restricted subsets of the language. For the complete language, we will again have to make do with monitoring selected runs of the system, verifying individual execution traces.

**Monitoring** can be performed either online or offline. By dissociating the evaluation of the constraints from the execution of the system, the latter eliminates performance issues but also increases space consumption, as the execution path (i.e. system states with time stamps) needs to be stored. Monitoring in real-time eliminates the need to cache the complete history and provides immediate feedback, but requires sufficient processing power. When monitoring a simulation whose execution speed can be controlled, even this requirement is eased.

In order to evaluate the graph patterns, we require direct access to the complete system state, which the runtime environment needs to make available using appropriate data structures. In a simulated environment, the simulation itself can provide these structures, whereas in a physical environment (or a software environment that cannot be instrumented), they need to be constructed through observation. This may be a complex task requiring a variety of sensors, ideally deployed redundantly – after all, the verification result is only as reliable as the underlying data. Regardless, the ability to perform agent verification based on such observations at all, which is due to the employed principle of physical grounding, is an asset in itself. When working with embedded systems, it is a significant advantage that we do not need to run the monitor on the embedded hardware itself, but can use a separate system that observes the common environment. As the environment is the only link between the two systems, this does not only avoid the usual resource issues, but also eliminates the distorting effect that the insertion of monitoring code into a real-time system potentially has on its timing.

A final issue is the evaluation frequency, which is of central importance for monitoring real-time scenarios. While time is dense, we can only observe the system in discrete intervals $\Delta t$ in practice, limiting the achievable sampling rate and making the evaluation only an approximation of the formal semantics. The ideal solution would be to perform the evaluation only on demand, which exactly reproduces the formal semantics. For simulations, this is actually feasible because we have the ability to instrument the monitored system so that change events are generated. If we lack such additional information, however, we have to explicitly set the evaluation frequency. If $\Delta t$ is too large, there might be intermediate states that are missed by the monitor, whereas a small $\Delta t$ increases the computational effort by triggering more evaluations. As a general rule, an appropriate compromise for $\Delta t$ should be adapted to the shortest expected interval between two situations. If a high resolution is only needed in specific areas, it would be possible to dynamically change the evaluation frequency, decreasing $\Delta t$ when a critical situation is observed.

#### 5.2.4.1 Story Decision Diagram Evaluation

Based on the semantics that we have defined in Chapter 3 and the requirements described above, we can realize a *property monitor* that is able to decide whether the specified property holds in the current state. In the context of scenario monitoring, the traditional operationalization of Story Patterns that halts at the first valid match is insufficient because *all* valid candidate sets are potentially relevant and might spawn new alternative traces. The monitor therefore needs an efficient way of generating and storing bindings, candidate sets and result sets as defined in Section 3.2.3.

**Evaluating the decision diagram.** The evaluation of SDDs closely follows the formal definitions, but is probably best characterized by the procedure used in our examples in Figures

## 5.2 Verification

3.2.21–3.2.26. The progress through the diagram is driven by individual bindings: Either starting from the empty binding or a given binding or candidate set, each binding is passed to the root node and subsequently traverses the diagram structure in a depth-first recursion following the respective then and else connectors. When multiple extensions for a binding are generated by a node, it iterates over all of them, passing each of them down the then connector; when no valid match is found, the original binding is passed down the else connector. Likewise, nodes loop over all alternatives when there are multiple connectors of the same type.

The fulfillment of the overall SDD is not determined by individual bindings, but sets thereof. The relationships between the generated bindings are handled in the background by a result manager, a separate data structure that is independent of the recursion dealing with the individual bindings. This is best explained by the illustrations for our last exemplary evaluation: The recursion generates all relevant bindings, as listed in Figure 3.2.25, whereas the result manager generates and stores candidate sets that only contain references to these bindings, as seen in Figure 3.2.26. When a binding is extended into a set of new bindings, the result manager merely needs to be informed whether this occurred in the context of a universal or an existential node in order to decide whether all candidate sets containing the binding need to be expanded or split into new alternatives, respectively. When a binding reaches a (0) node, all candidate sets containing it are eliminated; a (1) node requires no action at all. The result set of the SDD evaluation is then simply the set of all candidate sets remaining in the result manager after the recursion has finished. The relationship is not entirely unidirectional, though: As an optimization during the recursion, we can query the result manager whether there still is some candidate set containing the current binding, allowing us to discard bindings generated by a universally quantified node as soon as the first one of them fails.

By basing the evaluation primarily on bindings instead of candidate sets, we avoid multiple evaluations of the same condition and can minimize the number of performed pattern evaluations. It also allows us to concentrate most of the implementation effort within the generic parts of the monitor, reducing the specific parts of the diagram implementation to invoking the correct Story Pattern, passing bindings to the correct child nodes, and signaling the correct quantifier type to the result manager.

**Evaluating the patterns.** The evaluation of the Story Patterns themselves differs from the evaluation in other contexts, e.g. Story Diagrams, in two important points: We need to find *all* occurrences, and there is no fixed element this. As a logical consequence of the ability to specify properties for *all* entities of a type or about the existence of *some* specific entity, the evaluation always has to consider the system as a whole. This makes the required runtime environment more complex, but also opens up new opportunities for optimizations.

In classic Story Patterns, the order in which the elements are bound is static and fixed in the source code by the code generation, which may try to optimize this order based on the specified cardinalities. As the starting point is necessarily the this element and additional elements always need to be connected to previously bound elements, there are only few choices to be made in any case. In contrast, our access to the complete system graph gives us the freedom to bind the elements in any order we choose, apart from the evident restriction that edges cannot be bound independently of the nodes they connect. Though fixing an order based on the specified cardinalities during code generation may already accelerate the matching process, this only makes partial use of the flexibility afforded to us by the runtime environment. As it is possible to decide at runtime where we can reach a negative result by checking the fewest alternatives, we can significantly improve performance by using dynamically determined evaluation orders.

Finding the optimal order is not trivial. On the surface, the problem seems similar to finding a minimum spanning tree for the graph pattern, but the relevant algorithms are not applicable. For one, the cumulation of the edge weights is multiplicative, not additive, since we need to check all potential occurrences by backtracking through the graph pattern, and the overall cost not only depends on the chosen edges, but also the starting node. Besides, the cost of an edge is only known after the adjacent node has been bound, as it depends on the number of links the specific object has for the corresponding association. This means that the order needs to be context-sensitive and dynamically computed, which prohibits the use of complex algorithms that would nullify the intended performance gains.

As it turns out, there is a straight-forward greedy algorithm that yields near-optimal results. For typical sparse instance graphs as appear in our examples, it even produces the ideal solution, whereas deviations from the optimum have only been shown for heavily connected synthetic graphs. The approach is based on the assumption that the actual cardinalities are available at runtime: The number of links for a given association type between instances is generally available directly from the objects themselves as the size of the corresponding collection, and the number of instances for each type can be provided by the runtime environment, as an appropriate index is required for making available the entire system state anyway.

When applying a pattern, each of its elements needs to be confirmed as a match at least once. If a variable is already bound in the supplied initial binding, the corresponding element needs to be asserted, whereas elements representing free variables need to be bound. For confirming an element, multiple approaches are usually available. Nodes can either be bound in the traditional way by traversing an edge from a previously bound node, or by iterating over the list of instances provided by the runtime environment. Edges can be bound by traversing them in either direction, starting from a previously bound node. Asserting elements is simpler, as we merely have to check whether the object assigned to a node still exists and whether traversing an edge still leads to the expected result. In either case, it is obvious that following to-one associations entails fewer comparisons and less backtracking than iterating over to-many associations. A similar rationale applies to nodes: Starting with a type for which only a few instances exist allows quickly reducing the search space, whereas iterating over thousands of instances only to find that no relevant context exists for most of them is rarely productive. Based on these assessments, we arrive at the very straight-forward solution of always choosing the unprocessed element for which the approach with the least local weight, i.e. number of alternatives to consider, exists in the context of the current binding for processing.

Consider the pattern in Figure 5.2.7, which recognizes the fact that passengers and dangerous goods are in close proximity to each other, and a system consisting of 10000 tracks and 50 base stations. On a weekday morning, there might be 100 shuttles, 225 passengers, and 5 dangerous goods. In this case, we begin by binding $d$ (5 alternatives), look for a suitable shuttle $sd$ (0..1),

## 5.2 Verification

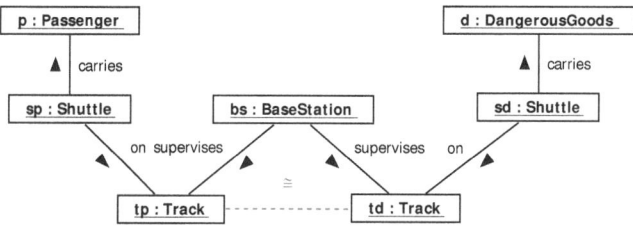

Figure 5.2.7: Pattern: passengers and dangerous goods in the same area

proceed to track td (1..2) and its supervisor bs (1..4). As base stations supervise hundreds of tracks in this example, it is then cheaper not to bind tp ($\sim$ 300), but to jump to p (225) and continue down to shuttle sp (0..1) and its tracks tp (1..2), finally checking whether tp is also supervised by bs. In all, the algorithm will have performed at most $5*1*2*4*225*1*2*4 = 72,000$ checks, out of a total of $5.625*10^{16}$ possible bindings and compared to $1,280,000$ comparisons when starting with the shuttles. In the early morning hours, there might be only 88 shuttles, carrying 10 passengers and 450 units of dangerous goods, changing the order to p, p-sp, sp-tp, tp-bs, sd, sd-td, sd-d, and td-bs. Note that these are only typical orders: If some base station is supervising only a small number of tracks, the algorithm would proceed via the base station, i.e. shuttle, track, base station, track, shuttle.

**Storing the results.** As the number of generated valid bindings may be quite large for complex system graphs, we also require an efficient way of storing them. As most bindings are only minor variations on other bindings, we can save much space by eliminating redundancies between them, storing the common part only once. One way of achieving this is to place them into a tree structure where each leaf represents a binding. While there will still be identical suffixes that are repeated throughout the tree and cannot be merged, the dynamic binding algorithm will have the positive side effect of pushing down elements with many alternatives, i.e a large fan out, towards the leaves of the tree, limiting the length of theses suffixes.

For most use cases, it is sufficient to only store the valid candidate sets and discard all intermediary results. When analyzing a specification, it may however be of interest to make information about failed attempts available, e.g. to show which specific element caused a universally quantified node to fail, as counterexamples are often the most direct way to identify the cause of a problem.

### 5.2.4.2 Timed Story Scenario Diagram Evaluation

Using *property monitors* for recognizing the intermediate states of a scenario, we can now realize a *behavior monitor* that is able to verify exhibited agent behavior against a TSSD. While we focused on a formally correct characterization, not approaches for their efficient evaluation, when defining their semantics in Chapter 3, we cannot do without optimized algorithms when using

**TSSDs in practice.** TSSDs combine graph patterns with path formulae, with the consequence that each system state may correspond to multiple observations and each observation may belong to multiple traces with different histories, leading to huge search spaces. Depending on the domain and the situation definitions of a TSSD, it is often possible to construct a worst case scenario which causes the number of traces to increase exponentially over time. In spite of this, typical TSSDs generate large, but reasonably limited trace trees. This is especially true of TSSDs describing sequential scenarios or closely following the actions of a specific agent, as observations ('turned left', 'rejected task X') are often final and exclude future alternative observations ('turned right', 'accepted task X') for the same agent in this case. Time constraints, which may be one of the motivations for using TSSDs in the first place, also limit the number of active traces by assigning a predetermined time to live to each incomplete trace after which it becomes irrelevant. Nonetheless, evaluation needs to be economic on all levels.

**Storing the trace graph.** The set of generated traces is stored in a bipartite graph consisting of *observation* and *transition* nodes. As in the formal definition, each trace is a sequence of related observations, starting at the root element. Similar to the technique used for storing bindings, the graph structure allows sharing common prefixes between traces. Common suffixes again have to be stored redundantly, as the concerned traces might diverge in the future due to their different histories, which would force us to separate the common segments again to avoid confounding the respective prefixes. Unlike the trace tree used in the formal definition, we allow observations with multiple direct predecessors, however, if the corresponding situation has multiple incoming connectors, i.e. is the result of an $\wedge$-join. This is different from the common suffix case because the branches of the TSSD do not represent alternatives, but parallel strands of the same process.

**Evaluating scenarios.** The formal semantics of TSSDs are defined recursively, both in terms of situations and time. In practice, this is too computationally expensive and besides would require caching the complete state history. For monitoring, it is preferable to recognize events as they happen and record their effect on the evaluation state immediately. We therefore need a modified algorithm that is designed for working in real-time, using a minimized history. We can, however, reuse all of the reductions that we used for transforming advanced syntactical features to a simplified core syntax above.

Two concepts aid us in building efficient monitors: Annotating *situations* and *connectors* with static properties derived by a preparatory analysis, and annotating *observation* and particularly *transition* nodes in the trace graph with state information for guiding the evaluation.

For each situation, we compute its *depth*, i.e. the length of the longest path from the initial node, and determine its *domain*, i.e. the names and types of its bound and unbound variables, by drilling down into its internal definition. The inbound connectors of a situation are partitioned according to their latest common ancestor, and each partition is marked as a *branch group* by annotating it with this ancestor. Each connector is annotated with the upper and lower bounds of the *time constraints* that come due at its destination and its *contributions*, i.e. the names and types of the bound elements it is expected to provide to its destination. We then perform a back-propagation of constraints. Branch group annotations are propagated up to the indicated ancestor. Upper bounds of time constraints and required contributions are passed backwards up to the *earliest*

## 5.2 Verification

*exclusive predecessor*, which is the connector right after the last situation with an alternative outgoing branch not belonging to the same branch group.

At runtime, *transition* nodes represent instances of a *connector*, just as *observation* nodes belong to a specific *situation*. Our goal is to invalidate these instance nodes as early as possible so that we can eliminate them from the trace graph again. We only use a less aggressive deletion strategy if we intend to display counterexamples or successful completions in detail.

Every time an evaluation step is triggered either by an event or due to a fixed evaluation frequency, the situations and connections of the diagram are visited using a breadth-first traversal respecting situation depth. If change events providing the delta between the current and the previous state are available, we can use our knowledge about the situation's domain to decide whether it may at all have been affected by the change at the type level. As validity may be affected by non-local changes, making such a decision at the instance level is only possible for specific cases and requires a more detailed analysis of the patterns.

**Processing situations.** For each potentially affected situation, we first iterate over the existing observations and assert whether the elements they have bound to variables still exist in the current system state. In this case, using updates about deletions is straight-forward. If variable bindings have become invalid, the enclosing observation is obsolete and eliminated, and the affected variable names are propagated forward to all reachable observation and transition nodes. Any observation whose domain contains the name (necessarily as a bound element) is eliminated using the same rationale, while any transition whose required contributions include the name is also eliminated because its branch leads to a situation which requires the invalidated binding and can therefore never be satisfied again.

Secondly, we check for valid transition nodes for the incoming connectors. If there is more than one precondition, transition nodes with compatible ancestors for each of their respective branch groups are required for every connector (excluding inhibitors), and the transported candidate sets need to be merged. For every candidate set, we then invoke the embedded structural diagram for identifying potential observations. The candidate sets of the generated result set needs to be explicitly checked against the existing observations ex post, as this is the only way of distinguishing new, persisting, and invalidated observations. Observations for pseudo states are special as, like the trivially true node, they match for any state graph. Furthermore, observations for termination nodes are eliminated after each evaluation. Each new observation is stored in a node containing its candidate set and time stamp. If the observation is completing a trigger, it is also assigned a unique root trace marker, which is registered in an index.

**Processing connectors.** When creating an observation, we simultaneously generate a new transition node for each outgoing connector. Each transition node stores a reference to the transported candidate set. If the connection is part of a split, the transition is annotated with the observation and the corresponding branch group. If a time constraint originates from the situation, the transition is furthermore marked with the earliest and latest permissible time derived from the constraint and the time stamp. If there is a time constraint between partially ordered elements, i.e. situations on parallel branches, the transition is marked with the time window into which the other observation must fall. Finally, root trace markers are passed on to subsequent transitions and observations.

When the breadth-first traversal visits a connector, all associated transitions are processed. We begin by checking their time constraints because this is the least expensive operation. If the connector is annotated with a lower bound time constraint, but the transition's earliest permissible time is in the future, it is marked as (currently) invalid. If the latest permissible time is in the past, the transition node is eliminated.

Secondly, if the transition is part of a branch group, but no transitions from a parallel branch are left in the group, the whole group can be eliminated. If there are time constraints between the branches, we can also eliminate transitions for which we can find no compatible observations after the time window has passed.

Finally, we evaluate any guards that are attached to the connector. As a guard is similar to a situation, the same filtering logic can be applied in order to decide whether the current update might have had an effect on the guard's domain, making it necessary to evaluate it. If the guard matches, the transition is eliminated. If a bound element from the guard's domain becomes invalid, the guard is permanently false and need not be evaluated again.

When a new observation is created, the annotations from the incoming transition nodes are copied to the generated outgoing transition nodes, albeit with some exceptions. Situations at the end of a time constraint consume the annotation and do not pass it on. Likewise, information about branch groups is stripped at the corresponding join.

The scenario then *holds* if there is an appropriately marked observation for a termination node for every root trace marker in the index at the end of an evaluation step. If the index contains a root trace marker without any associated transition nodes left, the scenario *fails*. Otherwise, it is *pending*. In the common case that there are no guards on the connector leading to the termination node, the root trace marker and all associated nodes are eliminated as soon as the node is observed, as this particular trace then *holds strongly*. The overall scenario only *holds strongly* if no transition nodes are left in the trace graph.

**Example.** We walk through a small example to illustrate the procedure. A shuttle receives a request to perform a task, sends an acknowledgment, then checks whether the task fits into the existing planning (feasible) and is sufficiently well remunerated (lucrative), and finally sends a reply containing its decision, unless the task has been canceled in the mean time.

In the annotated diagram (see Figure 5.2.8), the situations are named $U0$–$U6$ and the connectors are named $C0$–$C6$. For situations, $>$ marks the bound and $+$ the unbound elements of the *domain*, [ the begin and ] the end of a *time constraint*, and { the begin and } the end of a *branch group*. For connectors, / prefixes the relevant guards, $>$ marks the *contributions*, $l$ and $u$ the active bounds of *time constraints*, and {...} the *branch groups*.

Connectors $C1$–$C5$ are constrained by guard $G1$. Branch group $b1$ includes connectors $C2$–$C5$. There are time constraints between $U1$ and $U2$ and between $U1$ and $U5$. Most bindings are only required locally; only $s$ and $t$ are preserved throughout the whole scenario.

Initially, only $U0$ may be observed, as it is the only situation without preconditions. At time 0, observation $O0$ is generated, along with a transition for $C0$ (see Figure 5.2.9).

## 5.2 Verification

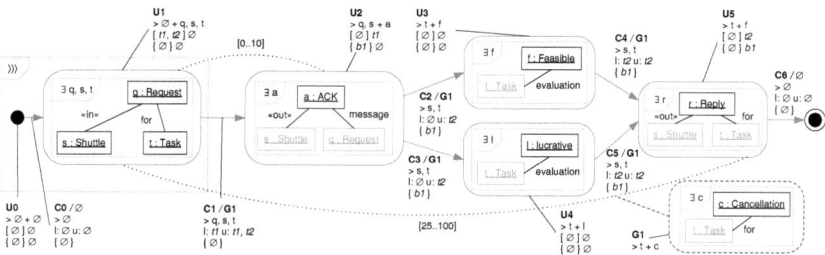

Figure 5.2.8: Scenario: A shuttle evaluates and replies to a query

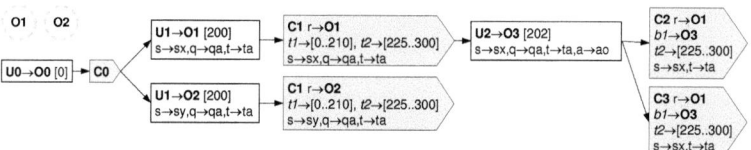

Figure 5.2.9: The evaluation at time 199

Figure 5.2.10: The evaluation at time 204

At time 200, a request $qa$ for task $ta$ is received by shuttles $sx$ and $sy$, leading to observations $O1$ and $O2$ for $U1$. Two transitions for $C1$ are created, one for each observation, and marked with the bindings and absolute time bounds. As the observations complete the scenario's trigger, the transitions also belong to the root traces $r \to O1$, respectively $r \to O2$.

At time 202, shuttle $sx$ has sent the required acknowledgment, which is observed as $O3$ for $U2$. The outgoing transitions for $C2$ and $C3$ belong to the branch group $b1 \to O3$ and may later only be joined with other transitions stemming from $O3$. The irrelevant bindings for $q$ and $a$ are not propagated, the time bound $t1$ has been consumed by $O3$ (see Figure 5.2.10).

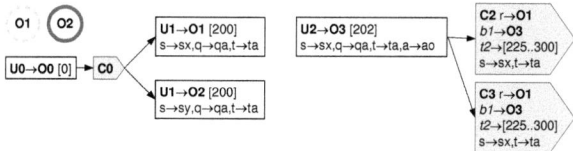

Figure 5.2.11: The evaluation at time 211

At time 211, the two transitions for $C1$ have been eliminated because their upper time bound 210 has been reached. As a result, there are now no active transitions for the root trace $r \to O2$ left (see Figure 5.2.11). While, formally, the scenario has failed now and we could simply stop the evaluation, it is more appropriate from an agent monitoring perspective to say that shuttle $sy$ has violated the specification, but continue the monitoring of $sx$.

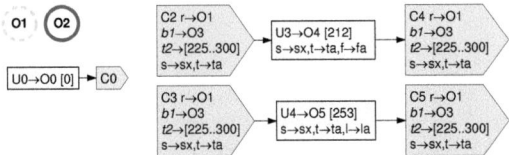

Figure 5.2.12: The evaluation at time 287

At time 212, $O4$ is observed for $U3$. As the annotations in the diagram indicate, $C2$ only passively transmits the lower bound of 225. For the newly created transition for $C4$, it becomes active though.

At time 222, the message $qa$ is garbage collected. The observations $O1$, $O2$, and $O3$ containing references to it are eliminated, but as the corresponding transitions for $C1$ have already been eliminated and no other transitions carry $qa$ as a contribution, no transitions are affected.

At time 253, $O5$ is observed for $U4$, and a transition for $C5$ is created (see Figure 5.2.12). The guard $G1$, which can be evaluated for all transitions at once in this case, continues not to match.

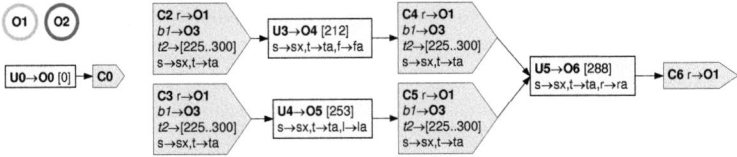

Figure 5.2.13: The evaluation at time 288

At time 288, two transitions for $C4$ and $C5$ from the branch group $b1 \to O3$ are available, and $O6$ for $U5$ can be observed. The branch group $b1$ is reunited, and the time constraint $t2$ is consumed. The resulting transition for $C6$ is therefore unconstrained, i.e. carries time constraints or branch information, but also no contributions or guards (see Figure 5.2.13), and will now and forever reach the termination node.

All nodes belonging to the completed root trace can now be eliminated, leading back to the state in Figure 5.2.9, except for the additional information that $r \to O2$ for $sy$ has failed and $r \to O1$ for $sx$ has succeeded.

The example illustrates our point about the size and complexity of the evaluation problem: Structural symmetries increase the problem size. Had the request been sent to one hundred shuttles, the trace would have been proportionally bigger. Meanwhile, the size of the trace for each shuttle was limited due to the fact that the agent can be expected not to send the same message multiple times, leading to a linear progression through the scenario. Such effects are neither rare nor random. In fact, we can systematically enforce less ramified trace trees by adding norms expressing suitable constraints, e.g. limiting an agent to a maximum number of concurrent commitments. Due to the resource restrictions that are typical of embedded systems, such constraints are often required to make the specification implementable in the first place.

#### 5.2.4.3 Usage

Continuing the evolution from techniques with a limited scope but full coverage to techniques with broader scope but weaker obtainable results, the use of TSSDs allows us to consider all of the properties that were previously discussed in this section, but definitely limits us to partial verification based on simulation or monitoring.

Using scenario-based verification, we can finally include the multi-agent system specification in its entirety in our considerations. As graph rules can be encoded as a TSSD consisting of two situations and a trigger, it is possible to freely combine both specification types in a culture and still use the above definition of GTS refinement for monitoring. As TSSDs are more expressive than graph rules, it is also possible to make further aspects such as the dependencies between commitments explicit by explicitly making the fulfillment of the lower-level commitment part of the scenario.

In the case study, we now also include the traffic routing culture in our analysis. While its central mechanism – vehicles have to reserve locations they want to use and commit to doing so at the indicated time – is inherently safe, developing the strategy used by the vehicles requires some care, as the agents need to carefully plan ahead in order to only make commitments they are actually able to keep. Although we have quickly found a working solution for which the system behaves correctly, thinking about this problem leads to the question whether the specified culture actually promotes an efficient solution and is not actually hampering the system.

## 5.3  Validation

Scenario-based verification allowed us to think about processes in the system at a larger scale and provides insights into the way different aspects of the system are interrelated. As the last example witnesses, the step from the question whether the system is behaving correctly to the question whether it actually achieves what we intend it to achieve is not a large one at this level.

In this chapter's introduction, we have discussed how Model-Driven Engineering can improve the development process and identified three main strategies for facilitating validation: Automation, reducing clerical errors and development times, simulation, allowing an inexpensive and early validation of a design, and iteration, based on meaningful feedback that is provided as early as possible. In the following sections, we will delve into each of these points.

Their common theme is the focus on timely and frequently repeated validation based on prototypes. The use of prototypes has a long tradition in software engineering, as evidenced by Fredrick Brooks' 1975 advice to 'plan to throw one away' [Bro95]. Since then, building prototypes has evolved from being considered as a painful but necessary learning experience into a methodology in its own right. This change is in part due to the fact that the tools and languages that are available today make the creation and later reuse of prototypes much easier. For object-oriented systems, methodologies based on rapid prototyping (cf. [Mul90, CS95]) have been proposed early on. In agent research, the importance of prototypes for testing emergent behavior appears evident. However, even though the training and evolving of designs is known from neural networks or genetic algorithms, rapid prototyping as a technique is not commonly cited, possibly because stressing the engineering aspect of agent-oriented software engineering is still a fairly recent trend.

We discuss these topics in the order in which they occur in the prototyping process. Synthesis is an optional step that may help to reduce development times, followed by the indispensable code generation. The essential phase is the experimental evaluation of the generated system by means of simulation. In order to validate that the system achieves its actual purpose, as opposed to the elicited requirements only, the ability to experience the system in action is crucial. The more complex and chaotic the system is, the more depends on the correct and intuitively accessible presentation of its behavior. If a simple visual inspection is insufficient to validate all requirements, the simulation environment may provide assistance in identifying and recording all relevant events, which can finally be subjected to a systematic in-depth analysis.

### 5.3.1 Automation

The two main motivations for automating parts of the development process are quality and speed. Where a step does not require creative input and can be performed by an algorithm, it is often more efficient to delegate it to an appropriate tool. If it is complex but systematic or simply tedious, automation can also help to avoid human errors.

There are two related, but distinct types of steps that can be automated: A transformation between models, deriving one specification from another, and code generation, deriving executable code from a model.

#### 5.3.1.1 Synthesis

There is a school of thought claiming that if we were only able to state our requirements precisely enough, it would be possible to automatically derive everything else from there. However, besides being a hard problem, behavioral synthesis is no magical silver bullet. The claim has thus prompted the rebuttal that this would result in simply shifting much of the original effort from implementation to meticulous requirements engineering – which need not be a bad idea in itself (cf. [Jac01]).

**Basic synthesis.** We follow more modest goals and simply aim to provide prototypical or partial agent implementations that can be refined or completed by the developer. In a first approxima-

## 5.3 Validation

tion, this may not even be difficult – we have actually already applied similar reasoning when performing verification. Given a community type specification, we can synthesize an agent representing a valid refinement by making all urgent norms mandatory in the agent implementation and otherwise letting it randomly apply the discretionary norms. This can be achieved using a quite simple controller design that tries to apply each rule in a round-robin fashion, which has the additional advantage of making the agent's behavior reproducible in subsequent tests.

The design of the agent introduces some additional complexity in comparison to the theoretical model because we cannot directly apply norms, but need to differentiate between the parts that correspond to effector and sensor applications and modifications to the agent's internal representation of the physical and social state of the environment. This can be achieved automatically based on the available mapping between behavioral norms and effectors.

The resulting agent is certainly not intelligent, but sufficient for testing many safety properties. It is also a convenient starting point for developing advanced designs that replace the random rule applications with more deliberate choices. The basic agent can also serve to provide a backdrop for testing these designs in their interactions with correct but otherwise unpredictable other implementations. When studying emergent effects with a probabilistic component, such as swarming behavior, it may even be as intelligent as it needs to be already.

**Goal-oriented behavior.** The basic synthesized agent will never exhibit strategic behavior, i.e. consciously pursue objectives as is characteristic of agents. Though acting in good faith, the agent is likely to break all of its commitments that cannot be fulfilled through direct action or inaction.

The strategies required for planning behavior that fulfills all requirements can be arbitrarily complex. The requirement itself may call for complex mathematical calculations or a semantic analysis of the context, and the interference of the environment and other agents can further complicate planning. Developing appropriate strategies is therefore often a creative process that cannot be automated, and synthesis is not possible unless the necessary creative input is provided by the requirements.

However, an algorithm may be able to guess the correct strategy without a deeper understanding of the problem if correct behavior can be achieved by merely applying effectors in the right order. If a shuttle commits to transporting a task to a destination, it may be able to reach the destination on time without understanding routing or shortest paths. The underlying idea is related to Live Sequence Chart (LSC) synthesis as performed in the Smart Playout approach (cf. [HM03]): Substituting brute force for problem-specific reasoning, the Play Engine uses model checking techniques for ensuring that the next message does not inevitably lead to constraint violations in the future. Likewise, an agent prototype could employ GROOVE in order to play out future execution paths and determine whether paths to a desirable outcome (destination reached on time) exist, choosing the shortest or most promising, i.e. least risky, one. As the search is not directed or guided by domain knowledge, such an implementation is much less computationally efficient than any specific one (a simple strategy 'move towards the destination' might achieve the same effect in the example), but its 'unsemantic' behavior might incidentally provide inspiration for innovative strategies in later designs.

If the requirements are given as TSSDs, the required computations may become less prohibitive. If the diagrams already provide a blueprint of the intended behavior, expressed as a sequence of snapshots that are not spaced too far apart, guessing the right actions for reaching the next 'checkpoint' requires a much shorter horizon because it can be decided whether certain behavior leads to a violation without looking very far into the future. The situation is reminiscent of interpolating missing frames in a movie – the more frames are available, the less potential for error there is. On the other hand, a more detailed specification also means that the developer has already put more effort into designing the desired behavior and has left less room for flexibility for the agents.

**Community type composition.** A second problem that surfaces when trying to synthesize agents that act as members of multiple community types is that the requirements of each may not be orthogonal, but affect each other. We have previously encountered this problem during verification and can, in fact, approach it in a similar way. As before, every action needs to be valid in all of an agent's communities, which means that where multiple constraint apply the most restrictive one needs to be respected. As a result of the verification, we know that there are no constraints that directly contradict each other, e.g. by not allowing an urgent action. It is therefore always possible to select an action that is locally valid. Nonetheless, there can be more subtle interactions between the community types at a larger scale, which can make determining the correct strategy even more difficult. For example, safety regulations might make a shorter route much slower than an apparent detour, causing a shuttle to constantly miss its delivery deadlines. As these effects may not be local or may spontaneously result from the interaction of multiple agents, synthesizing an agent may be hard, even though the basic algorithm still applies. We can still consider all possible actions and eliminate invalid behaviors until only valid options remain – but it may have become much more expensive to decide whether a behavior is ultimately valid.

**Coordination Patterns.** Synthesis can be extended to the coordination pattern level where agents interact by exchanging messages. Unlike synthesis from specifications based on GTS, the synthesis of automata from other types of specifications such scenarios has been studied intensively. While a program is ultimately an automaton, characterizing the desired behavior by means of expected scenarios is believed to be a more intuitive approach in many cases (cf. [HM03]).

However, it is generally easier to describe the desired behavior than to prevent undesired behavior in this way. The need to add additional constraints in order to avoid implied scenarios that unexpectedly result from the interaction of specified scenarios may therefore partially dilute their advantages. Regardless, scenarios are useful for understanding, visualizing, and monitoring behavior, even when they do not provide a complete specification but are combined with conventional specifications (cf. [GKKW05]).

While Message Sequence Charts are generally considered as too semantically weak for this purpose, there are approaches for controller synthesis based on Live Sequence Charts (LSC) and the related UML 2.0 Sequence Diagrams (cf. [HK02, BH04]). When implementing a coordination pattern, scenarios may be especially useful for choosing the right timing constraints based on the required message flow. For this use case, we have proposed an approach for synthesizing parametrized Real-Time Statecharts from scenarios that are annotated with concrete or symbolic

## 5.3 Validation

time constraints (cf. [GKB05]), which can then be used to test and iteratively refine the design (cf. [GHHK06]).

The problem that an agent has to fulfill multiple specifications may also occur at the pattern level. The approach presented in [GV06] describes an approach for handling non-orthogonal concerns that is applicable to the resulting composition problem.

### 5.3.1.2 Code Generation

The ability to generate code that actually implements the verified models is crucial for the validity of a model-driven approach. Code generation may appear more straight-forward than synthesis and arguably is the more mechanical task. However, the move from the abstract *platform-independent model* (PIM) to code that runs on a specific platform also entails modifications and design decisions that need to be made. We need a detailed understanding of our target platform, expressed as a *platform model* (PM), which explains why code generation is closely linked to our discussion of frameworks in the next section.

**Story-Driven Modeling.** In the context of Story-Driven Modeling, we can reuse or build on a wide selection of previous experiences and tools. When discussing the semantics of the associated notations, we have stressed their suitability for operationalization – starting with the original Story Diagrams (cf. [FNTZ98]), the ability to generate code from the diagrams has always been an essential quality of the notations. This is also true of the introduced extensions, as reflected by their use in the context of monitoring.

TSSDs cannot be used directly as the basis of an agent implementation but would require an additional synthesis step for deriving an implementable Story Diagram. SDDs, on the other hand, can serve as an implementation level technique that is able to act as a replacement for Story Patterns. When used in this way, e.g. for defining activities in a Story Diagram, we can switch to a simpler evaluation strategy because it suffices to identify a single valid occurrence to which the pattern can be applied – as opposed to all valid occurrences as required for monitoring. Otherwise, we can apply the same strategies and optimizations as above, in particular the dynamic determination of the binding order. Even though the diagrams have become more complex and expressive, the resulting code is therefore no less efficient than the code traditionally generated from Story Patterns.

There are some caveats to observe: Universal quantification may entail checks for a large number of elements. A single quantifier has the potential to replace an entire loop in a Story Diagram, which may be a more concise way of expressing the desired property, but may at the same time make the associated computational complexity less obvious. This is even more true of pattern references, which have to be used with some caution. The computational complexity of transitive conditions that are expressed using recursion depends on both the property and the size of the system and may be quite high. This complexity is, of course, not specific to the SDD, but would apply to any recursive definition of the property. For real-time applications where the WCET needs to be known, both recursion and universal quantification need to be used very judiciously and require tight upper bounds for the possible number of instances of the affected types.

Unlike their monitoring counterparts, SDDs that are used for implementation purposes may have side effects. In order to avoid problems when creating and deleting multiple elements, SDDs use a two-pass strategy: The code adds all created elements to the selected occurrences in the first pass, and only then performs all deletions in the second pass.

**Coordination patterns.** Code generation is also available for *Coordination Patterns*. As timing is usually critical, platform-specific technical aspects play a larger role for the generation process in this area. For a detailed discussion of code generation from Real-Time Statecharts, refer to [Bur06].

### 5.3.2 Simulation

Accelerating the creation of prototypes is only part of what is required for an effective iterative development process. Such a process is only possible if it is also possible to try out the generated prototypes.

It is hardly ever acceptable to start testing an embedded application by placing an early prototype into its production environment. Especially for safety-critical or mission-critical applications, this would be too risky, if not actually illegal. For physical systems, such a strategy might furthermore not scale because certain system-level effects resulting from interactions might only be observable once a minimum number of agents is present, and the time and cost required for building sufficiently many prototypes would be prohibitive. Even for purely virtual agents, setting up a large network may be costly.

Besides, the production environment may be difficult to control, in particular if it is distributed. Apart from introducing new sources of errors, physical distribution makes it much more difficult to obtain a consistent reading of the current system state for deciding correctness or analyzing the cause of identified errors.

Simulation is therefore a valuable approach for the evaluation of designs. Whether the results that are obtained by means of simulation are relevant to the production environment depends on the quality of the simulation. For an early design, even a crude simulation may provide valuable feedback, whereas fine tuning or the preparation for a release to the production environment require a sufficiently accurate representation. Like the models used for designing the system, any simulation will introduce a certain number of abstractions, and it is important to be aware of what they are and how they might affect the validity of the obtained results.

#### 5.3.2.1 Mechatronic Systems

Finding an appropriate compromise between the complexity and validity of a simulation is difficult for mechatronic multi-agent systems. However, the layered design of the *Operator-Controller-Module* (*OCM*) [HOG04, OHG04] that we use as the basic architecture of mechatronic agents alleviates this problem. By separating the different concerns real-time control (*Controller*), real-time communication and coordination (*Reflective Operator*), and strategic planning

## 5.3 Validation

and reasoning (*Cognitive Operator*), we do not only achieve a cleaner and more flexible design, but also gain the ability to study the layers in isolation. A simulation may thus focus on one layer and (partially or completely) abstract from the others. Typical aspects of interest are control engineering (*Controller* only), real-time reactive adaptive behavior and coordination (*Reflective Operator* and *Controller*), and deliberate agent behavior and communication (*Cognitive* and *Reflective Operators*).

The first aspect is the easiest to isolate, as control engineering is a discipline in its own right. It also enjoys the support of commercial Computer-Aided Engineering (CAE) tools such as Matlab Simulink [2] or CAMeL [3].

The *Reflective Operator* is the domain of *Coordination Patterns*. The Fujaba Real-Time Tool Suite[4] provides CASE tool support for the employed UML-based notations, i.e. Component Diagrams and Real-Time Statecharts. Based on a framework for component-based real-time communication (cf. [Hen05]), we are then able to execute and analyze the generated components.

However, in the design of self-optimizing systems that are able to adapt their control strategies, the separation between the lower levels is less clear-cut, and the *Reflective Operator* may need to react to the consequences of the *Controller*'s behavior. Using a unified component concept, we have therefore integrated Fujaba and CAMeL at the model level and employed the real-time runtime environment IPANEMA (cf. [Hon98]) as a common framework for running discrete, continuous and hybrid components on the same platform (cf. [BGK04]). This approach has since been refined and extended (cf. [Bur06, BGH$^+$07]).

If the *Cognitive Operator*'s function is merely to record, analyze, and learn from past behavior or to perform numerical optimizations, it is possible to directly extend this approach to the cognitive level. If, on the other hand, the OCM is used to implement an agent that is supposed to exhibit deliberate goal-driven behavior based on its analysis of its environment, the *Cognitive Operator* may have completely different requirements concerning the simulated environment than the other two levels. Typically, a mathematically less precise but more expansive, more semantically differentiated representation is necessary or preferred. This is true of all the application examples we have discussed thus far, which underlines the importance of this use case for our approach to multi-agent system design.

### 5.3.2.2 Multi-Agent Systems

At the University of Paderborn, a kernel for running a simulated shuttle system has been employed for educational purposes, in various student projects, and as part of a case study used in several workshops (cf. [GK05]). Another kernel was later written in the context of a bachelor's thesis studying the effects of different convoy formation strategies on the system's overall energy consumption (cf. [Bie04]). While dealing with related aspects of the same domain, both kernels were custom-built: The former focused on managing the execution and interaction of a set of

---
[2] Publisher's website: http://www.mathworks.de
[3] Publisher's website: http://www.ixtronics.de
[4] Fujaba project site: http://www.fujaba.de

concurrent shuttle agents as fairly as possible; the latter used a more detailed and physically correct model of shuttle movement and was optimized for simulating large numbers of shuttles and operating as fast as possible.

**Rapid Prototyping and Simulation Framework.** In [KG04], we have first discussed the necessity of a modular prototyping framework that combines an environment model with a set of libraries that provide a simulation infrastructure. Its purpose is to allow the generation of problem-adequate simulation environments while requiring minimal developer intervention. Instead of reimplementing a kernel for each new domain, a developer would simply generate domain-specific classes for use with a general purpose kernel. Likewise, different levels of detail would be achieved by replacing or reconfiguring the employed libraries. While certain use cases might still require dedicated coding, a wide spectrum of simulations could thus be created using a declarative approach. This basic idea is sketched in Figure 5.3.1.

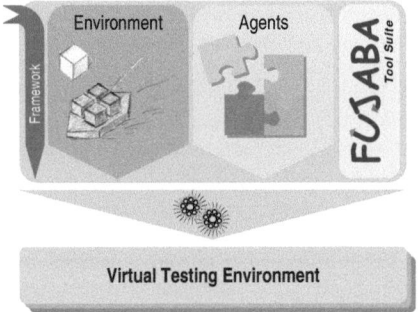

Figure 5.3.1: Rapid Prototyping Framework

The Intrapid project (cf. [ABB+06]), a large one-year student project, set out to implement such a framework consisting of a set of libraries with matching tool support. It is built around the principles of the CURCUMA framework from the ground up, but also integrates existing technologies from the context of Story-Driven Modeling and real-time *Coordination Patterns*.

**Core components.** The core of the framework is the *Simulation Kernel*, whose task is to manage the simulated environment. Its main functions are to store and expose a set of *entities* representing the current state of the environment model, to define a system clock, to provide a generic event mechanism based on the observer pattern, and to control the concurrent access to the environment. The kernel is the central component that connects and coordinates a set of specialized

## 5.3 Validation

components that are built around it, which allows deploying and configuring the system in a modular fashion.

The representation of the entities follows the theoretical model and divides them into active agents and passive items. We also distinguish logical and physical entities, the latter of which have a physical shape, a mass, and a position, orientation, and velocity in three-dimensional space. For physical entities, the modeled composition and aggregation relationships also carry additional semantics, determining how the entities are connected.

This is especially relevant to the *Physics Engine*, the component that needs the tightest integration with the kernel. The *Physics Engine* is implementing one of the most important aspects of the process model, the laws of nature that operate on the entities. There are two implementations: A rudimentary engine that provides basic movement and collision detection, and a more sophisticated engine based on the Open Dynamics Engine (ODE)[5], an open source library for simulating rigid body dynamics. ODE provides a realistic model based on the forces and torques acting on objects, including friction as determined by the integrated collision detection. It also supports various types of joints for connecting entities, which greatly facilitates the simulation of machines, such as vehicles. The library achieves a high level of realism and provides several mature and stable numerical methods for solving the associated differential equations, albeit its focus is on enabling large simulations in an efficient and user-friendly way, not providing the level of precision that is needed for CAE applications.

The most visible part of the framework is the *Visualization Component* that displays representations of the physical and logical entities of the model and allows interacting with the simulation. While there are also interesting use cases for two-dimensional visualizations, even if the simulation itself works with three dimensions, both of the frontends that were created by the project use three-dimensional graphics. They are based on the open source graphics engines OGRE [6] respectively Irrlicht [7]. The visualization primarily displays the physical entities using the positional information that is provided by the kernel, but may additionally display logical entities (e.g. a contract) that are associated with them. During the simulation, the observer can freely navigate through the virtual environment. In the more advanced version, it is also possible to manipulate the simulation at run-time by adding, moving, or removing entities and agents, which turns the *Visualization Component* into a visual scenario editor. Furthermore, the state of selected agents can be inspected. In order to enable the display of custom information, e.g. about an agent's internal reasoning processes, the windowed user interface provides generic interfaces and is configurable using XML.

**Agent infrastructure.** On top of this generic infrastructure, we provide dedicated interfaces and services to agents. Their purpose is both to facilitate agent implementations and to hide the underlying platform. Ideally, the nature of their environment should be completely transparent to the agents, making it possible to move a tested design over to the production environment with minimal changes simply by replacing the sensor and effector implementations and dropping the

---

[5] Open Dynamics Engine project site: http://www.ode.org
[6] OGRE project site: http://www.ogre3d.org
[7] Irrlicht project site: http://irrlicht.sourceforge.net

kernel. In order to make this vision achievable, the agents are based on the same real-time component framework (cf. [Hen05]) that is used in the context of the Fujaba Real-Time Tool Suite. They use it for communicating with each other, but also for interacting with their sensors and effectors, which are realized as dedicated components. This makes it particularly easy to replace the simulated version with the real ones later on. The platform offers services for instantiating, managing, and scheduling these components. It also offers basic support for deliberately introducing faults into the system by disabling components or communication channels.

From the point of view of Story-Driven Modeling, the perhaps most important service is provided by a module that adds an additional abstraction layer between the environment model and the agents. In a physical environment, there are very few associations besides composition relationships, which in turn only result from the deliberate conceptual decomposition of an entity (shuttle) into subentities (chassis and wheels). Most relationships in a physical environment are actually positional, i.e. concerned with objects' relative positions. This is most inconvenient when using a formalism for modeling that is based on the assumption that a system can be represented as a graph, as opposed to a set of isolated nodes whose relationships are implicit in their attributes.

The *Discretization Service* therefore performs a domain-specific translation from positional relationships into the semantic associations of the specified entity model. This is not only less tedious than doing this in the application code (although this advantage only carries over to the production system if a comparable service, such as the one presented in [SH04], is made available), but also more efficient, as it only needs to be done once for all agents.

In our application example in the previous chapter, we subdivided track blocks into track segments to allow making statements about a shuttle's location that are more precise than a simple using association to the track would be, but easier to interpret than the (quasi-)continuous relative position of the shuttle. As this is a common use case, the *Discretization Service* offers the rasterization of physical space, subdividing larger entities into a grid of smaller virtual entities. The service can then efficiently determine which cell an entity currently intersects and make this information available by means of the corresponding association.

The *Discretization Service* is also the foundation on which the *Monitoring Component* operates. Based on the defined community type specifications, it monitors the entities of the simulated environment and creates the appropriate social structures and entities, i.e. communities, roles, and professed intentions, in a separate internal model. As the *Simulation Kernel* provides access to the entire environment, and is even able to provide lists of all entities of a given type without overhead, the *Monitoring Component* acts as an omniscient observer that captures all theoretically indicated norm applications.

As both the size of the environment and the number of norms may be large, the *Monitoring Component* subscribes to change events from the kernel that allow it to narrow its focus down to those norms that might have been affected by the most recent update. For behavioral norms that are expressed as Story Patterns, there is the additional problem that the monitor would have to continuously check every one of their preconditions and cache the resulting occurrences in order to decide whether a rule application was valid once the corresponding postcondition is observed. In the framework, we therefore instrument the effector components in such a way that an event

## 5.3 Validation

is raised before the effector is actually applied, which makes a much leaner monitor that only performs the minimally necessary checks possible.

The *Monitoring Component* is itself a source of events, which a raised whenever a norm matches or a community, role, or professed intention is created or destroyed. The advanced *Visualization Component* listens for these events and is able to visualize the social state of the system by means of overlays that annotate the involved entities.

**Prototyping.** Beside its modular design, what most differentiates the framework from custom-built solutions is its tool integration. The ability to generate code that is designed to work with the framework and its features drastically reduces the need to write tedious boilerplate code.

This is especially true of the environment model. It is possible to describe the entities, their physical shape and attributes, their composition relationships with other entities, including the joint types that link them, and their visual representation in a completely declarative way, making the configuration of the framework's core components fully automatic. The same holds for the social model, as the code for each community type is completely determined by the specification.

For the agents, the basic infrastructure for each type and the external interfaces, i.e., the sensors and effectors, can be generated, as these parts are specified as diagrams. For the implementations of the agents' internals, there is a library of building blocks that provide common functionality such as managing perceptions or running and switching between different strategies, but no full tool integration to allow full flexibility concerning the employed libraries or techniques. With an appropriate adapted *Controller*, it would, for example, be possible to integrate an existing OCM implementation.

**Experiences.** In the course of the project, two application examples where implemented. Figure 5.3.2 shows screenshots from the two prototypes, a simulation of the behavior of a swarm of fish and a logistics scenario.

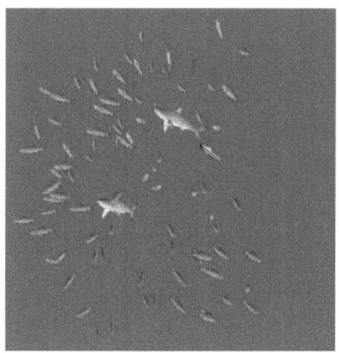
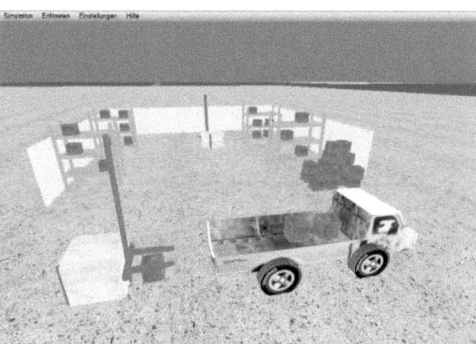

a. Fish swarm behavior          b. Logistics scenario

Figure 5.3.2: Visualization Engine

The swarming simulation was mainly designed as a proof of concept for the framework's core components. The scenario consists of an aquarium containing a swarm of fish hunted by sharks. The available sensors and effectors are quite basic: The sharks are faster and have greater long range vision, the prey is more agile and has a larger field of vision. User interaction is limited to dynamically adding obstacles to the simulation.

The prey fish emulate natural swarming behavior based on the boid paradigm [Rey87], three rules that cause fish to move towards the center of the swarm, to keep their distance from fish in close proximity and obstacles, and to align their velocities. They also avoid the sharks and the corners of the aquarium. As the visibility relation between fish is not symmetric, the overall shoal community is composed of subcommunities each consisting of one fish and its perceived neighbors, which govern the actual behavior. While these communities may appear like degenerate cases due to the asymmetry of the interaction, they illustrate an important design principle: Basing the required behavior on observable actions and states only works as intended if the concerned agents are actually able to make the observations that are supposed to trigger it. As the rules are operational and deterministic, it was trivial to use the community type specification itself as the prototypical agent controller.

The sharks are based on similar principles, with the notable difference that they are supposed to cooperate with the goal of cornering the prey. They were implemented explicitly in order to prove that it is possible to correctly implement a community type by implicitly considering it in the coding.

The prototype allowed experimenting on the emergent properties of the system. By changing sensor and effector parameters and varying the thresholds and intensities for the behavioral norms, the balance of the system could be shifted towards either party and diverse behavioral patterns could be induced.

The logistics scenario simulates a port with warehouses where forklifts load and unload cargo that is transported by trucks and ships. Its goal is to organize the transport of cargo from a source warehouse to a destination warehouse in a decentralized fashion. A broker publishes transportation tasks, for which trucks then bid. Where necessary, the trucks delegate the task to ships or other trucks as subcontractors, which is also organized via auctions. At the endpoints of each leg, the transporters need to procure the services of the local forklifts.

As this scenario is rather complex, designing coordination mechanisms that guarantee the efficient and timely execution of all or a high percentage of transportation tasks is far from trivial. As each case involves at least three different agent types, and as subcontracting can lead to complex, deeply nested community structures, designing the necessary cultures require the creation of many interrelated, carefully orchestrated norms. Since TSSDs were not yet invented, describing complex sequences of events was also unnecessarily tedious at times.

However, there was a sobering lesson to be learned from this case study: While building a sufficiently realistic simulation environment for mechatronic systems is hard, the framework does an excellent job making this easy for the developer. And while the coordination problem is sufficiently complex, the modeling approach was adequate for designing a solution that seemed sound. It was bringing the two together that caused the most problems.

## 5.3 Validation

In spite of the simplification that the *Discretization Service* offers, getting agents to behave correctly in an environment offering six degrees of freedom and a realistic physics model is very difficult. Even a basic task like picking up a crate poses many problems. Provided that the crate is still on the shelf where it was last recorded (it might have fallen down), the forklift needs to be positioned exactly to be able to reach it. If it turns out that the crate is slightly displaced or rotated with respect to its theoretical position (which is the norm), the forklift needs to align its position by maneuvering, in a limited space, which requires an algorithm that is able to dictate the correct sequence of movements. The agents also need an awareness of their own shape and the space around them and incorporate it in their decisions, as it is all too easy to inadvertently knock one crate from the shelf while retrieving another.

This is in itself not a surprising realization, as designing autonomous robots is a discipline in its own right into which much research was invested before the first moderate successes were obtained. After all, using a realistic simulation as the environment does not and should not eliminate all of the problems encountered in practice. However, the pretension to maximize the practical applicability of the obtained results incurs a steep initial penalty that is absent when using a much more abstract model, as is common in work on comparable application scenarios (see e.g. [KK07b]). The framework may indeed be well-suited to the problem of designing coordination mechanisms for autonomous mechatronic systems, but complicates the agent development because it requires diverting some attention to their mechanical aspects from the start. If the coordination between the agents depends on the exact physical characteristics of a situation, this may in fact be unavoidable. However, if these aspects can be separated to a certain degree, prematurely mixing them unduly complicates the design and evaluation of the agent coordination mechanisms.

In many cases, we find that it is more economical to use a higher level of abstraction, as in the application examples we have used throughout this thesis. When designing coordination mechanisms, every detail that is not strictly related to the agents' interaction introduces an unnecessary distraction. After migrating to the proposed extended language, we have therefore performed our evaluations based on a much simpler, completely ontology-driven kernel that drops the physics engine and all of the associated data structures and translation steps. We believe that developers should be free to decide which level of detail will actually be helpful for a specific task or phase. If a low level of abstraction is used, the developer, or rather team of developers, creating the agents needs to be willing and able to invest the additional effort that is required. This can be expected to be the case in later phases of the development process, as the specifics of the environment need to be accounted for before deploying an agent, but is not advisable for the initial design.

### 5.3.3 Analysis

The last, but not least important part of an experimental evaluation is to observe the system in action and obtain data which can then be analyzed. Meaningful feedback is indispensable for an efficient iterative process leading to incremental improvements.

### 5.3.3.1 Process Monitoring

When running a simulation, we are able to use the same code that was used earlier in the context of scenario-based verification for monitoring the system. For one, this allows us to keep verifying the system, as we are only able to achieve partial coverage during the initial verification and violations might, in principle, still surface in additional tests. But besides, TSSD monitoring can also help to make the system more transparent when analyzing it.

The sum of the trace trees that are currently active already gives a good impression of what is happening in the system. However, scanning through a large number of observations may still be impractical. If sequence labels have been defined in the scenarios, a more aggregated view can therefore be derived that abstracts from individual situations and only shows which phase of which scenarios an agent is currently in. If the sequence labels are defined in a way that, e.g., mirrors the commitments that are made and fulfilled, this list gives an immediate overview of an agent's open commitments.

When an in-depth analysis of some aspect of the system is needed, the trace tree of a TSSD provides a large repository of interesting data that can be mined. All process flows with all involved entities and exact time stamps are implicitly contained in it and can be extracted and processed. If our goal is to optimize the performance of the system, obtaining key performance indicators such as the minimum, average, or maximum time required to complete a certain scenario, the average time that passes between two specific situations, or the percentage of cases that corresponds to a specific variation of a branching scenario is quite helpful for spotting inefficiencies, focusing the further analysis, or simply gaining a better understanding of the events in the system. Even the most basic statistics such as the number of times a specific constraint has been violated may already be very helpful for pinpointing the problem.

### 5.3.3.2 Statistical Analysis

For some applications, we are less interested in the processes, but rather domain-specific indicators that need to be captured explicitly in order to enable their statistical analysis.

**Cooperative learning.** In [DGK+04], we have proposed a cooperative algorithm that allows shuttles to learn track usage profiles more quickly than would be possible in isolation. These profiles are then used for inferring the most efficient route from past utilization patterns. The algorithm was successively refined in a series of experiments that used the accumulated estimation error as a measure of profile quality. The resulting algorithm learned new patterns very quickly, was robust in the face of minor variations in the input data, but adapted quickly if the pattern was actually changed. In a second step, this algorithm was then used in an actual simulation of a shuttle system. In a bachelor's thesis ([Ren04]), shuttles using cooperative learning, individual learning, and no learning at all were compared and judged on the efficiency of their routing decisions, respectively the average generated profit, which was expected to be correlated to this.

**Convoy formation.** In the context of another bachelor's thesis ([Bie04]), we set out to validate one of the central assumptions of the RailCab project, namely the claim that the ability to form

## 5.3 Validation

convoys makes small shuttles competitive with larger trains in terms of energy consumption. For this purpose, the above-mentioned special-purpose simulation kernel which abstracts from most aspects of the system but uses a detailed model of the shuttles' relative positions and energy consumption was built. Actual technical data from the project was used except for the air resistance of shuttles in a convoy, for which an (optimistic) estimate had to be used because no experimental data is available thus far.

The shuttles were coordinated using a precursor of the positioning culture that was presented in the previous chapter. Shuttles placed marker objects at track junctions that indicated when they intended to pass or had passed that point. This information was then used by other shuttles for adapting their behavior, with the goal of determining the most energy-efficient schedule that their task list would allow. The approach was inspired by work on stigmergy, i.e. self-organization through indirect communication, which is best known in the guise of ant-type routing based on pheromones (cf. e.g. [PBS05, Bon99]).

Different synthetic and realistic track layouts with different numbers of shuttles were used for evaluating a set of possible strategies. The performance indicators that were recorded in the experiments included the expended energy, convoy sizes, the absolute and relative distance traveled in convoys, and the accumulated delay that was incurred while completing a predetermined task list.

The obtained results were quite intriguing. Most importantly, shuttle density is crucial, as the effect of convoys becomes negligible if the system is too sparsely populated. This means that for inter-city travel, where distances are large, the minimum number of shuttles that is required for achieving any effect at all is high, i.e. in the hundreds or thousands depending on the exact size and structure of the network. Even then, the chances of a random encounter between two shuttles, let alone at a junction, are low to infinitesimal, even more so if shuttle speeds are uniform. Shuttles have to actively seek out other shuttles if a significant number of convoys is to be formed.

The second, quite surprising result was that most advanced strategies performed worse in terms of energy consumption than a naive strategy that only forms convoys opportunistically when a shuttle with a tighter deadline catches up with a slower shuttle. Accepting a detour for joining up with other shuttles hardly ever seems to pay off. Even more importantly, all strategies that actively accelerated the shuttle in order to catch up with other shuttles out of visual range incurred moderate to large penalties. The only approach using strategic planning that was consistently beneficial was to scan the traffic *behind* the shuttle and actively wait for other shuttles by slowing down as much as the schedule permitted.

Most advanced strategies lead to more kilometers traveled in convoys, but meanwhile also increased the overall energy consumption because the additional effort expended for reaching convoys was not worthwhile. These results do not only stress the importance of empirical evaluation – especially when dealing with emergent phenomena in complex systems, which often contradict our intuition – but also underline how crucial it is to choose the right performance indicators.

**System reliability.** In another project, we studied strategies for achieving emergent fault-tolerance based on the behavior of communities of self-interested agents (cf. [KT06]). In order to make a signal processing (or production) network, in which agents can perform different functions, reliable without introducing a central authority or dedicated backup systems, our approach uses a market model where agents are paid (or pay) for performing a specific function and for reconfiguring, depending on the perceived social benefit of the action. The norms need to be designed in such a way as to make the desired fault-tolerant behavior the economically rational choice. The employed reward and reconfiguration cost functions tend to discourage gratuitous reconfiguration due to the associated downtime, but use strong incentives to steer agents towards functions where demand threatens to exceed supply in the near future.

The problem possesses two notable properties: Firstly, the quality of a solution can neatly be summed up in two related key figures, availability (percentage of successfully processed packets) and reliability (probability of a sequence of successfully processed packets). Secondly, there is an abundance of parameters that can be modified, including the structure of the network, the number of agents, the agent failure rate, the agent respawn rate, the packet arrival frequency, the size of the available buffers, the time required for reconfiguring an agent to the agents' strategy, and the shape and exact parametrization of the employed reward and reconfiguration cost functions. This predestines the problem for automated testing.

We consequently created a scriptable test driver for automatically running different variants of the simulation and recording the results. This allowed us to explore a wide spectrum of combinations of parameter settings. As random events play an important role for the evaluation, repeated runs with different seeds were performed for each set of parameters. After interesting cases and promising strategies had been identified in several thousand experiments, successively more detailed tests were performed to fine tune the cost functions. Ultimately, this lead to a system that operated close to the theoretical optimum.

While not all multi-agent systems may lend themselves to a differential analysis based on slightly varied repetitions of the same experiment in this way – e.g. because each run would take too long, because the conditions cannot be controlled as exactly, because results are not reproducible, or because the quality of a result cannot be judged or ranked automatically – our experiences suggest that the usefulness of the ability to quickly generate different prototypes is strongly linked to our ability to evaluate them.

**Strategy selection.** How can we evaluate a system when there are multiple, possibly conflicting criteria? And what if different solutions perform best under different environment conditions? When designing agents that are supposed to function in a variety of environments, this question almost invariably surfaces.

Any decision must then necessarily be a compromise that is shaped by our preferences and assumptions. Nonetheless, there should be an explicit, clearly defined procedure for performing the evaluation of a solution. As there is a loss of information whenever we aggregate values, such transformations should be selected consciously.

The quality of a result should depend on measurable indicators. If there are multiple criteria, these have to be weighted or ranked, which then allows computing some form of weighted average from the indicators. After this quality value has been measured for different environment conditions, a quality profile can be created (see Figure 5.3.3a for a diagram plotting quality values against two variable environmental parameters).

We could simply compute an average quality value from our measurements. However, not all environmental conditions may be equally probable. Where this is possible, we specify probability distributions for the environmental parameters, which can be combined into a probability profile (see Figure 5.3.3b). This profile is used to weight the quality profile. If a single overall quality value is required, it can be obtained by integrating over the weighted profile.

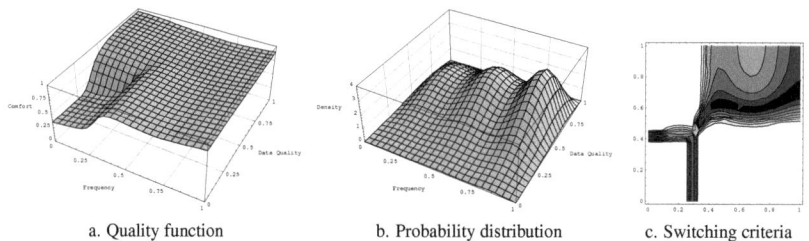

a. Quality function      b. Probability distribution      c. Switching criteria

Figure 5.3.3: Comparing and combining different strategies

In [AGKF06], we applied this idea in the context of a methodology for the design of self-optimizing mechatronic systems (see e.g. [GFG$^+$05]). When designing systems that are expected to be more flexible and versatile than traditional systems, a method for systematically choosing a design pattern or building block that is more differentiated than traditional scoring systems provides significant benefits.

In the specific case of adaptive systems, their very nature provides us with an additional option: not choosing at all. An adaptive system is characterized by its ability to modify its behavior - so why not simply use the optimal strategy at all times? If supporting several alternative solutions is possible technically, the differences are large enough to justify the more complex design, and robust criteria for switching between the strategies can be established, this results in a system that outperforms both original solutions. Based on the combined weighted quality profiles, both the achievable benefit and the switching criteria can be computed (see Figure 5.3.3c).

For situated multi-agent systems in general, what is considered a good solution depends on the environment to a large degree. However, the best solutions are those that are flexible enough to perform well under many different conditions, using the conceptual advantages of a loosely coupled system of autonomous actors to their best effect.

## 5.4 Conclusion

Throughout this chapter, numerous related publications that provided fundamental concepts or were closely related to a specific method were already presented. In the following section, we will take a more general look at agent verification and validation that is not limited to GTS.

## 5.4.1 Related Work

Approaches for the *formal verification* of multi-agent systems mostly focus on interaction protocols and the agents' mental state. In this vein, [BC03] applies conventional CTL model checking to specifically adapted models of the beliefs, desires and intentions of interacting agents. For systems modeled using the DESIRE methodology, [BCG+04] proposes a compositional verification approach that introduces a hierarchy of levels of abstraction for decomposing the problem into manageable subproblems. Due to their focus on cognitive agents and direct agent communication, these approaches are not suited for dealing with complex interactions based on the environment or ad-hoc cooperation as they lack support for the description and verification of structural adaptation.

Proposals such as [vdHRW05] are oriented towards games of a closed set of agents and answer the question whether a group of agents can achieve a specific goal, assuming that their coordination is perfect. Their premise is quite different from the one of our approach, which is concerned with the more pragmatic problem whether a given coordination mechanism is sufficient for guaranteeing the completion of the goal *within* the confines and limitations of the given environment.

Another approach that uses model checking in order to decide whether a set of social rules is effective is proposed in [vdHRW07]. The employed logic is notable for providing explicit support for considering the autonomy of the agents' decisions, but limits the approach to very restricted use cases.

Our work on GTS refinement and monitoring shows some similarities with the debugging support presented in [PWP05], where the agents' behavior is validated against Petri Net specifications, but explicitly factors in the agents' situatedness in the environment.

With respect to the problem of structural adaptation in software architectures, [BHTV03] parallels our approach in proposing the use of graph transformation systems for the verification of such systems. However, there is no explicit support for agents or higher-level control structures.

*Rapid prototyping* is in wide-spread use in many different areas. For embedded systems, a prototyping phase is actually considered an integral part of a proper development process (cf. [BN03]). In the specific context of mechatronic systems, it is often concerned with the design and incremental improvement of control laws (cf. [DRZH01]). For this purpose, it is combined with virtual prototyping (cf. [SJ99]) or, more frequently, dedicated prototyping hardware (e.g. FPGAs) that allows a quick implementation and reconfiguration. Here, the control structures and dataflow are usually rather static, however.

Software engineering, especially with proper CASE tool support, lends itself to rapid prototyping (cf. [Mul90]). Specifically, the use of Story-Driven Modeling for prototyping purposes has first been studied in the context of the ISILEIT project (cf. [GSEW05, SWGE04]), whose application area was the design of production control systems. While prototyping is generally seen as a useful method for early validation, as recently popularized by approaches like the test-driven Extreme Programming [Bec99], it is frequently not combined with a formal process. Where applied systematically, it is often primarily seen as a tool for requirements engineering [CS95].

## 5.4.2 Discussion

In this chapter, we have presented a wide spectrum of approaches for the verification and validation of multi-agent systems. The scope of the verification techniques we have discussed ranges from the verification of invariants over the model checking of generic safety properties and the analysis of agent behavior to the monitoring of complex scenarios. All of them have their merits due to the trade-off between expressiveness and computability that they offer: Do we need a basic but definite result for the entire system, or are we content with identifying and fixing counterexamples based on a complex specification until we consider it sufficiently probable that the agents will behave correctly?

Bound together by a common formal foundation and the principles of the CURCUMA framework, this collection of approaches constitutes a coherent method that is able to address a wide range of needs. The previously existing methods have been adapted and extended in this direction, while our original contributions were designed with the corresponding concepts in mind. The inherent support for decomposition that communities provide then turns an apparent weakness into a strength: Because we can assign different aspects of the problem to different communities, we can use the most appropriate method for each of them. The different methods have been applied to the application example and have proven effective at exposing even subtle flaws in the design in their respective domains.

When moving from models to concrete implementations, which are subject to additional problems and influences, the diversity of the applicable techniques further increases. With our focus on code generation and reusable modular frameworks that provide a basic infrastructure, we have however developed a concept that can cover a wide range of applications and offers great potential for future extensions in different directions. The spotlights on previous experiments have given a glimpse of the type of fascinating and practically relevant results that can be gained from multi-agent systems. Together, the extension of the infrastructure and the design of more complex or realistic application examples offer promising avenues for future research.

# Chapter 6

# Application

## 6.1 Introduction

One of the main motivations for using a model-driven approach is the expectation that it will boost productivity, either by making complex problems more manageable or by making the development process itself more efficient. In this thesis, we have presented the key ingredients of such an approach, namely a concept for structuring the models, a language for writing them, and a set of methods for improving and exploiting them. We have focused our discussion on the precise definition and illustration of our concepts and their formalizations, not pragmatic issues, thus far. Our running example and the projects that we have outlined in the previous chapter provide evidence that our approach is applicable to a wide range of domains and problems – but is it practical?

Experience teaches that usability is key for the success of a methodology, unless its adoption is forced by external constraints or sheer necessity. The practical value of a model-driven approach is directly correlated to the quality of the guidelines and the tool support that it provides to developers. In this chapter, we will therefore look into these topics and show how we support the application of our approach in practice.

**Chapter outline.** In the following section, we discuss the available tool support. We give an overview of the tool landscape and our specific contributions and then detail in what manner the different aspects of the approach are supported.

We then delve into questions concerning the usage of the proposed constraint languages in Section 6.3. We compare Timed Story Scenario Diagrams with a design pattern-based approach to the specification of temporal properties and discuss how the notations can provide support for deriving a formal model from textual requirements, using a self-contained example.

Finally, we discuss the possibilities of applying our approach in the context of the RailCab project, thus wrapping up our running application example.

## 6.2 Tool support

Many of the benefits of a model-driven approach are tied to proper tool support, and many eminent features such as formal verification or code generation directly depend on it. We therefore provide full end-to-end tool support for our constraint notations, from an advanced modeling environment to code generation for both the verification and the simulation use case. With respect to verification and validation, we do not provide the same level of support for the entire spectrum of approaches that were presented. In particular, the extended modeling tools are not fully integrated with all of the previously existing tools for verification and real-time modeling, which makes additional manual steps necessary for certain use cases. There is furthermore no support for automatic agent synthesis. In the following, we give a short overview of the different tool implementations before presenting our contributions in detail.

### 6.2.1 Tool Landscape

The centerpiece of the tool landscape is Fujaba[1], which provides an extensible platform for visual modeling, verification and code generation. Fujaba natively supports the key elements of Story-Driven Modeling, namely Class Diagrams and Story Diagrams, i.e. Activity Diagrams whose activities can be defined by means of Story Patterns.

The work on this thesis coincided with three major developments concerning Fujaba: The kernel underwent a major revision upgrade from version 4 to version 5, a new template-based code generation engine was introduced, and Fujaba was integrated into the open, plug-in-based Eclipse platform[2] as the Fujaba4Eclipse plug-in, which required a reimplementation of the graphical user interface. As Fujaba is currently used and developed at multiple universities and by projects with different priorities, not all of the available plug-ins are compatible with each other as a result of these changes.

**Related work.** In several areas, in particular in connection with *Coordination Patterns* and for purposes of verification and validation, we have referenced previous work for which tool support is available.

As mentioned in the previous chapter, *Coordination Patterns* can be modeled using the Fujaba Real-Time Suite, which provides support for Component Diagrams and Real-Time Statecharts (RTSC) with Java and C++ code generation for the employed component and runtime frameworks. The described synthesis of RTSC from annotated scenarios is implemented by a plug-in (cf. [GT05]). Another plug-in integrates the model checker UPPAAL (cf. [LPY97]) and thus enables the automatic verification of *Coordination Patterns* (cf. [Hir04]).

The verification of GTS is likewise supported through plug-ins. The GTS Model Checking plug-in (cf. [Neu06]) provides an interface to the model checker GROOVE (cf. [Ren03]). Specifications are augmented with the constraints that are required to simulate the use of graph isomorphisms

---
[1] Fujaba project site: http://www.fujaba.de
[2] Eclipse project site: http://www.eclipse.org

## 6.2 Tool support

and transformed to GROOVE's input format, the external tool is invoked, and the results and possible identified counterexamples are visualized in Fujaba. The Invariant Checking plug-in implements the algorithm for verifying invariants of systems with infinite state spaces and is also capable of displaying the generated counterexamples inside Fujaba. Finally, we have implemented the conversions that are required for exporting a specification to the relational calculator CrocoPat (cf. [BNL05]) for symbolic evaluation as a plug-in (cf. [BBG+06]).

**Intrapid Tools.** The concepts of the CURCUMA framework were first implemented and experimentally evaluated within the Intrapid project. A significant part of the implementation effort in that project went into the realization of the runtime framework that was described in the previous chapter. The implementation of the core components and the agent infrastructure consists of more than 300 classes containing several ten thousands of lines of C++ code. Nonetheless, matching tool support for modeling and generating environments, agents, and community types was also implemented in the form of four plug-ins consisting of more than 200 Java classes. The tool implementation is integrated into Fujaba4Eclipse, but uses the Fujaba 4 kernel and the original code generation engine.

The tool provides explicit support for many of the concepts of the CURCUMA framework in the form of specialized diagram types. These diagram types are based on the notations that were already supported by Fujaba4Eclipse, namely Class Diagrams and Story Diagrams, but not the extended constraint notations, as these had not been invented yet at the time. There are entity diagrams for modeling entities and their physical properties, agent-, sensor-, and effector type diagrams for defining the generated outer shell of the agent implementations, culture and norm diagrams for defining cultures, template types, roles, and professed intentions, with Story Patterns defining the different norms, and community type diagrams, which allow mapping template types to concrete entity types from the entity diagrams.

In order to enable the generation of C++ code from these diagrams, it was necessary to adapt the existing C++ code generation facilities, which had been designed for generating specific flavors of embedded applications. The specific semantics of the different diagram types also needed to be reflected in the generated code. This required the incorporation of a transformation engine which performed the corresponding modifications and substitutions before passing the derived model to the code generation engine.

**SDMX Tools.** This approach to code generation proved unnecessarily complex and inflexible. There were also limitations in the basic design of the employed diagrams. Notably, Story Patterns were only supported inside Activities as part of a Story Diagram, which was in turn required to be attached to some Method of a Class as its implementation. For the verification plug-ins, which called for stand-alone Story Patterns, this required workarounds based on conventions the user had to adhere to. The Intrapid tools hid this problem from the user by means of the dedicated diagram types, but did not solve the underlying problem, which again increased complexity.

When we implemented the extended constraint notations, we therefore chose to do so on a more solid foundation and switched to a new metamodel using the Fujaba 5 kernel and the revised code generation engine. We have also invested considerable effort into the Fujaba4Eclipse infrastructure in order to increase the flexibility and usability of the user interface. This has resulted in a set of Eclipse plug-ins, the Story-Driven Modeling Extensions (SDMX), which make up the current version of the tool. Not counting the generic contributions to the Fujaba4Eclipse infrastructure, the SDMX plug-ins consist of some 600 Java classes. Besides the above-mentioned end-to-end support for the new notations, there is a generic mechanism for attaching constraints to models and model entities, which, together with the extensive use of stereotypes, enables a much more light-weight implementation of the CURCUMA concepts.

## 6.2.2 Modeling

We now describe the features of the revised tool implementation and the extensions in the tool infrastructure they required in more detail. The new metamodel provides greater flexibility and does away with several assumptions that underlie previous versions, e.g. that a Story Pattern always occurs in the context of an Activity. This has consequences in many places, making it necessary to provide more generic implementations of features that were hard-coded before.

**Fujaba4Eclipse infrastructure.** The navigation tree that was used by Fujaba4Eclipse was implemented as a custom view. It also enforced a true tree structure, allowing each model element to appear at most once. Adding a new model element required implementing a custom adapter and registering it in the configuration files. The new Fujaba Explorer integrates the model outline into the Project Explorer that is provided by Eclipse. What is displayed is defined declaratively so that plug-ins only need to provide the desired configuration, but no custom adapters. The new navigator supports all of the features of the old one, but additionally allows displaying the same model element in multiple places and with different icons, labels, and children, depending on the context of the occurrence. As is customary in Eclipse, the status of a model element can be indicated by overlay icons or additional labels. Finally, the new Explorer allows modifying the model directly in the outline by dragging and dropping elements. The Explorer supports different view profiles that control what is displayed. The default view arranges the classes of a model according to the package structure, similar to the way this is done in the Eclipse Java IDE.

The wizards for creating new diagrams or model elements have been remodeled to use the Fujaba Explorer tree view for selections. During this modification, we have also introduced a new wiz-

## 6.2 Tool support

ard framework which allows defining labels, input fields, filters, selection criteria, and validity checks with only few lines of code, which drastically reduces the effort needed for implementing a custom wizard.

Another major improvement concerns the property editor that is used for viewing and modifying the properties of model elements. Originally, Eclipse only provided a table view with text input fields and drop-down selections for this purpose. While later versions introduced greater flexibility and allowed developing custom property pages, this required a custom implementation for every type of model element. We have therefore again realized a declarative solution that allows creating sophisticated, user-friendly property pages by means of simple annotations to the existing property definitions. Besides the standard text input and drop-down selection fields, the implementation offers modifiable drop-down selection fields that allow adding and removing entries, list fields that allow editing multi-valued properties, multiple selections fields that allow moving elements between a list of available elements and a list of selected elements, and nested fields that are populated depending on the selection in their master drop-down selection field. The property editors now also implement full undo support. Additionally, the design of the property adapters that handle the interaction between property editors and model elements was simplified by means of a new base class that offers a cleaner API hiding the complexity of providing input for the different field types that is compatible with Eclipse from the developer.

There are other less visible enhancements throughout the platform. The way model files are handled was changed, tying the loading and unloading of the model to the life cycle of the main editor. Loading and saving are now executed as background tasks. Utility methods for performing common tasks such as opening a diagram editor, managing the state of a model file, or displaying a selected model element in the editor have been added to the central infrastructure. An infrastructure for managing preferences based on the Eclipse preference mechanism with accompanying tool classes was put into place, and several pages with settings for Fujaba4Eclipse were added to the Eclipse preference dialog. The tool palettes of the diagram editors are now no longer hard-coded, but configured declaratively.

We have furthermore contributed to the graphics library that is used for laying out and displaying the diagrams by implementing Bezier curves that support static and interactive routing, a basic set of shapes whose visual style can be controlled in a unified manner, including the characteristic UML 2.0 box, support for shadows and decorations, and advanced label locators that keep labels from overlapping the connections which they annotate.

Figure 6.2.1 shows several of the enhancements, particularly the new Fujaba Explorer and the new property editor.

**Constraint modeling.** In order to provide a unified solution for attaching constraints to a model, we have created a constraint plug-in that provides the corresponding infrastructure. A *constraint* specifies a restriction on a set of model elements or the entire model. Its definition may be textual or of any supported diagram type. A *constraint set* aggregates a set of *constraints*. *Constraint sets* may contain other *constraint sets*, and each *constraint* may be included in multiple sets. Figure 6.2.2 shows the fully expanded constraint tree of a small example containing 6 *constraints* (expressed as SDDs) and 5 *constraint sets*.

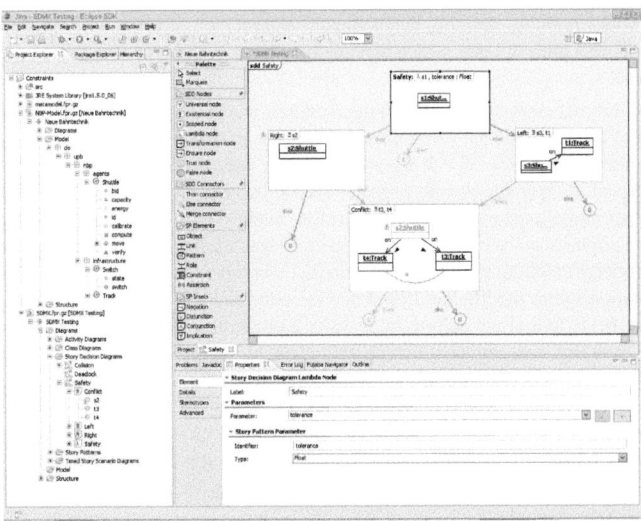

Figure 6.2.1: Screenshot showcasing several of the enhancements

By turning *constraints* into first class objects, there is now a clean way to mark the part of the model that represents the specification and persist this information in the model itself. This eliminates the need for the workarounds used by the existing verification plug-ins. The *constraint sets* make it convenient to restrict verification to part of a specification by exporting only the selected set to the verification tools, which makes it possible to explicitly maintain and compare different alternative solutions or to focus the evaluation on a specific concern.

**SDMX infrastructure.** SDDs and TSSDs make additional demands on the underlying infrastructure due to the syntax highlighting that is an integral part of their visual design. In order to correctly mark up bound and unbound pattern elements or forbidden scenarios, the tool needs a deeper understanding of the diagram and the underlying metamodel than is required for, e.g., Story Diagrams. Particularly deciding whether an element is bound or not is not trivial, as this depends both on the pattern itself and its context, which is different for a standalone pattern and one in a Story Diagram or TSSD.

This problem is solved by introducing three concepts: All named model elements are declared elements which may contain a reference to a definition of the same name and category. Elements without such a reference are themselves definitions and therefore unbound. The references are managed by each diagram's namespace, which processes and propagates all additions, deletions, and modifications. The namespace's relationship to other namespaces is made fully transparent by the diagram's context, which abstracts from the different surroundings and thus allows using the same diagram type both as a diagram in its own right and inside TSSD situations, scoped

## 6.2 Tool support 235

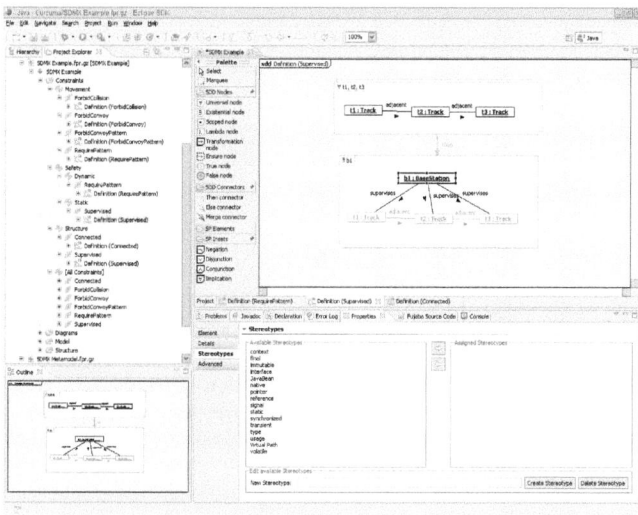

Figure 6.2.2: Constraints in Fujaba4Eclipse

SDD nodes, or Story Diagram activities. The specific context implementations need to know how to traverse transitions in a Story Diagram respectively connectors in a TSSD, but the interface used by the namespace is identical in all cases. When an element is added, the namespace asks the context for the preceding namespaces and then queries its predecessors for an existing definition of the same name and category. Changes in the structure of the host diagram trigger a complete reevaluation.

The infrastructure provides support for copying, pasting, and cloning elements, with fine-grained control over which elements should be copied by value or by reference, respectively whether a clone should be a deep or shallow copy. It also integrates the model elements with the Eclipse task and problem infrastructure. As in the Eclipse Java IDE, errors, warnings, and notices are displayed in a central problem view, as an overlay icon on the navigation tree, and in the editor, i.e. as an icon decorating the element in the diagram. Problem markers are persisted even when the referenced model file is unloaded and allow navigating to the diagram containing the marked element directly from the problem view.

**SDMX diagrams.** Based on this infrastructure, the three introduced diagram types were implemented. The SDD editor reuses the eSP editor for node definitions, and the TSSD editor in turn reuses the SDD editor for situation definitions. The TSSD editor was implemented as part of a master's thesis (cf. [Spi07]). The eSP and SDD editors also integrate into the existing Story Diagram editor.

The editors implement various features that are intended to increase productivity. Besides the generic mechanism for copying and pasting, common use cases such as propagating a pattern to a subsequent node in an SDD are supported explicitly. Leaf nodes are added and removed automatically as nodes and connectors are added. It is possible to change the type of a node in place, i.e. preserving its connections and content, using its context menu. Entire branches of the diagram can be moved together when laying out the diagram.

In eSPs, insets look and work similar to the way nodes operate in SDDs, but there is a notable difference: SDD nodes are created as empty containers to be later filled with content, whereas insets are added into an existing pattern, acquiring their content from what is already there. An inset does not own the enclosed elements, although they behave and move as parts of the inset. Unlike for nodes, elements can be removed from insets by resizing the inset or simply moving them outside of the box, and the contained elements are not deleted when the inset is deleted. Insets also support nesting. TSSD triggers are implemented in a similar way.

Along with the syntax highlighting, the editors perform various syntactic and semantic checks that generate error and warning annotations. They recognize incorrect graph structures, e.g. SDDs with multiple roots, disconnected TSSDs, and paradoxical or tautological statements, e.g. when all outgoing connectors of an SDD node lead to (1) nodes. They also warn when a node with multiple predecessors references a potentially unbound element. Ambiguous or intersecting insets are flagged, as are problematic trigger blocks in TSSDs.

In the preferences, the visual appearance of the diagrams can be tuned. Several options control the level of detail and redundant information, such as additional labels, that is displayed. The strategies for displaying leaf nodes in SDDs range from the bare semantically required minimum, over an adaptive strategy ensuring balanced layouts, to displaying all of them. In eSPs, it is possible to choose between ≪create≫/≪destroy≫, ++/−−, and ∗/∼ for indicating modified elements.

Figure 6.2.3 shows the diagram from Figure 4.3.16 in the context of the editor. Note the error annotation and the corresponding problem view. All of the application example diagrams that have appeared in the preceding chapters were created using the described editors.

### 6.2.3 Prototyping

The tool implementation supports the validation of models by enabling the generation, execution, and evaluation of prototypes. The corresponding functionality is provided by the SDMX Code Generation plug-in and the SDMX Runtime library.

**Code generation.** The code generation engine is based on the CodeGen2 plug-in (cf. [GSR05]), which in turn uses the Velocity template engine[3] for actually writing the code. The code generation engine works by creating tokens for all relevant model elements, reordering and modifying them, and then using them for populating the assigned Velocity templates, all based on the chain of responsibility pattern. This approach provides improved transparency and makes it straight-

---

[3]Velocity project site: http://velocity.apache.org

## 6.2 Tool support

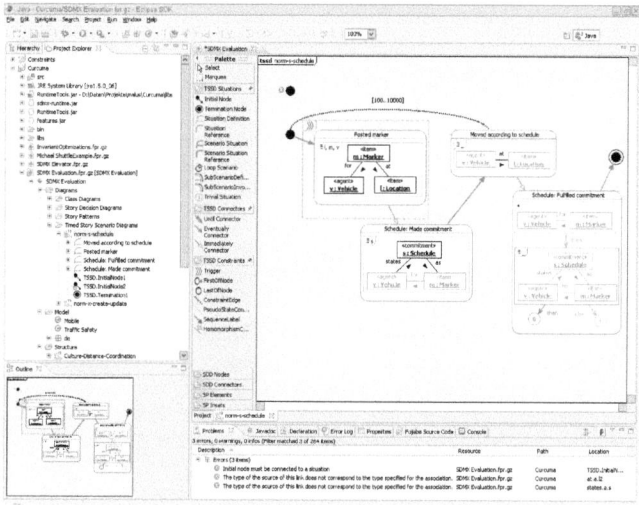

Figure 6.2.3: A Timed Story Scenario Diagram in Fujaba4Eclipse

forward to modify the result of the code generation by adapting the templates.

The SDMX Code Generation engine again introduces certain enhancements that have enabled us to quickly and efficiently implement the code generation support for the concrete diagram types and model elements. The engine needs to register with the CodeGen2 infrastructure and declare itself responsible for the model root element, as the standard implementation would merely traverse all classes and ignore constraints or standalone diagrams. The engine furthermore overrides the regular chain of responsibility mechanism in order to deal with another difference: The standard implementation assumes that the model corresponds to a tree structure, which implicitly ensures that every element is processed at most once. In our case, this is neither true of the overall model nor of the individual diagrams. To prevent the generation of superfluous tokens and infinite cycles, we therefore cache each generated token and reuse it when the corresponding model element is passed to the engine for processing again.

When formalizing the constraint languages, we have repeatedly handled syntactic features by mapping them to other constructs. This is particularly true of TSSDs, but also affects the other diagram types, e.g. when rewriting a scoped node as a SDD Pattern/Reference pair. Unfortunately, actually creating these auxiliary constructs as model elements incurs an undesirable overhead, requires a greater effort to ensure consistency, and may inadvertently pollute the model. We therefore only create tokens representing these virtual model elements and annotate them with the desired properties. While it is generally possible to access a model element through its token and directly query its methods from a template, this would fail for tokens representing virtual elements. In order to avoid having to write dedicated templates for the two cases, the corresponding properties of real model elements are also automatically added to their tokens as annotations by means of reflection. In this way, templates can access both types of elements in a unified fashion.

As the new notations introduce a multitude of new element types, we have made sure that only the token creators are specific to element types, but the same token type and code writer are reused for all element types. We also make it simple to control the generated file and folder structure and invoke dedicated special-purpose templates, e.g. for generating a basic infrastructure.

Both eSP and SDD code generation cover all introduced features of the notations. Code generation for TSSDs was again implemented in the context of a master's thesis (cf. [Spi07, GHH$^+$07]). The semantic kernel of the language is fully supported, with the exception of subscenarios.

The generated code heavily relies on abstract base classes, which has the advantage that the specific code for a diagram is much leaner than it would be otherwise. The diagram implementation only overrides certain hook methods that characterize the diagram and are called at the appropriate time by the base class. The base class, or rather framework of base classes, encapsulates the matching algorithm and all of the optimizations that are applied to it. In this manner, eSP matching is performed using the dynamic algorithm that was presented in the previous chapter. The SDD matching algorithm supports the adapted evaluation strategies for implementation or verification purposes, generating either at most one or all valid bindings.

**Runtime Framework.** The code generation works hand in hand with a matching runtime framework. The code generation instruments all entities in such a way that every new instance is registered with a central model directory, which is indispensable for matching patterns that do not contain a fixed this element that can serve as a starting point. Furthermore, the model directory listens for modifications in the model, which are invariably signaled by property change events. All changes that occur at the same point in time are collected into a single update, which is sent as soon as the system clock is advanced.

The selected *constraint sets* make up the specification that is used for monitoring the system. The generated specification is passed to an evaluator, which also receives the aggregated updates. Based on the update and the meta-information that has been added to each constraint by the code generator, the evaluator decides which of the available constraints have to be reevaluated, as described in the previous chapter. The evaluator records all constraint violations that are reported back to it and is thus able to provide the final verdict after an evaluation run.

The framework provides a system clock and a basic scheduler that allows running multiple agents or processes in parallel in simulated real-time. Each active process is queried for the action it would like to perform next. As graph transformations are instantaneous, whereas actions typically consume time, the invoked actions are queued and executed once the time required for completing them has passed. The actions that an agent performs can either be scripted or determined based on a state machine representing the agent's internal state. Besides templates for these two cases, the framework also provides support for the rudimentary synthesis strategy of randomly applying one of the permitted effectors.

## 6.3 Deriving Constraint Specifications

In previous chapters, we have defined the syntax and semantics of visual languages for the description of structural and temporal properties, discussed their expressiveness, and used them in the specification of multi-agent systems. While we have repeatedly emphasized that accessibility and intuitive ways of expressing real world properties were central design objectives of our constraint notations, we have so far not focused on the question of how such property specifications can be derived from informal requirements.

We first look at an approach that is based on design patterns that have been inspired by common temporal properties found in real-world applications. The patterns represent a cross-section of typical problems and can serve as a benchmark for gauging the applicability of TSSDs. We also consider whether the approach itself is helpful for the specification of TSSDs.

In the following section, we discuss how informal textual requirements can be translated into a set of formal constraints. We propose a systematic approach that is built around a set of basic principles and guided by the occurrence of certain keywords and apply it to a small, self-contained example.

### 6.3.1 Specification Pattern System

The Property Specification Pattern System presented in [DAC98] and extended in [DAC99] was proposed to address the problem of making formal specification techniques and thus formal verification accessible to practitioners, as even experts face problems when trying to encode moderately complex real-life properties using temporal logics such as LTL. The intention behind the Specification Pattern System is to enable users to construct more complex properties from basic, assuredly correct building blocks by providing generic specification patterns encoding certain elementary properties (existence, absence, universality, bounded existence, precedence (chains), and response (chains)), each specialized for a set of different scopes (globally, before R, after Q, between Q and R, after Q until R).

In the following, we demonstrate how the patterns of the Specification Pattern System can be encoded using Timed Story Scenario Diagrams. A convenient quality of TSSDs is that they allow us to define scopes and properties separately as orthogonal concepts and then simply plug the appropriate property into the desired scope.

**Scopes.** In Figure 6.3.1, we define the scopes as TSSDs. The original textual specification of the patterns is somewhat ambiguous – $\varphi$ exists before $R$ could be interpreted in two ways: $\varphi$ needs to exist before (possibly) $R$ is observed (putting the emphasis on *exists* $\varphi$), or $\varphi$ needs to exist whenever $R$ is observed afterwards (emphasizing *before R*). The latter is the interpretation that is encoded by the provided LTL pattern. The scopes *before*, *after*, *between*, and *until* are thus encoded using trigger blocks where $\varphi$ is the triggered scenario. As the table shows, all definitions except the definition of *until* are very compact. The last case requires an additional termination node because TSSDs provide no direct encoding of for the operator $\tilde{U}$ (weak until) so that the property that $R$ may occur or not needs to be encoded explicitly. This omission is intentional as

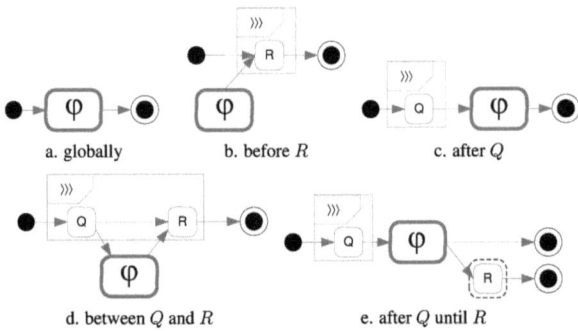

Figure 6.3.1: The scopes encoded as TSSDs (for a property $\varphi$)

we believe that, in the context of a scenario notation, it is more intuitive to explicitly specify that the scenario might be successfully completed in an earlier situation using the standard syntax for completion (⦿) instead of introducing a dedicated syntax for a $\tilde{U}$ connector.

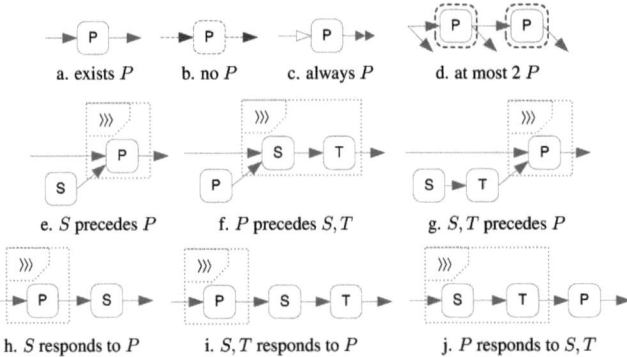

Figure 6.3.2: The properties $\varphi$ encoded as TSSDs)

**Properties.** In Figure 6.3.2, we define the ten different properties listed by the Specification Pattern System. Inbound connectors link to possible preconditions, outbound connectors encode success and lead to possible postconditions. *Existence*, *absence*, and *universality* are trivially encoded using the standard syntax for required and forbidden scenarios. *Bounded existence* is encoded by enumerating the acceptable sequences, i.e. 0, 1, or 2 occurrences. As the number of occurrences is relevant, all situations are strict so that no additional occurrences are permitted between the observations of a trace. Again, the weak progress (no occurrence of $P$ is also

## 6.3 Deriving Constraint Specifications

acceptable) is encoded by additional outbound connectors. When it comes to encoding response and precedence chains, the notation excels – quite unsurprisingly, as this is the use case for which it was designed. Triggers are designed for expressing response (and its dual, precedence), while sequences such as $S, T$ are *the* basic concept in TSSDs.

**Derivation.** These property definitions can now simply be substituted for $\varphi$ by completing them with an initial node as their precondition and termination nodes as their postcondition(s). While the trivial form of each combined pattern obtained using this mechanistic approach already yields usable results, simplified versions can be derived using two simple transformations that basically correspond to the elimination of redundant parentheses in mathematical expressions.

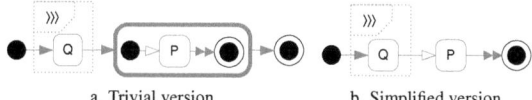

a. Trivial version    b. Simplified version

Figure 6.3.3: Always $P$ after $Q$

A scenario situation with a single termination node can be eliminated by connecting each situation inside the scope whose predecessor is the scope's initial node to each of the scope's predecessor nodes, and by connecting each situation inside the scope whose successor is the scope's termination node to each of the scope's successor nodes (see Figure 6.3.3).

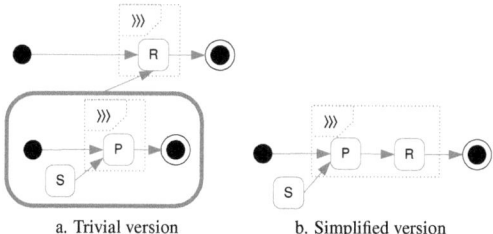

a. Trivial version    b. Simplified version

Figure 6.3.4: Always $S$ precedes $P$ before $R$

Secondly, if both the surrounding scenario and the scenario situation contain trigger blocks, these blocks are merged (see Figure 6.3.4).

Figure 6.3.5 lists all simplified variants of the (1,2) response chain pattern. For comparison, these are the corresponding LTL encodings as listed by the Specification Pattern System:

a. $\mathbf{G}(P \Rightarrow \mathbf{F}(S \wedge \mathbf{X}\,\mathbf{F}\,T))$
b. $\mathbf{F}\,R \Rightarrow (P \Rightarrow (\neg R\,\mathbf{U}(S \wedge \neg R \wedge \mathbf{X}(\neg R\,\mathbf{U}\,T))))\,\mathbf{U}\,R$
c. $\mathbf{G}(Q \Rightarrow \mathbf{G}(P \Rightarrow (S \wedge \mathbf{X}\,\mathbf{F}\,T)))$
d. $\mathbf{G}((Q \wedge \mathbf{F}\,R) \Rightarrow (P \Rightarrow (\neg R\,\mathbf{U}(S \wedge \neg R \wedge \mathbf{X}(\neg R\,\mathbf{U}\,T))))\mathbf{U}\,R)$

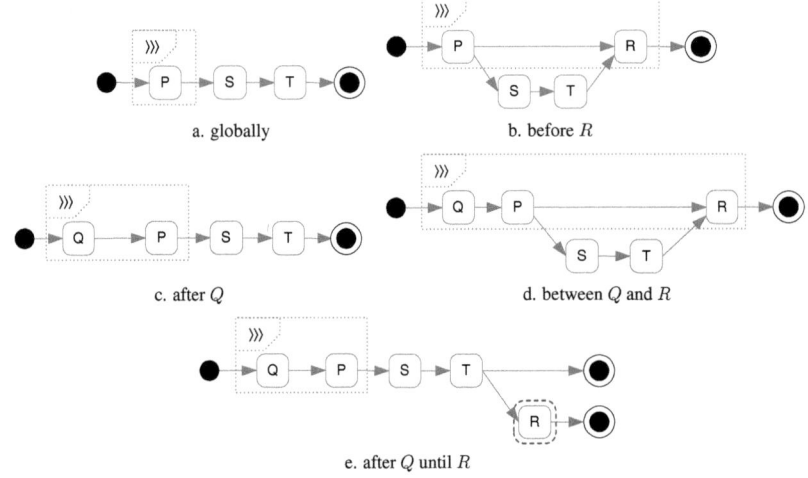

Figure 6.3.5: Response (1,2), simplified versions

e. $\mathbf{G}(Q \Rightarrow (P \Rightarrow (\neg R\, \mathbf{U}(S \wedge \neg R \wedge \mathbf{X}(\neg R\, \mathbf{U}\, T))))\mathbf{U}(R \vee \mathbf{G}(P \Rightarrow (S \wedge \mathbf{X}\, \mathbf{F}\, T))))$

**Discussion.** For response and precedence, the simplified forms are quite natural expressions of the original requirements. Disregarding the Specification Pattern System's distinction between scopes and properties, e.g. $S, T$ responds to $P$ after $Q$ actually translates to 'after the sequence $Q, P$, there needs to follow $S, T$', which is exactly what the TSSD expresses. In general, the resulting diagrams are compact and can be interpreted in a straight-forward manner without the context of the original specification pattern. TSSDs thus avoid the problem faced by the LTL that a correct formula may be derived using the appropriate patterns, but is still very hard to parse for any reader who does not know how it was originally derived.

While TSSDs provide a suitable way of encoding the patterns of the Specification Pattern System, we believe that TSSDs would not greatly benefit from using the Specification Pattern System in order to derive them. This is not due to any flaw or lack of usefulness in the pattern system itself, but to the fact that the intuitions it provides to designers are already directly integrated into the TSSD language.

## 6.3.2 Deriving Properties from Textual Requirements

We now discuss how structural and temporal property specifications can be derived from informal textual requirements in a systematic manner. We deliberately deviate from our running example in favor of a small, self-contained example: As our case study, we use an elevator system, which is in part inspired by the example property used in the motivation of [DAC99] and in part a reference to a classic example used for demonstrating Story-Driven Modeling with Fujaba. We extend both scenarios, however, from a house with a single elevator to a large building with an arbitrary number of floors and elevators. This flexibility illustrates one of the advantages of the approach in comparison with other logics: The ability to scale properties to any number of instances is implicitly provided as this is inherent in the patterns.

The following requirements are provided for the system:

1. **Safety**: Whenever an elevator is not at a floor, its doors may not be open.
2. **Responsive**: Every request for an elevator is assigned to exactly one elevator by the central dispatcher.
3. **Progress**: An elevator may not stay between floors for more than 30 seconds.
4. **Progress**: If requests have been assigned to an elevator, it may not be idle for more than 22 seconds.
5. **Purposeful**: An elevator may only move towards some assigned request.
6. **Fairness**: Concurrent requests must be fulfilled within 300 seconds of each other.
7. **Fairness**: When a request for a specific floor has been assigned to an elevator, it may only arrive at this floor at most twice before opening its doors.

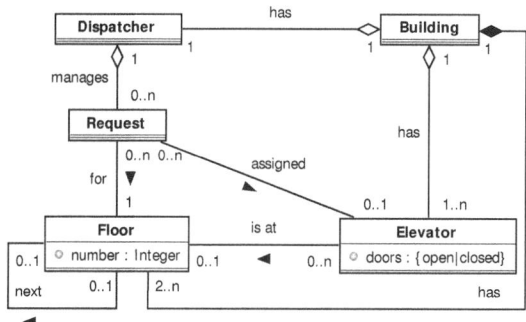

Figure 6.3.6: Elevator class diagram

Using standard object-oriented analysis techniques, we extract the classes elevator, floor, and request, and infer the existence of a building as the root of the composition hierarchy and a dispatcher, which is in charge of assigning requests to elevators. We also identify the dynamic associations is at, assigned, and for, and arrive at the class diagram in Figure 6.3.6 from the requirements.

We can now encode the constraints. The first step is to classify the type of requirement the constraint expresses and choose the appropriate notation. While constraints concerning the static structure ('there must always be at least one...') or safety properties ('there must never be...') can be expressed using SDDs, most behavioral constraints (such as requirements describing changes, sequences of events, or containing time constraints) require TSSDs.

**(1)** *Whenever an elevator is not at a floor, its doors may not be open.* Even though the requirement (1) appears to contain a temporal element (*whenever*), it is a static safety property and can therefore be encoded as a structural requirement. In order to derive the SDD structure, we decompose the textual specification: *whenever* or an initial *if* indicate universal quantification, as the property applies to any elevator at any time. We furthermore extract the basic, positive properties *at a floor* and *its doors are open*, noting but ignoring the negations expressed by *not* for now. These elements can now directly be translated into SDD nodes | ∀ elevator e |, | ∃ e is at a floor | and | • e's door = open |.

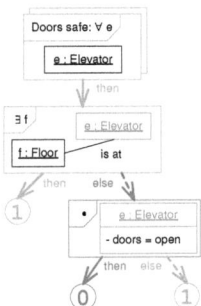

Figure 6.3.7: Property (1) encoded as an SDD

When connecting the nodes into a decision diagram, we reintroduce the negations: As the doors must *not* be open, we invert the outgoing connectors of the third node. Furthermore, as this condition only needs to hold if the elevator is *not* at a floor, we attach the third node to the second node's else connector. After adding the standard implied leaf nodes, this results in the SDD in Figure 6.3.7.

**(2)** *Every request for an elevator is assigned to exactly one elevator by the central dispatcher.* Property (2) could be interpreted as a structural constraint which could easily be encoded as a simple SDD or even eSP | ∀ requests | ⇒ | ∃ assigned elevator |. However, requests would have to be assigned upon creation to fulfill this property. We therefore conclude that the requirement actually describes the outcome of a process and interpret it as *Every time there is a request, it is eventually assigned to exactly one elevator.*

## 6.3 Deriving Constraint Specifications

The temporal keyword *eventually* separates the two relevant structural properties: | ∃ request | (Figure 6.3.8a) and | ∃ elevator that is assigned to the request | (Figure 6.3.8b). Keywords such as *exactly*, *at least*, *more than*, *at most*, and *less than* are indicators for a cardinality, in this case for the cardinality [1..1].

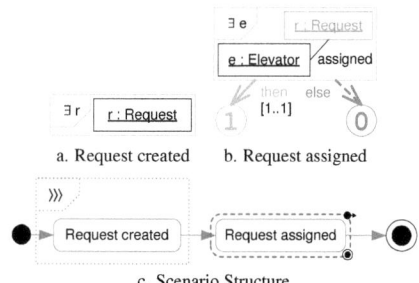

Figure 6.3.8: Deriving Property (2)

The basic structure of the TSSD follows naturally from the requirement: There are two situations connected by an *eventually* connector. The qualifier *every time* is a certain sign for a trigger block around the qualified property, in this case the first situation. Finally, we can also interpret the requirement that the request is assigned to *exactly one* elevator as a temporal constraint, namely that it can only be assigned *exactly once*. Whenever observations are counted (*once*, *twice*) or required to be the *first*, *last*, *next*, or *preceding* one in a scenario, this is indicative of *strict* situations. As the same request can never be reassigned, the second situation becomes *globally strict*, resulting in the temporal property in Figure 6.3.8c.

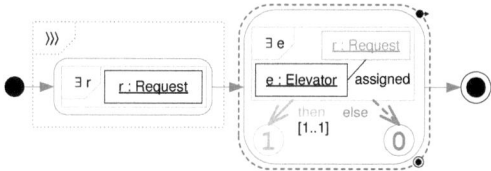

Figure 6.3.9: Property (2) encoded as a TSSD

Inserting the structural properties into the temporal constraint yields the final TSSD in Figure 6.3.9. Note that in this case, the cardinality is actually made redundant by the stronger strictness requirement.

**(3)** *An elevator may not stay between floors for more than 30 seconds.* Property (3) is clearly a temporal property. But what are the contained structural properties? Keywords such as *stay* that describe the persistence of a state indicate a situation with an *until* connector, or two situations with the second one expressing the negation of the original property. In this case, the properties are that the *elevator is between floors* (i.e. not at a floor) but afterwards not between floors (i.e. at a floor). We thus have |∃ elevator e| so that *not* |∃ e is at a floor| (Figure 6.3.10a) and |∃ e is at a floor| (Figure 6.3.10b). At the temporal level, we need to add the time constraint *no more than*

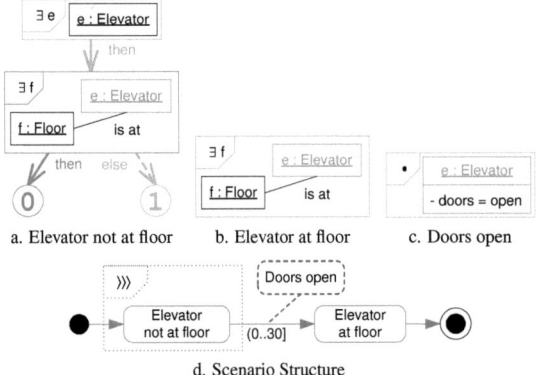

Figure 6.3.10: Deriving Property (3)

*30 seconds*, which can be directly translated into the constraint [0..30] between the two situations (Figure 6.3.10d). Textual time constraints typically have the form *less than t* ([0..t)), *no more than t* or *at most t* ([0..t]), *no less than t* or *at least t* ([t..∞)), *more than t* ((t..∞)), or *between a and b* ([a..b]). As the property needs to hold *every time* an elevator is not at a floor, we again have to add a trigger block.

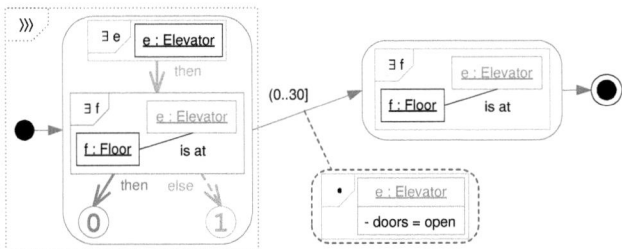

Figure 6.3.11: Property (3) encoded as a TSSD

We can easily integrate requirement (1) into our encoding of requirement (3) by adding a simple guard (Figure 6.3.10c) enforcing that the doors are not open, as the interval between the situations corresponds exactly to the scope of that requirement (*whenever...*). However, the structural

## 6.3 Deriving Constraint Specifications

encoding is useful because it is easier to verify. Combining the temporal and structural encodings yields Figure 6.3.11.

**(4)** *If requests have been assigned to an elevator, it may not be idle for more than 22 seconds.* Property (4) is again temporal. The first property (whether an elevator is requested) can be derived directly: Is there some request that is assigned to the elevator? As this property will appear again in subsequent properties, we encode it in an SDDP (Figure 6.3.12) that we reference in the first situation (Figure 6.3.13a). The question what *idleness* means requires more creativity. A

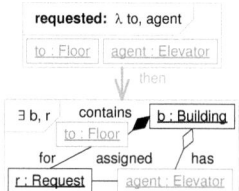

Figure 6.3.12: SDDP definition: Was the elevator requested on the floor?

straight-forward interpretation would be that elevator is *idle* if it is not moving, i.e. staying at a floor. We can thus use familiar definitions for an elevator that is at a floor (Figure 6.3.13b) and an elevator that has left that floor (Figure 6.3.13c). The temporal structure (Figure 6.3.13d) is simple:

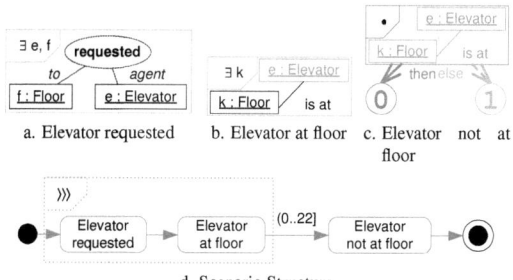

a. Elevator requested   b. Elevator at floor   c. Elevator not at floor

d. Scenario Structure

Figure 6.3.13: Deriving Property (4)

There is a request, the elevator arrives at a floor, the elevator has left the floor. There is furthermore a time constraint (0..22] between the latter situations. Writing [0..22] would have been equivalent as the elevator cannot possibly be at and not at the floor at the same time.

The only interesting aspect is the trigger block, which includes the first two situations as the property needs to hold *every time* there are requests *and* the elevator is idle. We could merge the two situations into one, but as the two conditions are conceptually independent, the diagram seems clearer if we do not. Combined, the properties yield the TSSD in Figure 6.3.14.

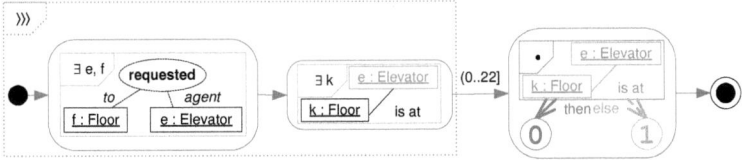

Figure 6.3.14: Property (4) encoded as a TSSD

**(5)** *An elevator may only move towards some assigned request.* If the direction of movement of an elevator was encoded by a state variable (e.g. for display to the users as commonly done), property (5) could be encoded as a structural property. Based on the chosen model, we will have to detect movement as a sequence of states and thus use a temporal property.

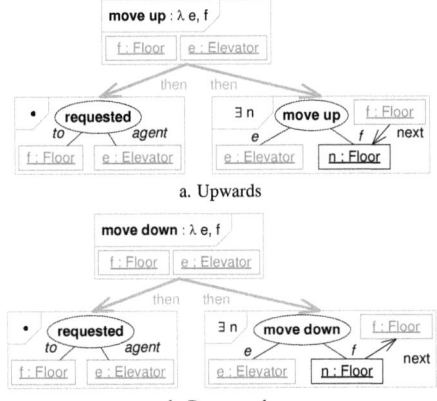

a. Upwards

b. Downwards

Figure 6.3.15: SDDP definitions: is there a request in the indicated direction?

We begin by encoding the condition *towards some assigned request*. For a given elevator, floor, and direction, there either is a matching request for the current floor (determined using the SDDP in Figure 6.3.12), or there is a request for some other floor in the indicated direction. As this is a transitive property, the corresponding SDD Patterns for the two possible directions (Figure 6.3.15a and 6.3.15b) are defined recursively, traversing the floors in the indicated direction until they find a request or fail.

We detect the direction of the movement by means of a sequence of situations in the trigger. The elevator initially is at floor (Figure 6.3.16a), but eventually either arrives at the next floor when moving up (Figure 6.3.16b) or the previous floor when moving down (Figure 6.3.16d). These two branches make up the trigger of the scenario (Figure 6.3.16f).

## 6.3 Deriving Constraint Specifications

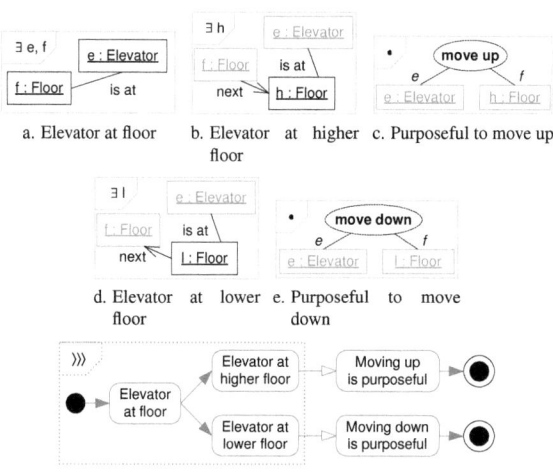

Figure 6.3.16: Deriving Property (5)

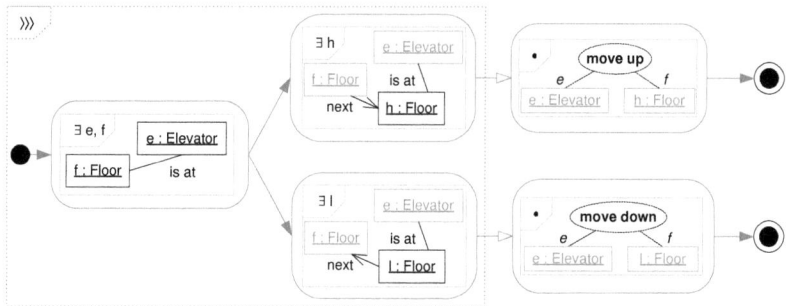

Figure 6.3.17: Property (5) encoded as a TSSD

As the central requirement (valid direction) is actually structural, it immediately needs to be acceptable for the elevator to move in the given direction once the trigger is completed. The two situations in Figure 6.3.16c and 6.3.16e reference the corresponding pattern, checking whether the movement was justified by a request. Together, this results in the TSSD in Figure 6.3.17.

**(6)** *Concurrent requests must be fulfilled within 300 seconds of each other.* Property (6), which is obviously temporal, can mostly be encoded reusing previous definitions. *Concurrent requests* are simply encoded as two simultaneous matches for the requested pattern (Figure 6.3.12), as shown in Figure 6.3.18a. If we do not want to assume that the dispatcher groups requests for the same floor, we would need a *homomorphism* constraint between $a$ and $b$ – on the other hand, property (6) is trivially true for requests for the same floor anyway. A request is considered *fulfilled*

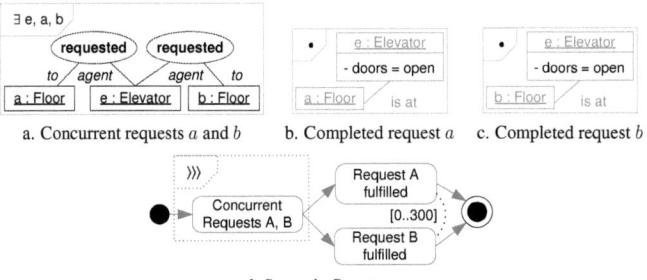

Figure 6.3.18: Deriving Property (6)

when the elevator opens it doors at the requested floor. This is recognized by the SDDs in Figures 6.3.18b and 6.3.18c, respectively.

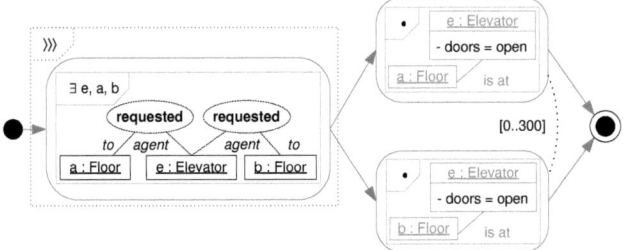

Figure 6.3.19: Property (6) encoded as a TSSD

In the temporal domain, the property implies the requirement that *every time* there are (concurrent) requests, they must *eventually be fulfilled*. There is no enforced order (e.g. first come, first served) in which the requests need to be fulfilled. Whenever there are only partially ordered *concurrent* processes, this induces a branch in the diagram (see Figure 6.3.18d). As the requests need to be completed *every time* a pair is found, there is a trigger block around the first situation. As *both* requests need to be completed to fulfill the requirement, the two branches are merged in an *and*-join.

The time constraint *within* limits the time that may elapse between the two observations. The fact that the situations are on two different branches is immaterial – we can simply add the constraint [0..300] to a constraint edge between them. Combined, this yields the TSSD in Figure 6.3.19.

## 6.3 Deriving Constraint Specifications 251

**(7)** *When a request for a specific floor has been assigned to an elevator, it may only arrive at this floor at most twice before opening its doors.* Property (7) is a well-known example (cf. [DAC99]) that results in a rather impressive LTL formula:

$$G\ ((requested \wedge F\ doorsOpen) \Rightarrow$$
$$((\neg atFloor \wedge \neg doorsOpen)\ U$$
$$(doorsOpen \vee ((atFloor \wedge \neg doorsOpen)\ U$$
$$(doorsOpen \vee ((\neg atFloor \wedge \neg doorsOpen)\ U$$
$$(doorsOpen \vee ((atFloor \wedge \neg doorsOpen)\ U$$
$$(doorsOpen \vee (\neg atFloor\ U\ doorsOpen))))))))))$$

The exact equivalent of that formula can be expressed using the bounded-existence/between Specification Pattern (see Section 6.3.1 the standard TSSD encoding of this pattern). However, we believe that a slightly stronger interpretation of the requirement better reflects what is expected of an elevator, namely that it eventually does open its doors at the floor where it was requested, which is not implied in the above formula.

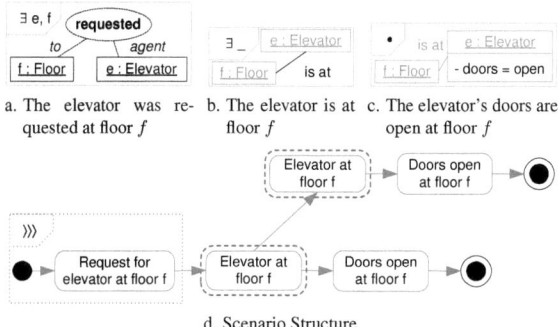

a. The elevator was requested at floor $f$
b. The elevator is at floor $f$
c. The elevator's doors are open at floor $f$

d. Scenario Structure

Figure 6.3.20: Deriving Property (7)

The structural properties have all been defined before: The elevator is requested for a floor (Figure 6.3.20a), it arrives at that floor (Figure 6.3.20b), and it opens its doors at that floor (Figure 6.3.20c).

As before, *when...* induces a trigger block around the first situation. For deriving the rest of the structure (Figure 6.3.20d), we can simply play out the possible scenarios: The elevator can arrive for the first time and then open its doors. Alternatively, it can leave, arrive again, and then open its doors. As the number of observations is obviously relevant, we follow the guideline we have introduced when discussing property (2) and make the corresponding situations *strict* so that no additional intermediate arrivals are accepted by the TSSD. Property (7) is then encoded by the TSSD in Figure 6.3.21. When composing the diagram, we have explicitly labeled the is at links with the variables $a1$ and $a2$ to underline the fact that the situations will only match distinct arrivals.

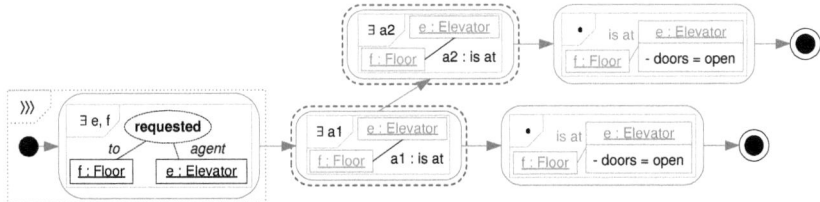

Figure 6.3.21: Property (7) encoded as a TSSD

The case that the elevator is at the floor, which is allowed by the last term of the LTL formula ($\neg atFloor$ U $doorsOpen$), is omitted in the TSSD because *being* at the floor is a logical precondition for opening the doors there. The encoding in the contained SDDs clearly indicates this property as the floor needs to be bound in the first pattern as a precondition for matching the second pattern. This illustrates the fact that the ability to integrate the modeling of structural properties into a scenario definition helps to make the dependencies between different properties explicit, which are lost when simply abstracting them by means of propositions such as $atFloor$ and $doorsOpen$.

**Discussion.** The presented examples illustrate that the notations allow expressing requirements in a formal format that provides support for many features that are commonly occurring in natural language specifications. It is therefore not as far removed from the informal requirements as many other formal techniques and allows a fairly direct translation. The examples, though limited in size and complexity, also show that the notations produce compact and readable specifications for non-trivial properties that are significantly harder to express using traditional temporal logic, even more so if the definitions of the structural properties and the unlimited size of the system are included in the consideration.

Practical experiences with students suggest that the general idea of the notations can be grasped quickly. They generally proved easy to use, although certain advanced features such as universal quantification in TSSDs are not without subtleties. While this is beyond the scope of this work, a systematic empirical evaluation of the notations' usability would be feasible by training randomly selected groups of students in the use of SDD/TSSD and OCL/LTL, presenting them with identical specification problems, and comparing the required effort and the quality (completeness and correctness) of the produced specifications. In the absence of such a study, we believe that our qualitative argument for the notations' usefulness stands.

## 6.4 Application in Practice

As stated in the introduction, the present work was created in the context of the Special Research Initiative 614 *Self-optimizing Concepts and Structures in Mechanical Engineering*. After presenting our approach in detail, we would like to use the following short section to take a step

## 6.4 Application in Practice

back and position our contributions in the context of the overall project. As the RailCab R&D project, from which our running application example was drawn, serves as a main motivating example to the Special Research Initiative, we wrap up our application example in doing so.

**An interdisciplinary problem.** Software-intensive systems embed software into real-world applications from different domains, which makes their development an interdisciplinary task almost by definition. In the case of mechatronic systems, many disciplines including mechanics, electronics, control engineering, software engineering, and operations research are involved. Traditionally, the development process for such systems follows a type of waterfall model with each discipline handing its finished design to the next, which makes iterations difficult and costly. As the design of the hardware is subject to the more rigid constraints, it typically takes precedence over the software design, at the expense of potential synergies to be gained from a holistic approach. But even between control and software engineering, which would appear to be more closely related, the different specific methodologies and terminologies that are employed create a gap.

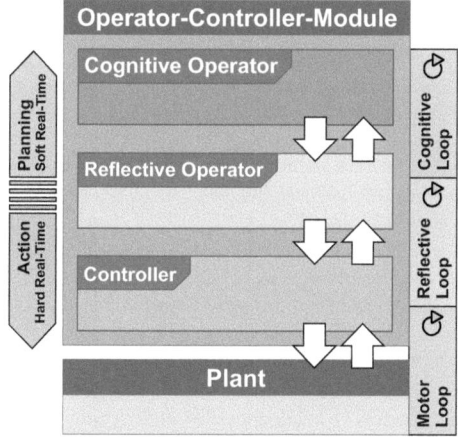

Figure 6.4.1: The Operator-Controller-Module architecture

One of the main objectives of the Special Research Initiative 614 is to propose an integrated design methodology that promotes interdisciplinary cooperation. As discussed before, the *Operator-Controller-Module* (*OCM*) [HOG04, OHG04] is a cornerstone of the concept that is being developed, as it provides a common architecture for software and control engineers and thus contributes to a solution of that particular issue.

The abstract architecture of an OCM is depicted in Figure 6.4.1. The *Controller* on the lowest level directly interacts with the hardware, the *plant*, in the *Motor Loop*. The *Reflective Operator* monitors the *Controller* and parametrizes or reconfigures it as necessary in reaction to changes in the environment or its internal priorities in the *Reflective Loop*. Finally, the *Cognitive Operator* performs complex planning and optimization tasks and considers user preferences. The resulting strategies and priorities are then passed down to the *Reflective Operator* in the *Cognitive Loop*. This distribution of tasks within a clearly structured architecture makes it possible to design an appropriate solution for each subproblem, while the defined interfaces ensure that these solutions integrate in order to solve the overall problem. The *Motor Loop* and the *Reflective Loop* are in charge of operative aspects and need to run in hard real-time, whereas the *Cognitive Loop* deals with planning aspects and only needs to meet soft real-time requirements.

Our definition of an *agent* makes it natural to consider each OCM as an agent. While the reverse does not follow, it is certainly an option to design each agent as an OCM, in particular if it is involved in real-time interactions.

When applying the CURCUMA framework, the focus is on the *Cognitive Operator*, as the coordination and planning level benefits most from the advanced concepts that are provided by cultures. The currently active roles and the professed intentions of users or other agents provide a context for adapting and evolving strategies that are passed down to the operative level.

Nonetheless, the approach also extends into the *Reflective Operator*, as there are cultures that require real-time communication, such as the update subculture of the positioning culture in our application example. Thanks to our efforts to integrate *Coordination Patterns* into a unified metamodel in Section 2.3, we are able to describe both operator levels in a single seamless model. Conversely, there is no reason why the design of the *Reflective Operator* should not benefit from the advanced concepts of our approach. After all, constructs such as professed intentions primarily serve to aid the understanding of the designer and may correspond to something as simple as the reception of a signal in the implementation.

Even though the environment model covers certain aspects of the mechanical and control design of the system, the *Controller* level and those parts of the *Reflective Operator* that interface with it are out of the scope of the approach as their design requires dedicated methods. However, if the pertinent hybrid techniques of the Special Research Initiative 614 are employed, the conceptual alignment of the approaches allows their tight integration within the proposed architecture.

The pretension of our environment models is to provide domain knowledge to the software engineers at a level of abstraction that is appropriate for their design task, the creation of the coordination and control architecture. To some degree, this operates in the opposite direction as well: Combined with the high level concepts of the CURCUMA framework and our reliance on visual specification languages, the incorporation of the domain model facilitates the communication with domain experts in a way that is accessible to them.

In the following, we revisit our example. As the shuttle system is quite complex, it can actually be decomposed into multiple perspectives that represent problems in their own right. Two possible views are the design of the system logistics, which concerns a network of agents, and the design of a single shuttle, which in itself can be conceived as a multi-agent system.

**Networked Mechatronic System: Logistics.** Thus far, our examples have focused on the interaction between multiple shuttles and the coordination of their movements. At this macroscopic

## 6.4 Application in Practice

level, the design is driven by our choice among the various coordination mechanisms that have been developed by logistics, economics, operations research, game theory, or agent research.

After identifying the essential elements such as shuttles, terminals, the track network, and passenger or cargo transportation tasks, we can collect an initial set of requirements and organize them using tentative cultures. In this, we may choose to build on existing analyses (e.g. cf. [Fah04]). Major objectives would be safety, i.e. avoiding excessive acceleration, derailments, collisions, and other accidents, effectiveness, i.e. the ability to achieve high throughput, low latency, and punctuality, and economy, i.e. minimizing energy consumption and maintenance cost. Subsequent design decisions or political or commercial considerations may add additional requirements, for example to ensure fairness if the shuttles are to be operated by multiple competing carriers.

We then apply suitable coordination mechanisms. As discussed in Section 4.1.1, we preferentially use decentralized designs, such as the described cooperative reasoning [DGK$^+$04, Ren04] and routing [Bie04] strategies, and market-based mechanisms. We can design the control software for the system quite freely, within the limits of the available bandwidth and computing power. The mechanics of the system only matter to the degree that the physical capabilities of the shuttles constrain possible solutions. Nonetheless, the ability to model the environment is crucial, as the physical design of the system and the logistic concept should influence each other. For example, the ability to overtake other shuttles in and between terminals is decisive for the system's capacity and the optimal routing algorithm. A terminal design with many parallel platforms (cf. [Fah04, Figure 64, p. 246]) decouples the stopover times of individual shuttles and provides greater planning flexibility, but is more costly than more basic designs. As this makes mixed infrastructures probable, the concept should provide support for both.

The design pattern that we employ most prominently is that of an agent economy, where services and resources are traded using (combinatorial) auctions or fixed pricing schemes. Transactions are mainly based on three types of professed intentions, as communicated by messages or actions: assertions about states and capabilities, declarations of intent, and commitments representing a mutually binding contract.

In the schematic in Figure 6.4.2, the key agents of the system design and their connections are listed. Task agents, brokers, and resource agents only need interactions in soft real-time and can do without the lower levels of the OCM. Strategic coordination between shuttles also takes place at the cognitive level. On the other hand, the interactions concerning the coordination of movements, especially in a convoy, need to happen in hard real-time, as does the communication with the base stations. They are consequently the responsibility of the *Reflective Operator*.

In the design, we may specify that a certain signal is a directive from the leading shuttle to initiate emergency braking procedures. The *Reflective Operator* will reflexively respond to this signal, switching to the corresponding state and triggering the required actions, without reasoning or caring about this. On the other hand, the periodical position updates that the *Reflective Operator* sends out correspond to assertions, which the *Cognitive Operator* will interpret as such and store for future reference, e.g. when computing whether a strategy adaptation will lead to a violation of previously asserted statements.

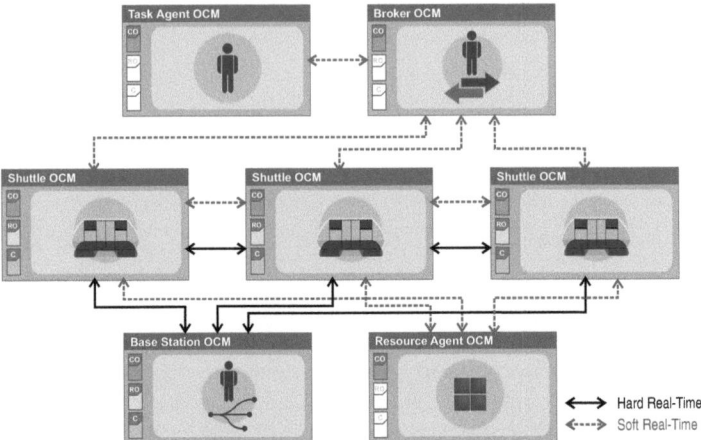

Figure 6.4.2: Schematic of the OCM network coordinating the overall system

As the design contains many safety-related aspects, a formal verification of certain parts such as the *Reflective Operators* is in order. On the other hand, the network of *Cognitive Operators* is more concerned with the efficiency of the system and primarily requires validation by means of simulation and statistical analysis, although the basic interaction protocols should of course also be verified.

**Autonomous Mechatronic System: Shuttle.** Thus far, the shuttles have always played the part of agents in our examples. However, an agent need not be a monolithic structure – in fact, it may even be composed of other agents itself. The design of the shuttle and its control systems is obviously much more directly driven by mechanical, electrical, and electronic concerns than the design of the system coordination, mandating the adoption of a slightly different approach to engineering the software. Nonetheless, there are striking conceptual similarities in spite of the differences.

Figure 6.4.3 shows the simplified OCM hierarchy of a shuttle. There is the energy management subsystem that is in control of the energy supply stored in the shuttle's batteries and capacitors, and a long list of consumers: Processors and transmitters as needed by the shuttle OCM that handles external interactions or the motion control module coordinating its children, the suspension tilt module that ensures a smooth ride, the critical track control module that keeps the shuttle's individually suspended wheels from derailing and steers the shuttle across junctions, and the linear drive module that is in charge of the propulsion system. The latter is exceptional because the linear drive is also the shuttle's sole energy source, drawing energy from the track's stator by means of induction when performing work, i.e. during acceleration and deceleration phases.

## 6.4 Application in Practice

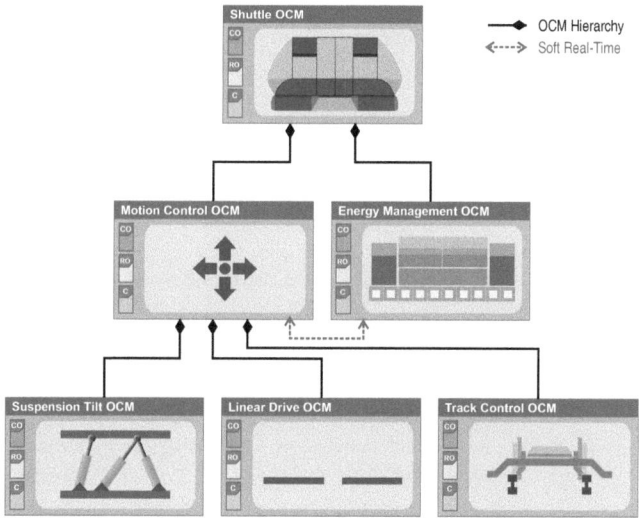

Figure 6.4.3: The OCM hierarchy of a shuttle

Energy management in the shuttle is a complex problem. There are two main circuits, a 680 volt loop for the main consumers and a 24 volt loop. In the prototype, the former powers the six large hydraulics cylinders of the suspension tilt module, four smaller cylinders for track control (2.5 kW peak consumption), and the linear drive (2.0 kW minimum, 2.2 kW peak consumption). The latter supplies 1.8 kW peak power, mainly to the valve control for the cylinders (1 kW peak consumption), but also to the main processing unit (400 W), the pneumatics compressor (140 W), and all other devices such as lights or, in the future, air conditioning. These consumers have very different requirements: The processor and compressor need to run at all times; the linear drive requires a steady supply within a narrow range when running; the hydraulics require high but short energy bursts. On the other side, the linear drive generates up to 4.0 kW, depending on speed, exerted force, and a complex equation involving rotor current, rotor frequency, and stator current. While the optimal combination of these can be computed, the only way to transfer energy into a shuttle moving steadily, e.g. down a slight slope, would be to waste energy through gratuitous acceleration cycles. Storing energy is therefore indispensable. The batteries store large amounts of energy, but prefer long discharge cycles, whereas the capacitors can only generate short but strong bursts, which requires sophisticated load balancing. We therefore face a resource allocation problem with many constraints, affecting the efficiency, safety, longevity, and comfort of the shuttle. It is clear that these goals are contradictory, and that whatever is locally optimal may be unacceptable for the overall shuttle.

Did we not face a similar resource allocation problem at the system level as well? Might we even apply the same culture? The problem is probably too specific for that, but we can apply the same design pattern and even reuse some of the pertinent subcultures. There is no replacement for the specialized algorithms needed in the local operations of energy management and linear drive, but the coordination between the components could work market-based, basically as a miniature version of the European Energy Exchange. The linear drive would offer energy cheaply while accelerating and raise the price while coasting. Energy management would be willing to pay high prices only if energy levels were critically low. On the consumer side, optional components like the active suspension might be powered down if energy prices are high. As the passive suspension is sufficient to protect the payload from shocks, this would only reduce the perceived comfort. The same goes for air conditioning, with the crucial difference that it is still effective when run intermittently, whereas an active suspension only has an effect when working in real-time. This approach has the additional advantage that the preferences of passengers that are willing to pay for a higher level of comfort can be considered directly by increasing the budget of the respective components. However, the system needs to include provisions for ensuring that the power supply for critical base functions is guaranteed at all times.

This problem is a showcase for the OCM architecture: The trading needs to be performed by the *Reflective Operator*, as balancing peak demands and reacting to fluctuations is only possible in real-time. On the other hand, the unique characteristics of the available energy sources make long term planning necessary. For example, the *Cognitive Operator* of the energy management module might query the shuttle for the upcoming track profile and direct the lower levels to invest in sufficient reserves when a long downward slope is approaching.

Such a design again calls for a mix of formal verification, guaranteeing that the system works reliably and predictably, and simulation, ascertaining that it is efficient.

## 6.5 Conclusion

In this chapter, we have discussed issues concerning the practical application of our approach. We have presented the implemented modeling and prototyping tools, comprising implementations of the new constraint notations, a constraint infrastructure, code generation facilities, and a runtime environment. We have also shown how our enhancements to the Fujaba4Eclipse infrastructure and user interface have improved usability.

We have then looked at the issue of whether the proposed notations are usable from a content perspective, i.e. whether they are comprehensible to the intended audience. We have shown that TSSDs provide clear benefits when writing and especially reading a catalog of patterns that is considered representative of the properties that occur most commonly in practice. We have demonstrated how both notations support the direct translation of informal requirements into a formal specification.

Finally, we have wrapped up our application example. In doing so, we have explained how our approach integrates into the overall vision of the Special Research Initiative 614, and have provided additional examples showing that it is applicable to a wide range of problems at different levels of granularity.

# Chapter 7
# Conclusion and Future Work

## 7.1 Conclusion

In this work, we have presented a comprehensive approach for the model-driven design of software intensive systems that integrates *component-oriented software engineering* with *Story-Driven Modeling* and concepts from *agent-oriented software engineering*. The CURCUMA framework, with communities, cultures, and legal stance as its key concepts, is the central innovation that has allowed us to build a bridge between two fields with quite different perspectives: On one side, software engineering for software intensive systems, which requires reliability, predictability, and verifiability; on the other, multi-agent system design, which takes inspiration from social or biological systems in order to create dynamic, flexible solutions, albeit often with an element of the chaotic. The resulting method combines desirable properties from both worlds: It provides abstractions for managing the complexity of design problems which are widely applicable and, in part even intuitively, accessible, but it is also formal and rigorous so that it supports the verification and validation of the design. It is capable of describing physical and social behavior and different types of behavioral and compositional adaptation by means of a system of contracts that make them predictable while leaving room for optimizations, autonomy, and artificial intelligence.

While the CURCUMA framework has provided the leverage for the conceptual integration, the formal integration at the metamodel level is achieved by using graph grammars as a common foundation. We propose a complete formalization of both *Story Patterns* and discrete real-time *Coordination Patterns*, which we then use to describe how the two perspectives interact both at the operational level (when *Story Patterns* are used to specify the side effects of a transition) and the meta level (when *Story Patterns* are used to instantiate *Coordination Patterns* or change control structures). Moreover, graph grammars are the foundation of the other key innovation of this thesis, the family of graphical constraint languages that we have developed. As a solution for modeling structural properties, *Story Decision Diagrams* (SDD) provide a first-order logic for graphs by embedding graph patterns into decision diagrams. Some of their enhancements are made available using a less revolutionary approach in the form of *enhanced Story Patterns*.

For modeling temporal properties, *Timed Story Scenario Diagrams* (TSSD) combine graph patterns with temporal logic into a highly expressive scenario language. Beside using the notations extensively throughout this thesis, we have explicitly studied their usability and expressiveness in comparison to related formalisms. Our tool implementation based on Fujaba4Eclipse offers advanced editors and code generation for all three notations.

The integration at the conceptual, formal, and tool level enables a wide range of verification and validation activities. We have adapted various techniques such as graph model checking, invariant checking, and different forms of monitoring to our modeling approach, which makes the formal analysis of a choice of properties from simple structural guarantees to complex scenarios with timing constraints possible. We have further strived to enable the iterative refinement of CURCUMA designs through rapid cycles of development, consisting of modeling, code generation, simulation, and analysis. Taken together, we provide the concepts that are needed to devise designs that solve complex coordination problems, with the instruments for vetting and evolving them using both formal analysis and practical experimentation.

## 7.2 Future Work

While this thesis has the ambition of providing a *comprehensive* approach to model-driven multi-agent system design, including specifications for conceptual framework, process, notations, formal methods, and infrastructure, it has no pretension of being *complete*. Although we have tried to be as thorough as possible in solving the involved theoretical issues, enough open questions remain, as answers have a tendency to bring up new questions. Besides, transcending its original context and inspiring new use cases is the mark of a good idea.

The coherent and comprehensive formalization of the different modeling techniques provides a starting point for various interesting extensions. In particular, the integration between component-based and story-driven techniques seems worth exploring: Taking inspiration from the way agents interact with their environment, do we increase the expressiveness of protocols by using graph patterns as conditions and actions? And to what extent can we reconfigure a component internally at runtime using structural patterns without descending into unpredictable chaos?

While we hope that all of the new notations will be found useful and manage to get adopted for other applications, it is the scenario notation that is the most innovative and promising for future research. Theoretical work on the analysis of TSSDs might make their verification and evaluation more efficient or point to possible limitations.

In the area of verification and validation, the composition of cultures poses a hard, but interesting problem that is relevant for both the compositional verification of designs and the agent synthesis problem. Is it perhaps possible to identify a set of design patterns that we can employ to make the reconciliation of multiple cultures easier for certain recurring types of interactions? To which degree can we automate these processes?

In the same area, there are also many opportunities for extending the available implementations. The tools that we have created support the core concepts of our approach and provide a solid

## 7.2 Future Work

infrastructure for extensions. The current set of verification tools would benefit from the new environment, e.g. by using the new constraint modeling infrastructure. At the same time, they should be extended to include all of the proposed features and optimizations.

Realizing fully integrated support for the envisioned iterative development model will still require a significant implementation effort, even though a proof of concept exists. For example, the Java framework lacks the service library and specific tool integration that would be required for supporting a realistic project involving mechatronic agents. The existing C++ simulation framework could act as a blueprint, but could also be put to use in its own right.

The CURCUMA framework itself is born out of a set of guiding principles that have been refined over the years. While the presented version can therefore be considered quite mature, it is likely to keep evolving in the future. However, the vital challenge is not theoretical, but practical in nature. As the approach is designed to deal with large, complex, dynamic, and heterogeneous systems, it cannot be conclusively evaluated using small, isolated examples, but needs to be applied to a real project with a suitable profile by a team of developers in order to prove that it actually delivers the benefits it promises. In these pages, we hope to have made a convincing argument that it would.

# Bibliography

[AAH+85]  Mack W. Alford, Jean-Pierre Ansart, Günter Hommel, Leslie Lamport, Barbara Liskov, Geoff P. Mullery, and Fred B. Schneider. Distributed systems: Methods and tools for specification. In *Advanced Course: Distributed Systems*, volume 190 of *Lecture Notes in Computer Science (LNCS)*. Springer Verlag, Berlin, Heidelberg, Germany, 1985.

[ABB+06]  Maik Anderka, Basil Becker, Thomas Bremes, Thomas Janson, Carsten Kröger, Nedim Lipka, Holger Mense, Stefan Neumann, Frank Nillies, Eike Rethmeier, Michael Schwier, Andreas Seibel, Sergej Tissen, Michael Spijkerman, Jens Wenner, Timo Wiesemann, Tao Xie, and Andrea Zschirnt. Abschlussbericht der Projektgruppe Intrapid: Iterativer Entwurf verteilter Multiagentensysteme, July 2006. (In German).

[ABKO04]  Alejandra Alfonso, Victor Braberman, Nicolas Kicillof, and Alfredo Olivero. Visual Timed Event Scenarios. In *ICSE '04: Proceedings of the 26th International Conference on Software Engineering*, pages 168–177, Washington, DC, USA, 2004. IEEE Computer Society.

[Ace04]  Acellera Organization, Napa, CA, USA. *Property Specification Language: Reference Manual V 1.1*, June 2004. Document formal/06-05-01.

[AD94]  Rajeev Alur and David L. Dill. A theory of timed automata. *Theoretical Computer Science*, 126(2):183–235, 1994.

[AGG]  Technical University of Berlin. *AGG, the Attributed Graph Grammar system*. Online at http://www.tfs.cs.tu-berlin.de/agg (last visited March 2008).

[AGKF06]  Björn Axenath, Holger Giese, Florian Klein, and Ursula Frank. Systematic requirements-driven evaluation and synthesis of alternative principle solutions for advanced mechatronic systems. In *Proceedings of the 14th IEEE International Requirements Engineering Conference (RE'06), Minneapolis/St. Paul, Minnesota, USA, September 11-15, 2006*, pages 156–165. IEEE Computer Society, September 2006.

[AH93]  Rajeev Alur and Thomas A. Henzinger. Real-time logics: Complexity and expressiveness. *Information and Computation*, 104(1):35–77, 1993.

[AH94]      Rajeev Alur and Thomas A. Henzinger. A really temporal logic. *Journal of the ACM*, 41(1):181–204, 1994.

[ASSB00]    Adnan Aziz, Kumud Sanwal, Vigyan Singhal, and Robert Brayton. Model-checking continuous-time markov chains. *ACMTCL: ACM Transactions on Computational Logic*, 1:162–170, 2000.

[BBB01]     Massimo Benerecetti, Paolo Bouquet, and Matteo Bonifacio. Distributed context-aware systems. *Human-Computer Interaction*, 16:213–228, 2001.

[BBG+06]    Basil Becker, Dirk Beyer, Holger Giese, Florian Klein, and Daniela Schilling. Symbolic Invariant Verification for Systems with Dynamic Structural Adaptation. In *Proceedings of the $28^{th}$ International Conference on Software Engineering (ICSE)*, Shanghai, China, pages 72–81. ACM Press, 2006.

[BBM95]     Saša Buvač, Vanja Buvač, and Ian Mason. Metamathematics of contexts. *Fundamenta Mathematicae*, 23(3), 1995. Available from http://www-formal.stanford.edu/buvac.

[BC03]      Massimo Benerecetti and Alessandro Cimattis. Validation of multiagent systems by symbolic model checking. In Fausto Giunchiglia, James Odell, and Gerhard Weiß, editors, *Agent-Oriented Software Engineering III: Third International Workshop, AOSE 2002, Bologna, Italy, July 2002*, volume 2585 of *Lecture Notes in Computer Science (LNCS)*, pages 32–46. Springer Verlag, Berlin, Heidelberg, Germany, July 2003.

[BCG+04]    Frances M. T. Brazier, Frank Cornelissen, Rune Gustavsson, Catholijn M. Jonker, Olle Lindeberg, Bianca Polak, and Jan Treur. Compositional Verification of a Multi-Agent System for One-to-Many Negotiation. *Applied Intelligence*, 20(2):95–117, 2004.

[BCM05]     Patricia Bouyer, Fabrice Chevalier, and Nicolas Markey. On the expressiveness of TPTL and MTL. Technical Report Research report LSV-2005-05, Laboratoire Spécification et Vérification, École Normale Supérieure de Cachan, May 2005.

[BDHK06]    Henrik C. Bohnenkamp, Pedro R. D'Argenio, Holger Hermanns, and Joost-Pieter Katoen. MODEST: A compositional modeling formalism for hard and softly timed systems. *IEEE Transactions on Software Engineering (TSE)*, 32(10):812–830, 2006.

[BDKJT97]   Frances M. T. Brazier, Barbara M. Dunin-Keplicz, Nicholas R. Jennings, and Jan Treur. DESIRE: Modelling Multi-Agent Systems in a Compositional Formal Framework. *International Journal of Cooperative Information Systems*, 6(1):67–94, 1997.

# BIBLIOGRAPHY 267

[Bec99]   Kent Beck. *Extreme Programming Explained: Embrace Change*. Addison-Wesley Professional, Reading, 1999.

[Bec07]   Basil Becker. Verifikation induktiver Invarianten in hybriden Graphtransformationssystemen. Master's thesis, University of Paderborn, Department of Computer Science, Paderborn, Germany, July 2007.

[BG02]    Paolo Bresciani and Paolo Giorgini. The TROPOS Analysis Process as Graph Transformation System. In *OOPSLA 2002 Workshop on Agent-Oriented Methodologies. COTAR (2002)*. ACM Press, 2002.

[BG03]    Sven Burmester and Holger Giese. The Fujaba Real-Time Statechart PlugIn. In Holger Giese and Albert Zündorf, editors, *Proceedings of the 1st International Fujaba Days 2003, Kassel, Germany*, volume tr-ri-04-247 of *Technical Reports of the Department of Computer Science*, pages 12–17. University of Paderborn, October 2003.

[BGG+04]  Paolo Bresciani, Paolo Giorgini, Fausto Giunchiglia, John Mylopoulos, and Anna Perini. TROPOS: An Agent-Oriented Software Development Methodology. *Journal of Autonomous Agents and Multiagent Systems*, 8(3):203–236, May 2004.

[BGH05]   Sven Burmester, Holger Giese, and Martin Hirsch. Syntax and Semantics of Hybrid Components. Technical Report tr-ri-05-264, Department of Computer Science, University of Paderborn, October 2005.

[BGH+07]  Sven Burmester, Holger Giese, Stefan Henkler, Martin Hirsch, Matthias Tichy, Alfonso Gambuzza, Eckehard Müch, and Henner Vöcking. Tool Support for Developing Advanced Mechatronic Systems: Integrating the Fujaba Real-Time Tool Suite with CAMeL-View. In *Proceedings of the 29th International Conference on Software Engineering (ICSE), Minneapolis, MN, USA*, pages 801–804. IEEE Computer Society Press, May 2007.

[BGK04]   Sven Burmester, Holger Giese, and Florian Klein. Design and Simulation of Self-Optimizing Mechatronic Systems with Fujaba and CAMeL. In Andy Schürr and Albert Zündorf, editors, *Proceedings of the 2nd International Fujaba Days 2004, Darmstadt, Germany*, volume tr-ri-04-253 of *Technical Reports of the Department of Computer Science*, pages 19–22. University of Paderborn, September 2004.

[BGM+08]  Sven Burmester, Holger Giese, Eckehard Münch, Oliver Oberschelp, Florian Klein, and Peter Scheideler. Tool Support for the Design of Self-Optimizing Mechatronic Multi-Agent Systems. *International Journal on Software Tools for Technology Transfer (STTT)*, 8(4):1–16, February 2008.

[BGN+03]  Sven Burmester, Holger Giese, Jörg Niere, Matthias Tichy, Jörg P. Wadsack, Robert Wagner, Lothar Wendehals, and Albert Zündorf. Tool Integration at the Meta-Model Level within the FUJABA Tool Suite. In *Proceedings of the Workshop* on *Tool-Integration in System Development (TIS), Helsinki, Finland, (ESEC / FSE 2003 Workshop 3)*. ACM Press, September 2003.

[BGS05]  Sven Burmester, Holger Giese, and Wilhelm Schäfer. Model-driven architecture for hard real-time systems: From platform independent models to code. In *Proceedings of the European Conference on Model Driven Architecture - Foundations and Applications (ECMDA-FA'05), Nürnberg, Germany*, volume 3748 of *Lecture Notes in Computer Science (LNCS)*, pages 25–40. Springer Verlag, Berlin, Heidelberg, Germany, November 2005.

[BGST05]  Sven Burmester, Holger Giese, Andreas Seibel, and Matthias Tichy. Story-Patterns for Hard Real-Time Systems. In Holger Giese and Albert Zündorf, editors, *Proceedings of the 3rd International Fujaba Days 2005, Paderborn, Germany*, Technical Reports of the Department of Computer Science, pages 1–8. University of Paderborn, September 2005.

[BH99]  Jonathan Bowen and Mike Hinchey. *High-Integrity System Specification and Design*. Springer Verlag, Berlin, Heidelberg, Germany, 1999.

[BH04]  Yves Bontemps and Patrick Heymans. As fast as sound (lightweight formal scenario synthesis and verification). In Holger Giese and Ingolf Krüger, editors, *Proceedings of the 3rd Int. Workshop on "Scenarios and State Machines: Models, Algorithms and Tools" (SCESM'04), Edinburgh*, pages 27–34. IEEE Computer Society Press, May 2004.

[BHTV03]  Luciano Baresi, Reiko Heckel, Sebastian Thöne, and Daniel Varro. Modeling and validation of service-oriented architectures: Aapplication vs. style. In *Proceedings of the 9th European software engineering conference held jointly with 10th ACM SIGSOFT international symposium on Foundations of software engineering*, pages 68–77. ACM Press, 2003.

[Bie04]  Dietmar Bielemeyer. Entwurf und Evaluation skalierbarer Algorithmen zur Konvoibildung für schienengebundene Shuttlesysteme, 2004. (In German).

[BKO05]  Victor Braberman, Nicolas Kicillof, and Alfredo Olivero. A scenario-matching approach to the description and model checking of real-time properties. *IEEE Transactions on Software Engineering (TSE)*, 31(12):1028–1041, December 2005.

[BKPPT01]  Paolo Bottoni, Manuel Koch, Francesco Parisi-Presicce, and Gabriele Taentzer. A visualization of OCL using collaborations. In Martin Gogolla and Cris Kobryn, editors, *Proceedings of the 4th International Conference on the Unified Modeling Language (UML'2001)*, volume 2185 of *Lecture Notes in Computer Science (LNCS)*, pages 257–271. Springer Verlag, Berlin, Heidelberg, Germany, 2001.

[BKS02]   Julian Bradfield, Juliana Kuester Filipe, and Perdita Stevens. Enriching OCL Using Observational mu-Calculus. In Ralf-Detlef Kutsche and Herbert Weber, editors, *Fundamental Approaches to Software Engineering (FASE 2002), Grenoble, France*, volume 2306 of *Lecture Notes in Computer Science (LNCS)*, pages 50–76. Springer Verlag, Berlin, Heidelberg, Germany, April 2002.

[BM03]    Bernhard Bauer and Jörg P. Müller. Using UML in the Context of Agent-Oriented Software Engineering: State of the Art. In *Agent-Oriented Software Engineering IV*, volume 2935 of *Lecture Notes in Computer Science (LNCS)*, pages 291–325. Springer Verlag, Berlin, Heidelberg, Germany, 2003.

[BMN00]   Pierfrancesco Bellini, Riccardo Mattolini, and Paolo Nesi. Temporal logics for real-time system specification. *ACM Computing Surveys*, 32(1):12–42, 2000.

[BN03]    Bart Broekman and Edwin Notenboom. *Testing Embedded Software*. Addison-Wesley, 2003.

[BNL05]   Dirk Beyer, Andreas Noack, and Claus Lewerentz. Efficient Relational Calculation for Software Analysis. *IEEE Transactions on Software Engineering (TSE)*, 31(2):137–149, February 2005.

[BO05]    Bernhard Bauer and James Odell. UML 2.0 and agents: how to build agent-based systems with the new UML standard. *Engineering Applications of Artificial Intelligence*, 18:141–157, March 2005.

[Bon99]   Eric Bonabeau. Editor's introduction: Stigmergy. *Artificial Life*, 5(2):95–96, 1999.

[Bro91]   Rodney A. Brooks. Intelligence Without Reason. In John Myopoulos and Ray Reiter, editors, *Proceedings of the 12th International Joint Conference on Artificial Intelligence (IJCAI-91)*, pages 569–595, Sydney, Australia, August 1991. Morgan Kaufmann publishers Inc.: San Mateo, CA, USA.

[Bro95]   Fredrick P. Brooks. *The Mythical Man-Month: Essays on Software Engineering, 20th Anniversary Edition*. Addison Wesley, Reading, MA, USA, second edition, 1995.

[BRS+00]  Klaus Bergner, Andreas Rausch, Marc Sihling, Alexander Vilbig, and Manfred Broy. A Formal Model for Componentware. In Gary T. Leavens and Murali Sitaraman, editors, *Foundations of Component-Based Systems*, chapter 9, pages 189–210. Cambridge University Press, New York, NY, USA, 2000.

[BSDB00]  David Bradley, Derek Seward, David Dawson, and Stuart Burge. *Mechatronics*. Stanley Thornes, Cheltenham, UK, 2000.

[Bur06]   Sven Burmester. *Model-Driven Engineering of Reconfigurable Mechatronic Systems*. Logos Verlag, Berlin, Germany, 2006.

[BY03]   Johan Bengtsson and Wang Yi. Timed automata: Semantics, algorithms and tools. In Jörg Desel, Wolfgang Reisig, and Grzegorz Rozenberg, editors, *Lectures on Concurrency and Petri Nets*, volume 3098 of *Lecture Notes in Computer Science*, pages 87–124. Springer Verlag, Berlin, Heidelberg, Germany, 2003.

[Cas00]   Cristiano Castelfranchi. Engineering social order. In *Engineering Societies in the Agent World, First International Workshop, ESAW 2000, Berlin, Germany, August 21, 2000, Revised Papers*, volume 1972 of *Lecture Notes in Computer Science (LNCS)*, pages 1–18. Springer Verlag, Berlin, Heidelberg, Germany, 2000.

[CCG+02]  Giovanni Caire, Wim Coulier, Francisco J. Garijo, Jorge Gomez, Juan Pavon, Francisco Leal, Paulo Chainho, Paul E. Kearney, Jamie Stark, Richard Evans, and Philippe Massonet. Agent Oriented Analysis Using Message/UML. In *Proceedings of the AOSE, 2001*, volume 2222 of *Lecture Notes in Computer Science (LNCS)*, pages 119–135. Springer Verlag, Berlin, Heidelberg, Germany, 2002.

[CCGR99]  Alessandro Cimatti, Edmund M. Clarke, Fausto Giunchiglia, and Marco Roveri. NuSMV: A new symbolic model verifier. In *Proceedings of the 11th International Computer Aided Verification Conference*, volume 1633 of *Lecture Notes in Computer Science (LNCS)*, pages 495–499. Springer Verlag, Berlin, Heidelberg, Germany, 1999.

[CGP00]   Edmund M. Clarke, Orna Grumberg, and Doron Peled. *Model Checking*. MIT Press, Cambridge, MA, USA, January 2000.

[CHOT99]  Siobhan Clarke, William Harrison, Harold Ossher, and Peri Tarr. Subject-Oriented Design: Towards Improved Alignment of Requirements, Design and Code. In *Conference on Object-Oriented Programming, Systems, Languages, and Applications, November 1-5, 1999, Denver, Colorado, USA*, pages 325–339. ACM SIGPLAN Notices, 1999.

[CK02]    María Victoria Cengarle and Alexander Knapp. Towards OCL/RT. In Lars-Henrik Eriksson and Peter A. Lindsay, editors, *Formal Methods – Getting IT Right, International Symposium of Formal Methods Europe, Copenhagen, Denmark*, volume 2391 of *Lecture Notes in Computer Science (LNCS)*, pages 389–408. Springer Verlag, Berlin, Heidelberg, Germany, 2002.

[CS95]    John Connell and Linda Shafer. *Object-Oriented Rapid Prototyping*. Yourdon Press, Englewood Cliffs, NJ, USA, 1995.

[CT07]    Radovan Cervenka and Ivan Trencansky. *The Agent Modeling Language - AML. A Comprehensive Approach to Modeling Multi-Agent Systems*. Birkhäuser, Basel, Switzerland, July 2007.

[CW96]    Edmund M. Clarke and Jeannette M. Wing. Formal methods: state of the art and future directions. *ACM Computing Surveys*, 28(4):626–643, December 1996.

# BIBLIOGRAPHY 271

[DAC98] Matthew B. Dwyer, George S. Avrunin, and James C. Corbett. Property Specification Patterns for Finite-state Verification. In *2nd Workshop on Formal Methods in Software Practice*. ACM Press, March 1998.

[DAC99] Matthew B. Dwyer, George S. Avrunin, and James C. Corbett. Patterns in property specifications for finite-state verification. In *ICSE '99: Proceedings of the 21st international conference on Software engineering*, pages 411–420, Los Alamitos, CA, USA, 1999. IEEE Computer Society Press.

[DFRdS03] Fernando Luís Dotti, Luciana Foss, Leila Ribeiro, and Osmar Marchi dos Santos. Verification of distributed object-based systems. In Elie Najm, Uwe Nestmann, and Perdita Stevens, editors, *Formal Methods for Open Object-Based Distributed Systems, 6th IFIP WG 6.1 International Conference, FMOODS 2003, Paris, France, November 19.21, 2003, Proceedings*, volume 2884 of *Lecture Notes in Computer Science (LNCS)*, pages 261–275. Springer Verlag, Berlin, Heidelberg, Germany, 2003.

[DGK$^+$04] Wilhelm Dangelmaier, Holger Giese, Florian Klein, Hendrik Renken, and Peter Scheideler. Shared Experiences In Intelligent Transportation Systems. In M. Ribeiro and J. Santos-Victor, editors, *Proceedings of the IAV 2004 - The 5th Symposium on Intelligent Autonomous Vehicles, Lisbon, Portugal*, pages 231–236. Elsevier Science Publishers B.V, Amsterdam, The Netherlands, July 2004.

[Dij76] Edsger Wybe Dijkstra. *A Discipline of Programming*. Prentice Hall, Englewood Cliffs, NJ, USA, 1976.

[DMY02] Alexandre David, Oliver Möller, and Wang Yi. Formal Verification of UML Statecharts with Real-Time Extensions. In Ralf-Detler Kutsche and Herbert Weber, editors, *Proceedings of 5th International Conference on Fundamental Approaches to Software Engineering (FASE 2002), Grenoble, France*, volume 2306 of *Lecture Notes in Computer Science (LNCS)*, pages 218–232. Springer Verlag, Berlin, Heidelberg, Germany, 2002.

[DRZH01] Markus Deppe, Michael Robrecht, Mauro Zanella, and Wolfram Hardt. Rapid prototyping of real-time control laws for complex mechatronic systems. In *Proceedings of the 12th IEEE International Workshop on Rapid System Prototyping (RSP 2001), 25-27 June 2001, Monterey, CA, USA*, pages 188–193. IEEE Computer Society Press, 2001.

[EDK89] Edmund M. Clarke, David E. Long, and Kenneth L. McMillan. Compositional Model Checking. In *Proceedings of the Fourth Annual Symposium on Logic in Computer Science*, pages 353–361, Washington D.C., June 1989. IEEE Computer Society Press.

[Edm02]  Bruce Edmonds. Learning and exploiting context in agents. In *Proceedings of the first international joint conference on Autonomous agents and multiagent systems (AAMAS 2002)*, pages 1231–1238. ACM Press, 2002.

[EEKR99a]  Hartmut Ehrig, Gregor Engels, Hans-Jörg Kreowski, and Grzegorz Rozenberg, editors. *Handbook of Graph Grammars and Computing by Graph Transformation: Applications, Languages and Tools.* World Scientific Publishing Corporation, Singapore, Singapore, October 1999. Volume 2.

[EEKR99b]  Hartmut Ehrig, Gregor Engels, Hans-Jörg Kreowski, and Grzegorz Rozenberg, editors. *Handbook of Graph Grammars and Computing by Graph Transformations: Concurrency, Parallelism, and Distribution.* World Scientific Publishing Corporation, Singapore, Singapore, October 1999. Volume 3.

[EJW95]  David W. Embley, Robert B. Jackson, and Scott N. Woodfield. OO systems analysis: is it or isn't it? *IEEE Software*, 12(4):19–33, July 1995.

[Fah04]  Markus Fahrentholz. *Konzeption eines Betriebskonzepts für ein bedarfsgesteuertes schienengebundenes Shuttlesystem.* Dissertation, Universität Paderborn, Heinz Nixdorf Institut, Wirtschaftsinformatik, insbesondere CIM, 2004. Volume 157 of HNI-Verlagsschriftenreihe. Bonifatius GmbH, Paderborn, Germany, first edition, 2004.(In German).

[FESS07]  Alexander Förster, Gregor Engels, Tim Schattkowsky, and Ragnhild Van Der Straeten. Verification of Business Process Quality Constraints Based on Visual Process Patterns. In *Proceedings of the 1st IEEE International Symposium on Theoretical Aspects of Stoftware Engineering (TASE) 2007, Shanghai, China*, pages 1–10. IEEE Computer Society Press, June 2007.

[FG98]  Jacques Ferber and Olivier Gutknecht. A meta-model for the analysis and design of organizations in multi-agent systems. In *Proceedings of the 3rd International Conference on Multi Agent Systems (ICMAS98), Paris , France*, pages 128–135. IEEE Computer Society Press, 1998.

[FGK+04]  Ursula Frank, Holger Giese, Florian Klein, Oliver Oberschelp, Andreas Schmidt, Bernd Schulz, Henner Vöcking, and Katrin Witting. *Selbstoptimierende Systeme des Maschinenbaus - Definitionen und Konzepte*, volume 155 of *HNI-Verlagsschriftenreihe*. Bonifatius GmbH, Paderborn, Germany, first edition, November 2004. (In German).

[FGM03]  Jacques Ferber, Olivier Gutknecht, and Fabien Michel. From Agents to Organizations: An Organizational View of Multi-agent Systems. In *Agent-Oriented Software Engineering IV, 4th International Workshop, AOSE 2003, Melbourne, Australia, July 15, 2003, Revised Papers*, volume 2935 of *Lecture Notes in Computer Science (LNCS)*, pages 214–230. Springer Verlag, Berlin, Heidelberg, Germany, September 2003.

# BIBLIOGRAPHY 273

[FKR95]   Maier Fenster, Sarit Kraus, and Jeffrey S. Rosenschein. Coordination without communication: Experimental validation of focal point techniques. In *Proceedings of the 1st Int. Conf. on Multiagent Systems (ICMAS), San Francisco, CA, USA*, pages 102–108. MIT Press, Cambridge, MA, USA, 1995.

[FM02]    Stephan Flake and Wolfgang Mueller. An OCL Extension for Real-Time Constraints. In *Object Modeling with the OCL: The Rationale behind the Object Constraint Language*, volume 2263 of *Lecture Notes in Computer Science (LNCS)*, pages 150–171. Springer Verlag, Berlin, Heidelberg, Germany, February 2002.

[FNTZ98]  Thorsten Fischer, Jörg Niere, Lars Torunski, and Albert Zündorf. Story Diagrams: A new Graph Rewrite Language based on the Unified Modeling Language. In Gregor Engels and Grzegorz Rozenberg, editors, *Theory and Application of Graph Transformations 6*, volume 1764 of *Lecture Notes in Computer Science (LNCS)*. Springer Verlag, Berlin, Heidelberg, Germany, 1998.

[Fra06]   Ursula Frank. *Spezifikationstechnik zur Beschreibung der Prinziplösung selbstoptimierender Systeme*. PhD thesis, Universität Paderborn, Heinz Nixdorf Institut, Rechnerintegrierte Produktion, 2006. Volume 175 of HNI-Verlagsschriftenreihe. Bonifatius GmbH, Paderborn, Germany, first edition, 2006.(In German).

[FSES06]  Alexander Förster, Tim Schattkowsky, Gregor Engels, and Ragnhild Van Der Straeten. A Pattern-driven Development Process for Quality Standard-conforming Business Process Models. In *Proceedings of the IEEE Symposium on Visual Languages and Human-Centric Computing (VL/HCC), Brighton 2006*, pages 135–142. IEEE Computer Society Press, September 2006.

[GB03]    Holger Giese and Sven Burmester. Real-Time Statechart Semantics. Technical Report tr-ri-03-239, Department of Computer Science, University of Paderborn, Paderborn, Germany, June 2003.

[GBK+03]  Holger Giese, Sven Burmester, Florian Klein, Daniela Schilling, and Matthias Tichy. Multi-Agent System Design for Safety-Critical Self-Optimizing Mechatronic Systems with UML. In *OOPSLA 2003 - Second International Workshop on Agent-Oriented Methodologies, Anaheim, CA, USA*, pages 21–32. ACM Press, October 2003.

[GFG+05]  Jürgen Gausemeier, Ursula Frank, Holger Giese, Florian Klein, Andreas Schmidt, Daniel Steffen, and Matthias Tichy. A design methodology for self-optimizing systems. In Gesamtzentrum für Verkehr Braunschweig e.V., editor, *Contributions to the 6th Braunschweig conference of Automation, Assistance and Embedded Real Time Platforms for Transportation - Air-planes, Vehicles, Trains - (AAET2005)*, volume II, pages 456–479. GZVB, February 2005.

[GG01]    Chiara Ghidini and Fausto Giunchiglia. Local models semantics, or contextual reasoning = locality + compatibility. *Artificial Intelligence*, 127(2):221–259, 2001.

[GH06]     Holger Giese and Stefan Henkler. A survey of approaches for the visual model-driven development of next generation software-intensive systems. *Journal of Visual Languages and Computing*, 17(6):528–550, December 2006.

[GHH+07]   Holger Giese, Stefan Henkler, Martin Hirsch, Florian Klein, and Michael Spijkerman. Monitoring of Structural and Temporal Properties. In Holger Giese and Albert Zündorf, editors, *Proceedings of the Fujaba Days 2007, Kassel, Germany*, Technical Reports of the Department of Computer Science. University of Paderborn, October 2007.

[GHHK06]   Holger Giese, Stefan Henkler, Martin Hirsch, and Florian Klein. Nobody's perfect: Interactive Synthesis from Parametrized Real-Time Scenarios. In *Proceedings of the $5^{th}$ ICSE 2006 Workshop on Scenarios and State Machines: Models, Algorithms and Tools (SCESM'06),Shanghai, China*, pages 67–74. ACM Press, May 2006.

[GHJV94]   Erich Gamma, Richard Helm, Ralph Johnson, and John Vlissides. *Design Patterns, Elements of Reusable Object-Oriented Software*. Addison-Wesley, Reading, MA, USA, 1994.

[GHK98]    Fabio Gadducci, Reiko Heckel, and Manuel Koch. A fully abstract model for graph-interpreted temporal logic. In Hartmut Ehrig, Gregor Engels, Hans-Jörg Kreowski, and Grzegorz Rozenberg, editors, *Theory and Application of Graph Transformations*, volume 1764 of *Lecture Notes in Computer Science (LNCS)*, pages 310–322. Springer Verlag, Berlin, Heidelberg, Germany, 1998.

[GHK00]    Fabio Gadducci, Reiko Heckel, and Manuel Koch. A fully abstract model for graph-interpreted temporal logic. In *Proceedings of the Theory and Application of Graph Transformations*, volume 1764 of *Lecture Notes in Computer Science (LNCS)*, pages 310–322. Springer Verlag, Berlin, Heidelberg, Germany, 2000.

[Gie03]    Holger Giese. A Formal Calculus for the Compositional Pattern-Based Design of Correct Real-Time Systems. Technical Report tr-ri-03-240, Department of Computer Science, University of Paderborn, Paderborn, Germany, July 2003.

[GK05]     Holger Giese and Florian Klein. Autonomous Shuttle System Case Study. In Stefan Leue and Tarja Systä, editors, *Scenarios: Models, Algorithms and Tools*, volume 3466 of *Lecture Notes in Computer Science (LNCS)*, pages 90–94. Springer Verlag, Berlin, Heidelberg, Germany, April 2005.

[GK06a]    Holger Giese and Florian Klein. Beyond Story Patterns: Story Decision Diagrams. In Holger Giese and Bernhard Westfechtel, editors, *Proceedings of the 4th International Fujaba Days 2006, Bayreuth, Germany*, volume tr-ri-06-275 of *Technical Reports of the Department of Computer Science*, pages 2–9. University of Paderborn, September 2006.

# BIBLIOGRAPHY 275

[GK06b]   Holger Giese and Florian Klein. Visual Specification of Structural and Temporal Properties. Technical Report tr-ri-06-276, Department of Computer Science, University of Paderborn, April 2006.

[GK06c]   Holger Giese and Florian Klein. Visual Specification of Structural and Temporal Properties. In Holger Giese and Bernhard Westfechtel, editors, *Proceedings of the 4th International Fujaba Days 2006, Bayreuth, Germany*, volume tr-ri-06-275 of *Technical Reports of the Department of Computer Science*, pages 23–30. University of Paderborn, September 2006.

[GK07]    Holger Giese and Florian Klein. Systematic Verification of Multi-Agent Systems based on Rigorous Executable Specifications. *International Journal on Agent-Oriented Software Engineering (IJAOSE)*, 1(1):28–62, April 2007.

[GKB05]   Holger Giese, Florian Klein, and Sven Burmester. Pattern Synthesis from Multiple Scenarios for Parameterized Real-Timed UML models. In Stefan Leue and Tarja Systä, editors, *Scenarios: Models, Algorithms and Tools*, volume 3466 of *Lecture Notes in Computer Science (LNCS)*, pages 193–211. Springer Verlag, Berlin, Heidelberg, Germany, April 2005.

[GKKW05] Holger Giese, Ekkart Kindler, Florian Klein, and Robert Wagner. Reconciling Scenario-Centered Controller Design with State-Based System Models. In Yves Bontemps and Alexander Egyed, editors, *Proceedings of the 4th Workshop on Scenarios and State Machines: Models, Algorithms, and Tools (in Conjunction with the International Conference on Software Engineering), St. Louis, MO, USA*, pages 1–5. ACM Press, May 2005.

[Gri98]   Frank Griffel. *Componentware: Konzepte und Techniken eines Softwareparadigmas*. dpunkt-Verlag, Heidelberg, Germany, 1998.

[Gru93]   Thomas Gruber. A Translation Approach to Portable Ontology Specifications. *Knowledge Aquisition*, 5:199–220, 1993.

[GS04]    Holger Giese and Daniela Schilling. Towards the Automatic Verification of Inductive Invariants for Infinite State UML Models. Technical Report tr-ri-04-252, Department of Computer Science, University of Paderborn, Paderborn, Germany, 2004.

[GSCL02]  Alessandro Garcia, Viviane Silva, Christina Chavez, and Carlos Lucena. Engineering multi-agent systems with aspects and patterns. *Journal of the Brazilian Computer Society*, 8(1):57–72, July 2002.

[GSEW05]  Jürgen Gausemeier, Wilhelm Schäfer, Raimund Eckes, and Robert Wagner. Ramp-Up and Maintenance with Augmented Reality in Development of Flexible Production Control Systems. In *Proceedings of the 1st International Conference on*

*Changeable, Agile, Reconfigurable and Virtual Production (CARV05), September 22-23, Technical University of Munich, Germany*, pages 201–206, München, September 2005. Herbert Utz Verlag GmbH.

[GSR05]  Leif Geiger, Christian Schneider, and Carsten Reckord. Template- and model based code generation for MDA-tools. In Holger Giese and Albert Zündorf, editors, *Proceedings of the 3rd International Fujaba Days 2005, Paderborn, Germany*, Technical Reports of the Department of Computer Science, pages 9–14. University of Paderborn, September 2005.

[GT05]  Holger Giese and Sergej Tissen. The SceBaSy PlugIn for the Scenario-Based Synthesis of Real-Time Coordination Patterns for Mechatronic UML. In Holger Giese and Albert Zündorf, editors, *Proceedings of the 3rd International Fujaba Days 2005, Paderborn, Germany*, Technical Reports of the Department of Computer Science, pages 67–70. University of Paderborn, September 2005.

[GTB+03]  Holger Giese, Matthias Tichy, Sven Burmester, Wilhelm Schäfer, and Stefan Flake. Towards the Compositional Verification of Real-Time UML Designs. In *Proceedings of the European Software Engineering Conference (ESEC), Helsinki, Finland*, pages 38–47. ACM Press, September 2003.

[Gup04]  Indranil Gupta. *Building scalable solutions to distributed computing problems using probabilistic components*. PhD thesis, Cornell University, 2004. Adviser-Ken Birman.

[GV06]  Holger Giese and Alexander Vilbig. Separation of Non-Orthogonal Concerns in Software Architecture and Design. *Software and System Modeling (SoSyM)*, 5(2):136–169, June 2006.

[HE00]  Reiko Heckel and Gregor Engels. Graph Transformation and Visual Modeling Techniques. *Bulletin of the European Association for Theoretical Computer Science (EATACS)*, (71), June 2000.

[Hen05]  Stefan Henkler. Laufzeitunterstützung für Test, überwachung und Diagnose bei der modellbasierten Entwicklung mit Mechatronic UML. Master's thesis, University of Paderborn, June 2005.

[Hir04]  Martin Hirsch. Effizientes Model Checking von UML-RT Modellen und Realtime Statecharts mit UPPAAL. Master's thesis, University of Paderborn, June 2004.

[HK02]  David Harel and Hillel Kugler. Synthesizing state-based object systems from LSC specifications. *International Journal of Foundations of Computer Science*, 13(1):5–51, 2002.

# BIBLIOGRAPHY 277

[HKT02] Reiko Heckel, Jochen Malte Küster, and Gabriele Taentzer. Confluence of Typed Attributed Graph Transformation Systems. In *Graph Transformation: First International Conference, ICGT 2002, Barcelona, Spain, October 7-12, 2002*, volume 2505 of *Lecture Notes in Computer Science (LNCS)*, pages 161–176. Springer Verlag, Berlin, Heidelberg, Germany, 2002.

[HM02] David Harel and Rami Marelly. Playing with Time: On the Specification and Execution of Time-Enriched LSCs. In *Proceedings of the 10th IEEE/ACM International Symposium on Modeling, Analysis and Simulation of Computer and Telecommunication Systems (MASCOTS 2002)*, Fort Worth, Texas, USA, 2002. IEEE Computer Society Press. Invited paper.

[HM03] David Harel and Rami Marelly. *Come, Let's Play: Scenario-Based Programming Using LSCs and the Play-Engine*. Springer Verlag, Berlin, Heidelberg, Germany, 2003.

[HO93] William Harrison and Harold Ossher. Subject-oriented programming (a critique of pure objects). In *Proceedings of the Conference on Object-Oriented Programming, Systems, Languages, and Applications (OOPSLA'93), Washington, D.C., USA*, volume 28 of *ACM SIGPLAN Notices*, pages 411–428, 1993.

[HOG04] Thorsten Hestermeyer, Oliver Oberschelp, and Holger Giese. Structured Information Processing For Self-optimizing Mechatronic Systems. In *Proceedings of 1st International Conference on Informatics in Control, Automation and Robotics (ICINCO 2004), Setubal, Portugal*. IEEE Computer Society Press, August 2004.

[Hol97] Gerard J. Holzmann. The model checker SPIN. *IEEE Transactions on Software Engineering (TSE)*, 23(5):279–295, May 1997.

[Hol03] Gerard J. Holzmann. *The SPIN Model Checker, Primer and Reference Manual*. Addison-Wesley, Reading, Massachusetts, 2003.

[Hon98] Uwe Honekamp. *IPANEMA - Verteilte Echtzeit-Informationsverarbeitung in mechatronischen Systemen*. PhD thesis, University of Paderborn, 1998.

[HP98] David Harel and Michal Politi. *Modeling Reactive Systems with Statecharts: The Statemate Approach*. McGraw-Hill Companies, Inc., New York, first edition, 1998.

[HS02] Brent Hailpern and Padmanabhan Santhanam. Software debugging, testing, and verification. *IBM Systems Journal*, 41(1), 2002.

[Int95] International Organization for Standardization. *ISO 12207 Information Technology Software Life Cycle Process*, 1995.

[Jac01] Michael Jackson. *Problem Frames : Analysing and structuring software development problems*. ACM Press, 2001.

[Jac02]  Daniel Jackson. Alloy: a lightweight object modelling notation. *ACM Transactions on Software Engineering and Methodology*, 11(2):256–290, 2002.

[JC97]  Nicholas R. Jennings and Jose R. Campos. Towards a social level characterisation of socially responsible agents. *IEEE Proceedings on Software Engineering*, 144(1):11–25, 1997.

[Jen00]  Nicholas R. Jennings. On agent-based software engineering. *Artificial Intelligence*, 117(2000):277–296, 2000.

[Kat06]  Mark Kattenbelt. Towards an explicit-state model checking framework. Master's thesis, Faculty of EEMCS, University of Twente, Enschede, The Netherlands, August 2006.

[KC05]  Sascha Konrad and Betty H. C. Cheng. Real-time specification patterns. In *Proceedings of the 27th international conference on Software engineering (ICSE 2005)*, pages 372–381, New York, NY, USA, 2005. ACM Press.

[KE01]  James Kennedy and Russell C. Eberhardt. *Swarm Intelligence*. Morgan Kaufmann publishers Inc.: San Mateo, CA, USA, 2001.

[Ken02]  Stuart Kent. Model Driven Engineering. In Michael Butler, Luigia Petre, and Kaisa Sere, editors, *Proceedings of the Third International Conference on Integrated Formal Methods (IFM 2002), Turku, Finland*, volume 2335 of *Lecture Notes in Computer Science (LNCS)*, pages 286 – 298. Springer Verlag, Berlin, Heidelberg, Germany, May 2002.

[KG97]  David Kinny and Michael P. Georgeff. Modelling and Design of Multi-Agent Systems. In Jörg P. Müller, Michael Wooldridge, and Nicholas R. Jennings, editors, *Intelligent Agents III, Agent Theories, Architectures, and Languages, ECAI '96 Workshop (ATAL), Budapest, Hungary, August 12-13, 1996, Proceedings*, volume 1193 of *Lecture Notes in Computer Science (LNCS)*. Springer Verlag, Berlin, Heidelberg, Germany, 1997.

[KG04]  Florian Klein and Holger Giese. Ontologiebasiertes Rapid Prototyping für kognitive Multiagentensysteme. In *Modellierung 2004 - Praktischer Einsatz von Modellen, Workshop W4: Ontologien in der und für die Softwaretechnik, Marburg, Germany, 2004*, pages 33–42. Conradin Verlag, Marburg, Germany, March 2004. (In German).

[KG05]  Florian Klein and Holger Giese. Separation of concerns for mechatronic multi-agent systems through dynamic communities. In Ricardo Choren, Alessandro Garcia, Carlos Lucena, and Alexander Romanovsky, editors, *Software Engineering for Multi-Agent Systems III: Research Issues and Practical Applications*, volume 3390 of *Lecture Notes in Computer Science (LNCS)*, pages 272–289. Springer Verlag, Berlin, Heidelberg, Germany, February 2005.

# BIBLIOGRAPHY

[KG06a] Florian Klein and Holger Giese. Analysis and Design of Physical and Social Contexts in MultiAgent Systems using UML. In Ricardo Choren, Alessandro Garcia, Carlos Lucena, Alexander Romanovsky, Tom Holvoet, and Paolo Giorgini, editors, *Proceedings of the 4th Workshop on Software Engineering for Large-Scale Multi-Agent Systems (in Conjunction with the International Conference on Software Engineering), St. Louis, MO, USA*, volume 3914 of *Lecture Notes in Computer Science (LNCS)*, pages 91–108. Springer Verlag, Berlin, Heidelberg, Germany, February 2006.

[KG06b] Florian Klein and Holger Giese. Grounding Social Interactions in the Environment. In Danny Weyns, Van Parunak, and Fabien Michel, editors, *Environments for Multiagent Systems II*, volume 3830 of *Lecture Notes in Artificial Intelligence (LNAI)*, pages 139–162. Springer Verlag, Berlin, Heidelberg, Germany, March 2006.

[KG06c] Florian Klein and Holger Giese. Integrated Visual Specification of Structural and Temporal Properties. Technical Report tr-ri-06-277, Department of Computer Science, University of Paderborn, October 2006.

[KG07] Florian Klein and Holger Giese. Joint Structural and Temporal Property Specification using Timed Story Sequence Diagrams. In Matt Dwyer and Antónia Lopes, editors, *Proceedings of 10th International Conference on Fundamental Approaches to Software Engineering (FASE) 2007, held as part of ETAPS 2007, Lisboa, Portugal, March 24-April 1, 2007*, volume 4422 of *Lecture Notes in Computer Science (LNCS)*, pages 185–199. Springer Verlag, Berlin, Heidelberg, Germany, March 2007.

[KH99] Stuart Kent and John Howse. Mixing visual and textual constraint languages. In Robert France and Bernhard Rumpe, editors, *UML'99, Fort Collins, CO, USA, October 28-30. 1999, Proceedings*, volume 1723 of *Lecture Notes in Computer Science (LNCS)*, pages 384–398. Springer Verlag, Berlin, Heidelberg, Germany, 1999.

[KH02] Stuart Kent and John Howse. Constraint trees. In Tony Clark and Jos Warmer, editors, *Object Modeling with the OCL*, pages 228–249. Springer Verlag, Berlin, Heidelberg, Germany, 2002.

[Kin06] Ekkart Kindler. On the semantics of EPCs: Resolving the vicious circle. *Data and Knowledge Engineering*, 56(1):23–40, January 2006.

[KK07a] Hans-Jörg Kreowski and Sabine Kuske. Autonomous Units and Their Semantics - The Parallel Case. In José Luiz Fiadeiro and Pierre-Yves Schobbens, editors, *Recent Trends in Algebraic Development Techniques, 18th International Workshop, WADT 2006*, volume 4409 of *Lecture Notes in Computer Science (LNCS)*, pages 56–73, 2007.

| | |
|---|---|
| [KK07b] | Hans-Jörg Kreowski and Sabine Kuske. Communities of Autonomous Units for Pickup and Delivery Vehicle Routing. In Manfred Nagl and Andy Schürr, editors, *Proceedings of the third International Workshop and Symposium on Applications of Graph Transformation with Industrial Relevance (AGTIVE 2007), Kassel, 2007*, pages 1–16, 2007. |
| [KKK02] | Renate Klempien-Hinrichs, Peter Knirsch, and Sabine Kuske. Modeling the Pickup-and-Delivery Problem with Structured Graph Transformation. In Hans-Jörg Kreowski and Peter Knirsch, editors, *Proceedings of the APPLIGRAPH Workshop on Applied Graph Transformation (Satellite Event of ETAPS 2002)*, pages 119–130, 2002. |
| [Kle03] | Florian Klein. Entwicklung eines Metamodells zur Agentenorientierten Softwareentwicklung. Master's thesis, University of Münster, Department of Information Systems, Münster, Germany, March 2003. (In German). |
| [KLM+97] | Gregor Kiczales, John Lamping, Anurag Mendhekar, Chris Maeda, Christina Videira Lopes, Jean-Marc Loingtier, and John Irwin. Aspect-Oriented Programming. In *Proceedings of the European Conference on Object-Oriented Programming (ECOOP), Jyväskylä, Finland, June 9-13, 1997*, volume 1241 of *Lecture Notes in Computer Science (LNCS)*, pages 220–242. Springer Verlag, Berlin, Heidelberg, Germany, 1997. |
| [KNNZ00] | Hans J. Köhler, Ulrich Nickel, Jörg Niere, and Albert Zündorf. Integrating UML Diagrams for Production Control Systems. In *Proceedings of the $22^{nd}$ International Conference on Software Engineering (ICSE), Limerick, Irland*, pages 241–251. ACM Press, 2000. |
| [KO04] | Manasawee Kaenampornpan and Eamonn O'Neill. Modelling context: An activity theory approach. In *Proceedings of the Second European Symposium on Ambient Intelligence (EUSAI 2004), Eindhoven, The Netherlands, November 8-11, 2004*, volume 3295 of *Lecture Notes in Computer Science (LNCS)*, pages 367–375. Springer Verlag, Berlin, Heidelberg, Germany, 2004. |
| [Koy90] | Ron Koymans. Specifying real-time properties with metric temporal logic. *Real-Time Systems*, 2(4):255–299, 1990. |
| [KS01] | Reinhard Kahle and Thomas Studer. Formalizing non-termination of recursive programs. *JLAP*, 49(1-2):1–14, 2001. |
| [KT06] | Florian Klein and Matthias Tichy. Building reliable systems based on self-organizing multi-agent systems. In Ricardo Choren, Alessandro F. Garcia, Holger Giese, Ho fung Leung, Carlos José Pereira de Lucena, and Alexander B. Romanovsky, editors, *Proceedings of the $5^{th}$ ICSE 2006 Workshop on Software Engineering for Large-scale Multi-Agent Systems (SELMAS'06), Shanghai, China*. ACM Press, May 2006. |

## BIBLIOGRAPHY

[Kwi03]  Marta Z. Kwiatkowska. Model checking for probability and time: From theory to practice. In *Proceedings of the 18th Annual IEEE Syposium on Logic in Computer Science (LICS-03), June 22–25, 2003, Los Alamitos, CA, USA*, pages 351–360. IEEE Computer Society Press, June 2003. Invited paper.

[Lam77]  Leslie Lamport. Proving the correctness of multiprocess programs. *IEEE Transactions on Software Engineering*, SE–3(2):125–143, 1977.

[Lev95]  Nancy G. Leveson. *Safeware: system safety and computers*. Addison-Wesley, Reading, MA, USA, 1995.

[LL99]  Xuandong Li and Johan Lilius. Timing Analysis of UML Sequence Diagrams. In Robert France and Bernhard Rumpe, editors, *UML'99 - The Second International Conference on The Unified Modeling Language Fort Collins, Colorado, USA*, volume 1723 of *Lecture Notes in Computer Science (LNCS)*. Springer Verlag, Berlin, Heidelberg, Germany, October 1999.

[LPY97]  Kim G. Larsen, Paul Pettersson, and Wang Yi. UPPAAL in a Nutshell. *Springer International Journal of Software Tools for Technology*, 1(1):134–152, October 1997.

[LvdBC00]  Gerald Lüttgen, Michael von der Beeck, and Rance Cleaveland. A Compositional Approach to Statecharts Semantics. In *Proceedings of the Eighth International Symposium on Foundations of Software Engineering for Twenty-first Century Applications, November 2000, San Diego, CA, USA*, pages 120–129. ACM SIGSOFT Software Engineering Notes, November 2000.

[Mey92]  Bertrand Meyer. *Eiffel: The Language*. Prentice Hall, Englewood Cliffs, NJ, USA, 1992.

[MGF02]  François Mekerke, Geri Georg, and Robert Franc. Tool Support for Aspect-Oriented Design. In *Proceedings of the Workshops on Advances in Object-Oriented Information Systems (OOIS 2002), Montpellier, France*, volume 2426 of *Lecture Notes in Computer Science (LNCS)*, pages 280 – 289. Springer Verlag, Berlin, Heidelberg, Germany, 2002.

[MU00]  Naftaly H. Minsky and Victoria Ungureanu. Law-governed interaction: a coordination and control mechanism for heterogeneous distributed systems. *ACM Transactions on Software Engineering and Methodology (TOSEM)*, 9(3):273–305, 2000.

[Mul90]  Mark Mullin. *Rapid prototyping for object oriented systems*. Addison-Wesley, Reading, MA, USA, 1990.

[Mur89]  Tadahiko Murata. Petri nets: Properties, analysis and applications. *Proceedings of the IEEE*, 77(4):541–574, April 1989.

[Neu06]  Victor Neumann. Model Checking von Storypattern, May 2006. (In German).

[NF92]    Bashar Nuseibeh and Anthony Finkelstein. Viewpoints: A vehicle for method and tool integration. In *Proceedings of 5th International Workshop on Computer-Aided Software Engineering*, pages 50–60. IEEE Computer Society Press, 1992.

[NSZ03]   Ulrich Nickel, Wilhelm Schäfer, and Albert Zündorf. Integrative Specification of Distributed Production Control Systems for Flexible Automated Manufacturing. In Manfred Nagl and Bernhard Westfechtel, editors, *DFG Workshop: Modelle, Werkzeuge und Infrastrukturen zur Unterstützung von Entwicklungsprozessen*, pages 179–195. Wiley-VCH Verlag GmbH and Co. KGaA, 2003.

[Obj03]   Object Management Group, Needham, MA, USA. *MDA Guide Version 1.0.1*, June 2003. Document omg/03-06-01.

[Obj06]   Object Management Group, Needham, MA, USA. *UML 2.0 Object Constraint Language*, May 2006. Document formal/06-05-01.

[Obj07]   Object Management Group, Needham, MA, USA. *UML 2.1.1 Superstructure Specification*, February 2007. Document formal/07-02-05.

[OHG04]   Oliver Oberschelp, Thorsten Hestermeyer, and Holger Giese. Strukturierte Informationsverarbeitung für selbstoptimierende mechatronische Systeme. In *Proceedings of the Second Paderborner Workshop Intelligente Mechatronische Systeme*, number 145 in HNI-Verlagsschriftenreihe, pages 43–56, Paderborn, Germany, 2004. (In German).

[OL82]    Susan S. Owicki and Leslie Lamport. Proving liveness properties of concurrent programs. *TOPLAS*, 4(3):455–495, 1982.

[OMG05]   OMG. *UML Profile for Schedulability, Performance, and Time Specification*. Object Management Group, Needham, MA, USA, January 2005. Document formal/05-01-02.

[ORV$^+$04]  Andrea Omicini, Alessandro Ricci, Mirko Viroli, Cristiano Castelfranchi, and Luca Tummolini. Coordination artifacts: Environment-based coordination for intelligent agents. In *Proceedings of the 3rd International Joint Conference on Autonomous Agents and Multiagent Systems (AAMAS 2004), 19-23 August 2004, New York, NY, USA*, pages 286–293. IEEE Computer Society Press, August 2004.

[Par72]   David L. Parnas. On the Criteria to be Used in Decomposing Systems into Modules. *Communications of the ACM*, 15(12):1053–1058, 1972.

[PBS05]   H. Van Dyke Parunak, Sven Brueckner, and John A. Sauter. Digital pheromones for coordination of unmanned vehicles. In Danny Weyns, H. Van Dyke Parunak, and Fabien Michel, editors, *Environments for Multi-Agent Systems, First International Workshop, New York, NY, USA, 2004*, volume 3374 of *Lecture Notes in Computer Science (LNCS)*, pages 246–263. Springer Verlag, Berlin, Heidelberg, Germany, 2005.

# BIBLIOGRAPHY 283

[Pet62]     Carl Adam Petri. *Kommunikation mit Automaten*. PhD thesis, University of Bonn, Bonn, Germany, 1962. (In German).

[PMS94]     Adriano Peron and Andrea Maggiolo-Schettini. Transitions as Interrupts: A New Semantics for Timed Statecharts. In Masami Hagiya and John C. Mitchell, editors, *Theoretical Aspects of Computer Software, International Conference TACS '94, Sendai, Japan, April 19-22, 1994, Proceedings*, volume 789 of *Lecture Notes in Computer Science (LNCS)*. Springer Verlag, Berlin, Heidelberg, Germany, 1994.

[PWP05]     Lin Padgham, Michael Winikoff, and David Poutakidis. Adding debugging support to the prometheus methodology. *Engineering Applications of Artificial Intelligence*, 18:173–190, March 2005.

[RDH03]     Robby, Matthew B. Dwyer, and John Hatcliff. Bogor: an extensible and highly-modular software model checking framework. In *Proceedings of the European Software Engineering Conference (ESEC), Helsinki, Finland*, pages 267–276, 2003.

[Rei85]     Wolfgang Reisig. Petri nets. An Introduction. In Wilfried Brauer, Grzegorz Rozenberg, and Arto Salomaa, editors, *EATCS Monographs on Theoretical Compute Science*, volume 4. Springer Verlag, Berlin, Heidelberg, Germany, 1985.

[Ren03]     Arend Rensink. Towards model checking graph grammars. In Michael Leuschel, Stefan Gruner, and Stephane Lo Presti, editors, *Workshop on Automated Verification of Critical Systems (AVoCS)*, Technical Report DSSE–TR–2003–2, pages 150–160. University of Southampton, 2003.

[Ren04]     Hendrik Renken. Cooperative Learning for Autonomous Shuttle Systems, 2004.

[Rey87]     Craig Reynolds. Flocks, herds, and schools: A distributed behavioral model. *Computer Graphics*, 21(4), July 1987.

[RG95]      Anand S. Rao and Michael P. Georgeff. BDI Agents: From Theory to Practice. In *Proceedings of the 1st International Conference On Multi Agent Systems*, San Francisco, USA, 1995.

[RK99]      Jürgen Ruf and Thomas Kropf. Modeling and Checking Networks of Communicating Real-Time Systems. In *Correct Hardware Design and Verification Methods (CHARME'99)*, pages 265–279. IFIP WG 10.5, Springer Verlag, Berlin, Heidelberg, Germany, September 1999.

[Roz97]     Grzegorz Rozenberg, editor. *Handbook of Graph Grammars and Computing by Graph Transformation: Foundations*. World Scientific Publishing Corporation, Singapore, Singapore, February 1997. Volume 1.

| | |
|---|---|
| [RR98] | Wolfgang Reisig and Grzegorz Rozenberg, editors. *Lectures on Petri Nets I: Basic Models, Advances in Petri Nets 1998*. Number 1491 in Lecture Notes in Computer Science (LNCS). Springer Verlag, Berlin, Heidelberg, Germany, 1998. |
| [RS06] | Tobias Rötschke and Andy Schürr. Temporal Graph Queries to Support Software Evolution. In *Graph Transformation: 5th International Conference, ICGT 2006, Rio Grande do Norte, Brazil, September 17-23, 2006*, volume 4178 of *LNCS*, pages 1–15. Springer Verlag, Berlin, Heidelberg, Germany, 2006. |
| [RSV04] | Arend Rensink, Ákos Schmidt, and Dániel Varró. Model Checking Graph Transformations: A Comparison of Two Approaches. In Hartmut Ehrig, Gregor Engels, Francesco Parisi-Presicce, and Grzegorz Rozenberg, editors, *International Conference on Graph Transformations (ICGT)*, volume 3256 of *Lecture Notes in Computer Science (LNCS)*, pages 226–241. Springer Verlag, Berlin, Heidelberg, Germany, 2004. |
| [Rud97] | Michael Rudolf. Concepts and Implementation of an Interpreter for Attributed Graph Transformation. Master's thesis, Technical University Berlin, 1997. (In German). |
| [RWL96] | Trygve Reenskaug, Per Wold, and Odd Arild Lehene. *Working with Objects: The OOram Software Engineering Method*. Addison-Wesley, Reading, MA, USA/ Manning Publications, Sound View, CT, USA, 1996. |
| [SB04] | Luciano Serafini and Paolo Bouquet. Comparing formal theories of context in ai. *Artificial Intelligence*, 155(1-2):41–67, 2004. |
| [SBG99] | Albrecht Schmidt, Michael Beigl, and Hans-Werner Gellersen. There is more to context than location. *Computers & Graphics*, 23(6):893–901, 1999. |
| [SC02] | Bikram Sengupta and Rance Cleaveland. Triggered Message Sequence Charts. In William G. Griswold, editor, *Proceedings of the Tenth ACM SIGSOFT Symposium on the Foundations of Softare Engineering (FSE-10)*, Charleston, South Carolina, USA, November 2002. ACM Press. |
| [Sch05] | Viktor Schuppan. *Liveness Checking as Safety Checking to Find Shortest Counterexamples to Linear Time Properties*. PhD thesis, Swiss Federal Institute Of Technology Zurich (ETH Zürich), 2005. |
| [Sch06] | Daniela Schilling. *Kompositionale Softwareverifikation mechatronischer Systeme*. University of Paderborn, 2006. (In German). |
| [Sek94] | Emil Sekerinski. *Object Refinement*. PhD thesis, University of Karlsruhe, 1994. |
| [SH04] | Kurt Schelfthout and Tom Holvoet. Objectplaces: An environment for situated multi-agent systems. In *Proceedings of the 3rd International Joint Conference on* |

# BIBLIOGRAPHY 285

*Autonomous Agents and Multiagent Systems (AAMAS 2004), 19-23 August 2004, New York, NY, USA*, pages 1500–1501. IEEE Computer Society Press, August 2004.

[Sin98a] M. P. Singh. Agent communication languages: Rethinking the principles. *IEEE Computer*, 31(12):40–47, December 1998.

[Sin98b] Munindar P. Singh. The intentions of teams: Team structure, endodeixis, and exodeixis. In Henri Prade, editor, *Proceedings of the 13th European Conference on Artificial Intelligence, Brighton, UK, August 23-28 1998*, pages 303–307. John Wiley and Sons, Chichester, 1998.

[SJ99] Gunter Schupp and Alfred Jaschinksi. Virtual prototyping: the future way of designing railway vehicles. *International Journal of Vehicle Design*, 22(1-2):93–115, 1999.

[Spi07] Michael Spijkerman. Monitoring gemischt struktureller und temporaler Eigenschaften von UML Modellen. Master's thesis, University of Paderborn, Department of Computer Science, Paderborn, Germany, September 2007. (In German).

[Sta00] Standards Coordinating Committee of the IEEE Computer Society, The Institute of Electrical and Electronics Engineers, Inc., 345 East 47th Street, New York, NY 10017-2394, USA. *Recommended Practice for Architectural Description of Software-Intensive Systems, IEEE-Std-1471-2000*, 2000.

[Ste07] Daniel Steffen. *Ein Verfahren zur Produktstrukturierung für fortgeschrittene mechatronische Systeme*. Dissertation, Universität Paderborn, Heinz Nixdorf Institut, Rechnerintegrierte Produktion, April 2007. Volume 207 of HNI-Verlagsschriftenreihe. Bonifatius GmbH, Paderborn, Germany, first edition, 2007.(In German).

[Sto96] Neil Storey. *Safety-Critical Computer Systems*. Addison-Wesley, Reading, MA, USA, 1996.

[SV03] Ákos Schmidt and Dániel Varró. CheckVML: A Tool for Model Checking Visual Modeling Languages. In *Proceedings of the 6th International Conference on the Unified Modeling Language, UML2003*, volume 2863 of *Lecture Notes in Computer Science (LNCS)*, pages 92–95. Springer Verlag, Berlin, Heidelberg, Germany, 2003.

[SWGE04] Wilhelm Schäfer, Robert Wagner, Jürgen Gausemeier, and Raimund Eckes. An Engineer's Workstation to support Integrated Development of Flexible Production Control Systems. In Hartmut Ehrig, Werner Damm, Jörg Desel, Martin Gröse-Rhode, Wolfgang Reif, Eckehard Schnieder, and Engelbert Westkämper, editors, *Integration of Software Specification Techniques for Applications in Engineering,* volume 3147 of *Lecture Notes in Computer Science (LNCS)*, pages 48–68. Springer Verlag, Berlin, Heidelberg, Germany, September 2004.

[SWZ95] Andy Schürr, Andreas J. Winter, and Albert Zündorf. Graph Grammar Engineering with PROGRES. In Wilhelm Schäfer, editor, *Proceedings of European Software Engineering Conference (ESEC/FSE)*, volume 989 of *Lecture Notes in Computer Science (LNCS)*. Springer Verlag, Berlin, Heidelberg, Germany, 1995.

[SWZ99] Andy Schürr, Andreas J. Winter, and Albert Zündorf. The PROGRES Approach: Language and Environment. In Hartmut Ehrig, Gregor Engels, Hans-Jörg Kreowski, and Grzegorz Rozenberg, editors, *Handbook of Graph Grammars and Computing by Graph Transformation, volume 2 - Application, Languages and tools.*, pages 487–546. World Scientific Publishing Corporation, Singapore, Singapore, 1999.

[Szy98] Clemens Szyperski. *Component Software, Beyond Object-Oriented Programming*. Addison-Wesley, Reading, MA, USA, 1998.

[TGS06] Matthias Tichy, Holger Giese, and Andreas Seibel. Story Diagrams in Real-Time Software. In Holger Giese and Bernhard Westfechtel, editors, *Proceedings of the 4th International Fujaba Days 2006, Bayreuth, Germany*, volume tr-ri-06-275 of *Technical Reports of the Department of Computer Science*, pages 15–22. University of Paderborn, September 2006.

[Var02] Dániel Varró. Towards Symbolic Analysis of Visual Modelling Languages. In Paolo Bottoni and Mark Minas, editors, *Proceedings of the GT-VMT 2002: International Workshop on Graph Transformation and Visual Modelling Techniques, Barcelona, Spain, October 11-12, 2002*, volume 72 of *ENTCS*, pages 57–70. Elsevier Science Publishers B.V, Amsterdam, The Netherlands, October 2002.

[Var03] Dániel Varró. Automated Formal Verification of Visual Modeling Languages by Model Checking. *Journal of Software and Systems Modelling*, 2003.

[Var04] Dániel Varró. Automated formal verification of visual modeling languages by model checking. *Software and System Modeling*, 3(2):85–113, May 2004.

[vdHRW05] Wiebe van der Hoek, Mark Roberts, and Michael Wooldridge. Knowledge and Social Laws. In Frank Dignum, Virginia Dignum, Sven Koenig, Sarit Kraus, Munidar P. Singh, and Michael Wooldridge, editors, *Proceedings of the Fourth International Joint Conference on Autonomous Agents and Multiagent Systems (AAMAS 2005), Utrecht, The Netherlands*, pages 674–681. ACM Press, July 2005.

[vdHRW07] Wiebe van der Hoek, Mark Roberts, and Michael Wooldridge. Social laws in alternating time: Effectiveness, feasibility, and synthesis. *Synthese*, 156(1):1–19, May 2007.

# BIBLIOGRAPHY

[VO02]  Mirko Viroli and Andrea Omicini. A specification language for agents observable behavior. In *Proceedings of the International Conference on Artificial Intelligence (ICAI) 2002 (Las Vegas, US)*, pages 321–327. CSREA Press, 2002.

[WD01]  Mark F. Wood and Scott A. DeLoach. An Overview of the Multiagent Systems Engineering Methodology. In *Agent-Oriented Software Engineering: First International Workshop, AOSE 2000, Limerick, Ireland*, volume 1957 of *Lecture Notes in Computer Science (LNCS)*, pages 207–221. Springer Verlag, Berlin, Heidelberg, Germany, September 2001.

[WJ95a]  Michael Wooldridge and Nicholas R. Jennings. Agent theories, architectures, and languages: a survey. In Michael Wooldridge and Nicholas R. Jennings, editors, *Intelligent Agents*, volume 890 of *Lecture Notes in Artificial Intelligence (LNAI)*, pages 1–39. Springer Verlag, Berlin, Heidelberg, Germany, 1995.

[WJ95b]  Michael Wooldridge and Nicholas R. Jennings. Intelligent agents: Theory and practice. *Knowledge Engineering Review*, 10(2):115–152, 1995.

[WJK99]  Michael Wooldridge, Nicholas R. Jennings, and David Kinny. A methodology for agent-oriented analysis and design. In Michael Wooldridge and Nicholas R. Jennings, editors, *Proceedings of the third annual conference on Autonomous Agents, Seattle, WA, USA, May 1999*, pages 69–76. ACM Press, 1999.

[Woo98]  Michael Wooldridge. Verifiable semantics for agent communication languages. In *Proceedings of the 3rd International Conference on Multi Agent Systems (ICMAS98), Paris , France*, pages 349–356. IEEE Computer Society Press, 1998.

[Woo00]  Michael J. Wooldridge. *Reasoning About Rational Agents (Intelligent Robotics and Autonomous Agents)*. MIT Press, Cambridge, MA, USA, 1 edition, January 2000.

[WPM+04]  Danny Weyns, H. Van Dyke Parunak, Fabien Michel, Tom Holvoet, and Jacques Ferber. Environments for multiagent systems state-of-the-art and research challenges. In Danny Weyns, H. Van Dyke Parunak, and Fabien Michel, editors, *Environment for multi-agent systems: first international workshop, 2004, New York, NY, USA*, volume 3374 of *Lecture Notes in Computer Science (LNCS)*, pages 1–47. Springer Verlag, Berlin, Heidelberg, Germany, 2004.

[WSHL05]  Danny Weyns, Kurt Schelfthout, Tom Holvoet, and Tom Lefever. Decentralized control of E'GV transportation systems. In Michal Pechoucek, Donald Steiner, and Simon Thompson, editors, *Proceedings of the 4rd International Joint Conference on Autonomous Agents and Multiagent Systems (AAMAS 2005), July 25-29, 2005, Utrecht, The Netherlands*, pages 67–74. ACM Press, July 2005.

[Yov96]  Sergio Yovine. Model checking timed automata. In Grzegorz Rozenberg and Frits W. Vaandrager, editors, *School on Embedded Systems*, volume 1494 of *Lecture Notes in Computer Science (LNCS)*, pages 114–152. Springer Verlag, Berlin, Heidelberg, Germany, 1996.

[Zün95]   Albert Zündorf. *PROgrammierte GRaphErsetzungsSysteme*. PhD thesis, RWTH Aachen, 1995.

[Zün01]   Albert Zündorf. *Rigorous Object Oriented Software Development*. University of Paderborn, 2001.

# Index

## A

affiliation norm, **144**, **156**
agent, **4**, 131, 138, **140**, **146**, 166, 254
agent design phase, **9**
agent specification, 140, **146**, **166**
alternative set, **77**
and inset, **60**
application graph, **30**
assertion, **143**, **158**
atomic proposition, **180**
attributed graph, **28**
attributed graph morphism, **29**
automaton, **42**
    extended, **43**
    hierarchical, **42**
    timed, **42**, 179

## B

behavior monitor, **203**
behavioral norm, **144**, **158**
behavioral state machines, **39**
binding, **75**
    valid, **75**

## C

candidate set, **76**
cardinalities, **66**

Class Diagram, **34**
Cognitive Loop, **254**
Cognitive Operator, **4**, 215, 254
commitment, **143**, **158**
community, 5, 10, 133, 139, **144**, 166
community specification, 139, 140, **144**, **164**
community type, 10, 139, 144, **144**, **164**
component, **37**, **44**
conjunction inset, **60**
connector
    else, **63**
    then, **63**
constraint, **233**
    edge, **99**
    homomorphism, **72**
    identity, **73**
    situation homomorphism, **103**
    time bound, **102**
constraint set, **233**
context, **140**, **147**
Controller, **4**, 214, 253
conventional norm, **144**, **158**
coordination pattern, 5, 17, 37, **40**, **44**, 163
    pattern constraint, **40**
    role, **40**
    role invariant, **40**

corresponding, **169**
culture, 5, 10, 133, 139, **145**, **154**
culture specification, 139, 140, **145**, **153**
CURCUMA, 6, **133**

## D

declaration, **158**
deployment phase, **9**
design process, **8**
direct transformation, **30**
directive, **143**, **158**
discretionary, **152**, 169
disjunction inset, **59**

## E

effector, 9, 138, **140**, **147**
effector specification, **147**
enhanced Story Pattern, **58**
entity, 9, 138, **140**, 146, 164
entity specification, **140**, **146**
environment, 9, **138**, 146
environment modeling phase, **9**
environment specification, 9, 138, 139, **140**, 146, **152**
equivalent, **168**
evolved from, **85**
excluding, **31**
existential, **104**
existential norm, **144**, 154, **155**
extended automaton, **43**

## F

facility, **141**

## G

globally strict, **102**
graph, 17, 26, **26**
   attributed, **28**
   compatible, **26**
   edge compatible, **26**
   inheritance type system, **27**
   intersection, **27**
   label compatible, **26**
   labeled, **26**
   subtraction, **27**
   type conformant, **27**
   type system, **27**
   typed, **27**
   union, **26**
graph grammar, 17
graph isomorphism, **29**
graph morphism, **29**
graph pattern, **30**, 35
   match, **30**
   simple, **29**
graph transformation rule, **30**
graph transformation system, 17, **32**, 92, 179
   constrained, **32**
   labeled, **32**
   prioritized, **32**
   typed, **32**
GTS refinement, **167**
guards, **99**

## H

hierarchical automaton, **42**

# I

if inset, **59**
implication inset, **59**
inheritance type system graph, **27**
inhibitors, **97**, **112**
inset
    and, **60**
    if, **59**
    not, **58**
    or, **59**
instantiation norm, **144**, **156**
interdiction, **143**, **158**
interface
    provided, **38**
    required, **38**
intersecting, **31**
invariant, **144**, **180**
    inductive, **191**
    operational, **191**
Invariant Story Pattern, **35**, 70
item, **140**, **146**

# J

joining, **31**

# L

labeled parallel composition, **196**
Labeled Transition System, **179**
legal stance, 133, **143**

# M

mechatronic system, **1**

merging, **31**
model, **178**
Motor Loop, **253**

# N

negation inset, **58**
negative application condition, **30**
node
    ensure, **70**
    existential guard, **65**
    existential quantified, **65**
    lambda, **67**
    leaf, **63**
    scoped, **69**
    transformation, **70**
    universal quantified, **66**
norm, 10, **144**, **154**, **155**
    affiliation, **144**, **156**
    behavioral, **144**, **158**
    conventional, **144**, **158**
    existential, **144**, **154**, **155**
    instantiation, **144**, **156**
    social, **144**, **154**, **157**
not inset, **58**

# O

Object Diagram, **35**
observation, **93**, **114**
observation compatible, **115**
occurrence, **30**
OCM, **4**, 253
Operator-Controller-Module, 253
Operator-Controller-Module, **4**, 214

or inset, **59**

## P

parallel composition, **32**
pattern references, **61**
perception, **140**
permission, **143**, **158**
port, **38**
process, 9, **141**, **149**
process specification, **141**, **149**
professed intention, 139, **143**, **144**, 154
professed intentions, **158**
propagation function, **77**
property monitor, **200**, 203
protocol state machines, **39**
pseudostate
    first of, **102**
    initial, **95**
    last of, **102**
    termination, **95**

## R

Real-Time Statecharts, **39**
realization, **44**
refinement, 6, **43**, **169**
Reflective Loop, **254**
Reflective Operator, **4**, 214, 253
requirement, 139
requirements, **10**
requirements modeling phase, **9**
restricted GTS refinement, **170**, 196
restricted refinement, **43**
result set, **77**

role, 10, 139, **144**, 154, **154**, 156
root trace, 104, **120**
RTSC, **39**

## S

satisfaction
    SDD, **75**
    TSSD, **120**
SDD, **62**
SDDP, **67**
SDDR, **67**
self-optimizing, **1**, 131
sensor, 9, 138, **140**, **147**
sensor specification, **147**
service, 9, 138, **141**, **151**
service specification, **141**, **151**
shuttles, **7**
simple graph pattern, 35
simple Story Pattern, **63**, 70
Single Pushout Approach, **30**
situation, **93**, **110**
    trivial, 106
social design phase, **9**
social norm, **144**, 154, **157**
social specification, 139, **143**, 153
software-intensive system, **1**
source graph, **30**
SP, **63**
specification, **178**
    agent, 140, **146**, **166**
    community, 139, 140, **144**, **164**
    culture, 139, 140, **145**, **153**
    effector, **147**
    entity, **140**, **146**

environment, 138, 139, **140**
process, **141**, **149**
sensor, **147**
service, **141**, **151**
social, 139, **143**, 153
system, 139, **171**
Story Decision Diagram, **62**
    Pattern, **67**
    Reference, **67**
Story Pattern, **22**, **36**
    enhanced, **58**
Story-Driven Modeling, **17**
strict, **101**
strictly next, **101**
strictly previous, **101**
subcommunity, 10, **144**
subculture, 154, **163**
subgraph, **28**
subpattern, **168**
subscenario, **107**, 124
subtype, **27**
system specification, 139, **171**

## T

target graph, **30**
target graph pattern, **191**
template type, 139, **145**, 154, **154**, 164
temporal connector
    eventually, **94**
    immediately, **94**
    until, **94**
timed automaton, **42**, 179
Timed Story Scenario Diagram, **92**
trace, 93, **95**, **114**

trace tree, **115**
trigger, **104**
TSSD, **92**
type, **27**
type conformant, **27**, 35
type system graph, **27**, 34, 35
typed graph, **27**, 35

## U

UML State Machine, **39**
universal, **104**
urgent, **152**, 169

## V

validation, **175**
verification, **175**
violation, **32**

## W

well-formed, **86**

Die VDM Verlagsservicegesellschaft sucht für wissenschaftliche Verlage abgeschlossene und herausragende

## Dissertationen, Habilitationen, Diplomarbeiten, Master Theses, Magisterarbeiten usw.

für die kostenlose Publikation als Fachbuch.

Sie verfügen über eine Arbeit, die hohen inhaltlichen und formalen Ansprüchen genügt, und haben Interesse an einer honorarvergüteten Publikation?

Dann senden Sie bitte erste Informationen über sich und Ihre Arbeit per Email an *info@vdm-vsg.de*.

**Sie erhalten kurzfristig unser Feedback!**

VDM Verlagsservicegesellschaft mbH
Dudweiler Landstr. 99
D - 66123 Saarbrücken
**www.vdm-vsg.de**

Telefon +49 681 3720 174
Fax +49 681 3720 1749

Die VDM Verlagsservicegesellschaft mbH vertritt

Printed by Books on Demand GmbH, Norderstedt / Germany